FLASHPOINT
CAPTAIN COLD

JOHN BROOME   GARDNER FOX   CARY BATES   WILLIAM MESSNER-LOEBS   GEOFF JOHNS
SCOTT KOLINS   FRANCIS MANAPUL   BRIAN BUCCELLATO   JOSHUA WILLIAMSON
writers

CARMINE INFANTINO   FRANK GIACOIA   MURPHY ANDERSON   BOB SMITH   GREG LaROCQUE   TIM DZON
SCOTT KOLINS   DAN PANOSIAN   FRANCIS MANAPUL   CARMINE DI GIANDOMENICO   DAVIDE GIANFELICE   NEIL GOOGE
artists

GENE D'ANGELO   CARL GAFFORD   JAMES SINCLAIR   MIKE ATIYEH   BRIAN BUCCELLATO
IVAN PLASCENCIA   CHRIS SOTOMAYOR
colorists

TODD KLEIN   AGUSTIN MAS   GASPAR SALADINO   DAVE SHARPE   WES ABBOTT   STEVE WANDS
letterers

BRIAN BOLLAND
collection cover artist

JULIUS SCHWARTZ, LEN WEIN, BRIAN AUGUSTYN, JOEY CAVALIERI, CHRIS CONROY,
BRIAN CUNNINGHAM Editors – Original Series
DARREN SHAN, AMEDEO TURTURRO, DIEGO LOPEZ Assistant Editors – Original Series
JEB WOODARD Group Editor – Collected Editions
SCOTT NYBAKKEN Editor – Collected Edition
STEVE COOK Design Director – Books
MEGEN BELLERSEN Publication Design

BOB HARRAS Senior VP – Editor-in-Chief, DC Comics
PAT McCALLUM Executive Editor, DC Comics

DIANE NELSON President
DAN DiDIO Publisher
JIM LEE Publisher
GEOFF JOHNS President & Chief Creative Officer
AMIT DESAI Executive VP – Business & Marketing Strategy,
Direct to Consumer & Global Franchise Management
SAM ADES Senior VP & General Manager, Digital Services
BOBBIE CHASE VP & Executive Editor, Young Reader & Talent Development
MARK CHIARELLO Senior VP – Art, Design & Collected Editions
JOHN CUNNINGHAM Senior VP – Sales & Trade Marketing
ANNE DePIES Senior VP – Business Strategy, Finance & Administration
DON FALLETTI VP – Manufacturing Operations
LAWRENCE GANEM VP – Editorial Administration & Talent Relations
ALISON GILL Senior VP – Manufacturing & Operations
HANK KANALZ Senior VP – Editorial Strategy & Administration
JAY KOGAN VP – Legal Affairs
JACK MAHAN VP – Business Affairs
NICK J. NAPOLITANO VP – Manufacturing Administration
EDDIE SCANNELL VP – Consumer Marketing
COURTNEY SIMMONS Senior VP – Publicity & Communications
JIM (SKI) SOKOLOWSKI VP – Comic Book Specialty Sales & Trade Marketing
NANCY SPEARS VP – Mass, Book, Digital Sales & Trade Marketing
MICHELE R. WELLS VP – Content Strategy

Color reconstruction by Rick Taylor, Tom McCraw, David Tanguay and Andrew Drace

FLASH ROGUES: CAPTAIN COLD

DC Comics, 2900 West Alameda Ave., Burbank, CA 91505
Printed by LSC Communications, Kendallville, IN, USA. 7/20/18. First Printing.
ISBN: 978-1-4012-8159-5

Library of Congress Cataloging-in-Publication Data is available.

TABLE OF CONTENTS

FLASH ROGUES
CAPTAIN COLD

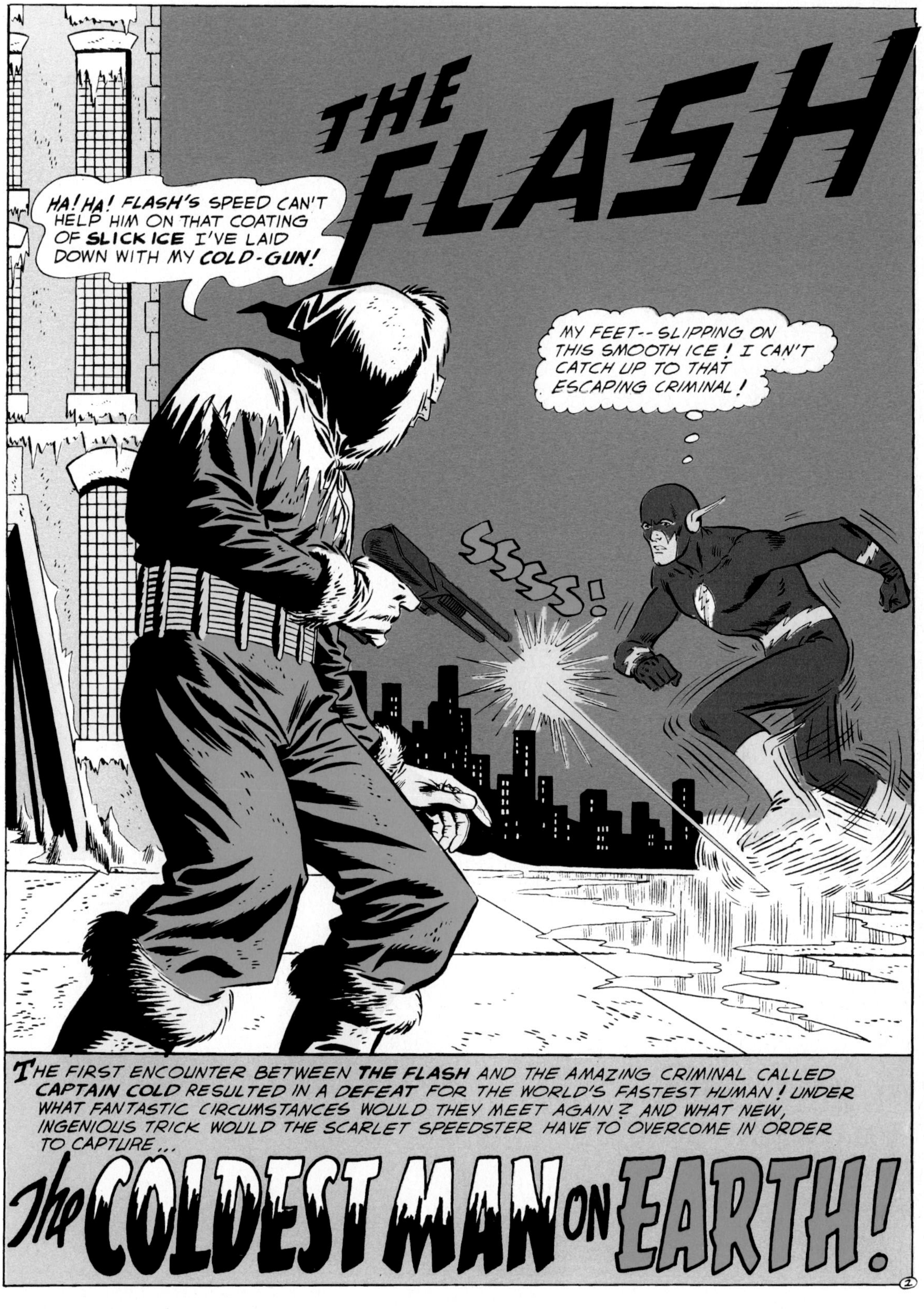
THE FLASH
HA! HA! FLASH'S SPEED CAN'T HELP HIM ON THAT COATING OF SLICK ICE I'VE LAID DOWN WITH MY COLD-GUN!
MY FEET--SLIPPING ON THIS SMOOTH ICE! I CAN'T CATCH UP TO THAT ESCAPING CRIMINAL!
SSSSS!
THE FIRST ENCOUNTER BETWEEN THE FLASH AND THE AMAZING CRIMINAL CALLED CAPTAIN COLD RESULTED IN A DEFEAT FOR THE WORLD'S FASTEST HUMAN! UNDER WHAT FANTASTIC CIRCUMSTANCES WOULD THEY MEET AGAIN? AND WHAT NEW, INGENIOUS TRICK WOULD THE SCARLET SPEEDSTER HAVE TO OVERCOME IN ORDER TO CAPTURE...
The COLDEST MAN ON EARTH!
2

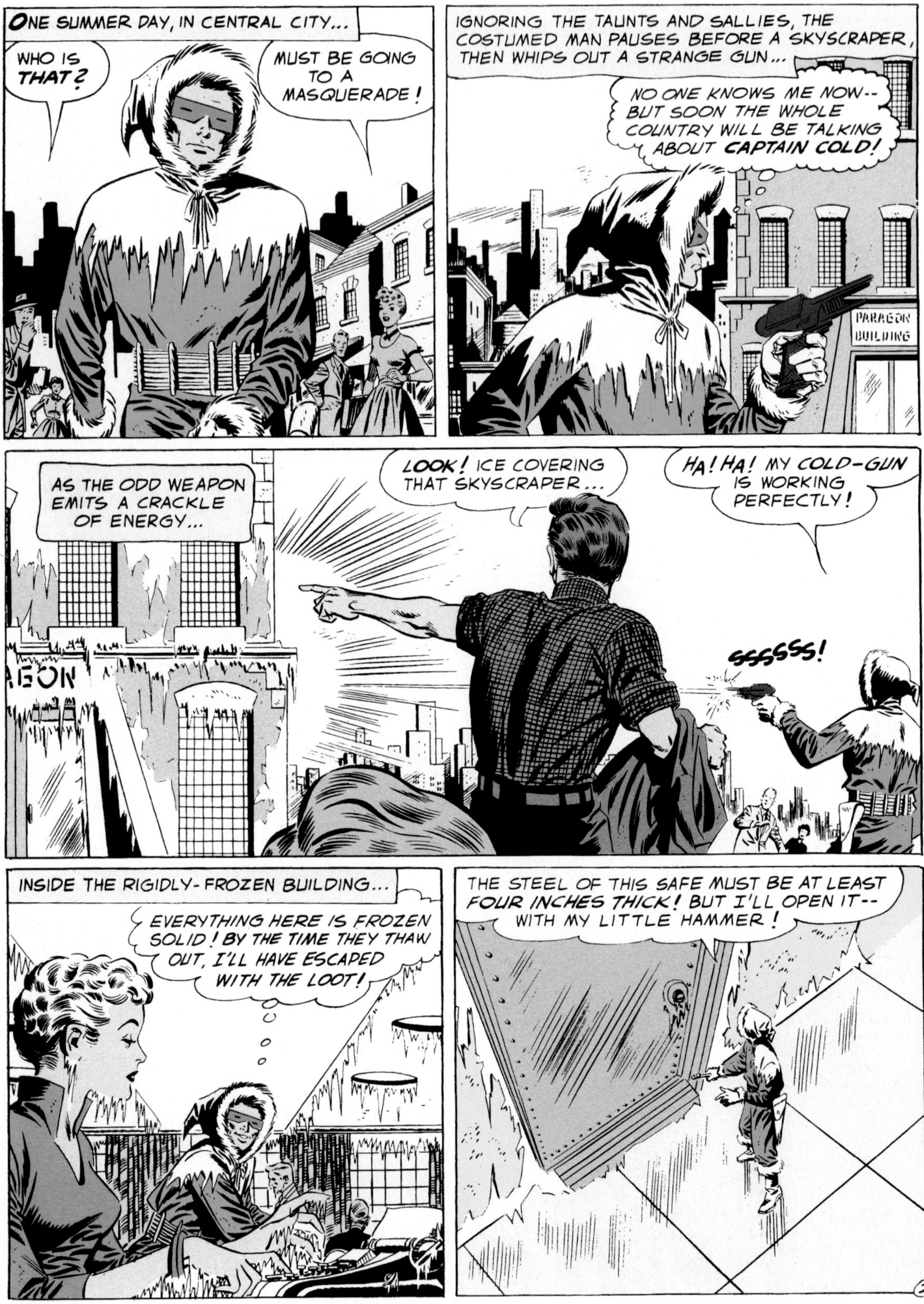
ONE SUMMER DAY, IN CENTRAL CITY...
WHO IS THAT?
MUST BE GOING TO A MASQUERADE!
IGNORING THE TAUNTS AND SALLIES, THE COSTUMED MAN PAUSES BEFORE A SKYSCRAPER, THEN WHIPS OUT A STRANGE GUN...
NO ONE KNOWS ME NOW-- BUT SOON THE WHOLE COUNTRY WILL BE TALKING ABOUT CAPTAIN COLD!
PARAGON BUILDING
AS THE ODD WEAPON EMITS A CRACKLE OF ENERGY...
LOOK! ICE COVERING THAT SKYSCRAPER...
HA! HA! MY COLD-GUN IS WORKING PERFECTLY!
SSSSSS!
AGON
INSIDE THE RIGIDLY-FROZEN BUILDING...
EVERYTHING HERE IS FROZEN SOLID! BY THE TIME THEY THAW OUT, I'LL HAVE ESCAPED WITH THE LOOT!
THE STEEL OF THIS SAFE MUST BE AT LEAST FOUR INCHES THICK! BUT I'LL OPEN IT-- WITH MY LITTLE HAMMER!
2

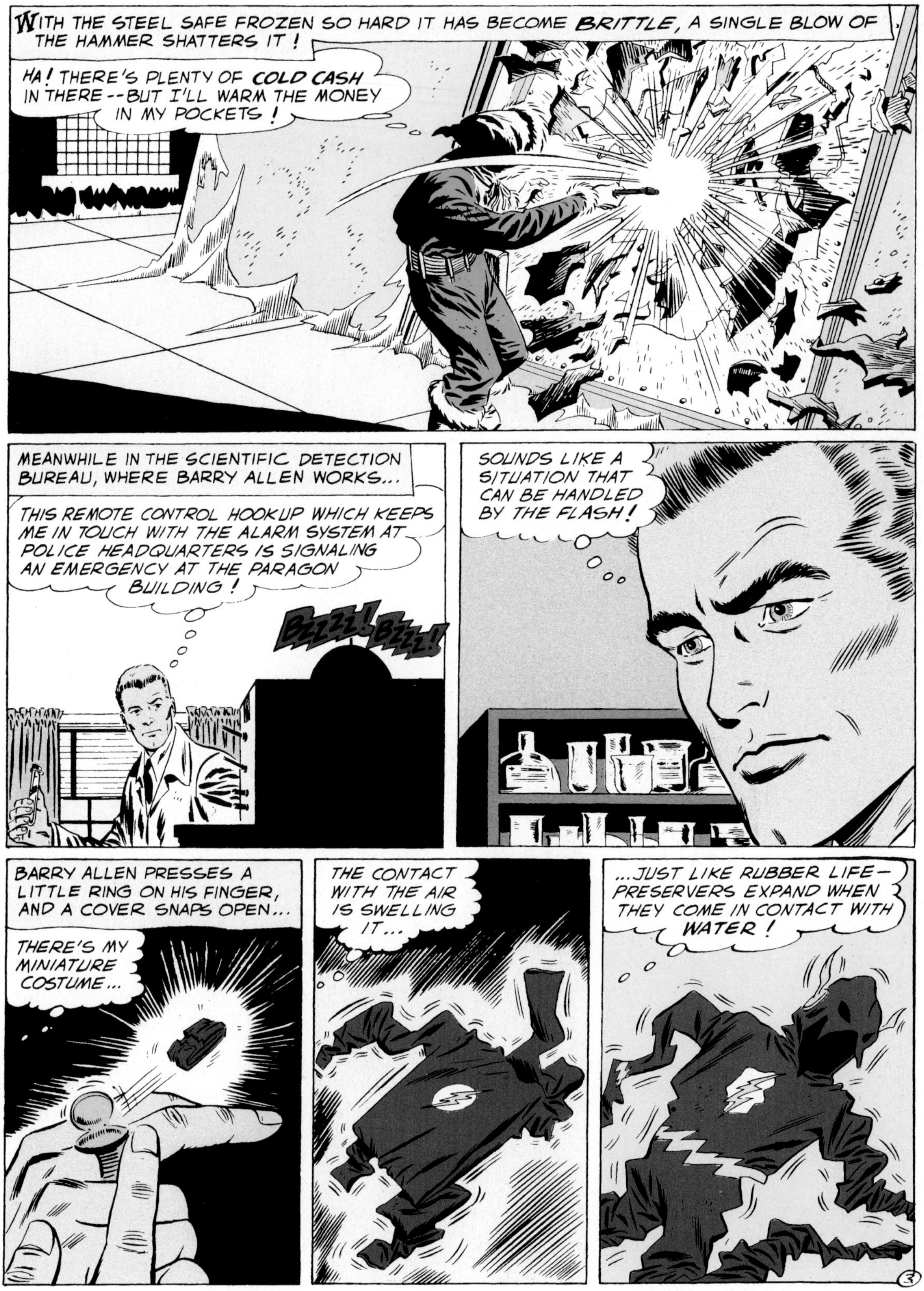
WITH THE STEEL SAFE FROZEN SO HARD IT HAS BECOME BRITTLE, A SINGLE BLOW OF THE HAMMER SHATTERS IT!
HA! THERE'S PLENTY OF COLD CASH IN THERE--BUT I'LL WARM THE MONEY IN MY POCKETS!
MEANWHILE IN THE SCIENTIFIC DETECTION BUREAU, WHERE BARRY ALLEN WORKS...
THIS REMOTE CONTROL HOOKUP WHICH KEEPS ME IN TOUCH WITH THE ALARM SYSTEM AT POLICE HEADQUARTERS IS SIGNALING AN EMERGENCY AT THE PARAGON BUILDING!
BZZZZ! BZZZ!
SOUNDS LIKE A SITUATION THAT CAN BE HANDLED BY THE FLASH!
BARRY ALLEN PRESSES A LITTLE RING ON HIS FINGER, AND A COVER SNAPS OPEN...
THERE'S MY MINIATURE COSTUME...
THE CONTACT WITH THE AIR IS SWELLING IT...
...JUST LIKE RUBBER LIFE-PRESERVERS EXPAND WHEN THEY COME IN CONTACT WITH WATER!
3

SOON, OVER THE ROOFTOPS OF THE CITY SPEEDS *THE FLASH*...

I GO SO FAST THAT I CAN "LEAP" DISTANCES OF A HUNDRED FEET WITH EASE!

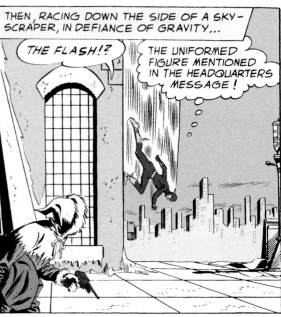

THEN, RACING DOWN THE SIDE OF A SKY-SCRAPER, IN DEFIANCE OF GRAVITY...

THE FLASH!?

THE UNIFORMED FIGURE MENTIONED IN THE HEADQUARTERS MESSAGE!

AS THE WORLD'S FASTEST HUMAN MOVES TOWARD HIS STRANGE ANTAGONIST...

YOU'LL NEVER DEFEAT *CAPTAIN COLD*, *FLASH*! I'M WELL-EQUIPPED FOR THIS MEETING WITH YOU!

ZZZZ!

THE NEXT MOMENT...

I-I HIT HIM WITH MY *COLD-GUN*--BUT HE'S STILL MOVING! WHY DIDN'T IT FREEZE HIM?

BECAUSE MY *SWIFT VIBRATIONS* OVERCOME YOUR COLD BLASTS!

IN A QUICK MANEUVER, THE FLEEING MASTER OF COLD LAYS DOWN A COATING OF ICE ON THE ROAD...

THIS ICE-- SO SLIPPERY THAT I CAN'T GET ANY FOOTING ON IT! I'M RUNNING AT JET SPEED-- IN THE SAME PLACE!

HA! HA! YOU'RE NOT SO *FAST* AS YOU THOUGHT YOU WERE, *FLASH*!

SSSS!

4

LATER, AS A SPEEDY SEARCH FAILS TO FIND A TRACE OF THE ELUSIVE CRIMINAL...

I NEVER EVEN GOT CLOSE ENOUGH TO LAY MY HANDS ON HIM! WILL I DO ANY BETTER THE NEXT TIME HE STRIKES--AS HE SURELY WILL?

HAS THE REDOUBTABLE FLASH TRULY MET HIS MATCH? IS THE FASTEST MAN ALIVE TOO "SLOW" TO BEAT CAPTAIN COLD?

BUT FIRST--JUST WHO IS THIS AMAZING CRIMINAL AND WHERE DOES HE COME FROM? FOR THE STARTLING ANSWER...

...LET US TURN BACK THE CLOCK A SHORT FEW WEEKS TO THE ROOM OF LEN SNART, AN AMBITIOUS CROOK...

IF ONLY I COULD FIND SOME WAY OF COPING WITH THE FLASH, NOTHING WOULD STOP ME! SAY, HERE'S SOMETHING IN TODAY'S PAPER THAT SUGGESTS A SOLUTION TO MY PROBLEM...

A SCIENTIFIC MAGAZINE HAS PREPARED A COMPREHENSIVE ARTICLE ON FLASH! IF I COULD GET A LOOK AT IT, I MIGHT GET A HINT HOW TO DEFEAT FLASH! WORTH A TRY...

THAT NIGHT, LEN SNART BREAKS INTO THE OFFICE OF THE MAGAZINE...

THIS IS IT! I'LL TAKE THE MANUSCRIPT HOME WITH ME--STUDY IT--FIGURE OUT HOW I CAN USE IT TO MY ADVANTAGE!

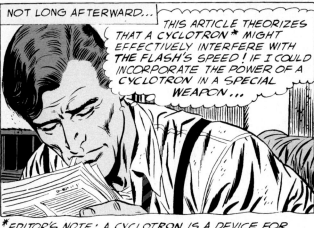

NOT LONG AFTERWARD...

THIS ARTICLE THEORIZES THAT A CYCLOTRON * MIGHT EFFECTIVELY INTERFERE WITH THE FLASH'S SPEED! IF I COULD INCORPORATE THE POWER OF A CYCLOTRON IN A SPECIAL WEAPON...

*EDITOR'S NOTE: A CYCLOTRON IS A DEVICE FOR IMPARTING VERY HIGH SPEED TO ELECTRIFIED PARTICLES BY SUCCESSIVE ELECTRIC IMPULSES AT HIGH FREQUENCY!

⑤

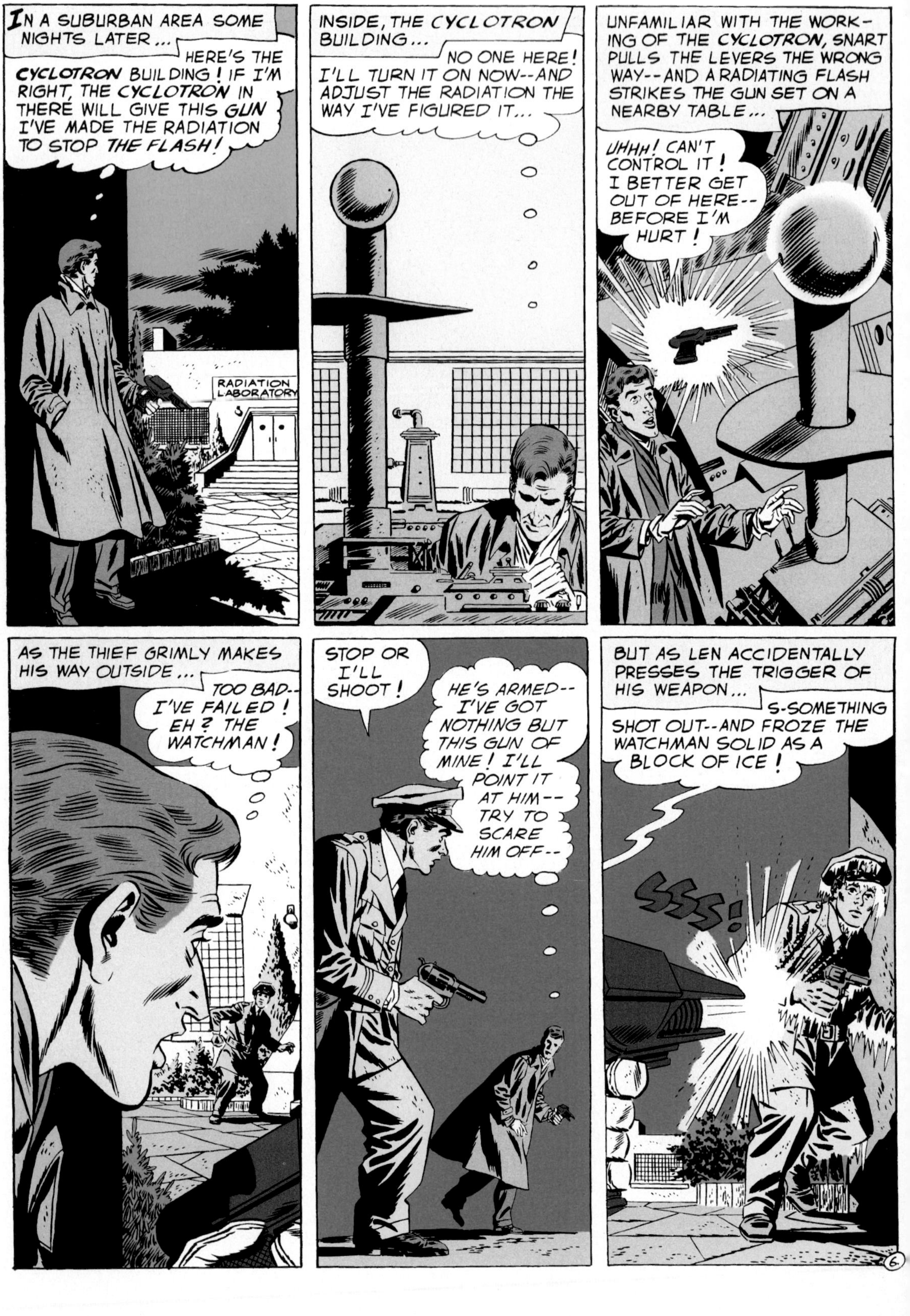
IN A SUBURBAN AREA SOME NIGHTS LATER...
HERE'S THE CYCLOTRON BUILDING! IF I'M RIGHT, THE CYCLOTRON IN THERE WILL GIVE THIS GUN I'VE MADE THE RADIATION TO STOP THE FLASH!
RADIATION LABORATORY
INSIDE, THE CYCLOTRON BUILDING...
NO ONE HERE! I'LL TURN IT ON NOW--AND ADJUST THE RADIATION THE WAY I'VE FIGURED IT...
UNFAMILIAR WITH THE WORKING OF THE CYCLOTRON, SNART PULLS THE LEVERS THE WRONG WAY--AND A RADIATING FLASH STRIKES THE GUN SET ON A NEARBY TABLE...
UHHH! CAN'T CONTROL IT! I BETTER GET OUT OF HERE--BEFORE I'M HURT!
AS THE THIEF GRIMLY MAKES HIS WAY OUTSIDE...
TOO BAD--I'VE FAILED! EH? THE WATCHMAN!
STOP OR I'LL SHOOT!
HE'S ARMED--I'VE GOT NOTHING BUT THIS GUN OF MINE! I'LL POINT IT AT HIM--TRY TO SCARE HIM OFF--
BUT AS LEN ACCIDENTALLY PRESSES THE TRIGGER OF HIS WEAPON...
S-SOMETHING SHOT OUT--AND FROZE THE WATCHMAN SOLID AS A BLOCK OF ICE!
SSSS!
6

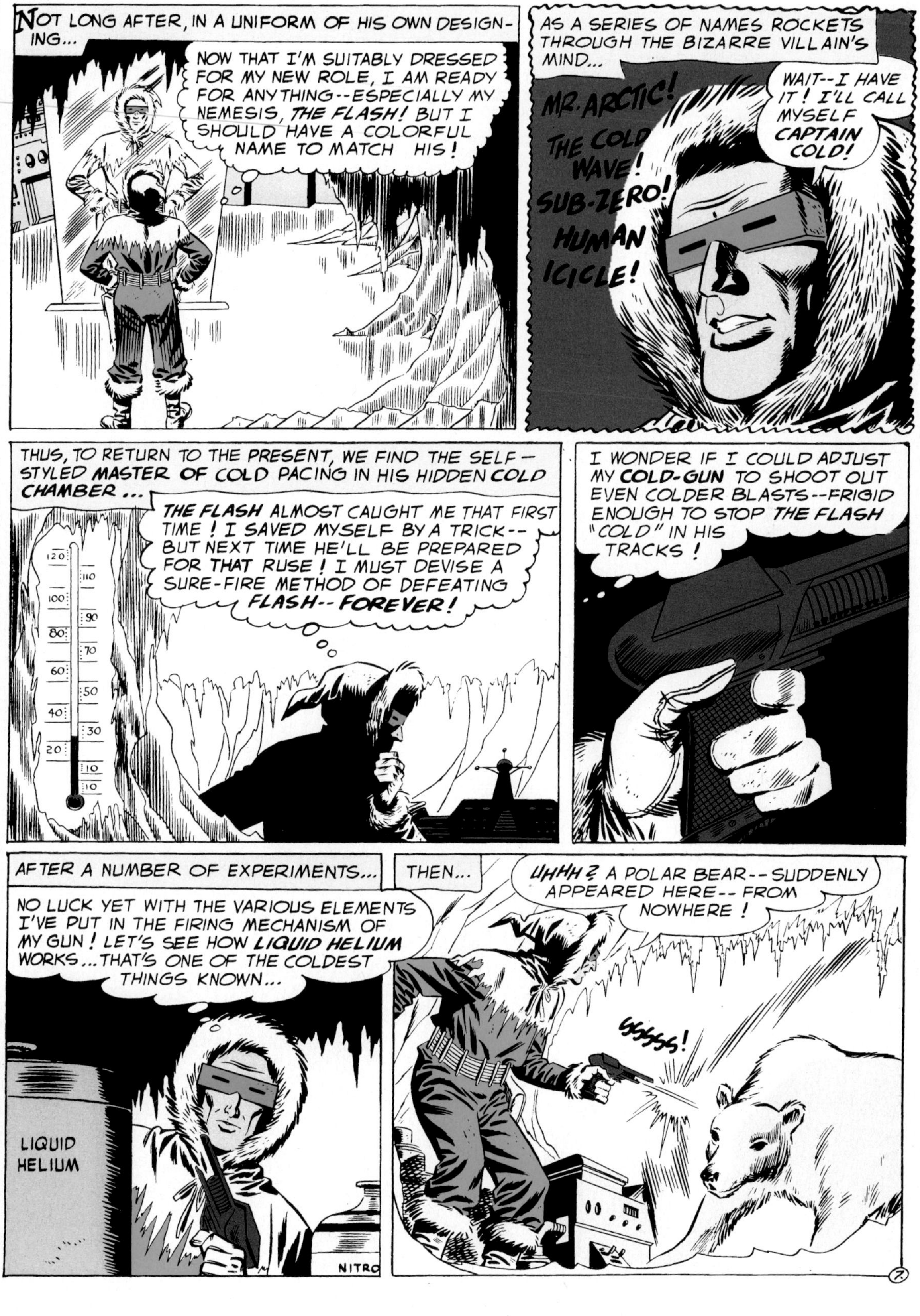
NOT LONG AFTER, IN A UNIFORM OF HIS OWN DESIGNING...
NOW THAT I'M SUITABLY DRESSED FOR MY NEW ROLE, I AM READY FOR ANYTHING--ESPECIALLY MY NEMESIS, THE FLASH! BUT I SHOULD HAVE A COLORFUL NAME TO MATCH HIS!
AS A SERIES OF NAMES ROCKETS THROUGH THE BIZARRE VILLAIN'S MIND...
MR. ARCTIC!
THE COLD WAVE!
SUB-ZERO!
HUMAN ICICLE!
WAIT--I HAVE IT! I'LL CALL MYSELF CAPTAIN COLD!
THUS, TO RETURN TO THE PRESENT, WE FIND THE SELF-STYLED MASTER OF COLD PACING IN HIS HIDDEN COLD CHAMBER...
THE FLASH ALMOST CAUGHT ME THAT FIRST TIME! I SAVED MYSELF BY A TRICK--BUT NEXT TIME HE'LL BE PREPARED FOR THAT RUSE! I MUST DEVISE A SURE-FIRE METHOD OF DEFEATING FLASH--FOREVER!
I WONDER IF I COULD ADJUST MY COLD-GUN TO SHOOT OUT EVEN COLDER BLASTS--FRIGID ENOUGH TO STOP THE FLASH "COLD" IN HIS TRACKS!
AFTER A NUMBER OF EXPERIMENTS...
NO LUCK YET WITH THE VARIOUS ELEMENTS I'VE PUT IN THE FIRING MECHANISM OF MY GUN! LET'S SEE HOW LIQUID HELIUM WORKS... THAT'S ONE OF THE COLDEST THINGS KNOWN...
LIQUID HELIUM
NITRO
THEN...
UHHH? A POLAR BEAR--SUDDENLY APPEARED HERE--FROM NOWHERE!
SSSSS!
7

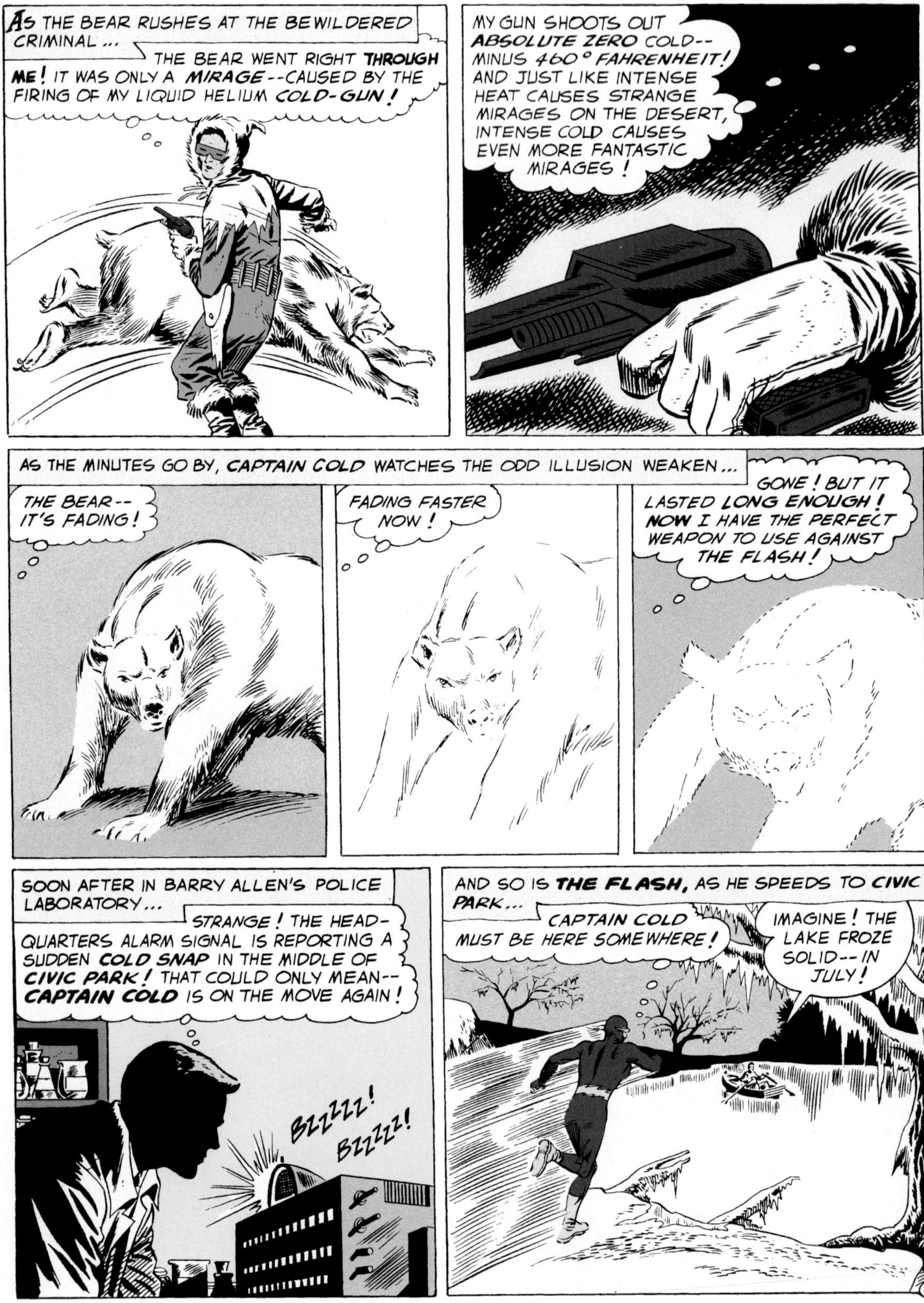

AS THE BEAR RUSHES AT THE BEWILDERED CRIMINAL ...
THE BEAR WENT RIGHT THROUGH ME! IT WAS ONLY A MIRAGE--CAUSED BY THE FIRING OF MY LIQUID HELIUM COLD-GUN!
MY GUN SHOOTS OUT ABSOLUTE ZERO COLD-- MINUS 460° FAHRENHEIT! AND JUST LIKE INTENSE HEAT CAUSES STRANGE MIRAGES ON THE DESERT, INTENSE COLD CAUSES EVEN MORE FANTASTIC MIRAGES!
AS THE MINUTES GO BY, CAPTAIN COLD WATCHES THE ODD ILLUSION WEAKEN ...
THE BEAR-- IT'S FADING!
FADING FASTER NOW!
GONE! BUT IT LASTED LONG ENOUGH! NOW I HAVE THE PERFECT WEAPON TO USE AGAINST THE FLASH!
SOON AFTER IN BARRY ALLEN'S POLICE LABORATORY...
STRANGE! THE HEAD-QUARTERS ALARM SIGNAL IS REPORTING A SUDDEN COLD SNAP IN THE MIDDLE OF CIVIC PARK! THAT COULD ONLY MEAN-- CAPTAIN COLD IS ON THE MOVE AGAIN!
BZZZZZ! BZZZZZ!
AND SO IS THE FLASH, AS HE SPEEDS TO CIVIC PARK...
CAPTAIN COLD MUST BE HERE SOMEWHERE!
IMAGINE! THE LAKE FROZE SOLID-- IN JULY!
8

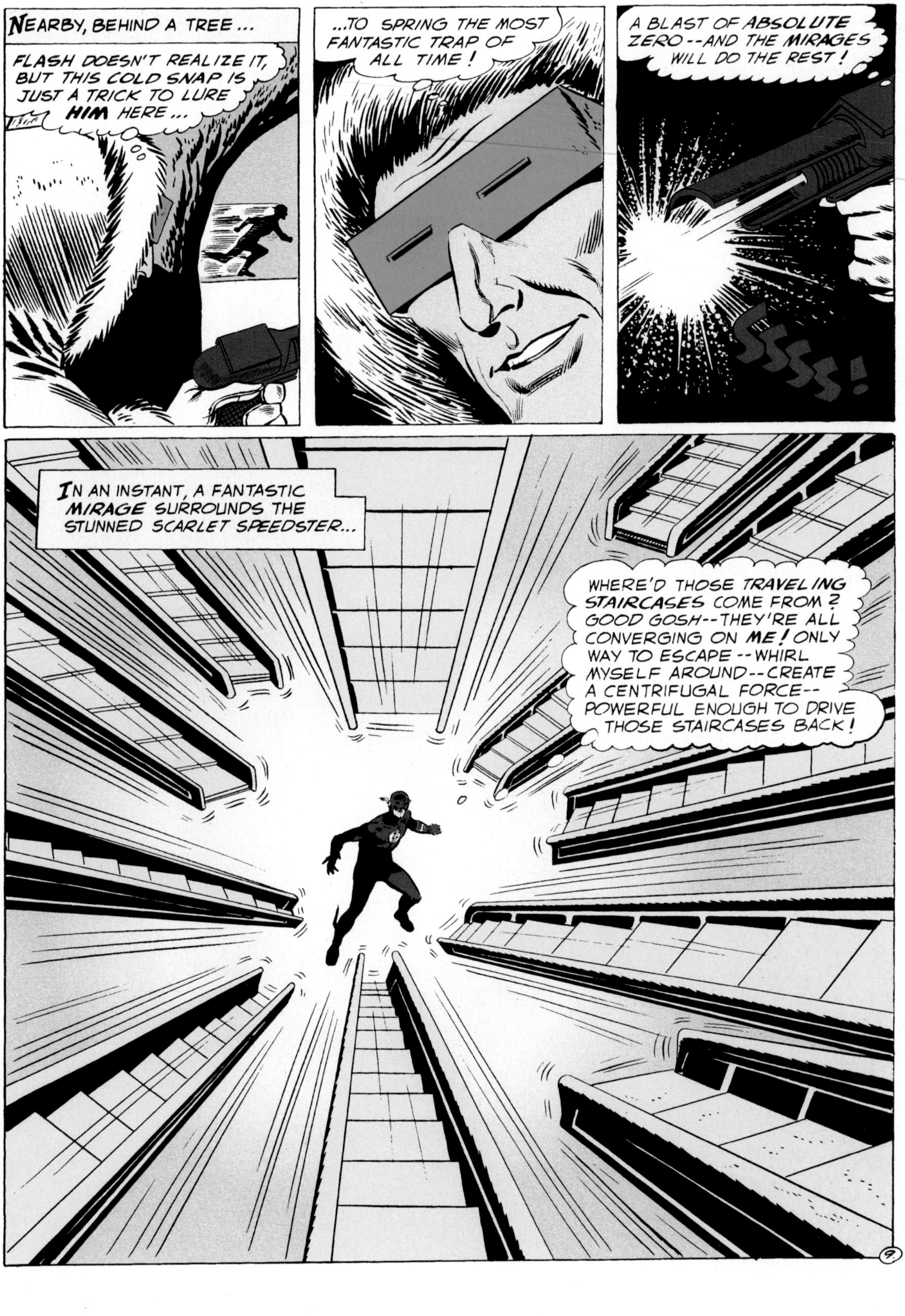
NEARBY, BEHIND A TREE ...
FLASH DOESN'T REALIZE IT, BUT THIS COLD SNAP IS JUST A TRICK TO LURE HIM HERE ...
...TO SPRING THE MOST FANTASTIC TRAP OF ALL TIME!
A BLAST OF ABSOLUTE ZERO--AND THE MIRAGES WILL DO THE REST!
SSSSS!
IN AN INSTANT, A FANTASTIC MIRAGE SURROUNDS THE STUNNED SCARLET SPEEDSTER...
WHERE'D THOSE TRAVELING STAIRCASES COME FROM? GOOD GOSH--THEY'RE ALL CONVERGING ON ME! ONLY WAY TO ESCAPE--WHIRL MYSELF AROUND--CREATE A CENTRIFUGAL FORCE--POWERFUL ENOUGH TO DRIVE THOSE STAIRCASES BACK!
9

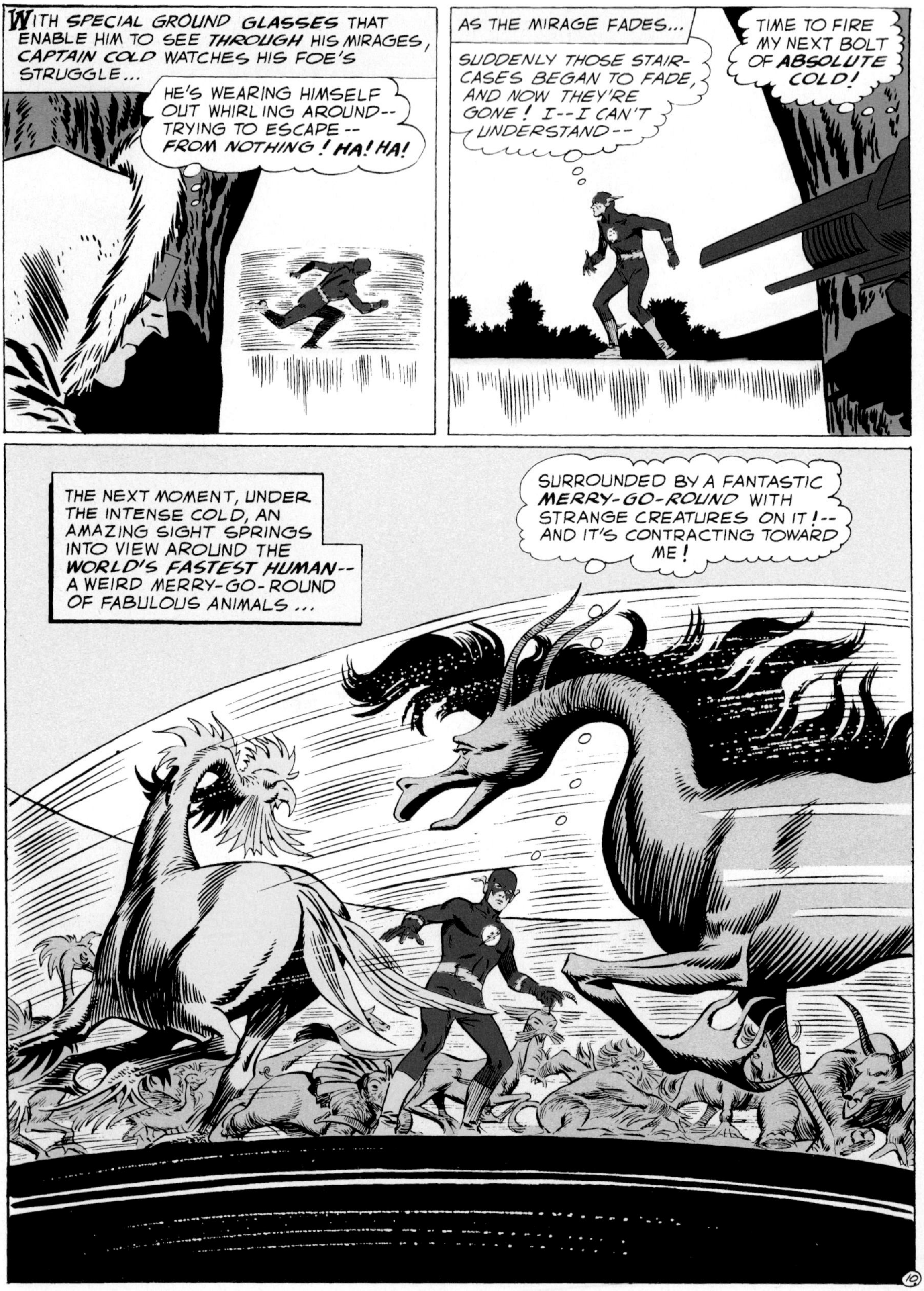
WITH SPECIAL GROUND GLASSES THAT ENABLE HIM TO SEE THROUGH HIS MIRAGES, CAPTAIN COLD WATCHES HIS FOE'S STRUGGLE...
HE'S WEARING HIMSELF OUT WHIRLING AROUND-- TRYING TO ESCAPE -- FROM NOTHING! HA! HA!
AS THE MIRAGE FADES...
SUDDENLY THOSE STAIR-CASES BEGAN TO FADE, AND NOW THEY'RE GONE! I--I CAN'T UNDERSTAND--
TIME TO FIRE MY NEXT BOLT OF ABSOLUTE COLD!
THE NEXT MOMENT, UNDER THE INTENSE COLD, AN AMAZING SIGHT SPRINGS INTO VIEW AROUND THE WORLD'S FASTEST HUMAN-- A WEIRD MERRY-GO-ROUND OF FABULOUS ANIMALS...
SURROUNDED BY A FANTASTIC MERRY-GO-ROUND WITH STRANGE CREATURES ON IT!-- AND IT'S CONTRACTING TOWARD ME!
10

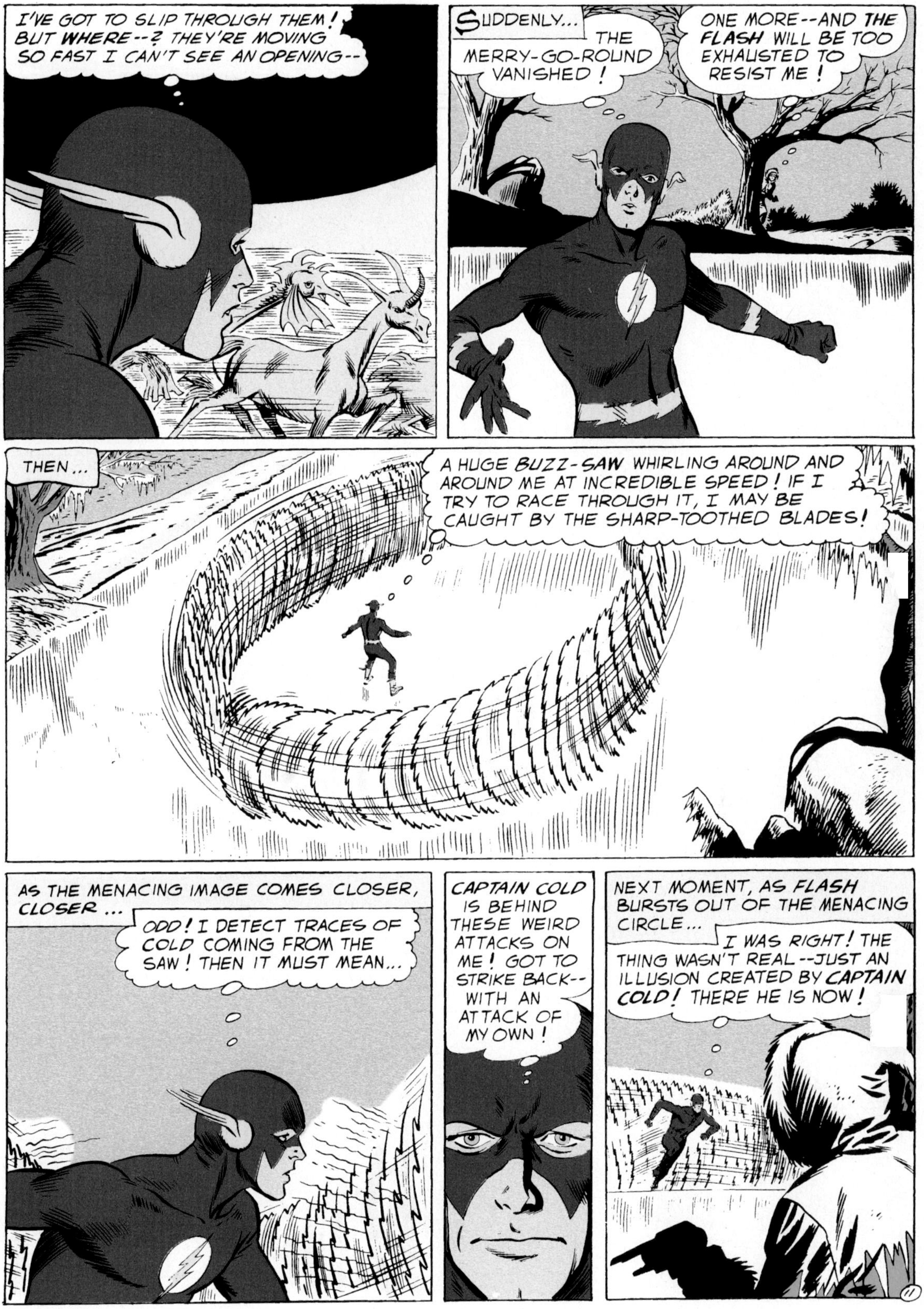
I'VE GOT TO SLIP THROUGH THEM! BUT WHERE--? THEY'RE MOVING SO FAST I CAN'T SEE AN OPENING--
SUDDENLY...
THE MERRY-GO-ROUND VANISHED!
ONE MORE--AND THE FLASH WILL BE TOO EXHAUSTED TO RESIST ME!
THEN...
A HUGE BUZZ-SAW WHIRLING AROUND AND AROUND ME AT INCREDIBLE SPEED! IF I TRY TO RACE THROUGH IT, I MAY BE CAUGHT BY THE SHARP-TOOTHED BLADES!
AS THE MENACING IMAGE COMES CLOSER, CLOSER...
ODD! I DETECT TRACES OF COLD COMING FROM THE SAW! THEN IT MUST MEAN...
CAPTAIN COLD IS BEHIND THESE WEIRD ATTACKS ON ME! GOT TO STRIKE BACK--WITH AN ATTACK OF MY OWN!
NEXT MOMENT, AS FLASH BURSTS OUT OF THE MENACING CIRCLE...
I WAS RIGHT! THE THING WASN'T REAL--JUST AN ILLUSION CREATED BY CAPTAIN COLD! THERE HE IS NOW!
11

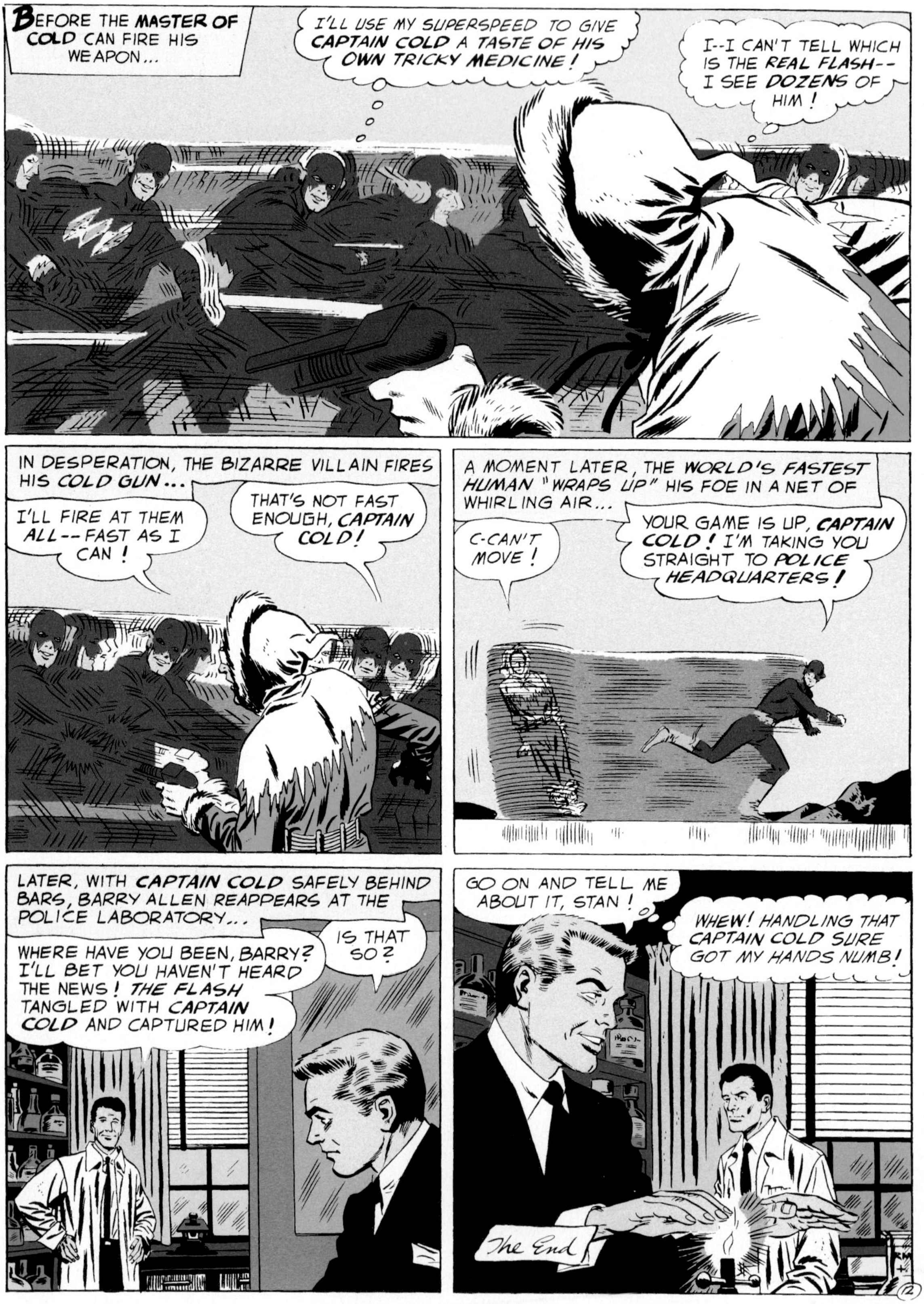
BEFORE THE MASTER OF COLD CAN FIRE HIS WEAPON...
I'LL USE MY SUPERSPEED TO GIVE CAPTAIN COLD A TASTE OF HIS OWN TRICKY MEDICINE!
I--I CAN'T TELL WHICH IS THE REAL FLASH-- I SEE DOZENS OF HIM!
IN DESPERATION, THE BIZARRE VILLAIN FIRES HIS COLD GUN...
I'LL FIRE AT THEM ALL--FAST AS I CAN!
THAT'S NOT FAST ENOUGH, CAPTAIN COLD!
A MOMENT LATER, THE WORLD'S FASTEST HUMAN "WRAPS UP" HIS FOE IN A NET OF WHIRLING AIR...
C-CAN'T MOVE!
YOUR GAME IS UP, CAPTAIN COLD! I'M TAKING YOU STRAIGHT TO POLICE HEADQUARTERS!
LATER, WITH CAPTAIN COLD SAFELY BEHIND BARS, BARRY ALLEN REAPPEARS AT THE POLICE LABORATORY...
WHERE HAVE YOU BEEN, BARRY? I'LL BET YOU HAVEN'T HEARD THE NEWS! THE FLASH TANGLED WITH CAPTAIN COLD AND CAPTURED HIM!
IS THAT SO?
GO ON AND TELL ME ABOUT IT, STAN!
WHEW! HANDLING THAT CAPTAIN COLD SURE GOT MY HANDS NUMB!
The End
12

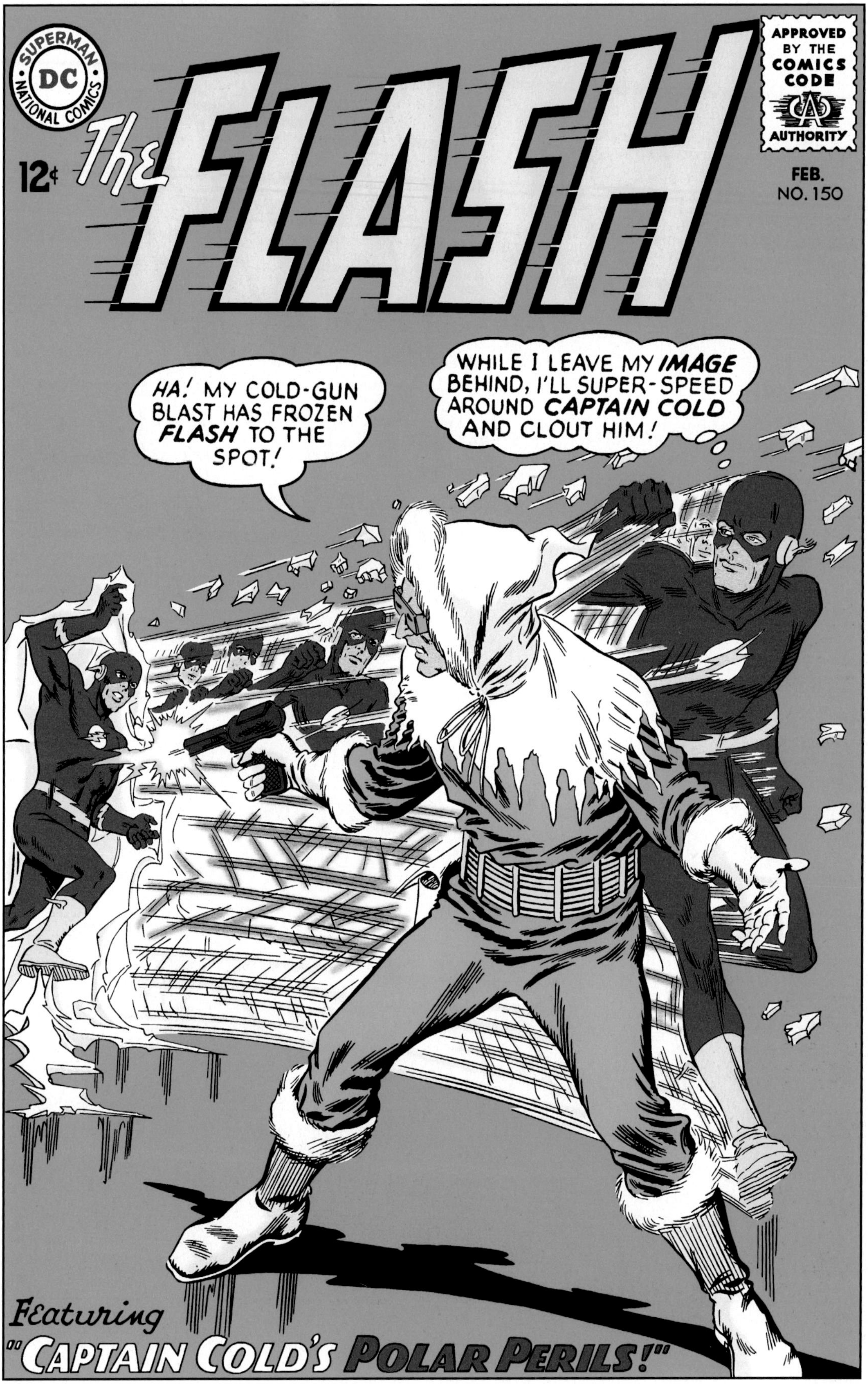

SUPERMAN DC NATIONAL COMICS
12¢
The FLASH
APPROVED BY THE COMICS CODE AUTHORITY
FEB. NO. 150
HA! MY COLD-GUN BLAST HAS FROZEN FLASH TO THE SPOT!
WHILE I LEAVE MY IMAGE BEHIND, I'LL SUPER-SPEED AROUND CAPTAIN COLD AND CLOUT HIM!
Featuring "CAPTAIN COLD'S POLAR PERILS!"

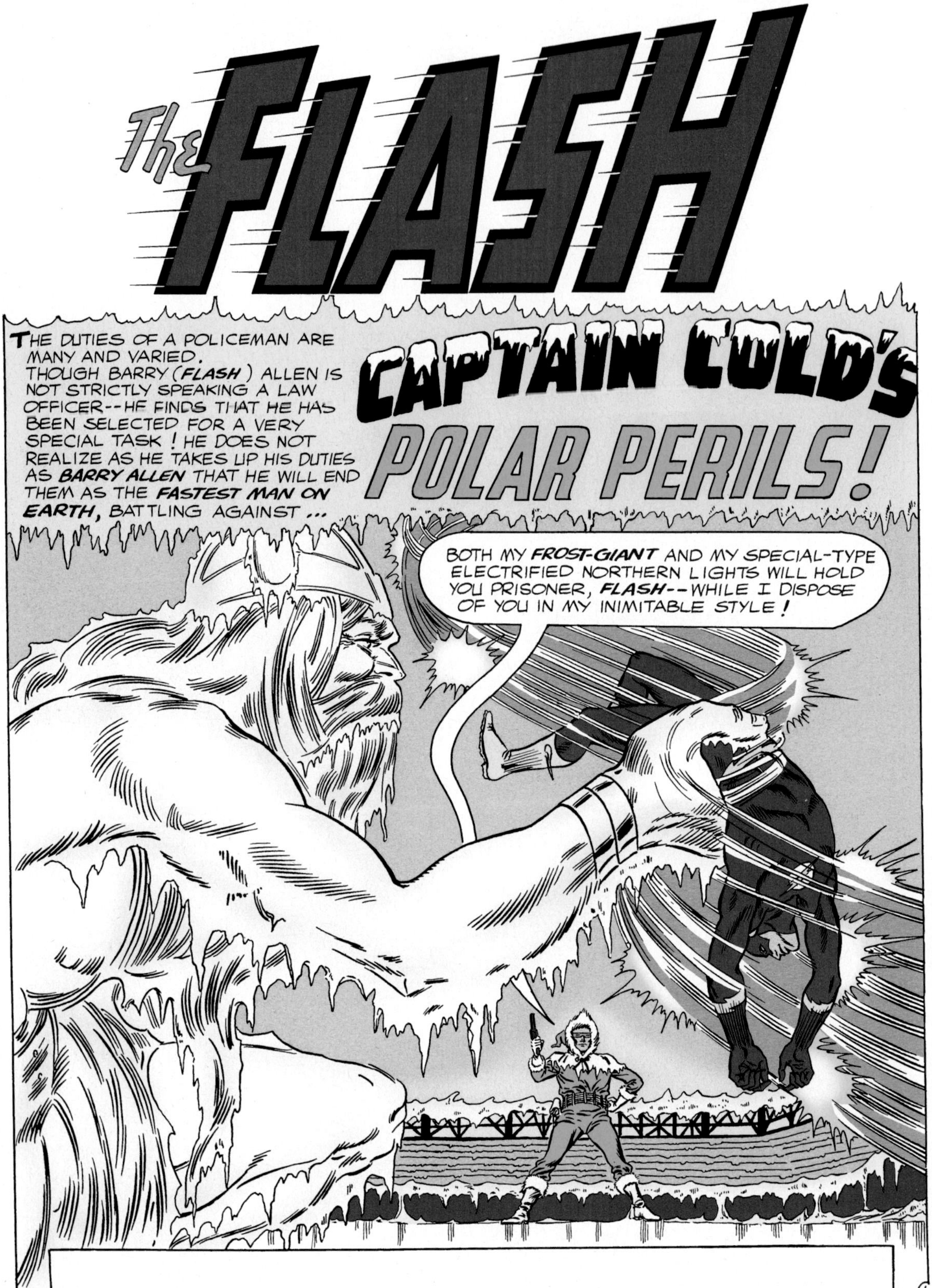
The FLASH
THE DUTIES OF A POLICEMAN ARE MANY AND VARIED. THOUGH BARRY (FLASH) ALLEN IS NOT STRICTLY SPEAKING A LAW OFFICER--HE FINDS THAT HE HAS BEEN SELECTED FOR A VERY SPECIAL TASK! HE DOES NOT REALIZE AS HE TAKES UP HIS DUTIES AS BARRY ALLEN THAT HE WILL END THEM AS THE FASTEST MAN ON EARTH, BATTLING AGAINST...
CAPTAIN COLD'S POLAR PERILS!
BOTH MY FROST-GIANT AND MY SPECIAL-TYPE ELECTRIFIED NORTHERN LIGHTS WILL HOLD YOU PRISONER, FLASH--WHILE I DISPOSE OF YOU IN MY INIMITABLE STYLE!

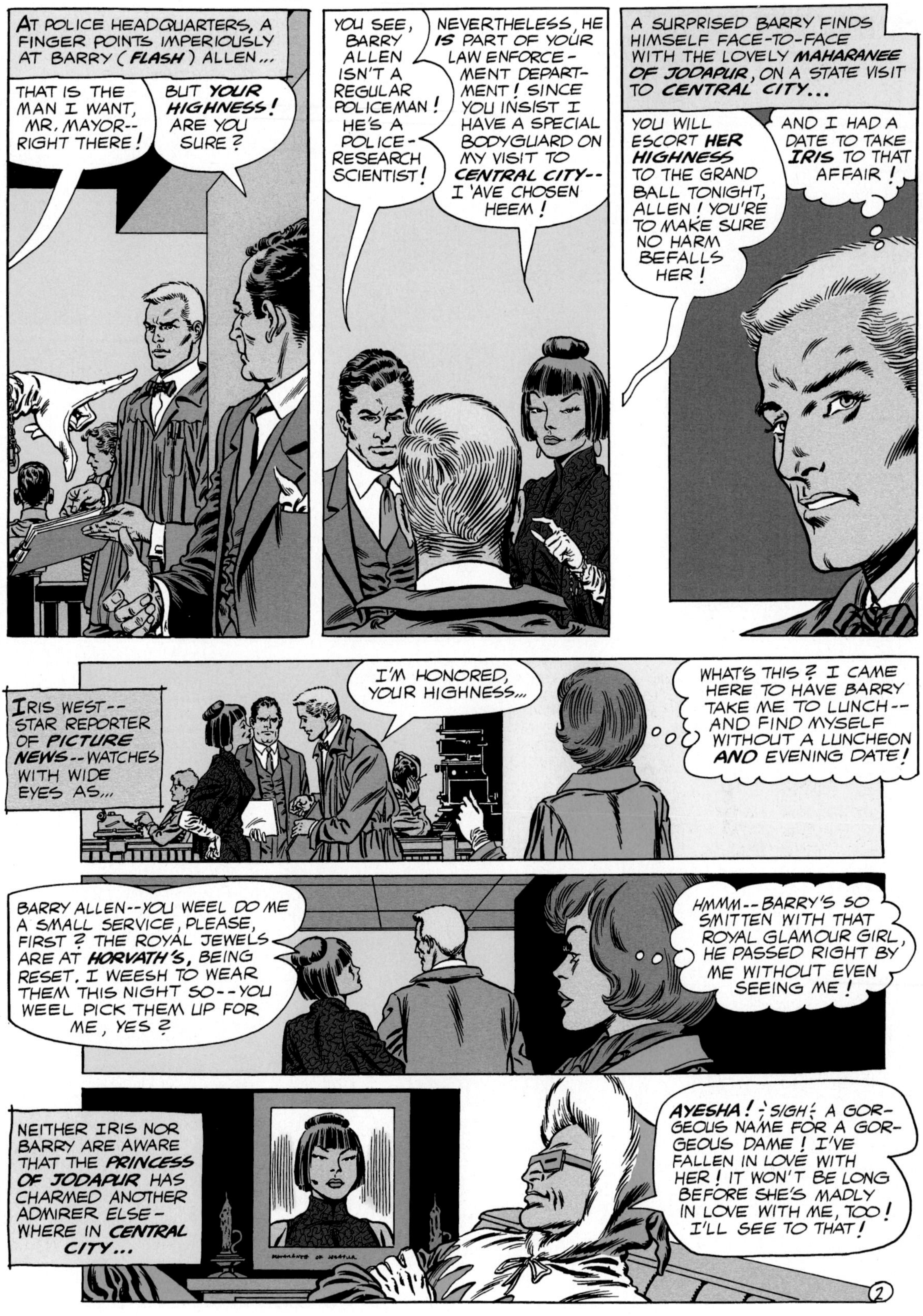
AT POLICE HEADQUARTERS, A FINGER POINTS IMPERIOUSLY AT BARRY (FLASH) ALLEN...
THAT IS THE MAN I WANT, MR. MAYOR-- RIGHT THERE!
BUT YOUR HIGHNESS! ARE YOU SURE?
YOU SEE, BARRY ALLEN ISN'T A REGULAR POLICEMAN! HE'S A POLICE-RESEARCH SCIENTIST!
NEVERTHELESS, HE IS PART OF YOUR LAW ENFORCE-MENT DEPART-MENT! SINCE YOU INSIST I HAVE A SPECIAL BODYGUARD ON MY VISIT TO CENTRAL CITY-- I 'AVE CHOSEN HEEM!
A SURPRISED BARRY FINDS HIMSELF FACE-TO-FACE WITH THE LOVELY MAHARANEE OF JODAPUR, ON A STATE VISIT TO CENTRAL CITY...
YOU WILL ESCORT HER HIGHNESS TO THE GRAND BALL TONIGHT, ALLEN! YOU'RE TO MAKE SURE NO HARM BEFALLS HER!
AND I HAD A DATE TO TAKE IRIS TO THAT AFFAIR!
IRIS WEST-- STAR REPORTER OF PICTURE NEWS--WATCHES WITH WIDE EYES AS...
I'M HONORED, YOUR HIGHNESS...
WHAT'S THIS? I CAME HERE TO HAVE BARRY TAKE ME TO LUNCH-- AND FIND MYSELF WITHOUT A LUNCHEON AND EVENING DATE!
BARRY ALLEN--YOU WEEL DO ME A SMALL SERVICE, PLEASE, FIRST? THE ROYAL JEWELS ARE AT HORVATH'S, BEING RESET. I WEESH TO WEAR THEM THIS NIGHT SO--YOU WEEL PICK THEM UP FOR ME, YES?
HMMM--BARRY'S SO SMITTEN WITH THAT ROYAL GLAMOUR GIRL, HE PASSED RIGHT BY ME WITHOUT EVEN SEEING ME!
NEITHER IRIS NOR BARRY ARE AWARE THAT THE PRINCESS OF JODAPUR HAS CHARMED ANOTHER ADMIRER ELSE-WHERE IN CENTRAL CITY...
AYESHA! -SIGH- A GOR-GEOUS NAME FOR A GOR-GEOUS DAME! I'VE FALLEN IN LOVE WITH HER! IT WON'T BE LONG BEFORE SHE'S MADLY IN LOVE WITH ME, TOO! I'LL SEE TO THAT!
2

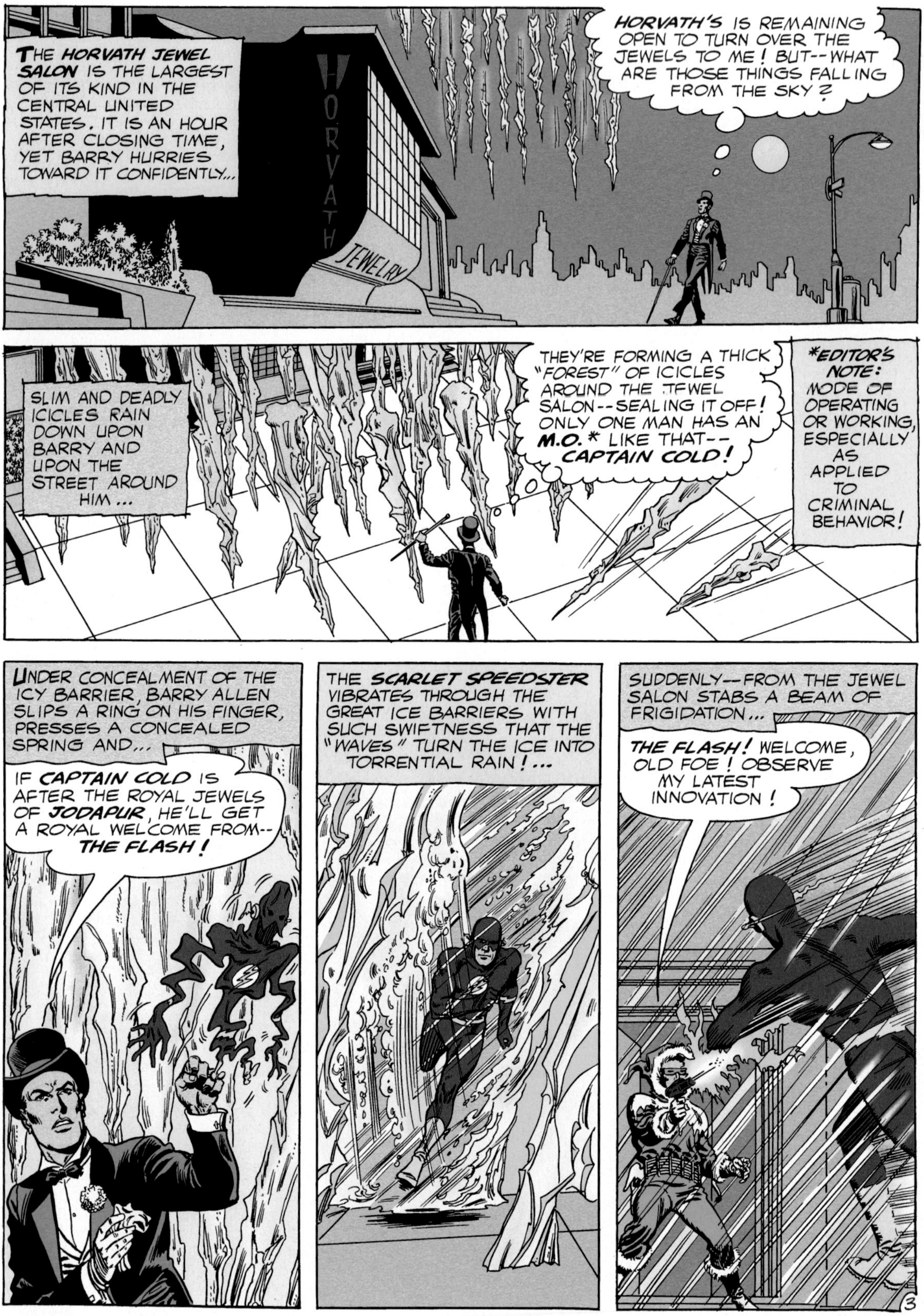
THE HORVATH JEWEL SALON IS THE LARGEST OF ITS KIND IN THE CENTRAL UNITED STATES. IT IS AN HOUR AFTER CLOSING TIME, YET BARRY HURRIES TOWARD IT CONFIDENTLY...
HORVATH
JEWELRY
HORVATH'S IS REMAINING OPEN TO TURN OVER THE JEWELS TO ME! BUT--WHAT ARE THOSE THINGS FALLING FROM THE SKY?
SLIM AND DEADLY ICICLES RAIN DOWN UPON BARRY AND UPON THE STREET AROUND HIM...
THEY'RE FORMING A THICK "FOREST" OF ICICLES AROUND THE JEWEL SALON--SEALING IT OFF! ONLY ONE MAN HAS AN M.O.* LIKE THAT--CAPTAIN COLD!
*EDITOR'S NOTE: MODE OF OPERATING OR WORKING, ESPECIALLY AS APPLIED TO CRIMINAL BEHAVIOR!
UNDER CONCEALMENT OF THE ICY BARRIER, BARRY ALLEN SLIPS A RING ON HIS FINGER, PRESSES A CONCEALED SPRING AND...
IF CAPTAIN COLD IS AFTER THE ROYAL JEWELS OF JODAPUR, HE'LL GET A ROYAL WELCOME FROM--THE FLASH!
THE SCARLET SPEEDSTER VIBRATES THROUGH THE GREAT ICE BARRIERS WITH SUCH SWIFTNESS THAT THE "WAVES" TURN THE ICE INTO TORRENTIAL RAIN!...
SUDDENLY--FROM THE JEWEL SALON STABS A BEAM OF FRIGIDATION...
THE FLASH! WELCOME, OLD FOE! OBSERVE MY LATEST INNOVATION!
3

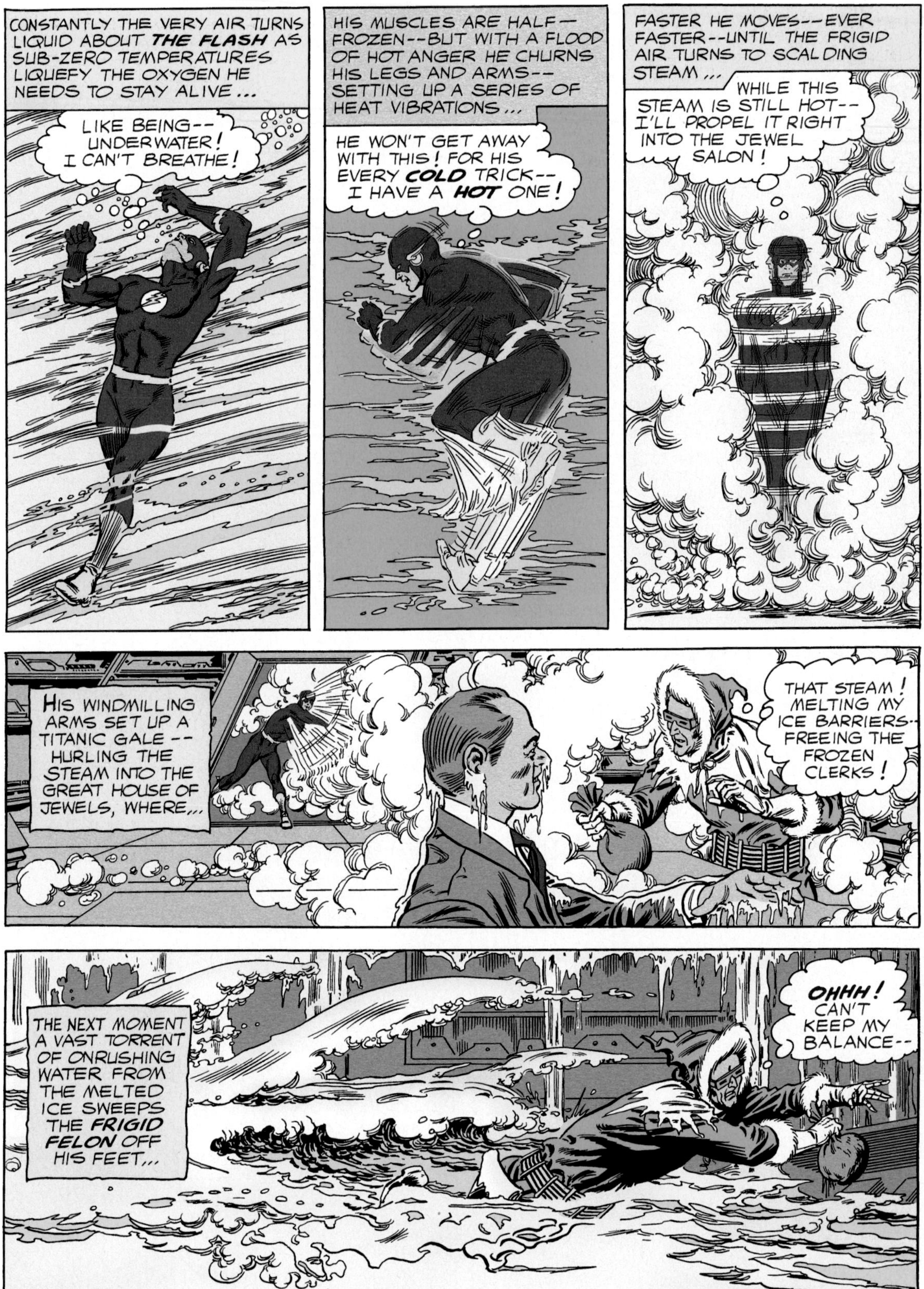
CONSTANTLY THE VERY AIR TURNS LIQUID ABOUT THE FLASH AS SUB-ZERO TEMPERATURES LIQUEFY THE OXYGEN HE NEEDS TO STAY ALIVE...
LIKE BEING-- UNDERWATER! I CAN'T BREATHE!
HIS MUSCLES ARE HALF-FROZEN--BUT WITH A FLOOD OF HOT ANGER HE CHURNS HIS LEGS AND ARMS--SETTING UP A SERIES OF HEAT VIBRATIONS...
HE WON'T GET AWAY WITH THIS! FOR HIS EVERY COLD TRICK-- I HAVE A HOT ONE!
FASTER HE MOVES--EVER FASTER--UNTIL THE FRIGID AIR TURNS TO SCALDING STEAM...
WHILE THIS STEAM IS STILL HOT-- I'LL PROPEL IT RIGHT INTO THE JEWEL SALON!
HIS WINDMILLING ARMS SET UP A TITANIC GALE--HURLING THE STEAM INTO THE GREAT HOUSE OF JEWELS, WHERE...
THAT STEAM! MELTING MY ICE BARRIERS--FREEING THE FROZEN CLERKS!
THE NEXT MOMENT A VAST TORRENT OF ONRUSHING WATER FROM THE MELTED ICE SWEEPS THE FRIGID FELON OFF HIS FEET...
OHHH! CAN'T KEEP MY BALANCE--
4

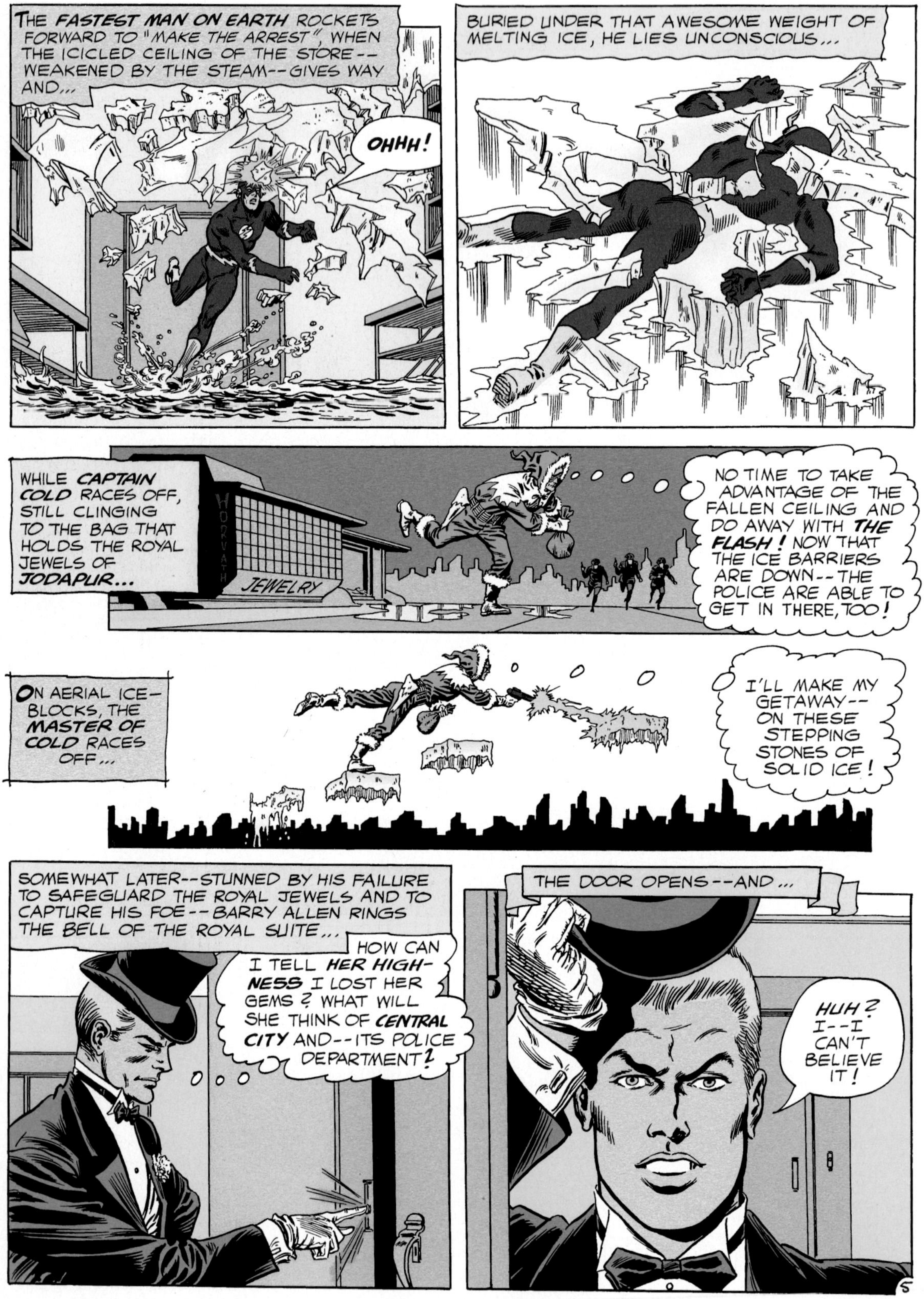
THE FASTEST MAN ON EARTH ROCKETS FORWARD TO "MAKE THE ARREST", WHEN THE ICICLED CEILING OF THE STORE--WEAKENED BY THE STEAM--GIVES WAY AND...
OHHH!
BURIED UNDER THAT AWESOME WEIGHT OF MELTING ICE, HE LIES UNCONSCIOUS...
WHILE CAPTAIN COLD RACES OFF, STILL CLINGING TO THE BAG THAT HOLDS THE ROYAL JEWELS OF JODAPUR...
HORVATH
JEWELRY
NO TIME TO TAKE ADVANTAGE OF THE FALLEN CEILING AND DO AWAY WITH THE FLASH! NOW THAT THE ICE BARRIERS ARE DOWN--THE POLICE ARE ABLE TO GET IN THERE, TOO!
ON AERIAL ICE-BLOCKS, THE MASTER OF COLD RACES OFF...
I'LL MAKE MY GETAWAY--ON THESE STEPPING STONES OF SOLID ICE!
SOMEWHAT LATER--STUNNED BY HIS FAILURE TO SAFEGUARD THE ROYAL JEWELS AND TO CAPTURE HIS FOE--BARRY ALLEN RINGS THE BELL OF THE ROYAL SUITE...
HOW CAN I TELL HER HIGHNESS I LOST HER GEMS? WHAT WILL SHE THINK OF CENTRAL CITY AND--ITS POLICE DEPARTMENT?
THE DOOR OPENS--AND...
HUH? I--I CAN'T BELIEVE IT!
5

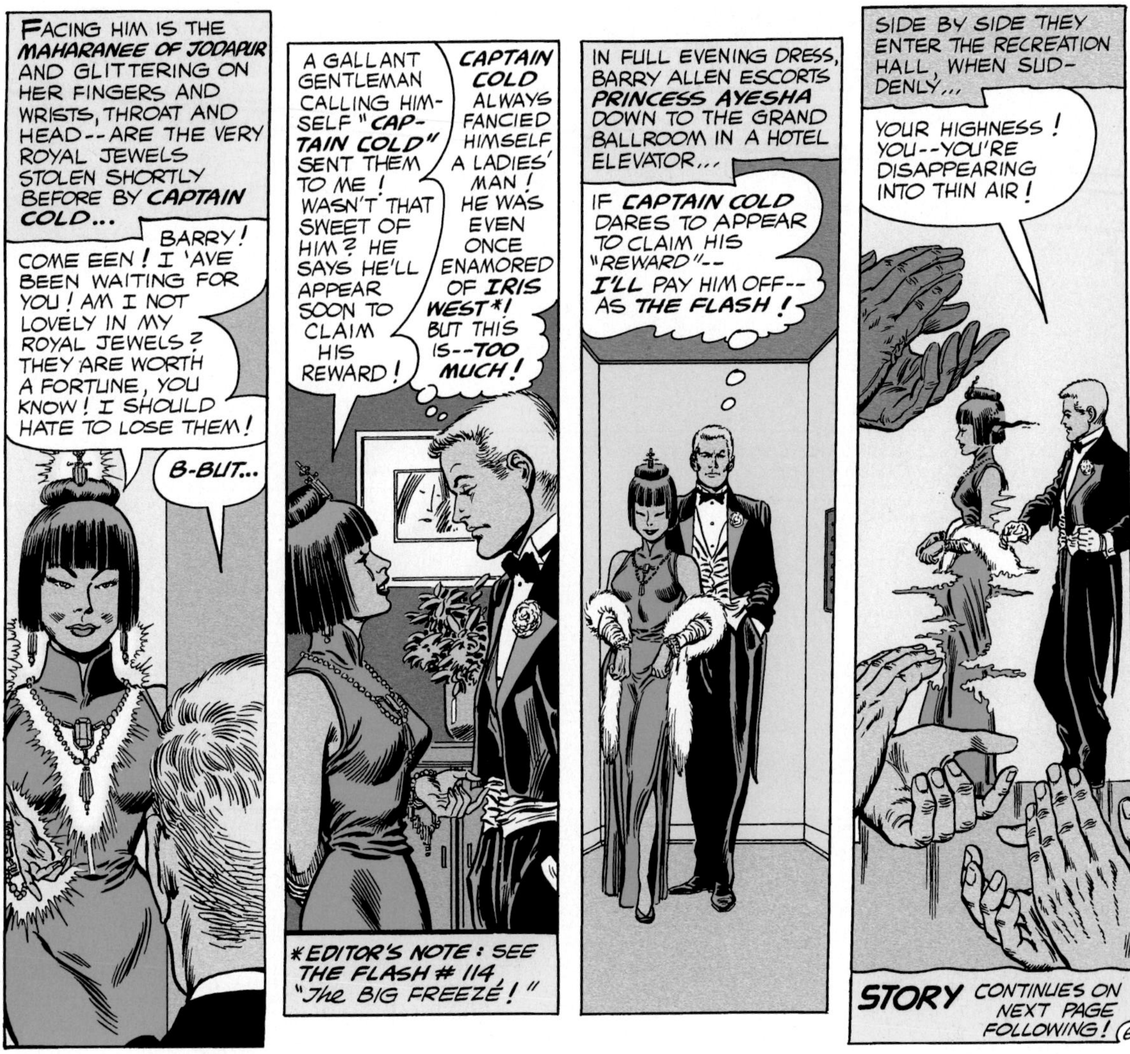

FACING HIM IS THE MAHARANEE OF JODAPUR AND GLITTERING ON HER FINGERS AND WRISTS, THROAT AND HEAD--ARE THE VERY ROYAL JEWELS STOLEN SHORTLY BEFORE BY CAPTAIN COLD...
BARRY! COME EEN! I 'AVE BEEN WAITING FOR YOU! AM I NOT LOVELY IN MY ROYAL JEWELS? THEY ARE WORTH A FORTUNE, YOU KNOW! I SHOULD HATE TO LOSE THEM!
B-BUT...
A GALLANT GENTLEMAN CALLING HIMSELF "CAPTAIN COLD" SENT THEM TO ME! WASN'T THAT SWEET OF HIM? HE SAYS HE'LL APPEAR SOON TO CLAIM HIS REWARD!
CAPTAIN COLD ALWAYS FANCIED HIMSELF A LADIES' MAN! HE WAS EVEN ONCE ENAMORED OF IRIS WEST*! BUT THIS IS--TOO MUCH!
*EDITOR'S NOTE: SEE THE FLASH # 114, "The BIG FREEZE!"
IN FULL EVENING DRESS, BARRY ALLEN ESCORTS PRINCESS AYESHA DOWN TO THE GRAND BALLROOM IN A HOTEL ELEVATOR...
IF CAPTAIN COLD DARES TO APPEAR TO CLAIM HIS "REWARD"--I'LL PAY HIM OFF--AS THE FLASH!
SIDE BY SIDE THEY ENTER THE RECREATION HALL, WHEN SUDDENLY...
YOUR HIGHNESS! YOU--YOU'RE DISAPPEARING INTO THIN AIR!
STORY CONTINUES ON NEXT PAGE FOLLOWING!
6

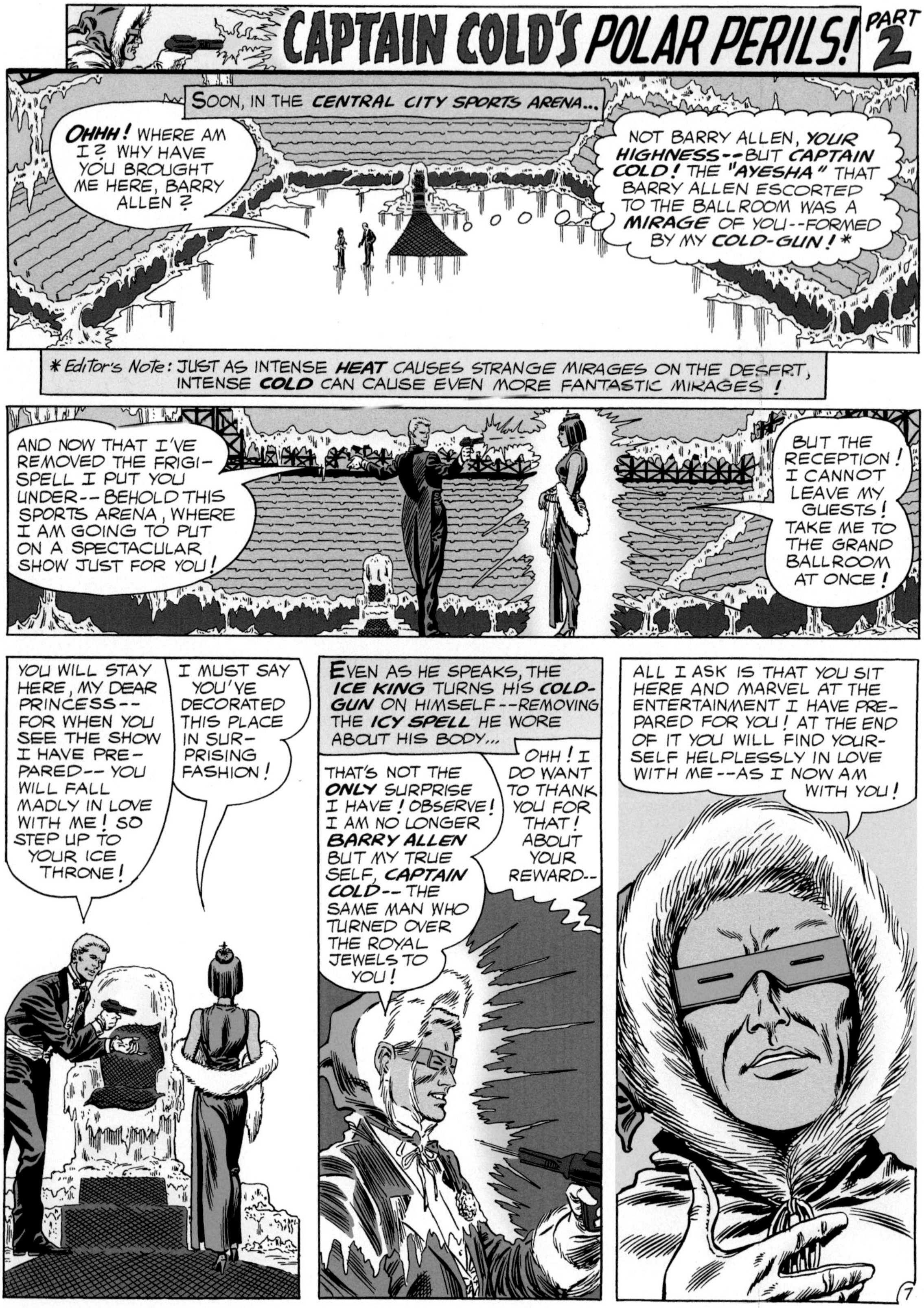
CAPTAIN COLD'S POLAR PERILS! PART 2
SOON, IN THE CENTRAL CITY SPORTS ARENA...
OHHH! WHERE AM I? WHY HAVE YOU BROUGHT ME HERE, BARRY ALLEN?
NOT BARRY ALLEN, YOUR HIGHNESS--BUT CAPTAIN COLD! THE "AYESHA" THAT BARRY ALLEN ESCORTED TO THE BALLROOM WAS A MIRAGE OF YOU--FORMED BY MY COLD-GUN! *
* Editor's Note: JUST AS INTENSE HEAT CAUSES STRANGE MIRAGES ON THE DESERT, INTENSE COLD CAN CAUSE EVEN MORE FANTASTIC MIRAGES!
AND NOW THAT I'VE REMOVED THE FRIGI-SPELL I PUT YOU UNDER-- BEHOLD THIS SPORTS ARENA, WHERE I AM GOING TO PUT ON A SPECTACULAR SHOW JUST FOR YOU!
BUT THE RECEPTION! I CANNOT LEAVE MY GUESTS! TAKE ME TO THE GRAND BALLROOM AT ONCE!
YOU WILL STAY HERE, MY DEAR PRINCESS-- FOR WHEN YOU SEE THE SHOW I HAVE PREPARED-- YOU WILL FALL MADLY IN LOVE WITH ME! SO STEP UP TO YOUR ICE THRONE!
I MUST SAY YOU'VE DECORATED THIS PLACE IN SURPRISING FASHION!
EVEN AS HE SPEAKS, THE ICE KING TURNS HIS COLD-GUN ON HIMSELF--REMOVING THE ICY SPELL HE WORE ABOUT HIS BODY...
THAT'S NOT THE ONLY SURPRISE I HAVE! OBSERVE! I AM NO LONGER BARRY ALLEN BUT MY TRUE SELF, CAPTAIN COLD-- THE SAME MAN WHO TURNED OVER THE ROYAL JEWELS TO YOU!
OHH! I DO WANT TO THANK YOU FOR THAT! ABOUT YOUR REWARD--
ALL I ASK IS THAT YOU SIT HERE AND MARVEL AT THE ENTERTAINMENT I HAVE PREPARED FOR YOU! AT THE END OF IT YOU WILL FIND YOURSELF HELPLESSLY IN LOVE WITH ME--AS I NOW AM WITH YOU!
7

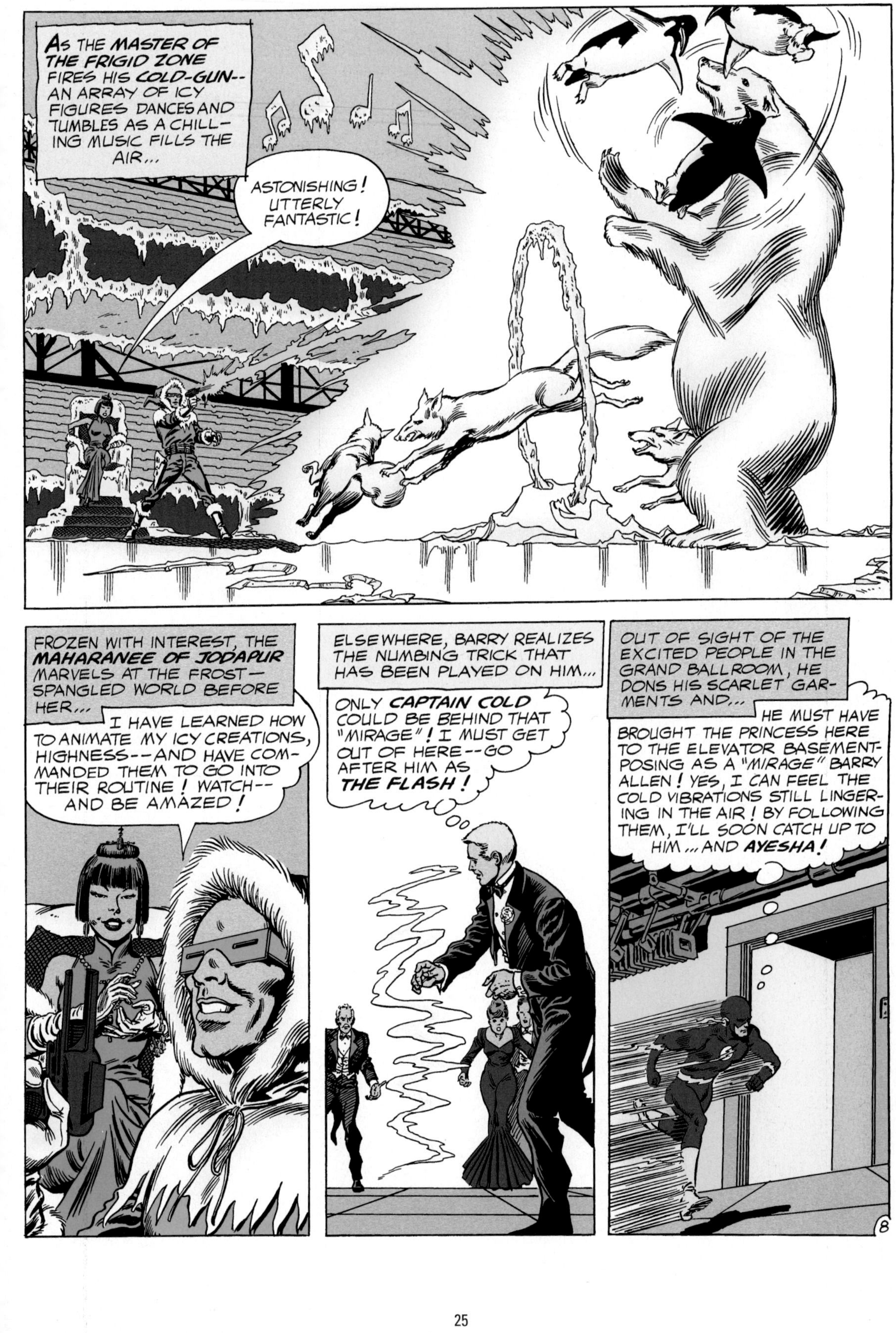

AS THE MASTER OF THE FRIGID ZONE FIRES HIS COLD-GUN-- AN ARRAY OF ICY FIGURES DANCES AND TUMBLES AS A CHILLING MUSIC FILLS THE AIR...
ASTONISHING! UTTERLY FANTASTIC!
FROZEN WITH INTEREST, THE MAHARANEE OF JODAPUR MARVELS AT THE FROST-SPANGLED WORLD BEFORE HER...
I HAVE LEARNED HOW TO ANIMATE MY ICY CREATIONS, HIGHNESS--AND HAVE COMMANDED THEM TO GO INTO THEIR ROUTINE! WATCH-- AND BE AMAZED!
ELSEWHERE, BARRY REALIZES THE NUMBING TRICK THAT HAS BEEN PLAYED ON HIM...
ONLY CAPTAIN COLD COULD BE BEHIND THAT "MIRAGE"! I MUST GET OUT OF HERE--GO AFTER HIM AS THE FLASH!
OUT OF SIGHT OF THE EXCITED PEOPLE IN THE GRAND BALLROOM, HE DONS HIS SCARLET GARMENTS AND...
HE MUST HAVE BROUGHT THE PRINCESS HERE TO THE ELEVATOR BASEMENT-POSING AS A "MIRAGE" BARRY ALLEN! YES, I CAN FEEL THE COLD VIBRATIONS STILL LINGERING IN THE AIR! BY FOLLOWING THEM, I'LL SOON CATCH UP TO HIM... AND AYESHA!
8

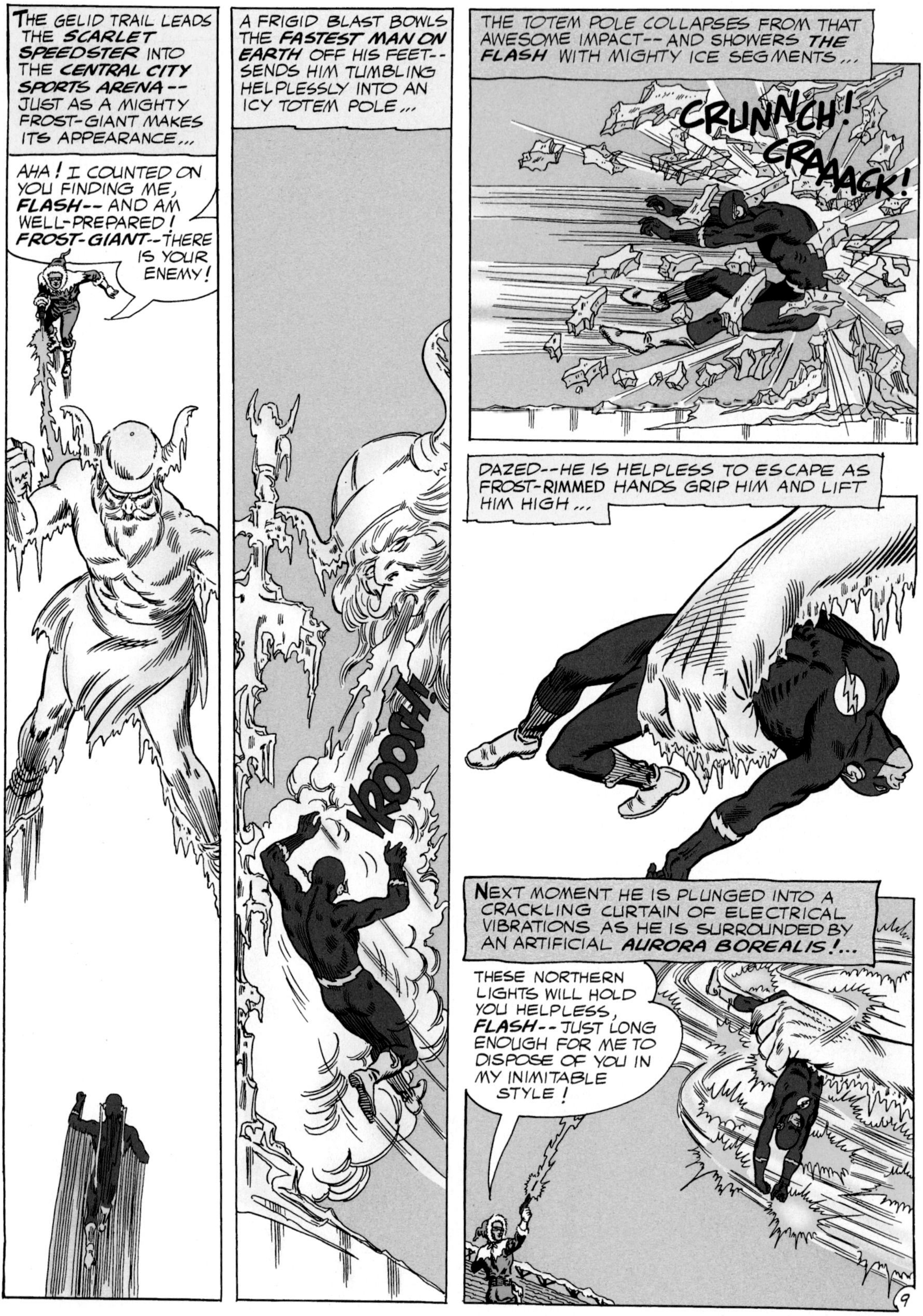
THE GELID TRAIL LEADS THE SCARLET SPEEDSTER INTO THE CENTRAL CITY SPORTS ARENA -- JUST AS A MIGHTY FROST-GIANT MAKES ITS APPEARANCE...
AHA! I COUNTED ON YOU FINDING ME, FLASH-- AND AM WELL-PREPARED! FROST-GIANT--THERE IS YOUR ENEMY!
A FRIGID BLAST BOWLS THE FASTEST MAN ON EARTH OFF HIS FEET-- SENDS HIM TUMBLING HELPLESSLY INTO AN ICY TOTEM POLE...
VROOSH!
THE TOTEM POLE COLLAPSES FROM THAT AWESOME IMPACT-- AND SHOWERS THE FLASH WITH MIGHTY ICE SEGMENTS...
CRUNNCH! CRAAACK!
DAZED--HE IS HELPLESS TO ESCAPE AS FROST-RIMMED HANDS GRIP HIM AND LIFT HIM HIGH...
NEXT MOMENT HE IS PLUNGED INTO A CRACKLING CURTAIN OF ELECTRICAL VIBRATIONS AS HE IS SURROUNDED BY AN ARTIFICIAL AURORA BOREALIS!...
THESE NORTHERN LIGHTS WILL HOLD YOU HELPLESS, FLASH-- JUST LONG ENOUGH FOR ME TO DISPOSE OF YOU IN MY INIMITABLE STYLE!
9

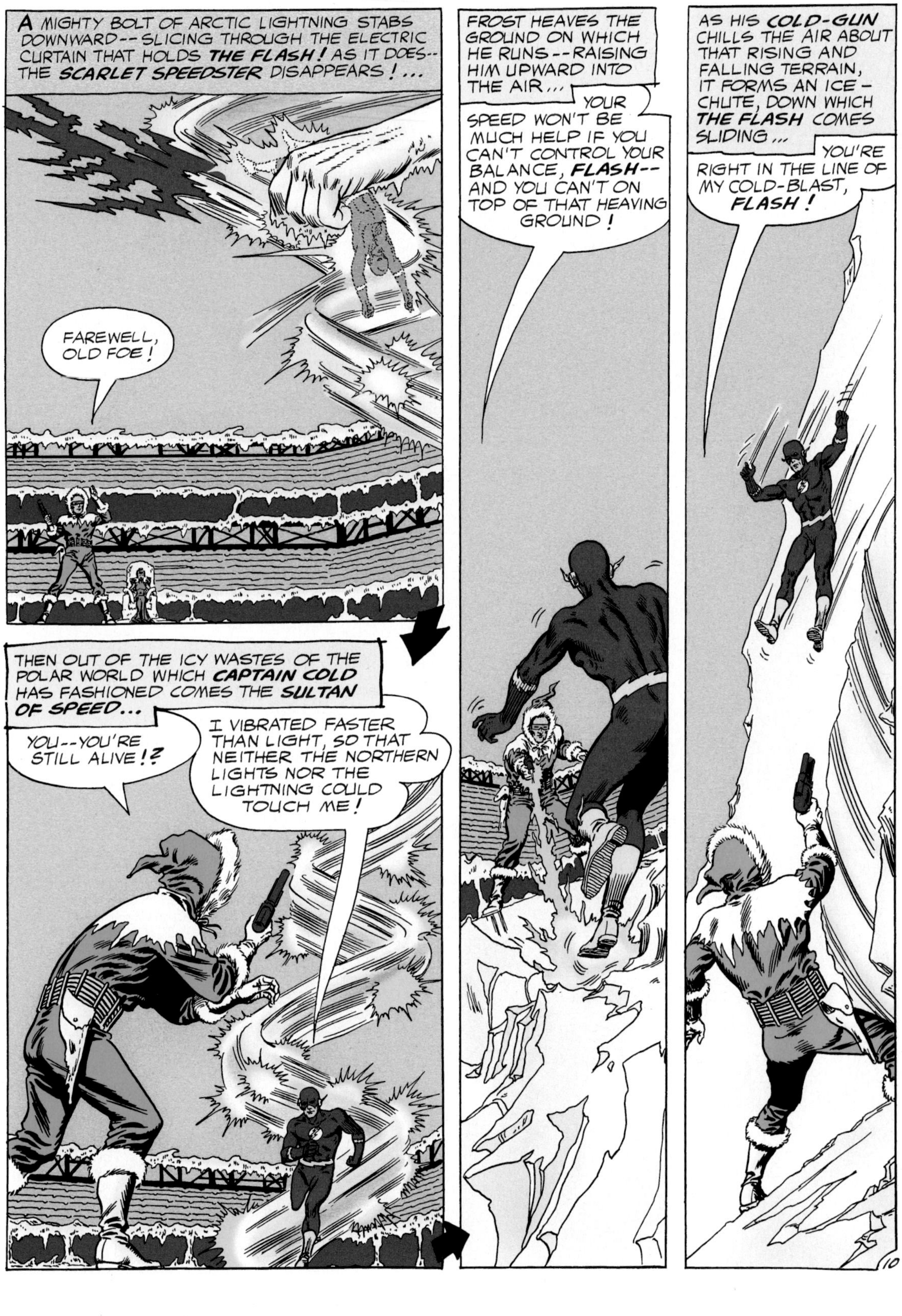

A MIGHTY BOLT OF ARCTIC LIGHTNING STABS DOWNWARD--SLICING THROUGH THE ELECTRIC CURTAIN THAT HOLDS THE FLASH! AS IT DOES--THE SCARLET SPEEDSTER DISAPPEARS!...
FAREWELL, OLD FOE!
THEN OUT OF THE ICY WASTES OF THE POLAR WORLD WHICH CAPTAIN COLD HAS FASHIONED COMES THE SULTAN OF SPEED...
YOU--YOU'RE STILL ALIVE!?
I VIBRATED FASTER THAN LIGHT, SO THAT NEITHER THE NORTHERN LIGHTS NOR THE LIGHTNING COULD TOUCH ME!
FROST HEAVES THE GROUND ON WHICH HE RUNS--RAISING HIM UPWARD INTO THE AIR...
YOUR SPEED WON'T BE MUCH HELP IF YOU CAN'T CONTROL YOUR BALANCE, FLASH--AND YOU CAN'T ON TOP OF THAT HEAVING GROUND!
AS HIS COLD-GUN CHILLS THE AIR ABOUT THAT RISING AND FALLING TERRAIN, IT FORMS AN ICE-CHUTE, DOWN WHICH THE FLASH COMES SLIDING...
YOU'RE RIGHT IN THE LINE OF MY COLD-BLAST, FLASH!
10

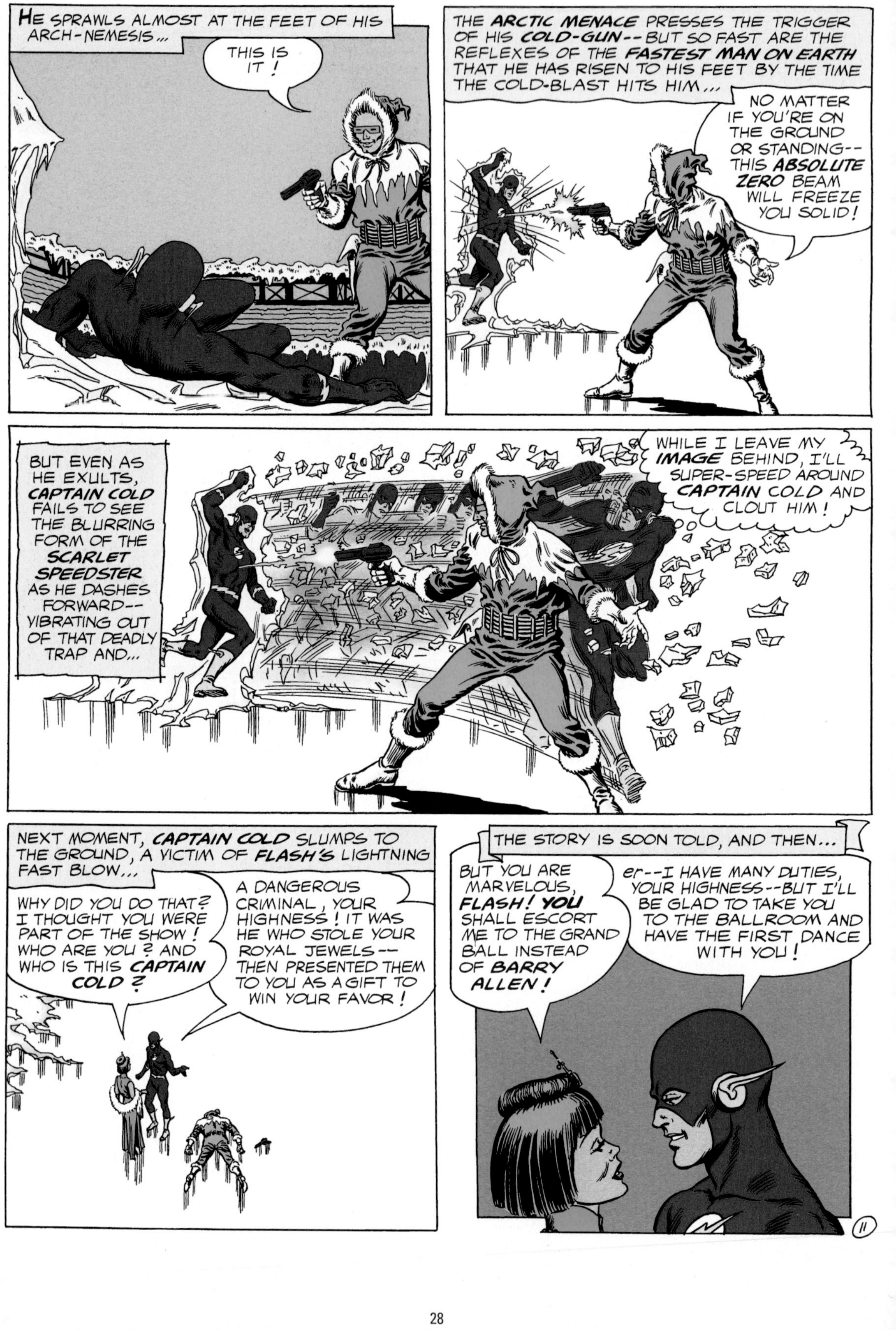

HE SPRAWLS ALMOST AT THE FEET OF HIS ARCH-NEMESIS...
THIS IS IT!
THE ARCTIC MENACE PRESSES THE TRIGGER OF HIS COLD-GUN--BUT SO FAST ARE THE REFLEXES OF THE FASTEST MAN ON EARTH THAT HE HAS RISEN TO HIS FEET BY THE TIME THE COLD-BLAST HITS HIM...
NO MATTER IF YOU'RE ON THE GROUND OR STANDING--THIS ABSOLUTE ZERO BEAM WILL FREEZE YOU SOLID!
BUT EVEN AS HE EXULTS, CAPTAIN COLD FAILS TO SEE THE BLURRING FORM OF THE SCARLET SPEEDSTER AS HE DASHES FORWARD--VIBRATING OUT OF THAT DEADLY TRAP AND...
WHILE I LEAVE MY IMAGE BEHIND, I'LL SUPER-SPEED AROUND CAPTAIN COLD AND CLOUT HIM!
NEXT MOMENT, CAPTAIN COLD SLUMPS TO THE GROUND, A VICTIM OF FLASH'S LIGHTNING FAST BLOW...
WHY DID YOU DO THAT? I THOUGHT YOU WERE PART OF THE SHOW! WHO ARE YOU? AND WHO IS THIS CAPTAIN COLD?
A DANGEROUS CRIMINAL, YOUR HIGHNESS! IT WAS HE WHO STOLE YOUR ROYAL JEWELS--THEN PRESENTED THEM TO YOU AS A GIFT TO WIN YOUR FAVOR!
THE STORY IS SOON TOLD, AND THEN...
BUT YOU ARE MARVELOUS, FLASH! YOU SHALL ESCORT ME TO THE GRAND BALL INSTEAD OF BARRY ALLEN!
er--I HAVE MANY DUTIES, YOUR HIGHNESS--BUT I'LL BE GLAD TO TAKE YOU TO THE BALLROOM AND HAVE THE FIRST DANCE WITH YOU!
11

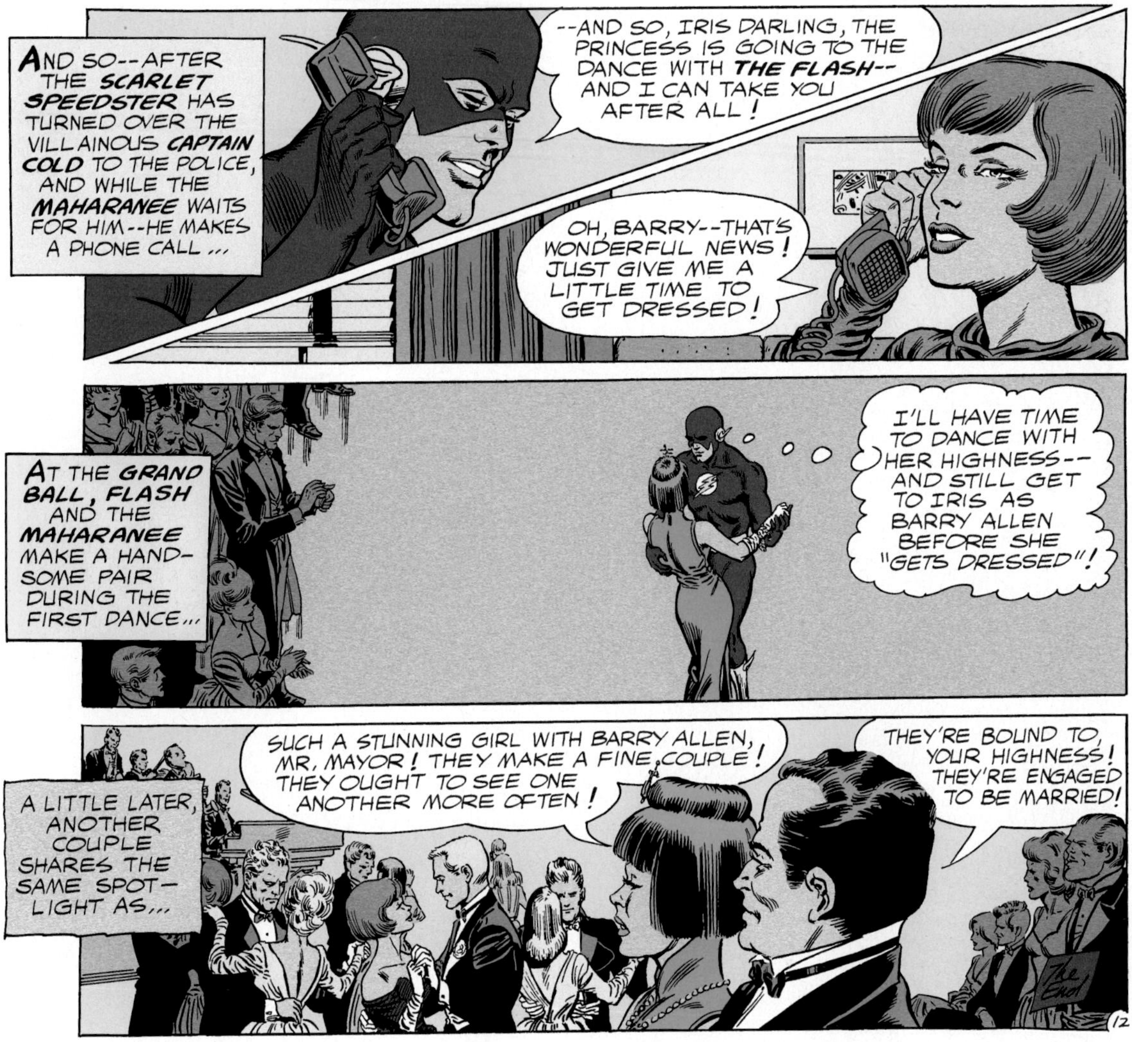

AND SO--AFTER THE SCARLET SPEEDSTER HAS TURNED OVER THE VILLAINOUS CAPTAIN COLD TO THE POLICE, AND WHILE THE MAHARANEE WAITS FOR HIM--HE MAKES A PHONE CALL ...
--AND SO, IRIS DARLING, THE PRINCESS IS GOING TO THE DANCE WITH THE FLASH-- AND I CAN TAKE YOU AFTER ALL!
OH, BARRY--THAT'S WONDERFUL NEWS! JUST GIVE ME A LITTLE TIME TO GET DRESSED!
AT THE GRAND BALL, FLASH AND THE MAHARANEE MAKE A HANDSOME PAIR DURING THE FIRST DANCE...
I'LL HAVE TIME TO DANCE WITH HER HIGHNESS-- AND STILL GET TO IRIS AS BARRY ALLEN BEFORE SHE "GETS DRESSED"!
A LITTLE LATER, ANOTHER COUPLE SHARES THE SAME SPOTLIGHT AS...
SUCH A STUNNING GIRL WITH BARRY ALLEN, MR. MAYOR! THEY MAKE A FINE COUPLE! THEY OUGHT TO SEE ONE ANOTHER MORE OFTEN!
THEY'RE BOUND TO, YOUR HIGHNESS! THEY'RE ENGAGED TO BE MARRIED!
The End
12

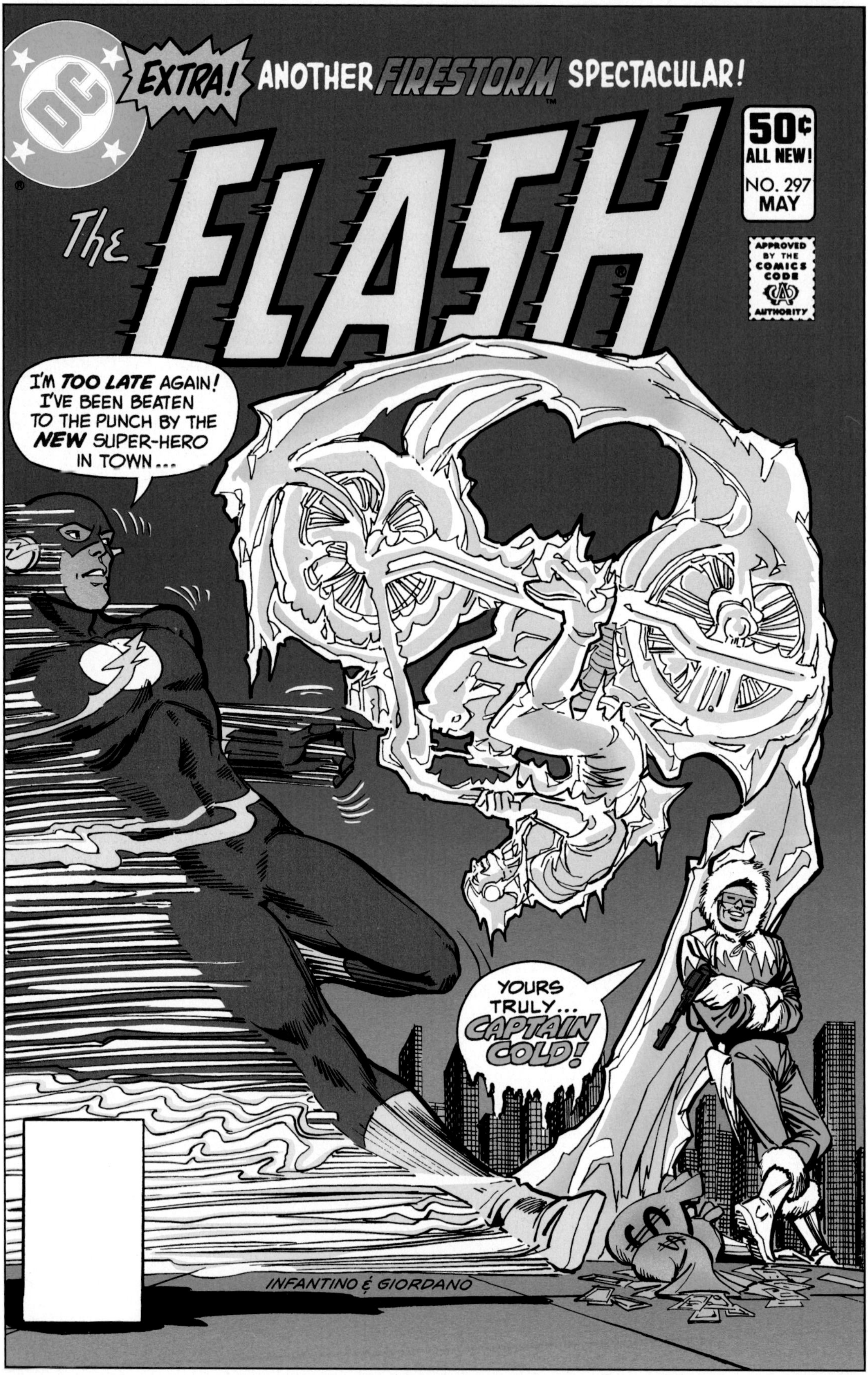

EXTRA!
ANOTHER FIRESTORM SPECTACULAR!
50¢ ALL NEW!
NO. 297 MAY
The FLASH
APPROVED BY THE COMICS CODE AUTHORITY
I'M TOO LATE AGAIN! I'VE BEEN BEATEN TO THE PUNCH BY THE NEW SUPER-HERO IN TOWN...
YOURS TRULY... CAPTAIN COLD!
INFANTINO & GIORDANO

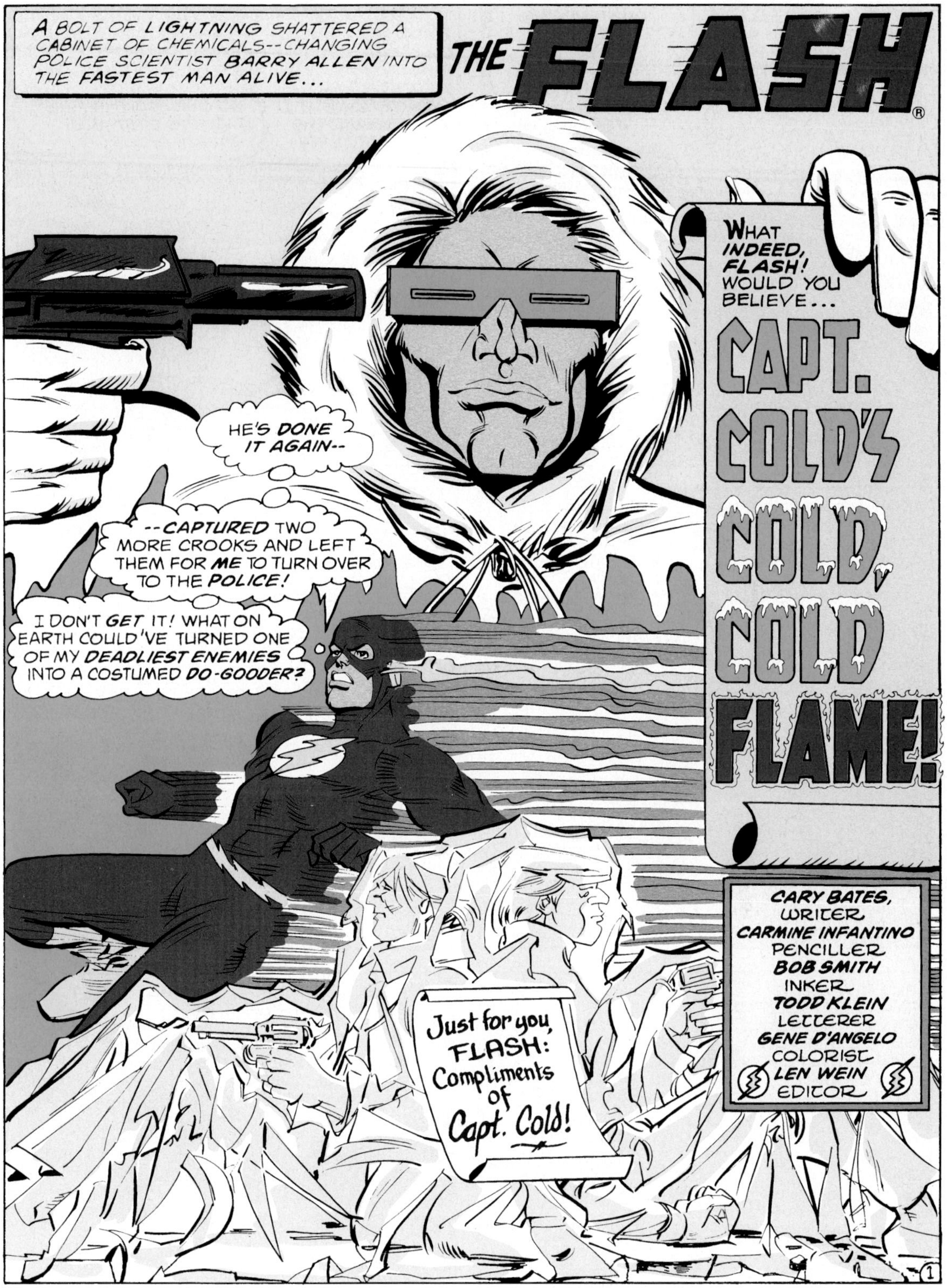
A BOLT OF LIGHTNING SHATTERED A CABINET OF CHEMICALS--CHANGING POLICE SCIENTIST BARRY ALLEN INTO THE FASTEST MAN ALIVE...
THE FLASH®
WHAT INDEED, FLASH! WOULD YOU BELIEVE... CAPT. COLD'S COLD, COLD FLAME!
HE'S DONE IT AGAIN--
--CAPTURED TWO MORE CROOKS AND LEFT THEM FOR ME TO TURN OVER TO THE POLICE!
I DON'T GET IT! WHAT ON EARTH COULD'VE TURNED ONE OF MY DEADLIEST ENEMIES INTO A COSTUMED DO-GOODER?
CARY BATES, WRITER
CARMINE INFANTINO PENCILLER
BOB SMITH INKER
TODD KLEIN LETTERER
GENE D'ANGELO COLORIST
LEN WEIN EDITOR
Just for you, FLASH: Compliments of Capt. Cold!
1

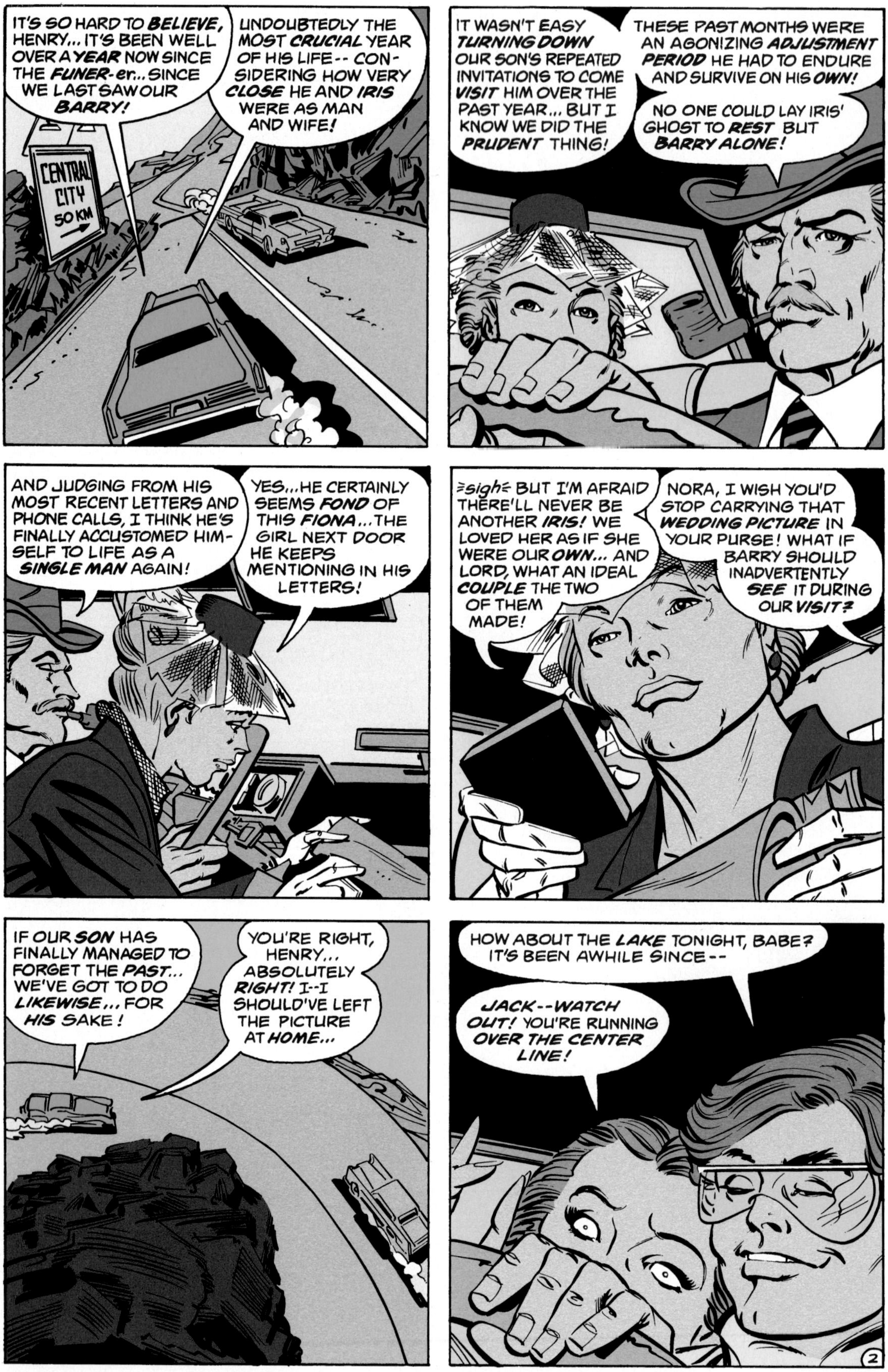
IT'S SO HARD TO BELIEVE, HENRY... IT'S BEEN WELL OVER A YEAR NOW SINCE THE FUNER-er... SINCE WE LAST SAW OUR BARRY!
UNDOUBTEDLY THE MOST CRUCIAL YEAR OF HIS LIFE-- CONSIDERING HOW VERY CLOSE HE AND IRIS WERE AS MAN AND WIFE!
CENTRAL CITY 50 KM
IT WASN'T EASY TURNING DOWN OUR SON'S REPEATED INVITATIONS TO COME VISIT HIM OVER THE PAST YEAR... BUT I KNOW WE DID THE PRUDENT THING!
THESE PAST MONTHS WERE AN AGONIZING ADJUSTMENT PERIOD HE HAD TO ENDURE AND SURVIVE ON HIS OWN!
NO ONE COULD LAY IRIS' GHOST TO REST BUT BARRY ALONE!
AND JUDGING FROM HIS MOST RECENT LETTERS AND PHONE CALLS, I THINK HE'S FINALLY ACCUSTOMED HIMSELF TO LIFE AS A SINGLE MAN AGAIN!
YES... HE CERTAINLY SEEMS FOND OF THIS FIONA... THE GIRL NEXT DOOR HE KEEPS MENTIONING IN HIS LETTERS!
≈sigh≈ BUT I'M AFRAID THERE'LL NEVER BE ANOTHER IRIS! WE LOVED HER AS IF SHE WERE OUR OWN... AND LORD, WHAT AN IDEAL COUPLE THE TWO OF THEM MADE!
NORA, I WISH YOU'D STOP CARRYING THAT WEDDING PICTURE IN YOUR PURSE! WHAT IF BARRY SHOULD INADVERTENTLY SEE IT DURING OUR VISIT?
IF OUR SON HAS FINALLY MANAGED TO FORGET THE PAST... WE'VE GOT TO DO LIKEWISE... FOR HIS SAKE!
YOU'RE RIGHT, HENRY... ABSOLUTELY RIGHT! I--I SHOULD'VE LEFT THE PICTURE AT HOME...
HOW ABOUT THE LAKE TONIGHT, BABE? IT'S BEEN AWHILE SINCE--
JACK--WATCH OUT! YOU'RE RUNNING OVER THE CENTER LINE!
2

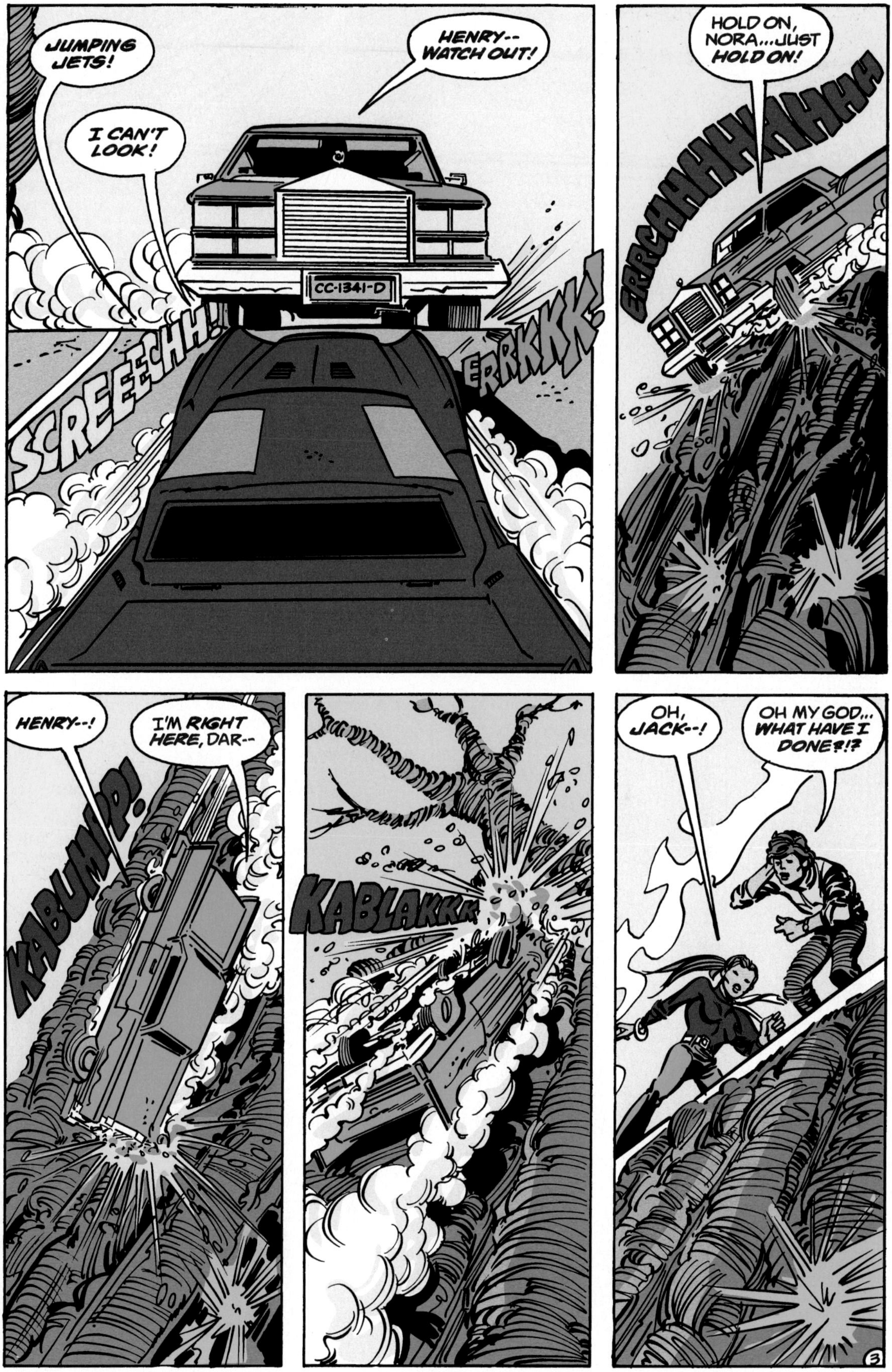
JUMPING JETS!
I CAN'T LOOK!
HENRY-- WATCH OUT!
CC-1341-D
SCREEEECHH!
ERRKKK!
HOLD ON, NORA...JUST HOLD ON!
ERRCHHHHHHHHHH
HENRY--!
I'M RIGHT HERE, DAR--
KABUMPP!
KABLAKKK
OH, JACK--!
OH MY GOD... WHAT HAVE I DONE?!?
3

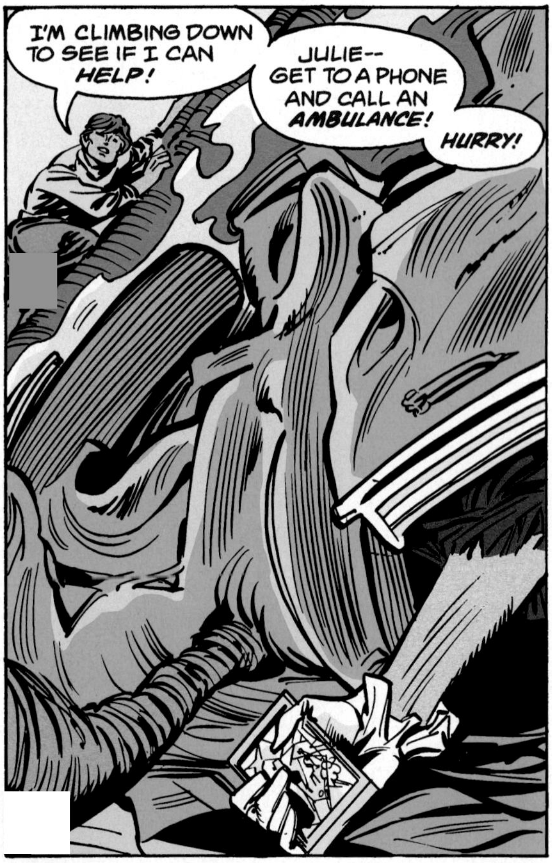
I'M CLIMBING DOWN TO SEE IF I CAN HELP!
JULIE-- GET TO A PHONE AND CALL AN AMBULANCE!
HURRY!

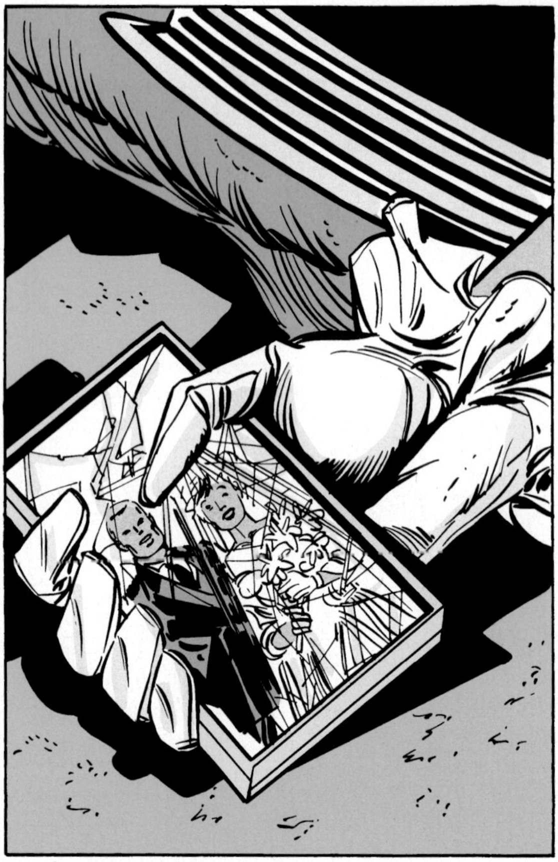

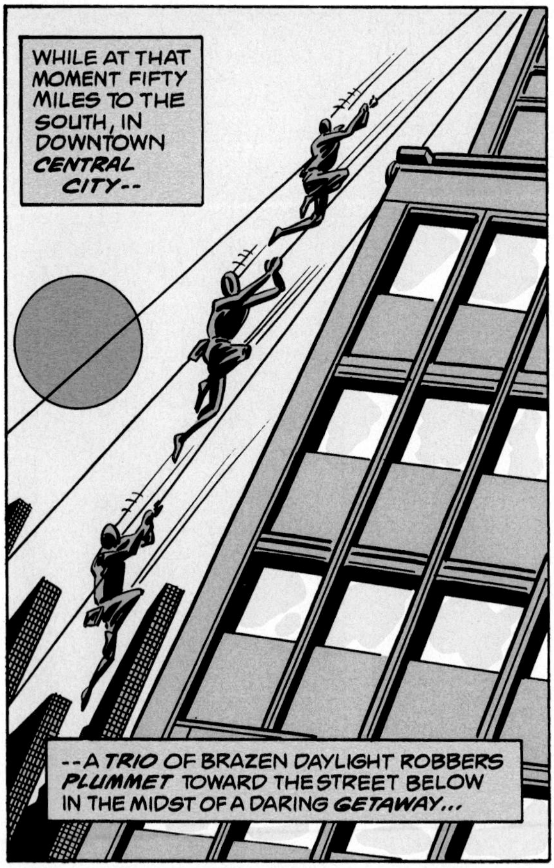
WHILE AT THAT MOMENT FIFTY MILES TO THE SOUTH, IN DOWNTOWN CENTRAL CITY--
--A TRIO OF BRAZEN DAYLIGHT ROBBERS PLUMMET TOWARD THE STREET BELOW IN THE MIDST OF A DARING GETAWAY...

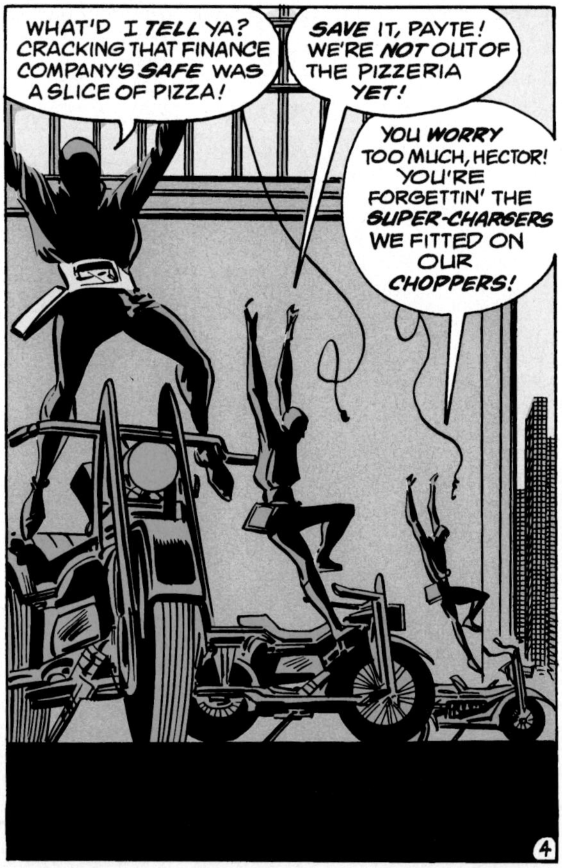
WHAT'D I TELL YA? CRACKING THAT FINANCE COMPANY'S SAFE WAS A SLICE OF PIZZA!
SAVE IT, PAYTE! WE'RE NOT OUT OF THE PIZZERIA YET!
YOU WORRY TOO MUCH, HECTOR! YOU'RE FORGETTIN' THE SUPER-CHARGERS WE FITTED ON OUR CHOPPERS!
4

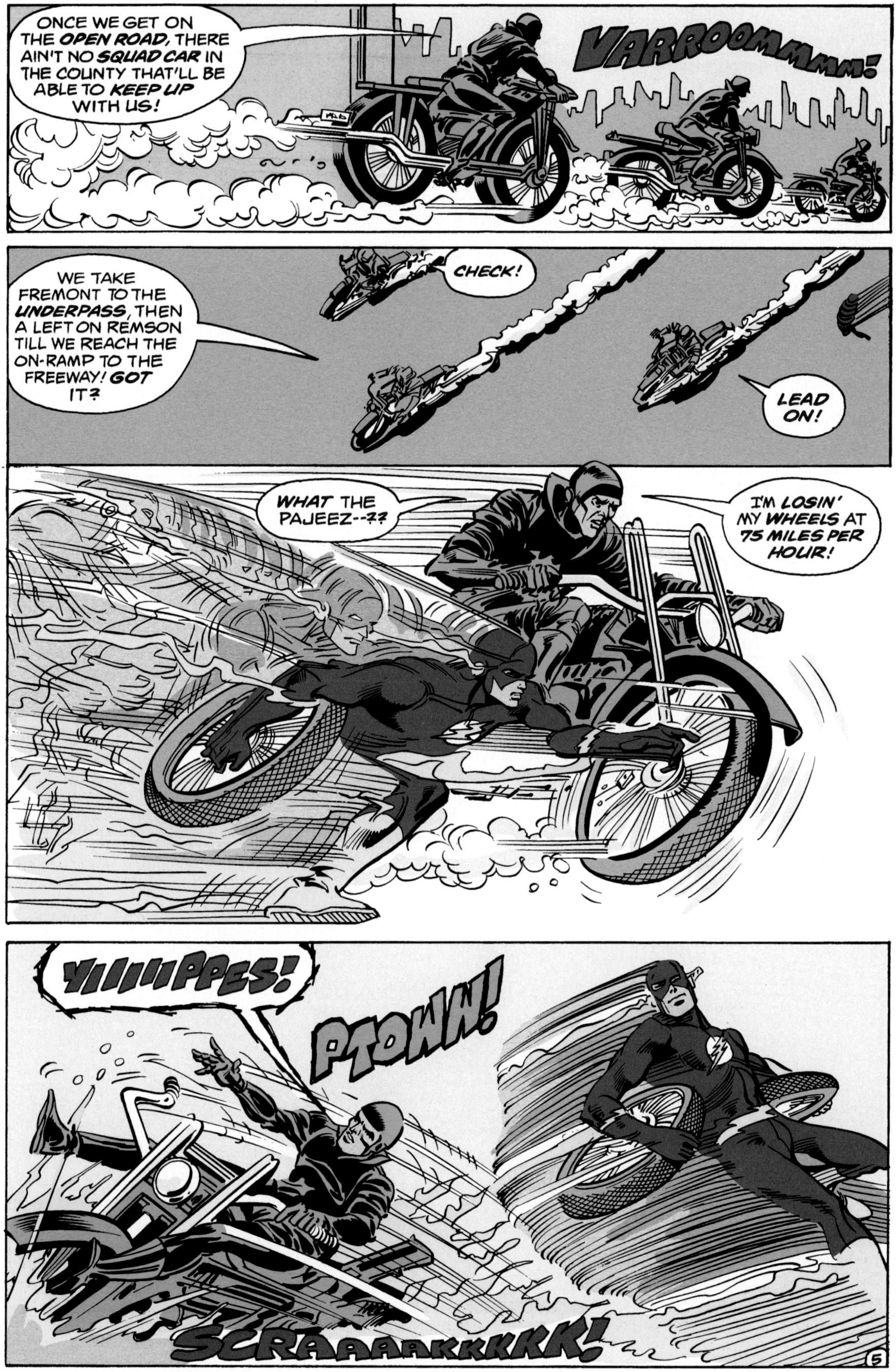
ONCE WE GET ON THE OPEN ROAD, THERE AIN'T NO SQUAD CAR IN THE COUNTY THAT'LL BE ABLE TO KEEP UP WITH US!
VARROOMMMM!
WE TAKE FREMONT TO THE UNDERPASS, THEN A LEFT ON REMSON TILL WE REACH THE ON-RAMP TO THE FREEWAY! GOT IT?
CHECK!
LEAD ON!
WHAT THE PAJEEZ--??
I'M LOSIN' MY WHEELS AT 75 MILES PER HOUR!
YIIIIIPPES!
PTOWN!
SCRAAAAKKKKK!
5

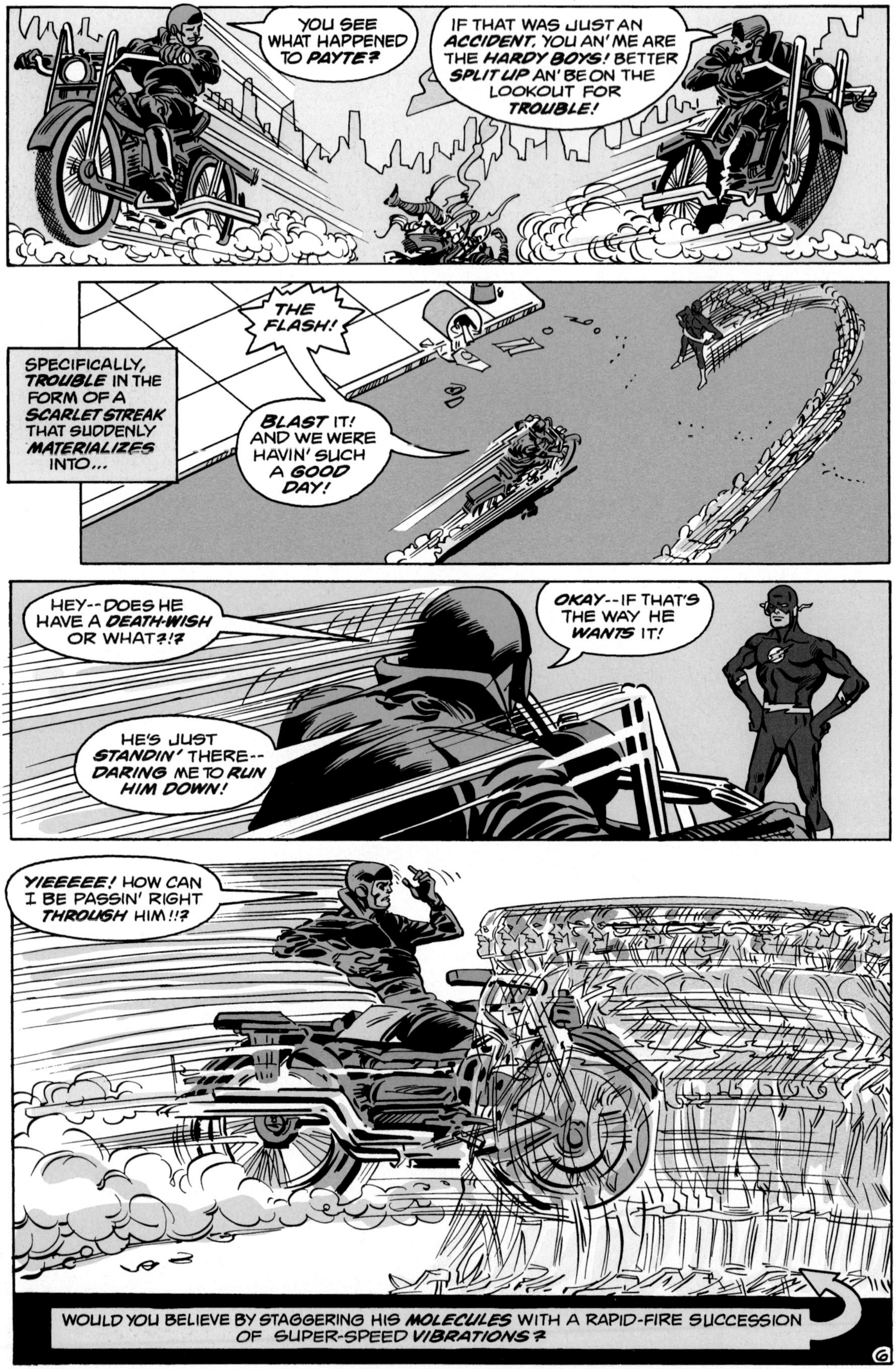

YOU SEE WHAT HAPPENED TO PAYTE?
IF THAT WAS JUST AN ACCIDENT, YOU AN' ME ARE THE HARDY BOYS! BETTER SPLIT UP AN' BE ON THE LOOKOUT FOR TROUBLE!
SPECIFICALLY, TROUBLE IN THE FORM OF A SCARLET STREAK THAT SUDDENLY MATERIALIZES INTO...
THE FLASH!
BLAST IT! AND WE WERE HAVIN' SUCH A GOOD DAY!
HEY--DOES HE HAVE A DEATH-WISH OR WHAT?!?
HE'S JUST STANDIN' THERE--DARING ME TO RUN HIM DOWN!
OKAY--IF THAT'S THE WAY HE WANTS IT!
YIEEEEE! HOW CAN I BE PASSIN' RIGHT THROUGH HIM!!?
WOULD YOU BELIEVE BY STAGGERING HIS MOLECULES WITH A RAPID-FIRE SUCCESSION OF SUPER-SPEED VIBRATIONS?
6

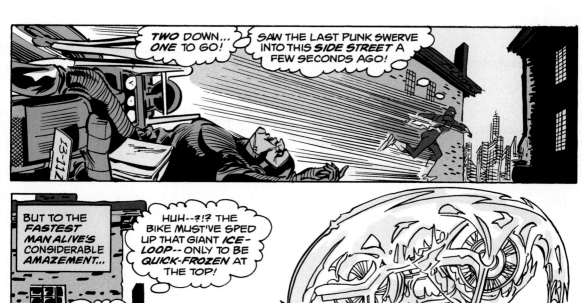

TWO DOWN... ONE TO GO!

SAW THE LAST PUNK SWERVE INTO THIS *SIDE STREET* A FEW SECONDS AGO!

BUT TO THE *FASTEST MAN ALIVE'S* CONSIDERABLE AMAZEMENT...

HUH--?!? THE BIKE MUST'VE SPED UP THAT GIANT *ICE-LOOP*-- ONLY TO BE *QUICK-FROZEN* AT THE TOP!

FRIGID GRANDSTANDING LIKE THAT CAN ONLY BE THE HANDIWORK OF *ONE MAN*--

--*CAPTAIN COLD*, AT OUR GOOD CITY'S *SERVICE* ONCE AGAIN, IT WOULD SEEM!

HERE'S THIS ONE'S SHARE OF THE *LOOT!* I *ASSURE* YOU IT'S *ALL HERE*, DOWN TO THE LAST *DOLLAR!*

I'VE BEEN *DOGGING* THIS TRIO FOR DAYS NOW, EVER SINCE ONE OF MY *INFORMANTS* TIPPED ME THEY WERE PLANNING A *BIG JOB!*

I WAS PREPARED TO NAB ALL *THREE* OF THEM WITH THE EVIDENCE *MYSELF* --TILL *YOU* SHOWED UP AND RAN *INTERFERENCE*, OLD BOY!

NO HARD FEELINGS, THOUGH-- SINCE *YOU* AND I ARE ON THE *SAME TEAM* NOW! *JUSTICE* WAS DONE TODAY AND, AFTER ALL, *THAT'S* WHAT COUNTS!

LISTEN, SNART* ...I'M NOT GOING TO BE ANYTHING LESS THAN *UP FRONT* WITH YOU!

LEN SNART IS CAPTAIN COLD'S TRUE NAME--*LEN.*

⑦

37

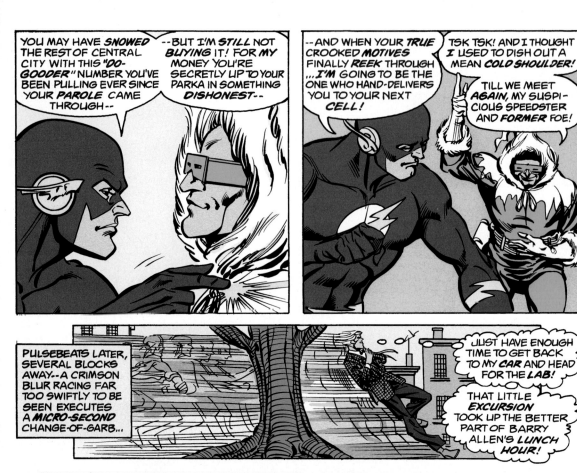

YOU MAY HAVE *SNOWED* THE REST OF CENTRAL CITY WITH THIS *"DO-GOODER"* NUMBER YOU'VE BEEN PULLING EVER SINCE YOUR *PAROLE* CAME THROUGH--

--BUT I'M *STILL* NOT *BUYING* IT! FOR *MY* MONEY YOU'RE SECRETLY UP TO YOUR PARKA IN SOMETHING *DISHONEST*--

--AND WHEN YOUR *TRUE* CROOKED *MOTIVES* FINALLY *REEK* THROUGH ...*I'M* GOING TO BE THE ONE WHO HAND-DELIVERS YOU TO YOUR NEXT *CELL!*

TSK TSK! AND I THOUGHT *I* USED TO DISH OUT A MEAN *COLD SHOULDER!*

TILL WE MEET *AGAIN,* MY SUSPI-CIOUS SPEEDSTER AND *FORMER* FOE!

PULSEBEATS LATER, SEVERAL BLOCKS AWAY--A CRIMSON BLUR RACING FAR TOO SWIFTLY TO BE SEEN EXECUTES A *MICRO-SECOND* CHANGE-OF-GARB...

JUST HAVE ENOUGH TIME TO GET BACK TO MY *CAR* AND HEAD FOR THE *LAB!*

THAT LITTLE *EXCURSION* TOOK UP THE BETTER PART OF BARRY ALLEN'S *LUNCH HOUR!*

CENTRAL TO *BARRY ALLEN*...*URGENT* YOU RESPOND...I REPEAT ...I REPEAT, URGENT! OVER!

OH, *TERRIFIC!* CAPTAIN FRYE PROBABLY HAS SOME NEW BRAIN-BUSTER OF A *CASE* TO DUMP IN MY LAP!

BUT WHEN THE UNPREPARED POLICE SCIENTIST HEARS THE *GRAVE NATURE* OF THE GRIM MESSAGE FROM HEADQUARTERS...

--*SKIP* THE CONDOLENCES! JUST TELL ME *WHICH HOSPITAL!* OVER!

DR. BURGESS? THEY TOLD ME AT THE FRONT DESK *YOU* WERE IN CHARGE OF THE *EMERGENCY WARD* WHEN MY *PARENTS* WERE BROUGHT IN!

BARRY ALLEN--?

YOU CERTAINLY CAME DOWN HERE *FAST* ENOUGH, MAN... NURSE RATCHET ONLY PHONED YOUR *PRECINCT STATION* A FEW *MINUTES* AGO!

DOCTOR...IF WE COULD DISCUSS MY *PARENTS*... PLEASE!

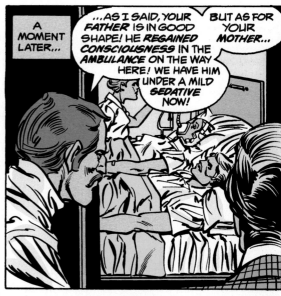

A MOMENT LATER...

...AS I SAID, YOUR *FATHER* IS IN GOOD SHAPE! HE *REGAINED CONSCIOUSNESS* IN THE *AMBULANCE* ON THE WAY HERE! WE HAVE HIM UNDER A MILD *SEDATIVE* NOW!

BUT AS FOR YOUR *MOTHER*...

...I'M AFRAID *HER* CONDITION IS FAR *MORE CRITICAL*! HER MULTIPLE CRANIAL *CONTUSIONS* HAVE PLUNGED HER INTO A DEEP *COMA*!

AT THE MOMENT WE HAVE NO WAY OF KNOWING *WHEN* SHE WILL *REVIVE*! IT COULD BE A MATTER OF *HOURS*...*DAYS*... EVEN *WEEKS*...

≷choke≷ OR SHE MAY *NOT REVIVE AT ALL*...

THAT'S WHAT YOU'RE *TELLING* ME, ISN'T IT?

FIFTEEN MILES TO THE NORTH-EAST OF *CENTRAL CITY*, YOU WILL FIND *COLBY HILLS ESTATES* --A MOST EXCLUSIVE NEIGHBORHOOD POPULATED BY THE VERY *WEALTHY*...

IT'S *ME*, HONEYBUNCH! YOUR DARLING *POPSICLE* IS *HOME*!

DID YOU HAVE A GOOD *CRIME-FIGHTING* DAY, SWEETHEART?

TELL YOU ABOUT IT *LATER*!

RIGHT NOW ALL I WANT IS TO WRAP MY ARMS AROUND THE *MOST BEAUTIFUL GIRL IN THE WORLD*!

OH, *LENNY*...

9

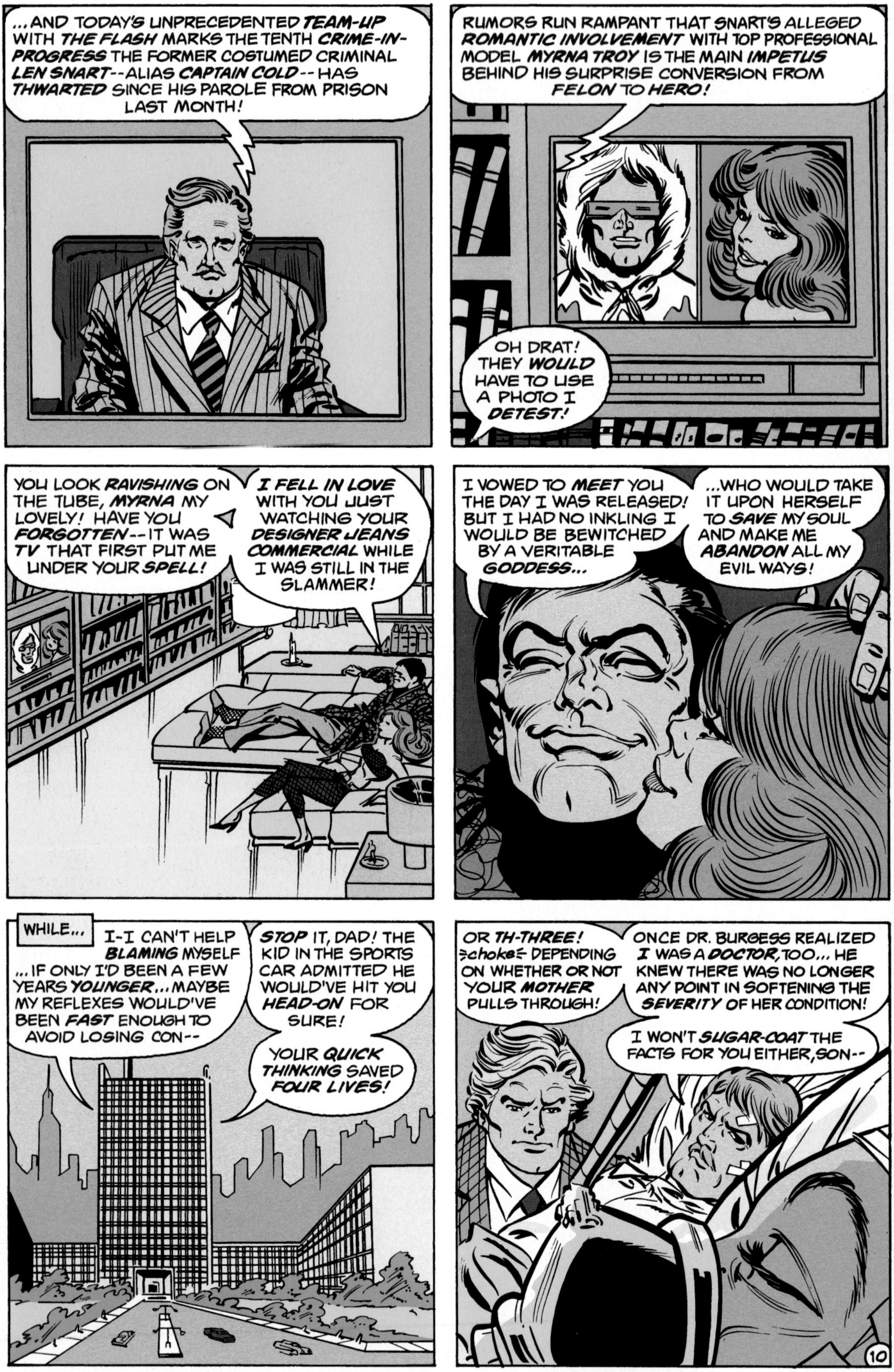
...AND TODAY'S UNPRECEDENTED TEAM-UP WITH THE FLASH MARKS THE TENTH CRIME-IN-PROGRESS THE FORMER COSTUMED CRIMINAL LEN SNART--ALIAS CAPTAIN COLD--HAS THWARTED SINCE HIS PAROLE FROM PRISON LAST MONTH!
RUMORS RUN RAMPANT THAT SNART'S ALLEGED ROMANTIC INVOLVEMENT WITH TOP PROFESSIONAL MODEL MYRNA TROY IS THE MAIN IMPETUS BEHIND HIS SURPRISE CONVERSION FROM FELON TO HERO!
OH DRAT! THEY WOULD HAVE TO USE A PHOTO I DETEST!
YOU LOOK RAVISHING ON THE TUBE, MYRNA MY LOVELY! HAVE YOU FORGOTTEN--IT WAS TV THAT FIRST PUT ME UNDER YOUR SPELL!
I FELL IN LOVE WITH YOU JUST WATCHING YOUR DESIGNER JEANS COMMERCIAL WHILE I WAS STILL IN THE SLAMMER!
I VOWED TO MEET YOU THE DAY I WAS RELEASED! BUT I HAD NO INKLING I WOULD BE BEWITCHED BY A VERITABLE GODDESS...
...WHO WOULD TAKE IT UPON HERSELF TO SAVE MY SOUL AND MAKE ME ABANDON ALL MY EVIL WAYS!
WHILE...
I-I CAN'T HELP BLAMING MYSELF ...IF ONLY I'D BEEN A FEW YEARS YOUNGER...MAYBE MY REFLEXES WOULD'VE BEEN FAST ENOUGH TO AVOID LOSING CON--
STOP IT, DAD! THE KID IN THE SPORTS CAR ADMITTED HE WOULD'VE HIT YOU HEAD-ON FOR SURE!
YOUR QUICK THINKING SAVED FOUR LIVES!
OR TH-THREE! =choke= DEPENDING ON WHETHER OR NOT YOUR MOTHER PULLS THROUGH!
ONCE DR. BURGESS REALIZED I WAS A DOCTOR, TOO... HE KNEW THERE WAS NO LONGER ANY POINT IN SOFTENING THE SEVERITY OF HER CONDITION!
I WON'T SUGAR-COAT THE FACTS FOR YOU EITHER, SON--
10

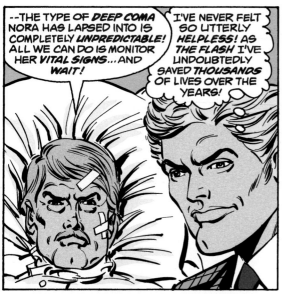

--THE TYPE OF *DEEP COMA* NORA HAS LAPSED INTO IS COMPLETELY *UNPREDICTABLE!* ALL WE CAN DO IS MONITOR HER *VITAL SIGNS*...AND *WAIT!*

I'VE NEVER FELT SO UTTERLY *HELPLESS!* AS *THE FLASH* I'VE UNDOUBTEDLY SAVED *THOUSANDS* OF LIVES OVER THE YEARS!

BUT *NOW,* WHEN ONE OF THE LIVES I CARE ABOUT THE *MOST* IS HANGING BY A MERE *THREAD*--MY *SUPER-SPEED* TURNS OUT TO BE ABSOLUTELY *USELESS!*

THE ONLY *POWERS* I CAN TURN TO ARE *HOPE*--AND *PRAYER!*

MUCH LATER THAT EVENING, ELSEWHERE IN THE CITY--THE STILL OF THE NIGHT IS *BROKEN* BY...

CENTRAL CITY JEWELERY EXCHANGE

KA-BRAACCCKKKKK!!

THE DEVASTATING *ICE-BOLT* BUCKLES THE REINFORCED SOLID STEEL DOORS AS IF THEY WERE NO MORE THAN MERE *TINSEL*--

--AUTOMATICALLY TRIGGERING THE INTRICATE *BURGLAR ALARM SYSTEM* THAT ENCOMPASSES THE ENTIRE JEWELRY EXCHANGE...

AND YET *NO ALARM* CAN BE SOUNDED--NOT THROUGH ELECTRICAL CIRCUITS THAT HAVE BEEN *QUICK-FROZEN* TO SUB-ZERO TEMPERATURES!

INSIDE, THE FIRST OF MANY ELEGANT DISPLAY CASES IS SHATTERED *OPEN* WITH GREAT HASTE, NOT TO MENTION *LUST*...

...AS A FAMILIAR *COSTUMED CRIMINAL* FEASTS A PAIR OF *GREED*-GLAZED EYES ON THE PRICELESS SPARKLING *SPOILS* OF A NIGHT'S WORK!

11

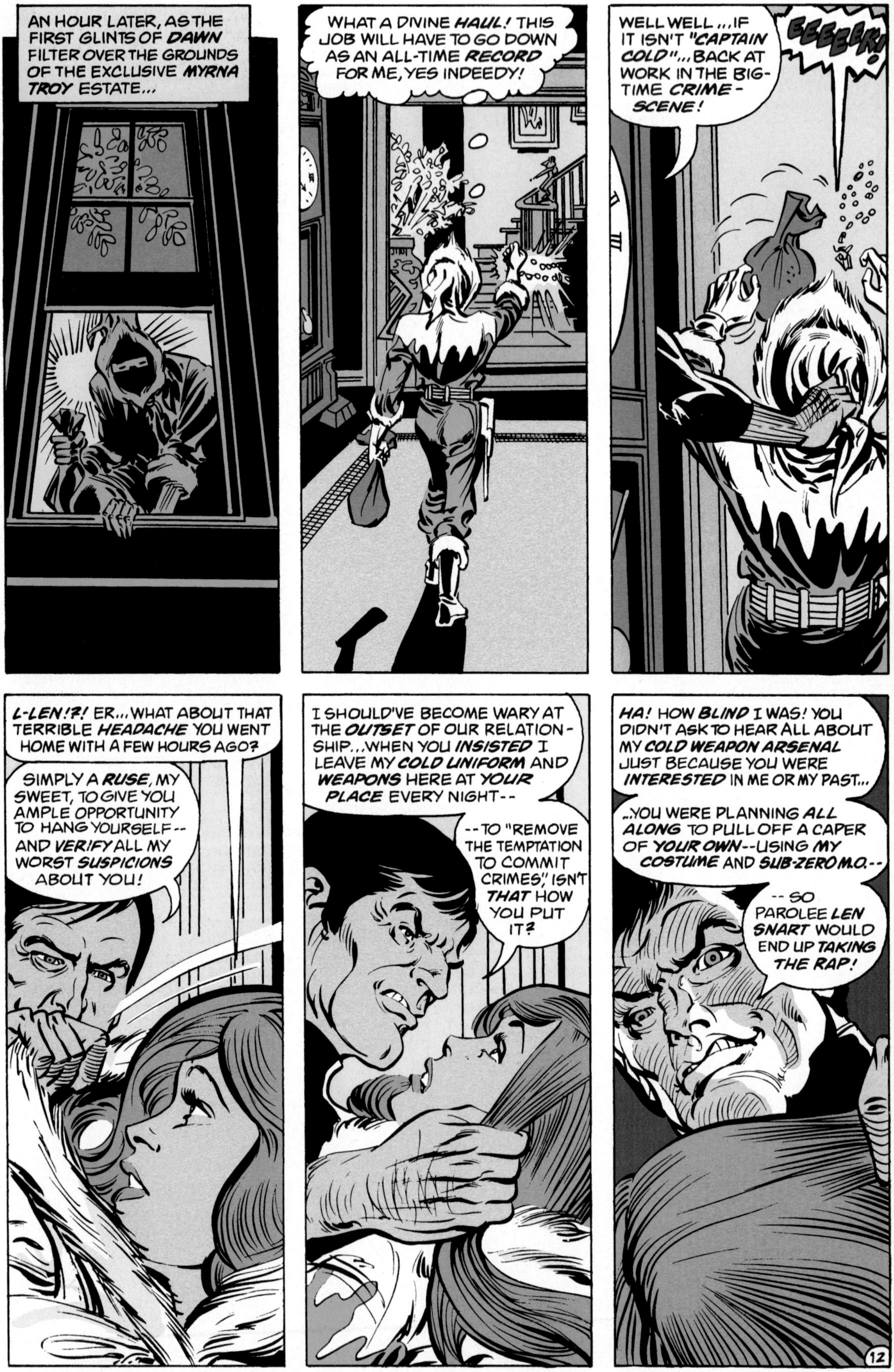
AN HOUR LATER, AS THE FIRST GLINTS OF DAWN FILTER OVER THE GROUNDS OF THE EXCLUSIVE MYRNA TROY ESTATE...
WHAT A DIVINE HAUL! THIS JOB WILL HAVE TO GO DOWN AS AN ALL-TIME RECORD FOR ME, YES INDEEDY!
WELL WELL...IF IT ISN'T "CAPTAIN COLD"...BACK AT WORK IN THE BIG-TIME CRIME-SCENE!
EEEEEK!
L-LEN!?! ER...WHAT ABOUT THAT TERRIBLE HEADACHE YOU WENT HOME WITH A FEW HOURS AGO?
SIMPLY A RUSE, MY SWEET, TO GIVE YOU AMPLE OPPORTUNITY TO HANG YOURSELF--AND VERIFY ALL MY WORST SUSPICIONS ABOUT YOU!
I SHOULD'VE BECOME WARY AT THE OUTSET OF OUR RELATIONSHIP...WHEN YOU INSISTED I LEAVE MY COLD UNIFORM AND WEAPONS HERE AT YOUR PLACE EVERY NIGHT--
--TO "REMOVE THE TEMPTATION TO COMMIT CRIMES," ISN'T THAT HOW YOU PUT IT?
HA! HOW BLIND I WAS! YOU DIDN'T ASK TO HEAR ALL ABOUT MY COLD WEAPON ARSENAL JUST BECAUSE YOU WERE INTERESTED IN ME OR MY PAST...
..YOU WERE PLANNING ALL ALONG TO PULL OFF A CAPER OF YOUR OWN--USING MY COSTUME AND SUB-ZERO M.O.--
--SO PAROLEE LEN SNART WOULD END UP TAKING THE RAP!
12

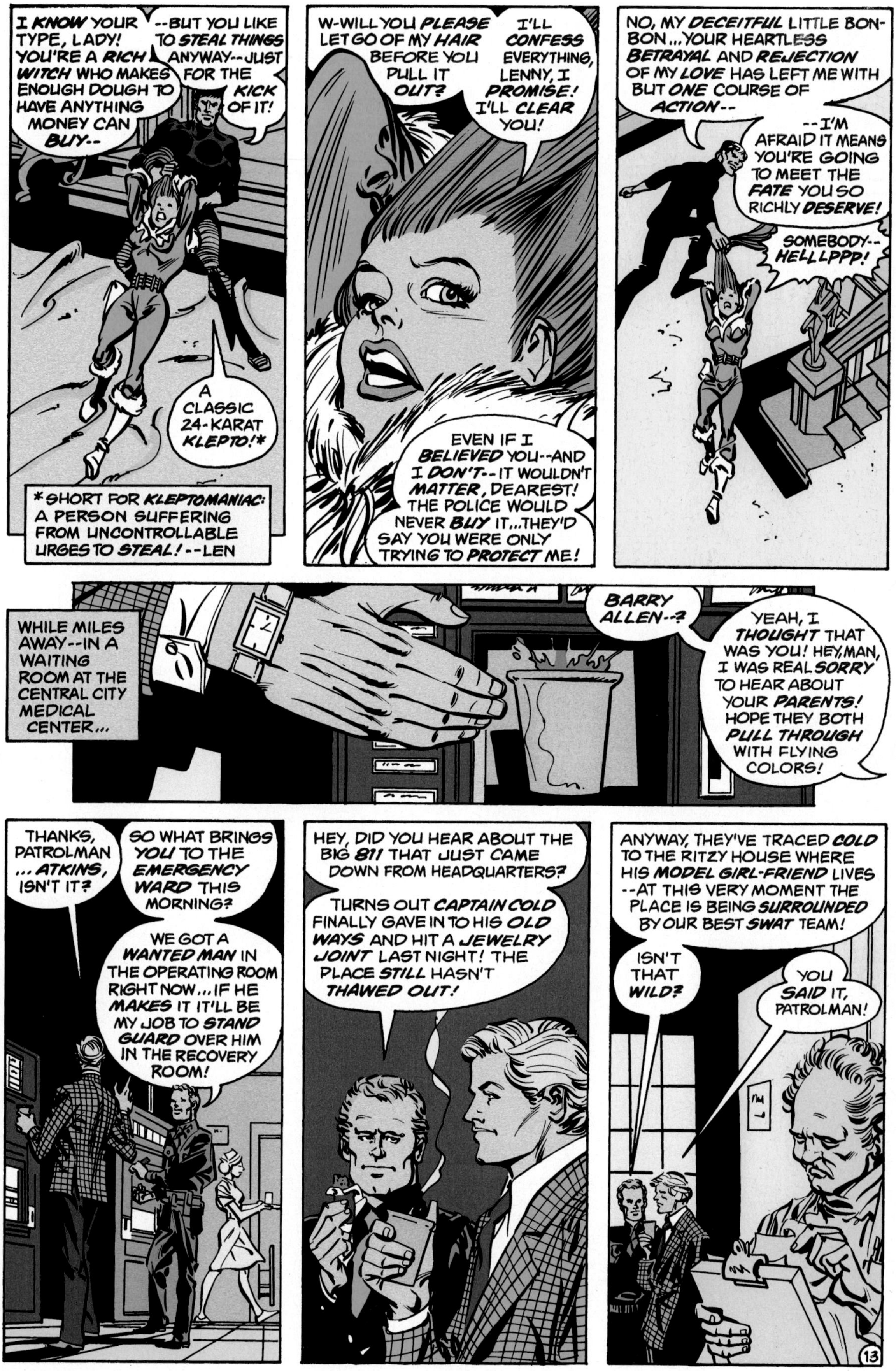

I KNOW YOUR TYPE, LADY! YOU'RE A RICH WITCH WHO MAKES ENOUGH DOUGH TO HAVE ANYTHING MONEY CAN BUY--
--BUT YOU LIKE TO STEAL THINGS ANYWAY--JUST FOR THE KICK OF IT!
A CLASSIC 24-KARAT KLEPTO!*
*SHORT FOR KLEPTOMANIAC: A PERSON SUFFERING FROM UNCONTROLLABLE URGES TO STEAL! --LEN
W-WILL YOU PLEASE LET GO OF MY HAIR BEFORE YOU PULL IT OUT?
I'LL CONFESS EVERYTHING, LENNY, I PROMISE! I'LL CLEAR YOU!
EVEN IF I BELIEVED YOU--AND I DON'T--IT WOULDN'T MATTER, DEAREST! THE POLICE WOULD NEVER BUY IT...THEY'D SAY YOU WERE ONLY TRYING TO PROTECT ME!
NO, MY DECEITFUL LITTLE BON-BON...YOUR HEARTLESS BETRAYAL AND REJECTION OF MY LOVE HAS LEFT ME WITH BUT ONE COURSE OF ACTION--
--I'M AFRAID IT MEANS YOU'RE GOING TO MEET THE FATE YOU SO RICHLY DESERVE!
SOMEBODY--HELLLPPP!
WHILE MILES AWAY--IN A WAITING ROOM AT THE CENTRAL CITY MEDICAL CENTER...
BARRY ALLEN--?
YEAH, I THOUGHT THAT WAS YOU! HEY, MAN, I WAS REAL SORRY TO HEAR ABOUT YOUR PARENTS! HOPE THEY BOTH PULL THROUGH WITH FLYING COLORS!
THANKS, PATROLMAN ...ATKINS, ISN'T IT?
SO WHAT BRINGS YOU TO THE EMERGENCY WARD THIS MORNING?
WE GOT A WANTED MAN IN THE OPERATING ROOM RIGHT NOW...IF HE MAKES IT IT'LL BE MY JOB TO STAND GUARD OVER HIM IN THE RECOVERY ROOM!
HEY, DID YOU HEAR ABOUT THE BIG 811 THAT JUST CAME DOWN FROM HEADQUARTERS?
TURNS OUT CAPTAIN COLD FINALLY GAVE IN TO HIS OLD WAYS AND HIT A JEWELRY JOINT LAST NIGHT! THE PLACE STILL HASN'T THAWED OUT!
ANYWAY, THEY'VE TRACED COLD TO THE RITZY HOUSE WHERE HIS MODEL GIRL-FRIEND LIVES --AT THIS VERY MOMENT THE PLACE IS BEING SURROUNDED BY OUR BEST SWAT TEAM!
ISN'T THAT WILD?
YOU SAID IT, PATROLMAN!
13

SCANT SECONDS LATER, ELSEWHERE ON THE SAME FLOOR...

THIS *DESERTED STOREROOM* ROUTINE IS STRAIGHT OUT OF MY OLD PAL *CLARK KENT'S* REPERTOIRE --

SUPPLIES

STAFF ONLY

--BUT IT PROVIDES THE 3/10ths OF A SECOND'S WORTH OF *PRIVACY* I NEED TO *SUIT-UP* FOR ACTION!

AT THE PRESS OF A BUTTON, A COMPRESSED *SCARLET UNIFORM* IS EJECTED FROM A SECRET COMPARTMENT IN THE POLICE SCIENTIST'S *RING* -- INSTANTLY *EXPANDING* ON CONTACT WITH THE AIR!

THEN, MOVING FAR TOO *FAST* TO BE *PERCEIVED* BY THE HUMAN EYE, A *CRIMSON BLUR* HARMLESSLY VIBRATES HIS MOLECULES *THROUGH* THE CLOSED DOOR IN HIS PATH...

AS MUCH AS I *HATE* LEAVING MY PARENTS' SIDE RIGHT NOW, I CAN'T ALLOW *BARRY ALLEN'S* PERSONAL PROBLEMS TO *INTERFERE* WITH MY *FLASH*-DUTIES...

...NOT AS LONG AS I'VE PLEDGED TO *PROTECT* THE PEOPLE OF THIS CITY FROM DANGEROUS FELONS LIKE *CAPTAIN COLD!*

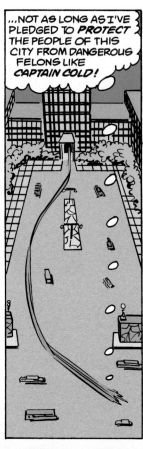

PULSEBEATS LATER...

THIS IS YOUR *LAST CHANCE*, SNART! RELEASE MISS TROY AND COME OUT WITH YOUR HANDS UP... OR WE'RE COMING IN!

THAT'S WHAT *THEY* THINK! EVEN THOUGH THIS IS THE DEPARTMENT'S CRACK *SWAT** TEAM OUT HERE--

*SPECIAL WEAPONS AND TACTICAL. --LEN

--NOT EVEN *THEIR* KIND OF *FIREPOWER* WILL STAND UP TO SNART'S FANTASTIC *COLD WEAPONS* ARSENAL IF HE DECIDES TO *LET LOOSE!*

14

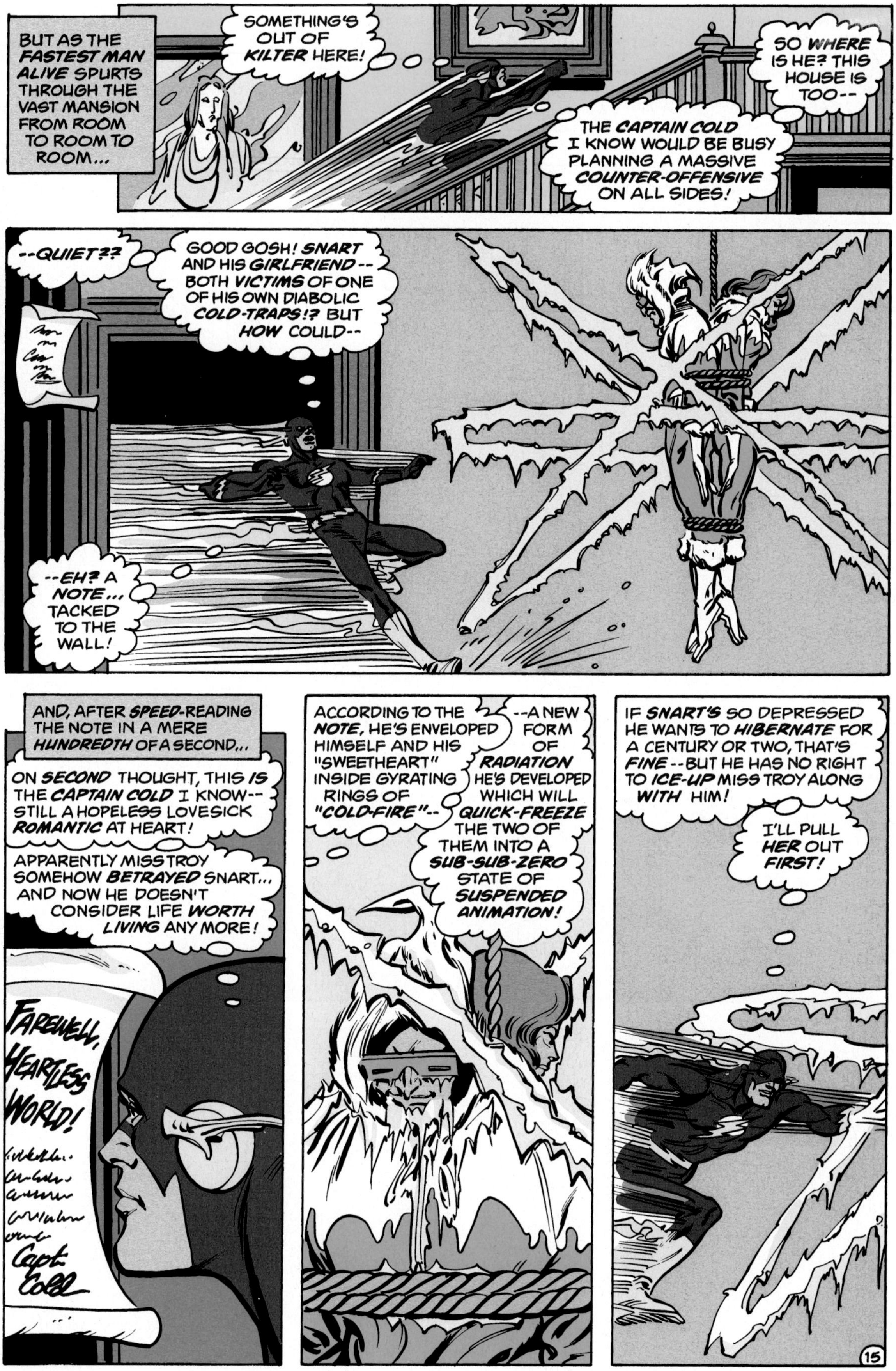

BUT AS THE FASTEST MAN ALIVE SPURTS THROUGH THE VAST MANSION FROM ROOM TO ROOM TO ROOM...
SOMETHING'S OUT OF KILTER HERE!
SO WHERE IS HE? THIS HOUSE IS TOO--
THE CAPTAIN COLD I KNOW WOULD BE BUSY PLANNING A MASSIVE COUNTER-OFFENSIVE ON ALL SIDES!
--QUIET??
GOOD GOSH! SNART AND HIS GIRLFRIEND-- BOTH VICTIMS OF ONE OF HIS OWN DIABOLIC COLD-TRAPS!? BUT HOW COULD--
--EH? A NOTE... TACKED TO THE WALL!
AND, AFTER SPEED-READING THE NOTE IN A MERE HUNDREDTH OF A SECOND...
ON SECOND THOUGHT, THIS IS THE CAPTAIN COLD I KNOW-- STILL A HOPELESS LOVESICK ROMANTIC AT HEART!
APPARENTLY MISS TROY SOMEHOW BETRAYED SNART... AND NOW HE DOESN'T CONSIDER LIFE WORTH LIVING ANY MORE!
FAREWELL, HEARTLESS WORLD!
Capt. Cold
ACCORDING TO THE NOTE, HE'S ENVELOPED HIMSELF AND HIS "SWEETHEART" INSIDE GYRATING RINGS OF "COLD-FIRE"--
--A NEW FORM OF RADIATION HE'S DEVELOPED WHICH WILL QUICK-FREEZE THE TWO OF THEM INTO A SUB-SUB-ZERO STATE OF SUSPENDED ANIMATION!
IF SNART'S SO DEPRESSED HE WANTS TO HIBERNATE FOR A CENTURY OR TWO, THAT'S FINE--BUT HE HAS NO RIGHT TO ICE-UP MISS TROY ALONG WITH HIM!
I'LL PULL HER OUT FIRST!
15

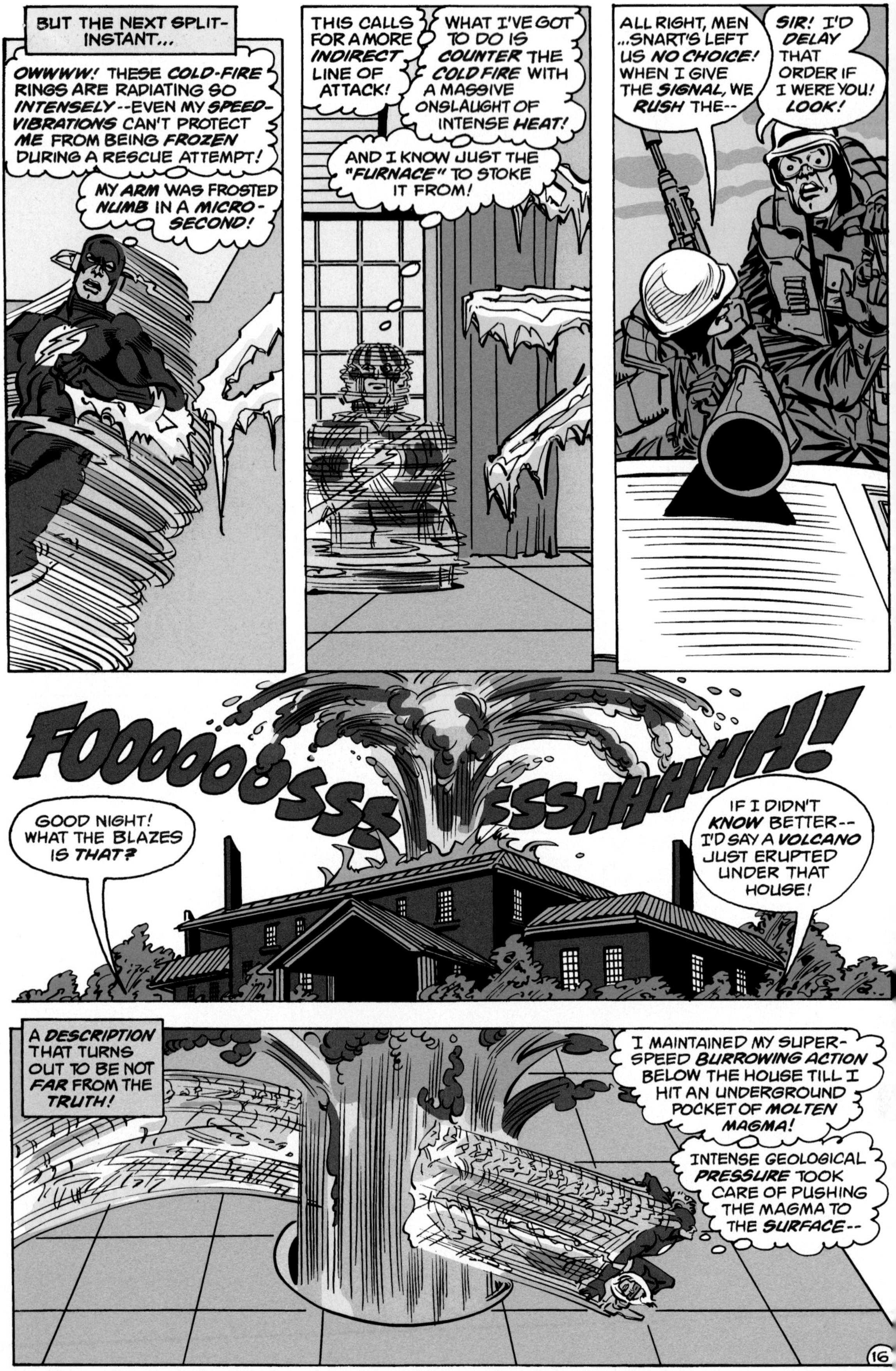
BUT THE NEXT SPLIT-INSTANT...
OWWWW! THESE COLD-FIRE RINGS ARE RADIATING SO INTENSELY--EVEN MY SPEED-VIBRATIONS CAN'T PROTECT ME FROM BEING FROZEN DURING A RESCUE ATTEMPT!
MY ARM WAS FROSTED NUMB IN A MICRO-SECOND!
THIS CALLS FOR A MORE INDIRECT LINE OF ATTACK!
WHAT I'VE GOT TO DO IS COUNTER THE COLD FIRE WITH A MASSIVE ONSLAUGHT OF INTENSE HEAT!
AND I KNOW JUST THE "FURNACE" TO STOKE IT FROM!
ALL RIGHT, MEN ...SNART'S LEFT US NO CHOICE! WHEN I GIVE THE SIGNAL, WE RUSH THE--
SIR! I'D DELAY THAT ORDER IF I WERE YOU! LOOK!
FOOOOOOOSSSSSSSHHHHHH!
GOOD NIGHT! WHAT THE BLAZES IS THAT?
IF I DIDN'T KNOW BETTER--I'D SAY A VOLCANO JUST ERUPTED UNDER THAT HOUSE!
A DESCRIPTION THAT TURNS OUT TO BE NOT FAR FROM THE TRUTH!
I MAINTAINED MY SUPER-SPEED BURROWING ACTION BELOW THE HOUSE TILL I HIT AN UNDERGROUND POCKET OF MOLTEN MAGMA!
INTENSE GEOLOGICAL PRESSURE TOOK CARE OF PUSHING THE MAGMA TO THE SURFACE--
16

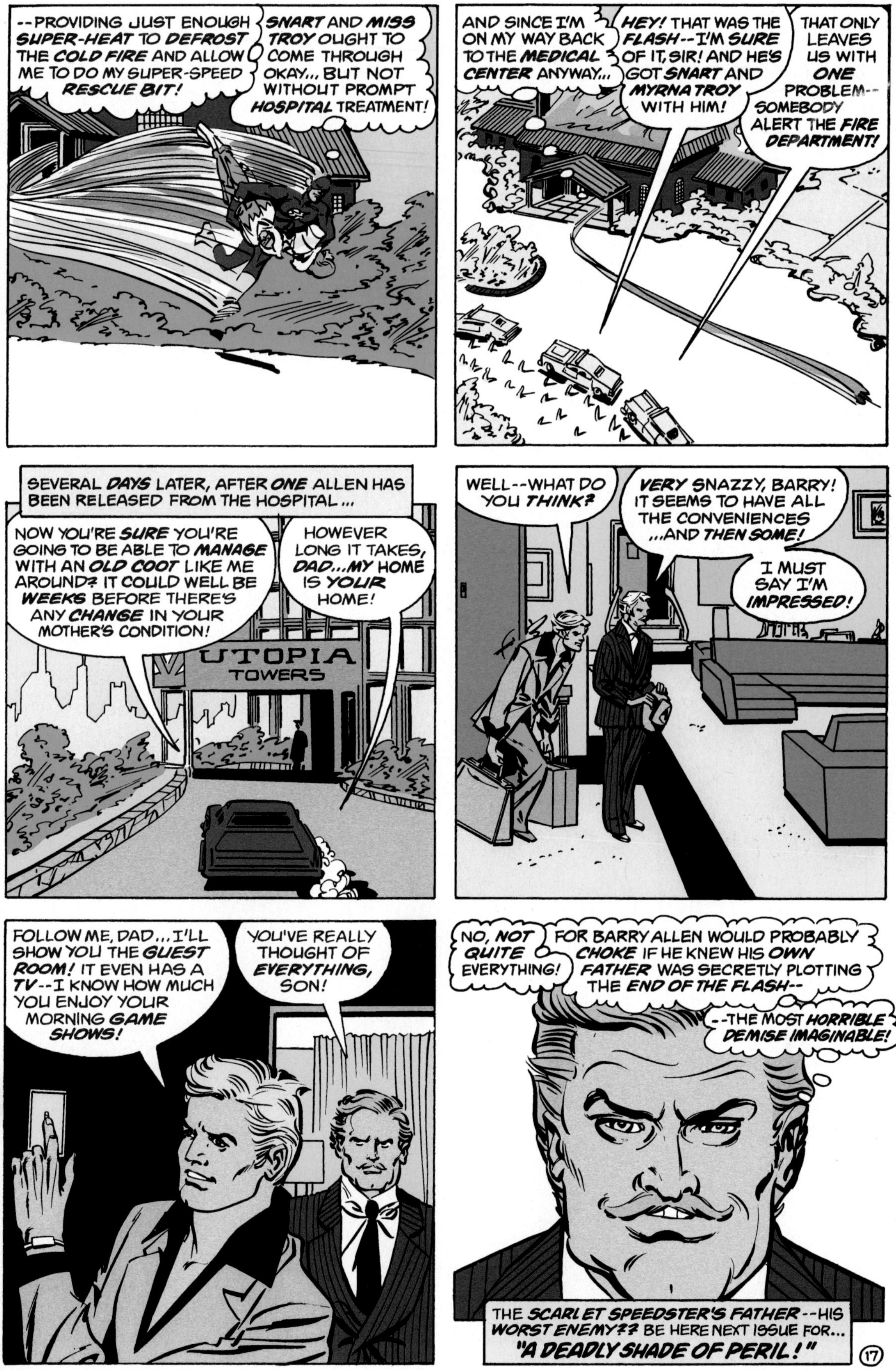
--PROVIDING JUST ENOUGH SUPER-HEAT TO DEFROST THE COLD FIRE AND ALLOW ME TO DO MY SUPER-SPEED RESCUE BIT!
SNART AND MISS TROY OUGHT TO COME THROUGH OKAY... BUT NOT WITHOUT PROMPT HOSPITAL TREATMENT!
AND SINCE I'M ON MY WAY BACK TO THE MEDICAL CENTER ANYWAY...
HEY! THAT WAS THE FLASH--I'M SURE OF IT, SIR! AND HE'S GOT SNART AND MYRNA TROY WITH HIM!
THAT ONLY LEAVES US WITH ONE PROBLEM--SOMEBODY ALERT THE FIRE DEPARTMENT!
SEVERAL DAYS LATER, AFTER ONE ALLEN HAS BEEN RELEASED FROM THE HOSPITAL...
NOW YOU'RE SURE YOU'RE GOING TO BE ABLE TO MANAGE WITH AN OLD COOT LIKE ME AROUND? IT COULD WELL BE WEEKS BEFORE THERE'S ANY CHANGE IN YOUR MOTHER'S CONDITION!
HOWEVER LONG IT TAKES, DAD...MY HOME IS YOUR HOME!
UTOPIA TOWERS
WELL--WHAT DO YOU THINK?
VERY SNAZZY, BARRY! IT SEEMS TO HAVE ALL THE CONVENIENCES ...AND THEN SOME!
I MUST SAY I'M IMPRESSED!
FOLLOW ME, DAD... I'LL SHOW YOU THE GUEST ROOM! IT EVEN HAS A TV--I KNOW HOW MUCH YOU ENJOY YOUR MORNING GAME SHOWS!
YOU'VE REALLY THOUGHT OF EVERYTHING, SON!
NO, NOT QUITE EVERYTHING!
FOR BARRY ALLEN WOULD PROBABLY CHOKE IF HE KNEW HIS OWN FATHER WAS SECRETLY PLOTTING THE END OF THE FLASH--
--THE MOST HORRIBLE DEMISE IMAGINABLE!
THE SCARLET SPEEDSTER'S FATHER--HIS WORST ENEMY?? BE HERE NEXT ISSUE FOR...
"A DEADLY SHADE OF PERIL!"
17

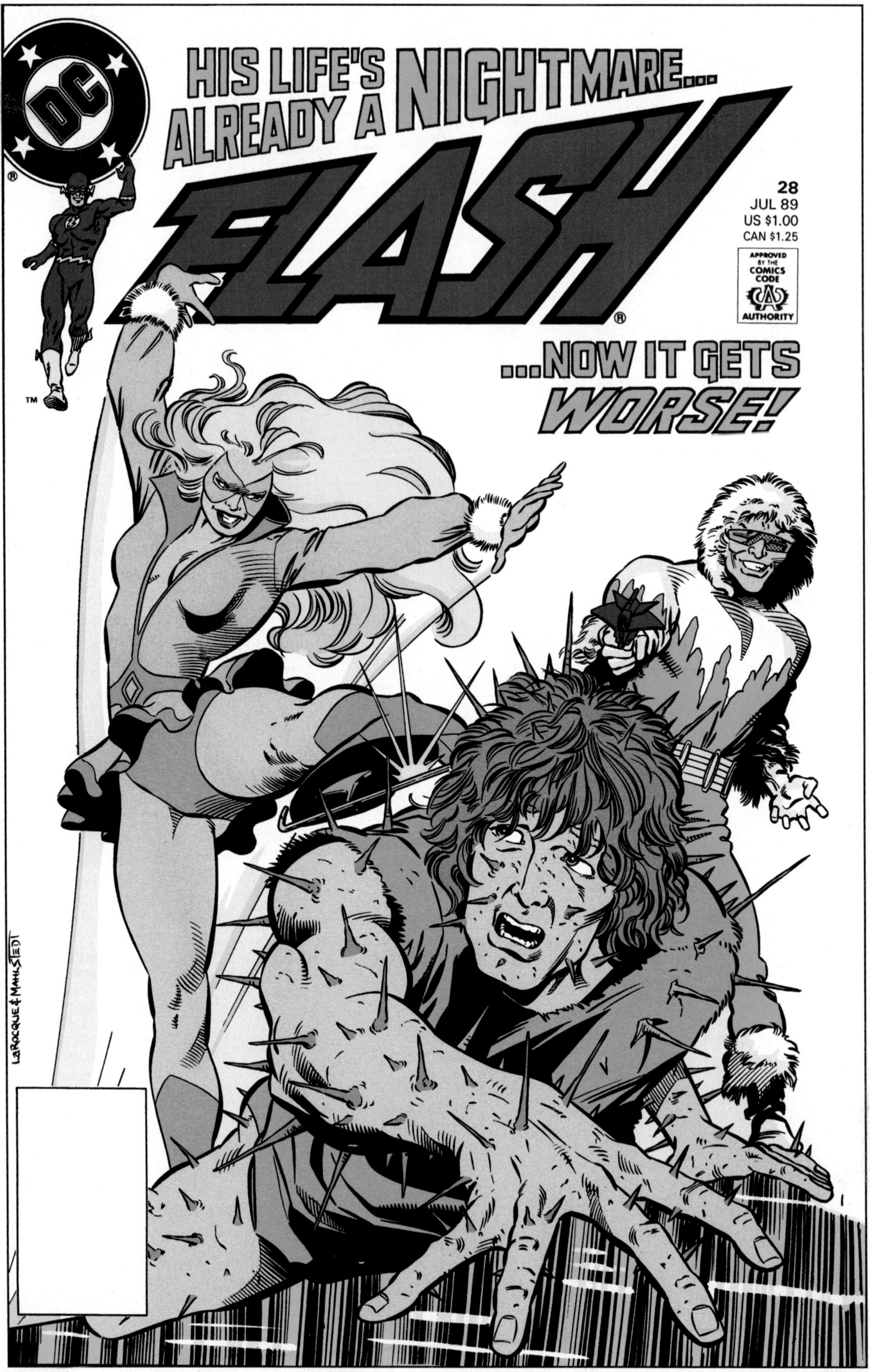
DC
HIS LIFE'S ALREADY A NIGHTMARE...
FLASH
28
JUL 89
US $1.00
CAN $1.25
APPROVED BY THE COMICS CODE AUTHORITY
...NOW IT GETS WORSE!
LaROCQUE & MAHLSTEDT

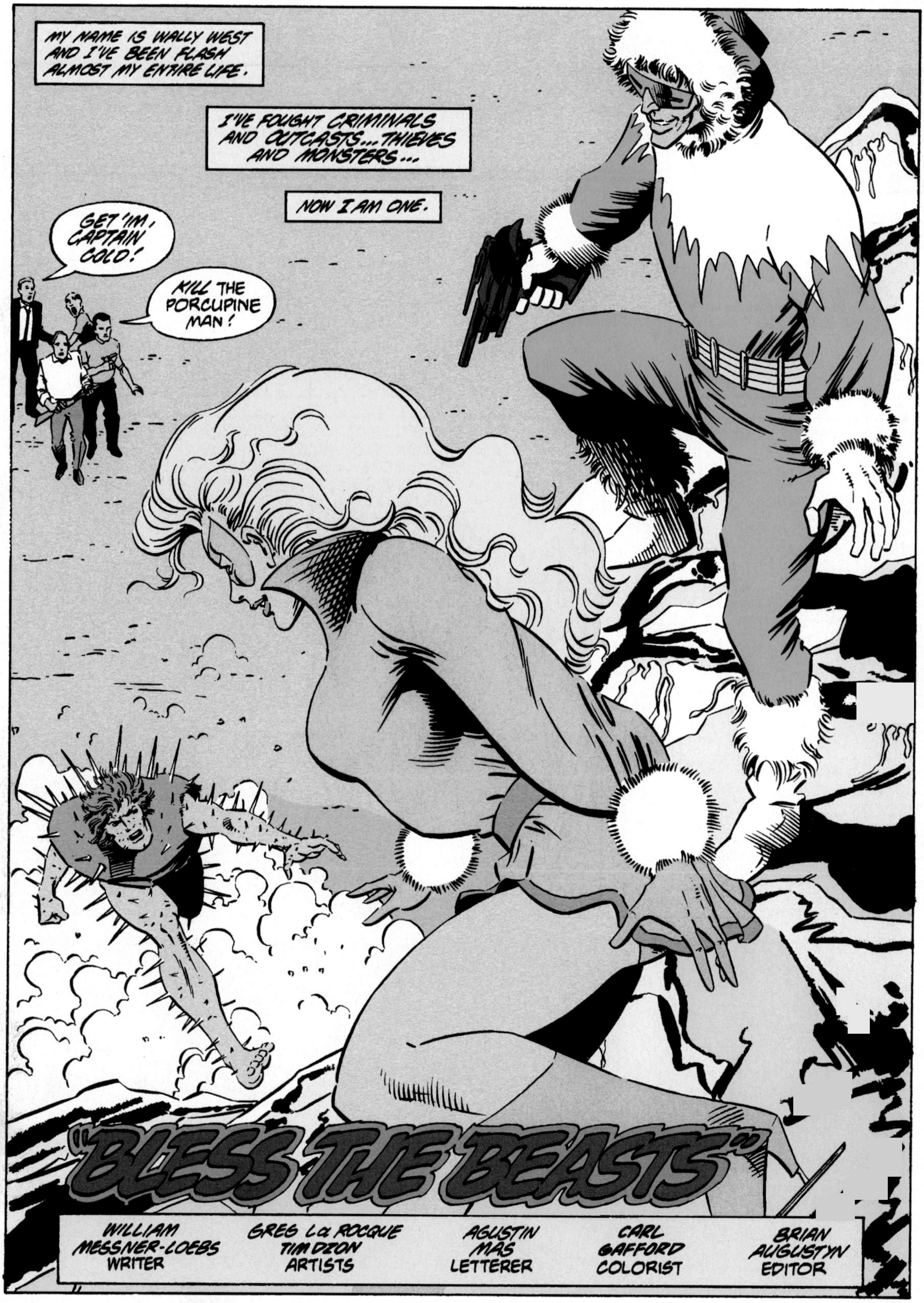

MY NAME IS WALLY WEST AND I'VE BEEN FLASH ALMOST MY ENTIRE LIFE.
I'VE FOUGHT CRIMINALS AND OUTCASTS... THIEVES AND MONSTERS...
NOW I AM ONE.
GET 'IM, CAPTAIN COLD!
KILL THE PORCUPINE MAN!
"BLESS THE BEASTS"
WILLIAM MESSNER-LOEBS WRITER
GREG LaROCQUE TIM DZON ARTISTS
AGUSTIN MAS LETTERER
CARL GAFFORD COLORIST
BRIAN AUGUSTYN EDITOR

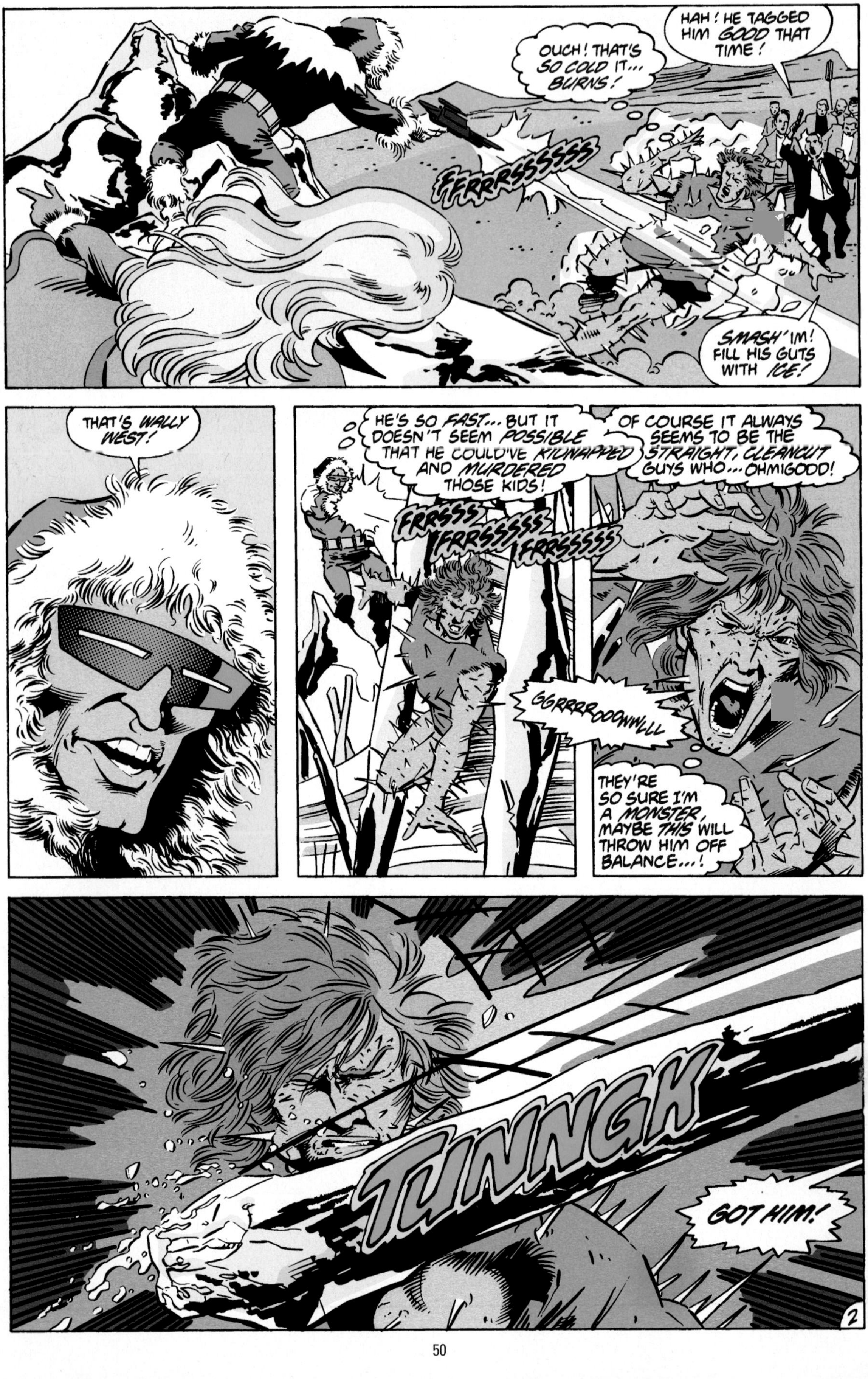

OUCH! THAT'S SO COLD IT... BURNS!
HAH! HE TAGGED HIM GOOD THAT TIME!
FFRRRRSSSSSSS
SMASH 'IM! FILL HIS GUTS WITH ICE!
THAT'S WALLY WEST!
HE'S SO FAST... BUT IT DOESN'T SEEM POSSIBLE THAT HE COULD'VE KIDNAPPED AND MURDERED THOSE KIDS!
OF COURSE IT ALWAYS SEEMS TO BE THE STRAIGHT, CLEANCUT GUYS WHO... OHMIGODD!
FRRSSS
FRRSSSSSS
FRRSSSSS
GGRRRRROOOWWLLL
THEY'RE SO SURE I'M A MONSTER, MAYBE THIS WILL THROW HIM OFF BALANCE...!
TUNNGK
GOT HIM!
2

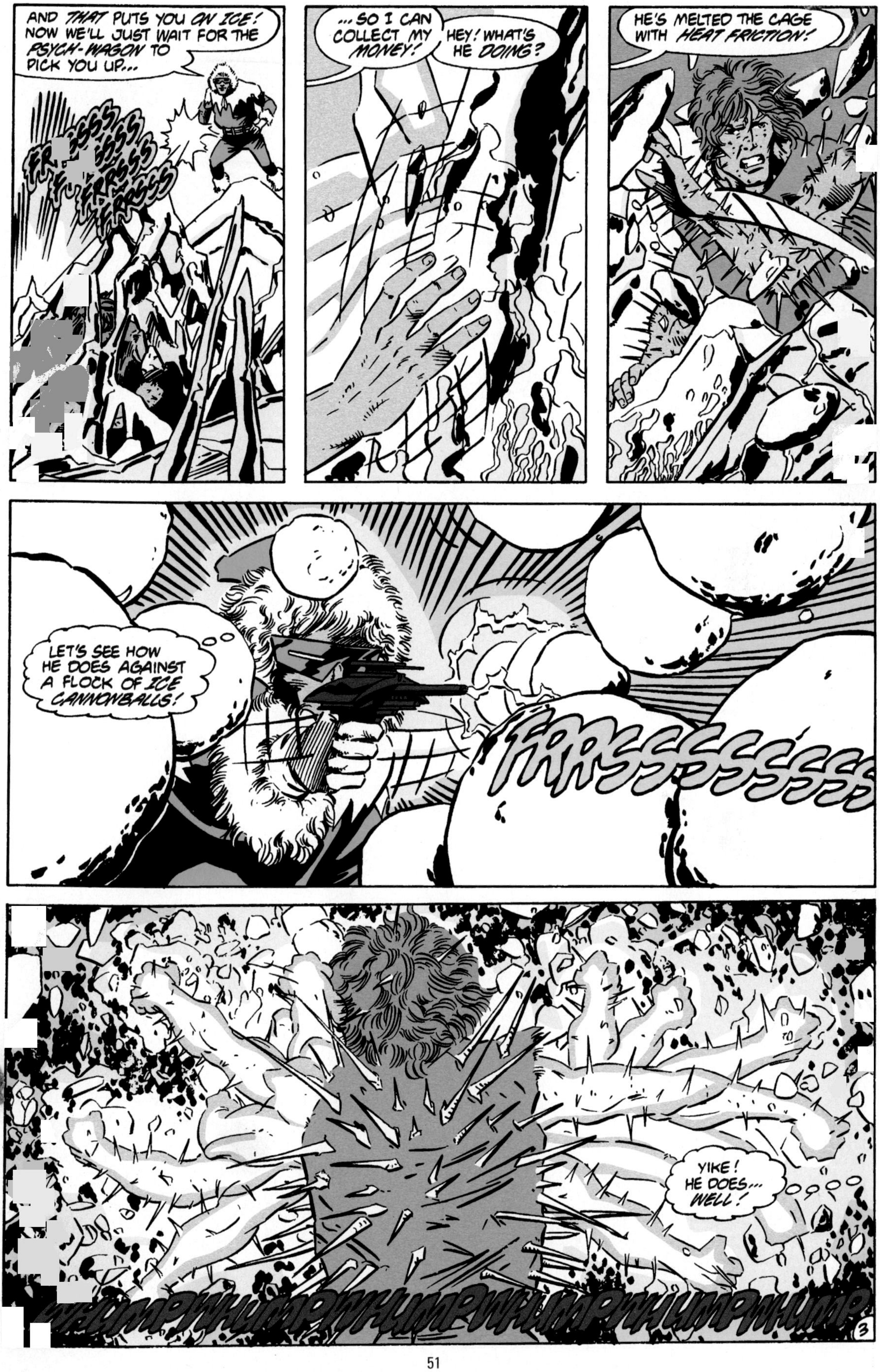
AND THAT PUTS YOU ON ICE! NOW WE'LL JUST WAIT FOR THE PSYCH-WAGON TO PICK YOU UP...
FRSSSS FRSSSS FRSSSS FRSSSS
...SO I CAN COLLECT MY MONEY!
HEY! WHAT'S HE DOING?
HE'S MELTED THE CAGE WITH HEAT FRICTION!
LET'S SEE HOW HE DOES AGAINST A FLOCK OF ICE CANNONBALLS!
FRRSSSSSSSSS
YIKE! HE DOES... WELL!
WHUMPWHUMPWHUMPWHUMPWHUMPWHUMPWHUMP
3

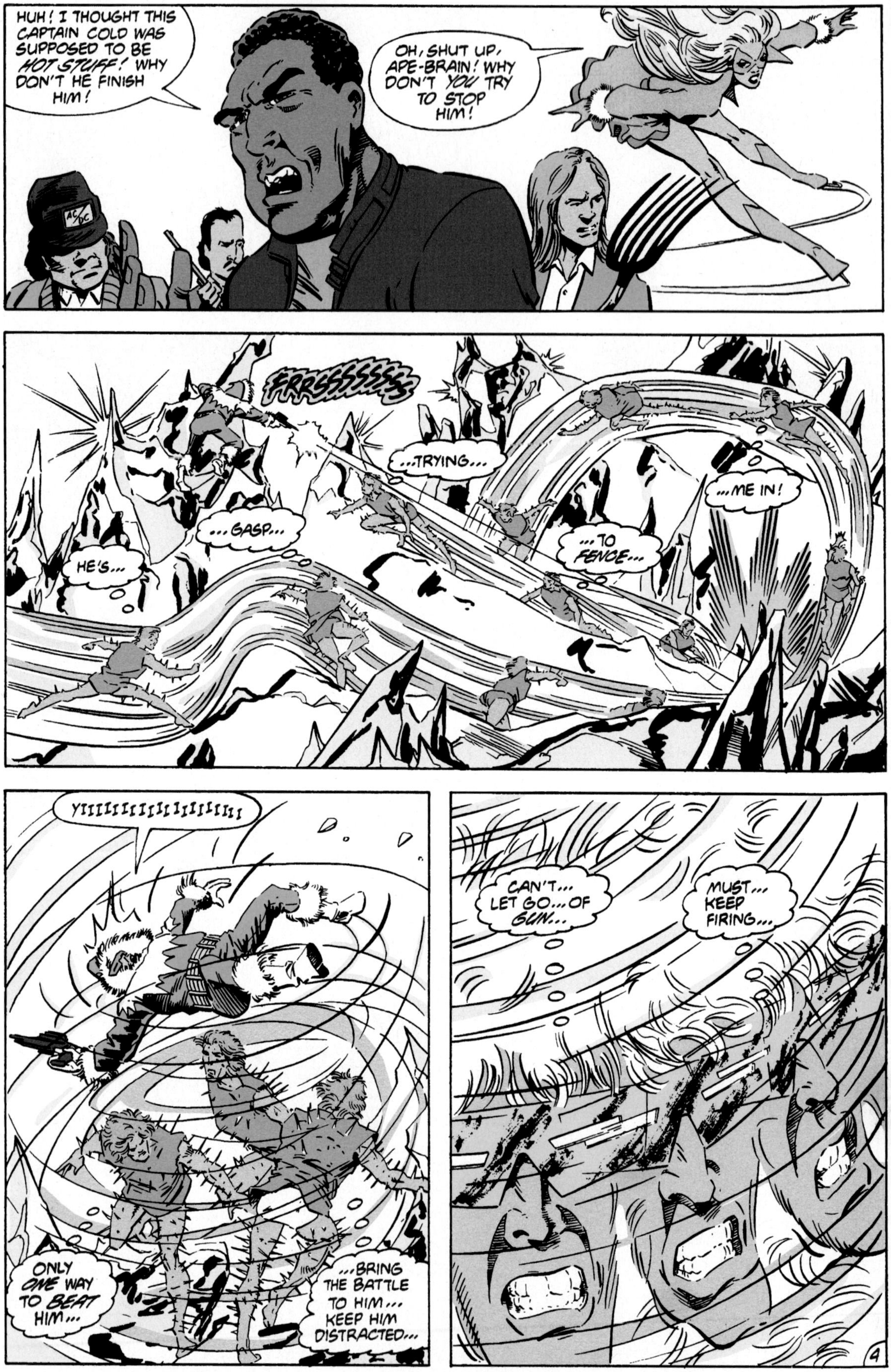
HUH! I THOUGHT THIS CAPTAIN COLD WAS SUPPOSED TO BE HOT STUFF! WHY DON'T HE FINISH HIM!
OH, SHUT UP, APE-BRAIN! WHY DON'T YOU TRY TO STOP HIM!
FRRSSSSSSSS
...TRYING...
...ME IN!
...GASP...
...TO FENCE...
HE'S...
YIIIIIIIIIIIIIIIIIII
CAN'T... LET GO... OF GUN...
MUST... KEEP FIRING...
ONLY ONE WAY TO BEAT HIM...
...BRING THE BATTLE TO HIM... KEEP HIM DISTRACTED...
4

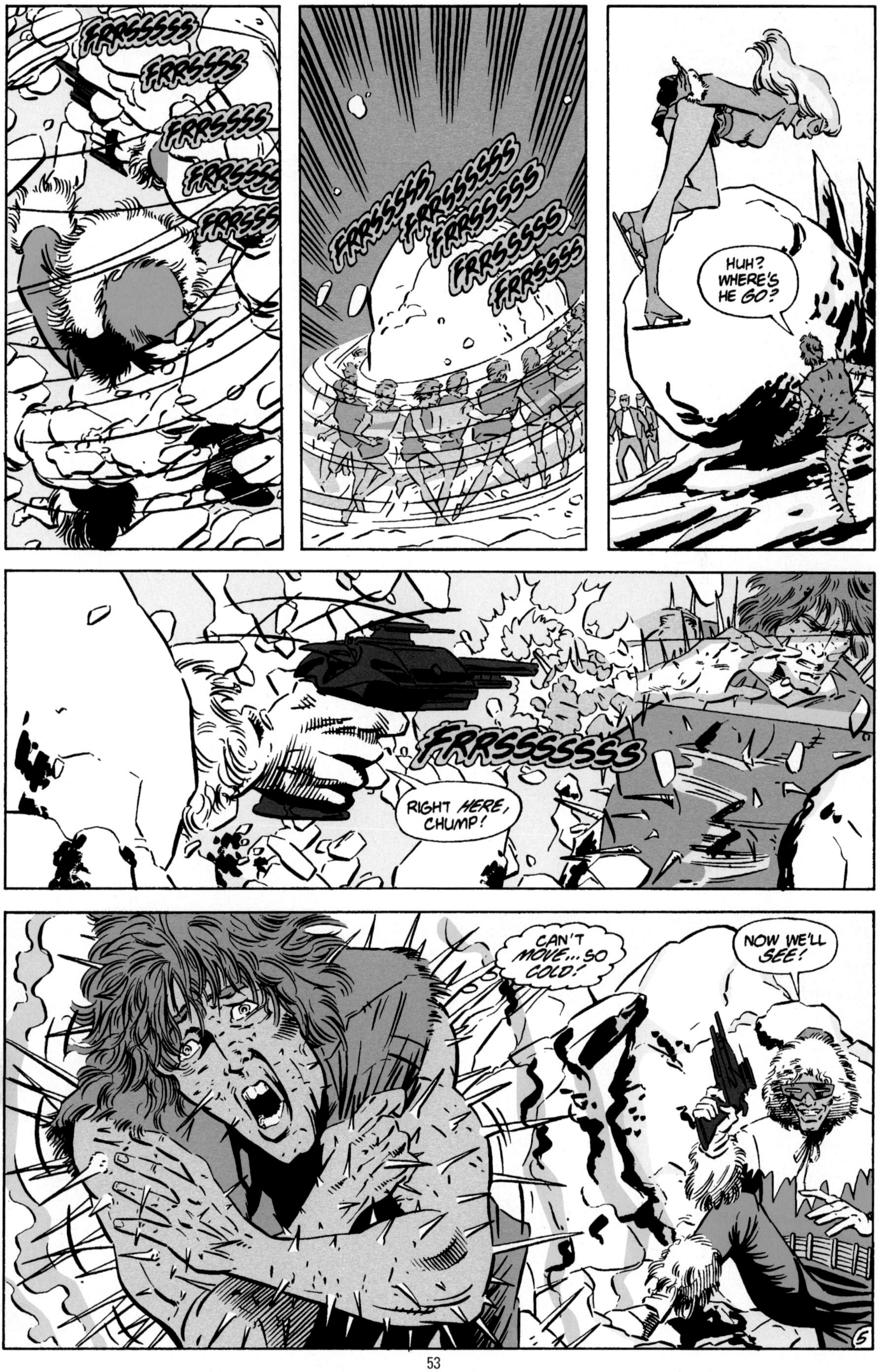
FRRSSSSS
FRRSSSS
FRRSSSS
FRRSSSS
FRRSSS
FRRSSSS
FRRSSSSSS
FRRSSSSS
FRRSSSSS
FRRSSSS
HUH? WHERE'S HE GO?
FRRSSSSSSS
RIGHT HERE, CHUMP!
CAN'T MOVE... SO COLD!
NOW WE'LL SEE!
5

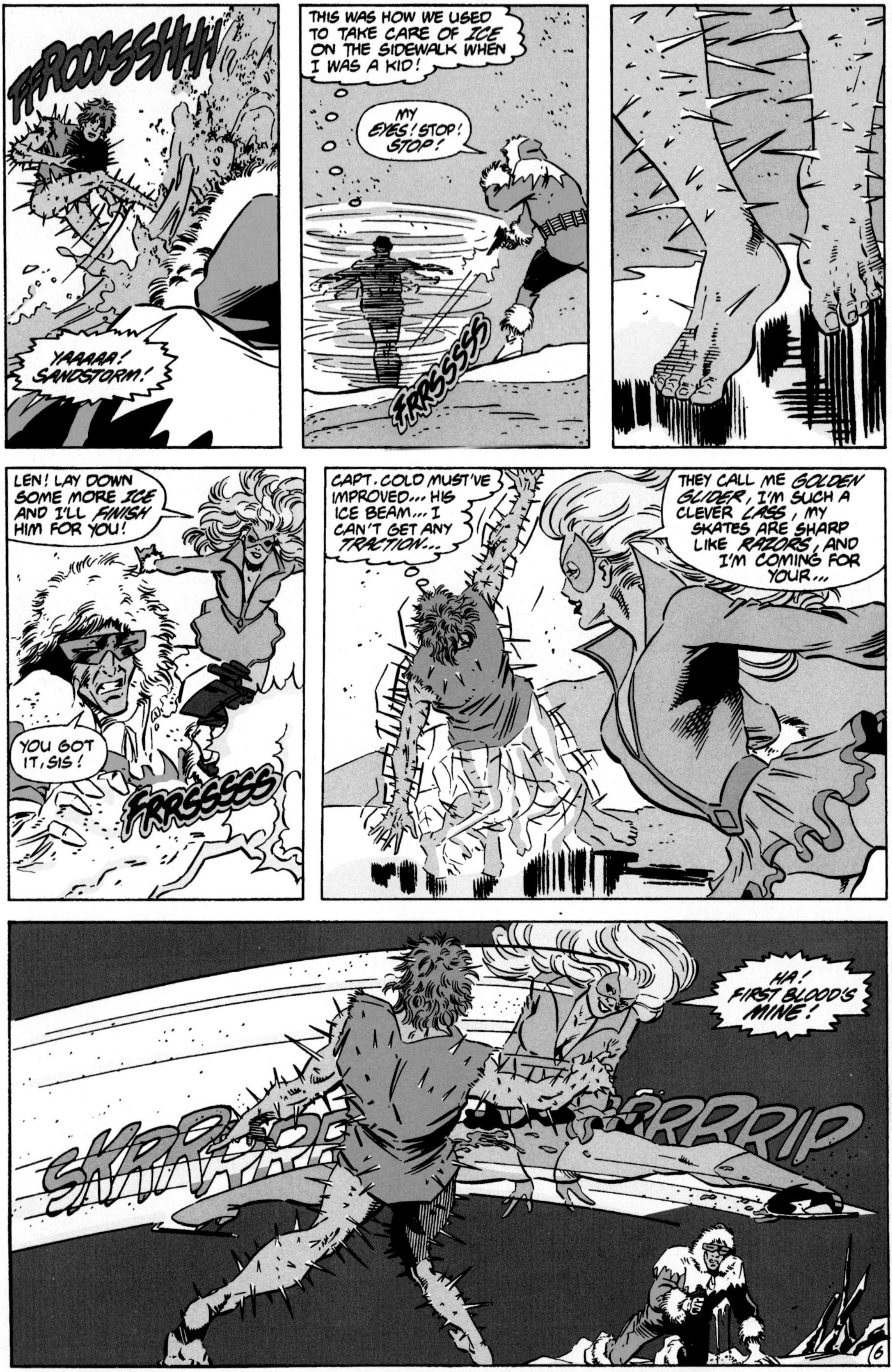
FFROOOSSHHH
YAAAAA! SANDSTORM!
THIS WAS HOW WE USED TO TAKE CARE OF ICE ON THE SIDEWALK WHEN I WAS A KID!
MY EYES! STOP! STOP!
FRRSSSSS
LEN! LAY DOWN SOME MORE ICE AND I'LL FINISH HIM FOR YOU!
YOU GOT IT, SIS!
FRRSSSSS
CAPT. COLD MUST'VE IMPROVED... HIS ICE BEAM... I CAN'T GET ANY TRACTION...
THEY CALL ME GOLDEN GLIDER, I'M SUCH A CLEVER LASS, MY SKATES ARE SHARP LIKE RAZORS, AND I'M COMING FOR YOUR...
HA! FIRST BLOOD'S MINE!
SKRRRRRRRRRRRRIP
6

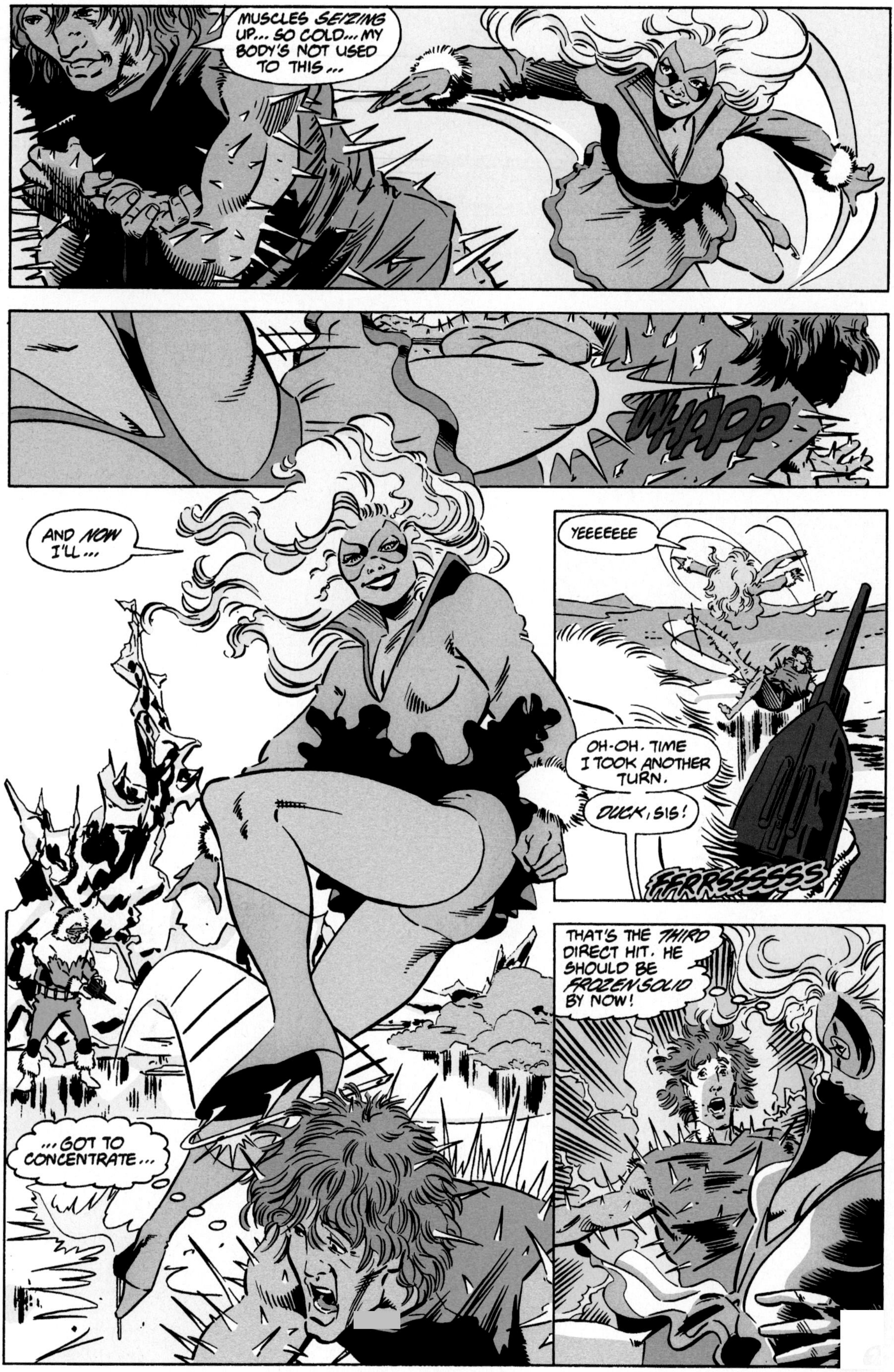
MUSCLES SEIZING UP... SO COLD... MY BODY'S NOT USED TO THIS...
WHAPP
AND NOW I'LL...
YEEEEEEE
OH-OH. TIME I TOOK ANOTHER TURN.
DUCK, SIS!
FFRRSSSSSS
...GOT TO CONCENTRATE...
THAT'S THE THIRD DIRECT HIT. HE SHOULD BE FROZEN SOLID BY NOW!

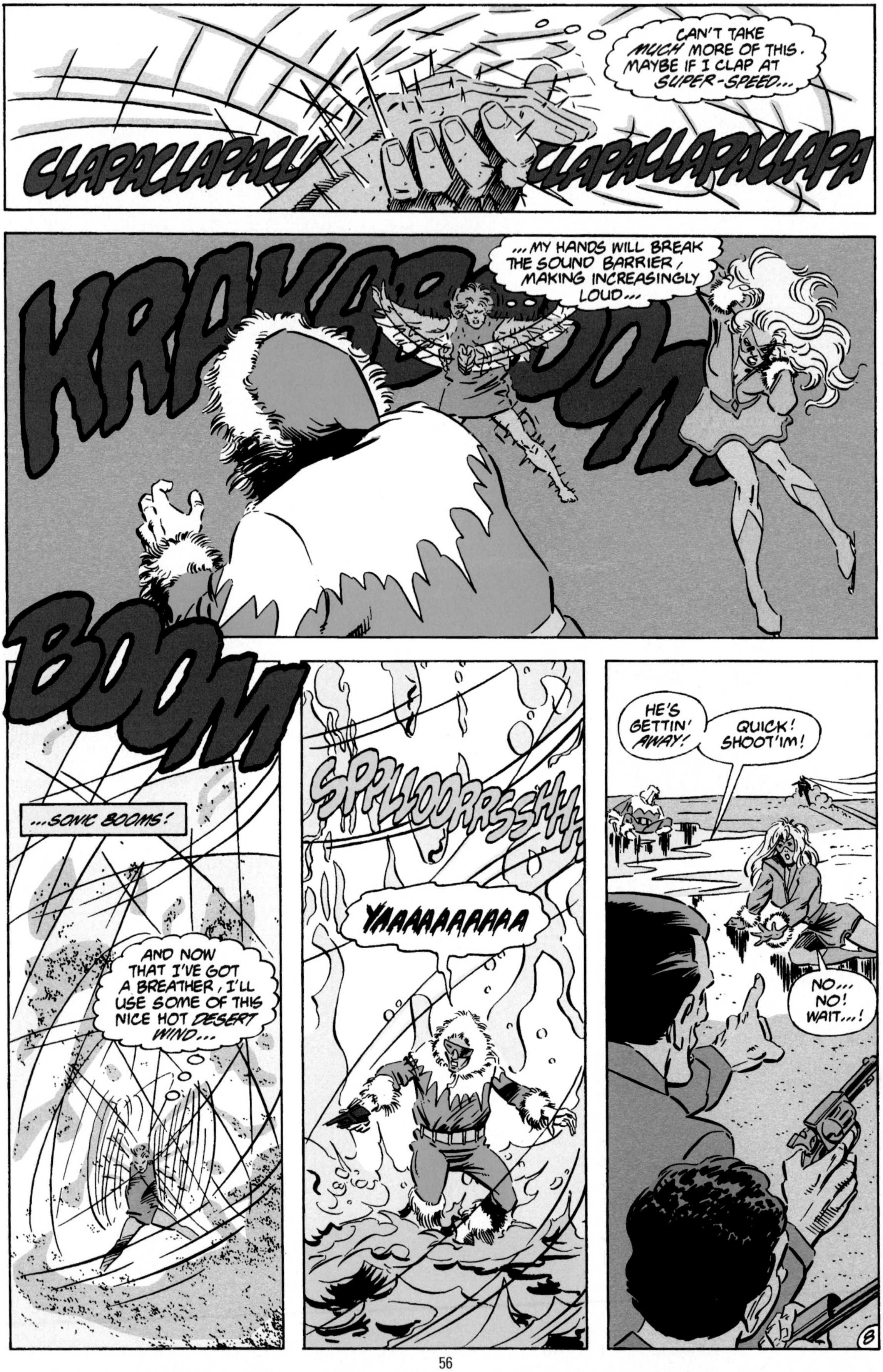
CAN'T TAKE MUCH MORE OF THIS. MAYBE IF I CLAP AT SUPER-SPEED...
CLAPACLAPACLAPACLL
CLAPACLAPACLAPACLAPA
...MY HANDS WILL BREAK THE SOUND BARRIER, MAKING INCREASINGLY LOUD...
KRAKAKOOOOM
BOOM
...SONIC BOOMS!
AND NOW THAT I'VE GOT A BREATHER, I'LL USE SOME OF THIS NICE HOT DESERT WIND...
SPPLLOORRSSHH
YAAAAAAAAAA
HE'S GETTIN' AWAY!
QUICK! SHOOT'IM!
NO... NO! WAIT...!
8

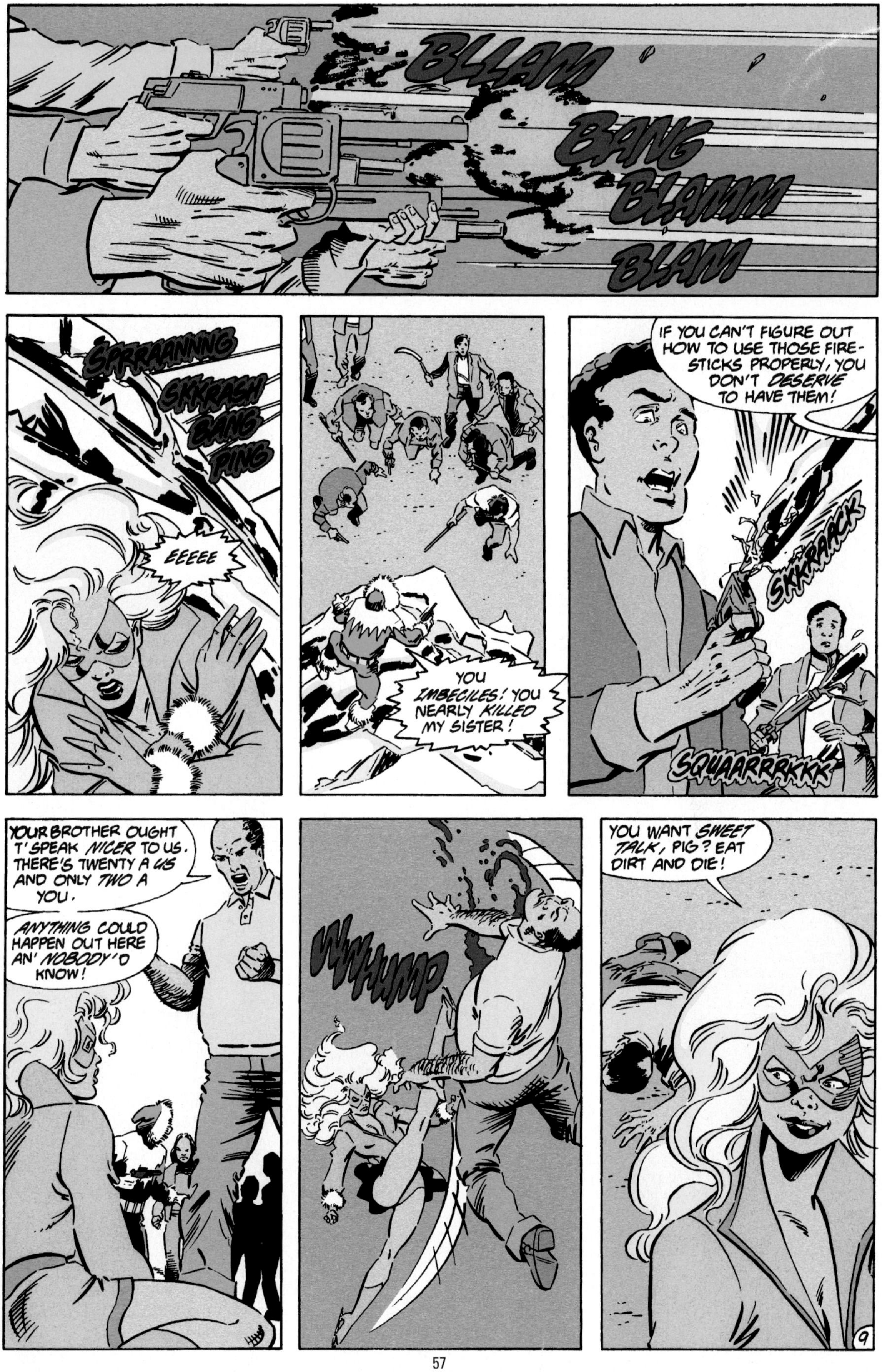
BLLAM
BANG
BLAMM
BLAM
SPRRAANNNG
SKKRASH
BANG
PING
EEEEE
YOU IMBECILES! YOU NEARLY KILLED MY SISTER!
IF YOU CAN'T FIGURE OUT HOW TO USE THOSE FIRE-STICKS PROPERLY, YOU DON'T DESERVE TO HAVE THEM!
SKKRAACK
SQUAARRRKKK
YOUR BROTHER OUGHT T'SPEAK NICER TO US. THERE'S TWENTY A US AND ONLY TWO A YOU.
ANYTHING COULD HAPPEN OUT HERE AN' NOBODY'D KNOW!
WHHUMP
YOU WANT SWEET TALK, PIG? EAT DIRT AND DIE!
9

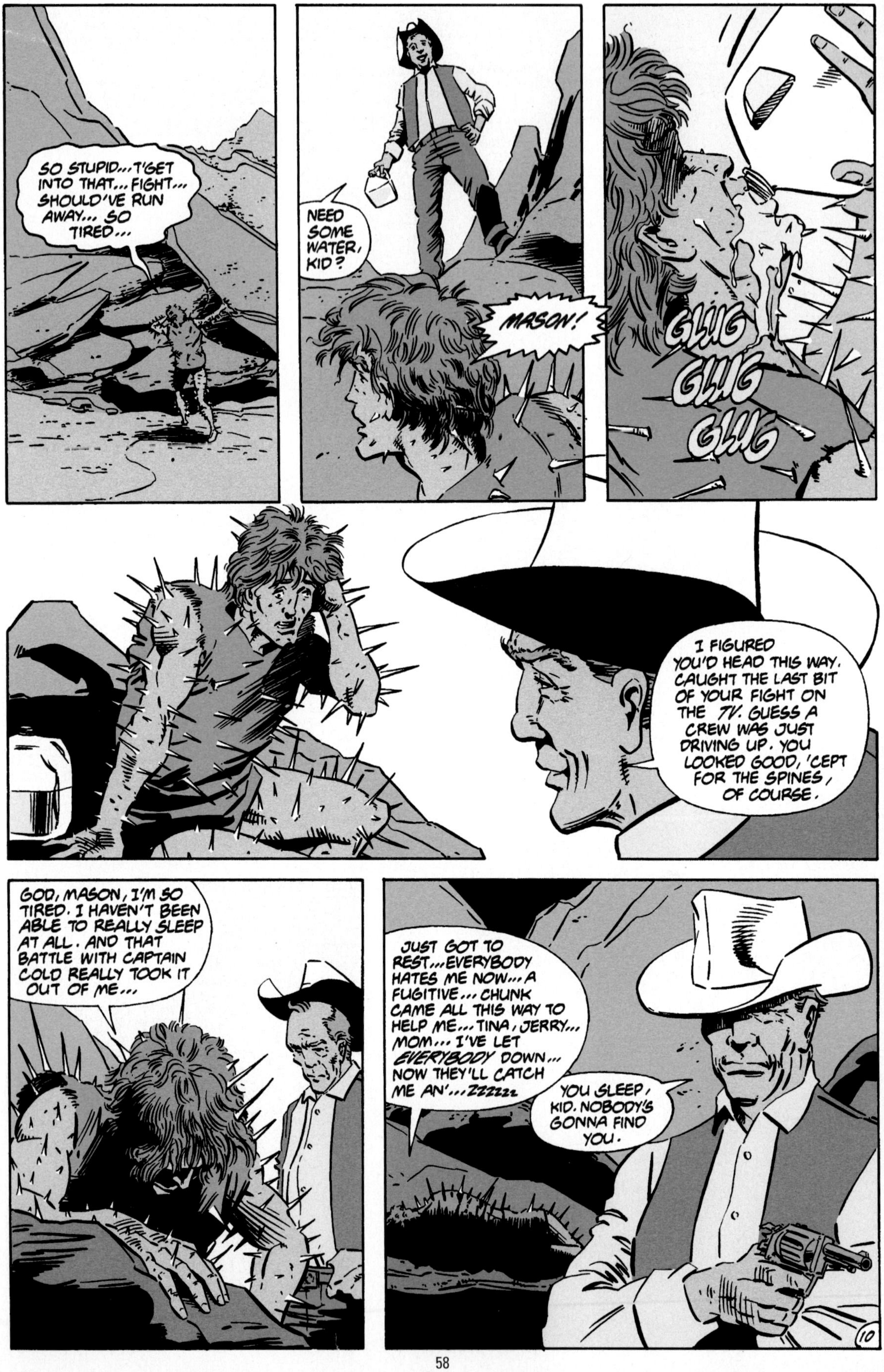
SO STUPID...T'GET INTO THAT... FIGHT... SHOULD'VE RUN AWAY... SO TIRED...
NEED SOME WATER, KID?
MASON!
GLUG GLUG GLUG
I FIGURED YOU'D HEAD THIS WAY. CAUGHT THE LAST BIT OF YOUR FIGHT ON THE TV. GUESS A CREW WAS JUST DRIVING UP. YOU LOOKED GOOD, 'CEPT FOR THE SPINES, OF COURSE.
GOD, MASON, I'M SO TIRED. I HAVEN'T BEEN ABLE TO REALLY SLEEP AT ALL. AND THAT BATTLE WITH CAPTAIN COLD REALLY TOOK IT OUT OF ME...
JUST GOT TO REST... EVERYBODY HATES ME NOW... A FUGITIVE... CHUNK CAME ALL THIS WAY TO HELP ME... TINA, JERRY... MOM... I'VE LET EVERYBODY DOWN... NOW THEY'LL CATCH ME AN'...Zzzzzz
YOU SLEEP, KID. NOBODY'S GONNA FIND YOU.
10

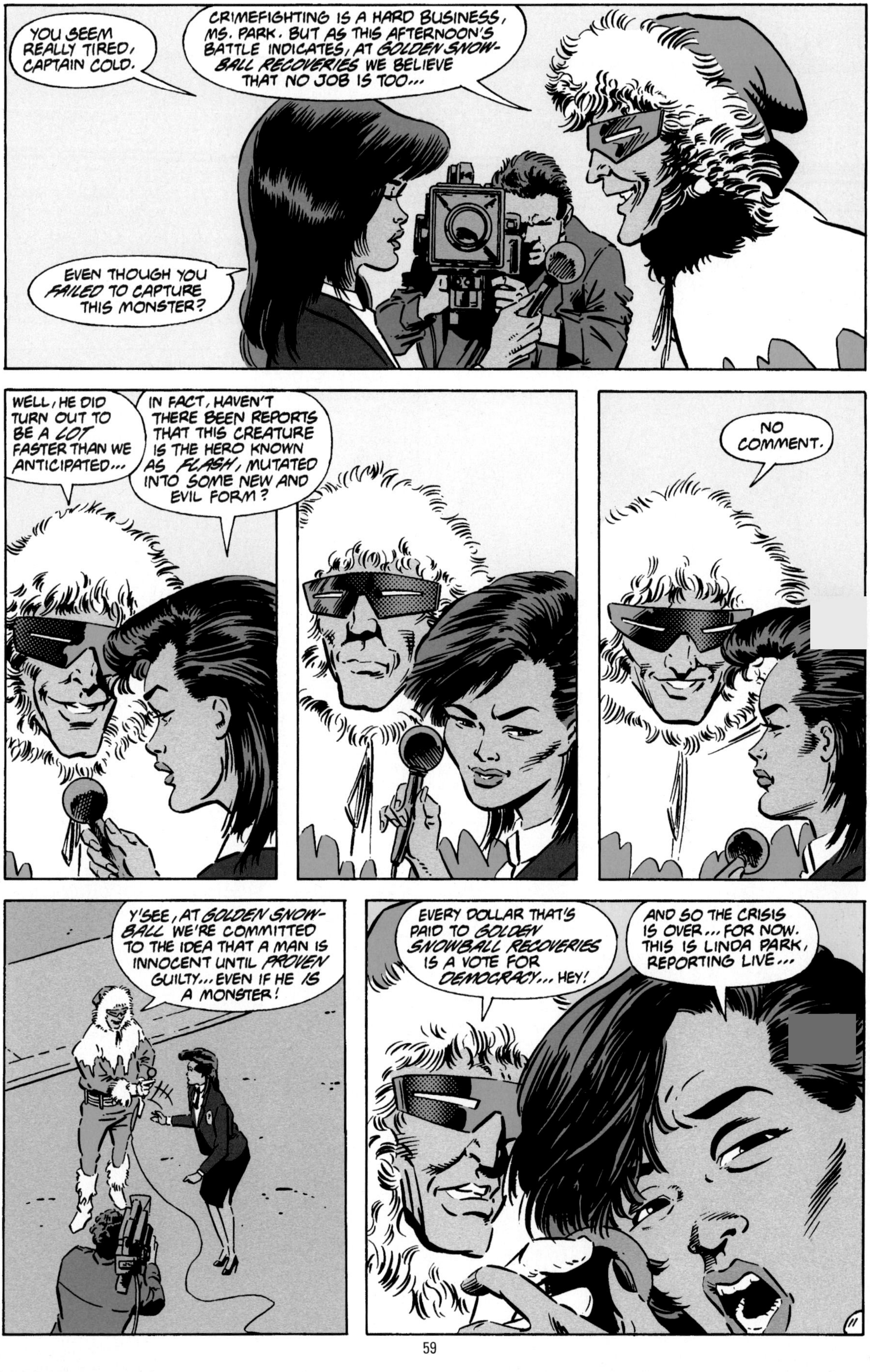
YOU SEEM REALLY TIRED, CAPTAIN COLD.
CRIMEFIGHTING IS A HARD BUSINESS, MS. PARK. BUT AS THIS AFTERNOON'S BATTLE INDICATES, AT GOLDEN SNOW-BALL RECOVERIES WE BELIEVE THAT NO JOB IS TOO...
EVEN THOUGH YOU FAILED TO CAPTURE THIS MONSTER?
WELL, HE DID TURN OUT TO BE A LOT FASTER THAN WE ANTICIPATED...
IN FACT, HAVEN'T THERE BEEN REPORTS THAT THIS CREATURE IS THE HERO KNOWN AS FLASH, MUTATED INTO SOME NEW AND EVIL FORM?
NO COMMENT.
Y'SEE, AT GOLDEN SNOW-BALL WE'RE COMMITTED TO THE IDEA THAT A MAN IS INNOCENT UNTIL PROVEN GUILTY... EVEN IF HE IS A MONSTER!
EVERY DOLLAR THAT'S PAID TO GOLDEN SNOWBALL RECOVERIES IS A VOTE FOR DEMOCRACY... HEY!
AND SO THE CRISIS IS OVER... FOR NOW. THIS IS LINDA PARK, REPORTING LIVE...

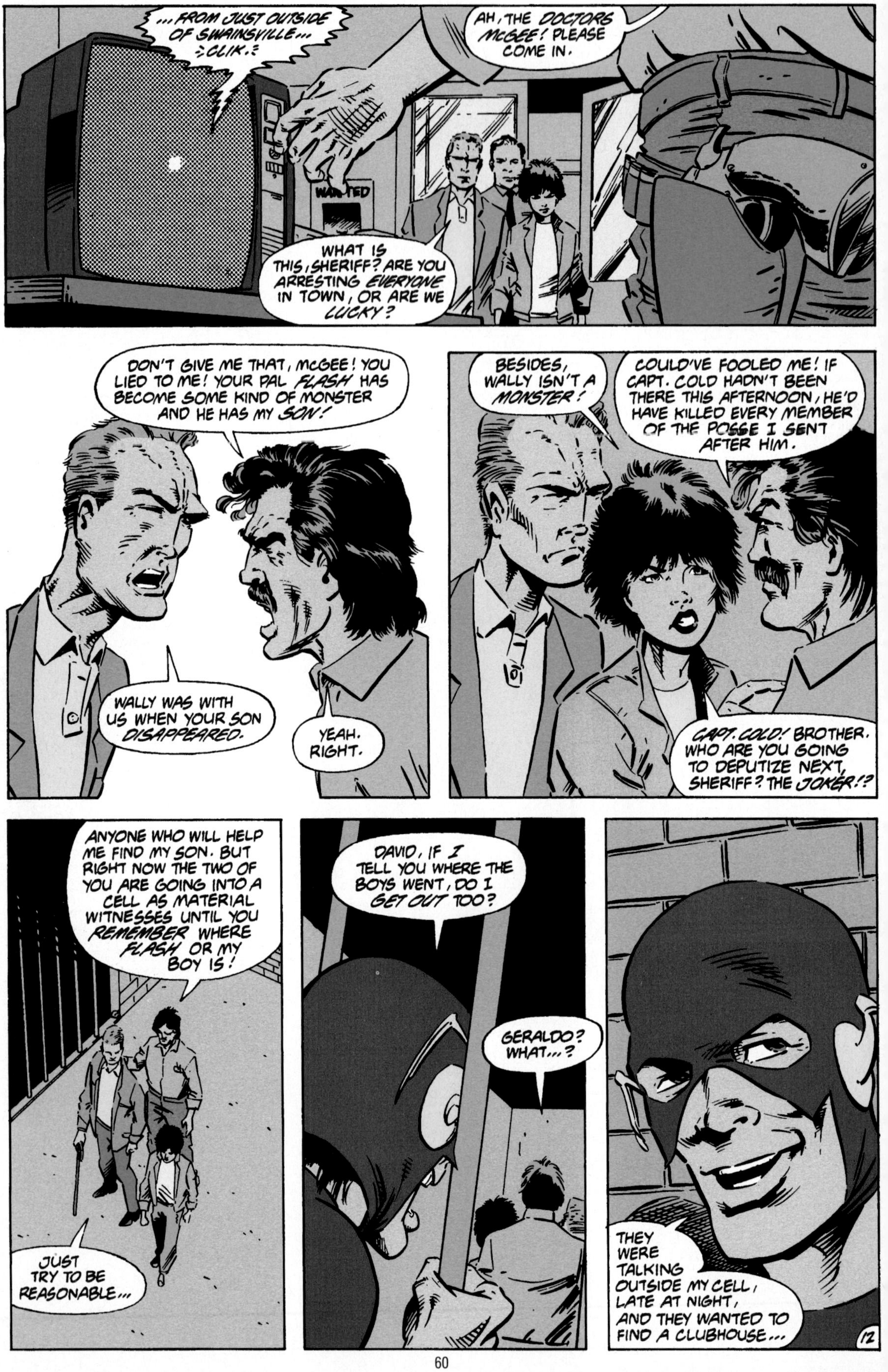
...FROM JUST OUTSIDE OF SWAINSVILLE... :CLIK.:
AH, THE DOCTORS McGEE! PLEASE COME IN.
WANTED
WHAT IS THIS, SHERIFF? ARE YOU ARRESTING EVERYONE IN TOWN, OR ARE WE LUCKY?
DON'T GIVE ME THAT, McGEE! YOU LIED TO ME! YOUR PAL FLASH HAS BECOME SOME KIND OF MONSTER AND HE HAS MY SON!
WALLY WAS WITH US WHEN YOUR SON DISAPPEARED.
YEAH. RIGHT.
BESIDES, WALLY ISN'T A MONSTER!
COULD'VE FOOLED ME! IF CAPT. COLD HADN'T BEEN THERE THIS AFTERNOON, HE'D HAVE KILLED EVERY MEMBER OF THE POSSE I SENT AFTER HIM.
CAPT. COLD! BROTHER. WHO ARE YOU GOING TO DEPUTIZE NEXT, SHERIFF? THE JOKER!?
ANYONE WHO WILL HELP ME FIND MY SON. BUT RIGHT NOW THE TWO OF YOU ARE GOING INTO A CELL AS MATERIAL WITNESSES UNTIL YOU REMEMBER WHERE FLASH OR MY BOY IS!
JUST TRY TO BE REASONABLE...
DAVID, IF I TELL YOU WHERE THE BOYS WENT, DO I GET OUT TOO?
GERALDO? WHAT...?
THEY WERE TALKING OUTSIDE MY CELL, LATE AT NIGHT, AND THEY WANTED TO FIND A CLUBHOUSE...
12

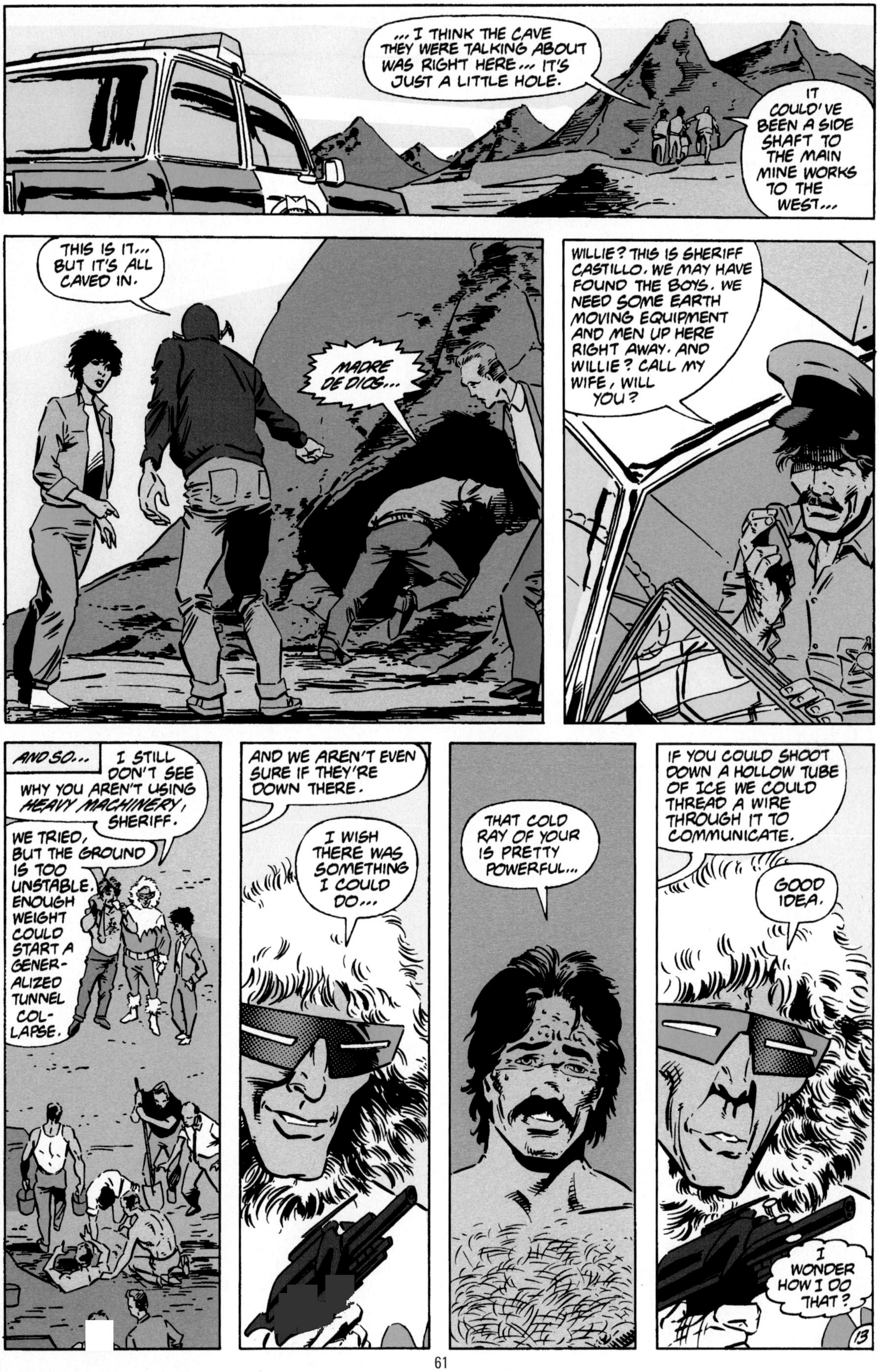

...I THINK THE CAVE THEY WERE TALKING ABOUT WAS RIGHT HERE... IT'S JUST A LITTLE HOLE.
IT COULD'VE BEEN A SIDE SHAFT TO THE MAIN MINE WORKS TO THE WEST...
THIS IS IT... BUT IT'S ALL CAVED IN.
MADRE DE DIOS...
WILLIE? THIS IS SHERIFF CASTILLO. WE MAY HAVE FOUND THE BOYS. WE NEED SOME EARTH MOVING EQUIPMENT AND MEN UP HERE RIGHT AWAY. AND WILLIE? CALL MY WIFE, WILL YOU?
AND SO...
I STILL DON'T SEE WHY YOU AREN'T USING HEAVY MACHINERY, SHERIFF.
WE TRIED, BUT THE GROUND IS TOO UNSTABLE. ENOUGH WEIGHT COULD START A GENERALIZED TUNNEL COLLAPSE.
AND WE AREN'T EVEN SURE IF THEY'RE DOWN THERE.
I WISH THERE WAS SOMETHING I COULD DO...
THAT COLD RAY OF YOUR IS PRETTY POWERFUL...
IF YOU COULD SHOOT DOWN A HOLLOW TUBE OF ICE WE COULD THREAD A WIRE THROUGH IT TO COMMUNICATE.
GOOD IDEA.
I WONDER HOW I DO THAT?
13

AND ELSEWHERE...

TWINGGG

OUCH. OUCH. OUCH. OUCH. OUCH.

JUST ANOTHER SEC, KID. ONCE THESE SPINES'RE OUT, YOU WON'T BE SO CONSPICUOUS!

OUCH.

NOTHING TO IT. IT'S JUST LIKE FISHIN' FOR BUCKSHOT WHEN I WAS A KID!

SWELL. THEN I'LL DO IT T'YOU FOR A WHILE!

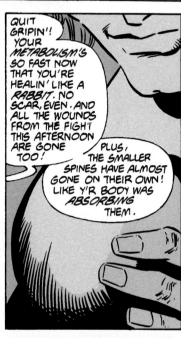

QUIT GRIPIN'! YOUR METABOLISM'S SO FAST NOW THAT YOU'RE HEALIN' LIKE A RABBIT. NO SCAR, EVEN. AND ALL THE WOUNDS FROM THE FIGHT THIS AFTERNOON ARE GONE TOO!

PLUS, THE SMALLER SPINES HAVE ALMOST GONE ON THEIR OWN! LIKE Y'R BODY WAS ABSORBING THEM.

GEEZ.

MAKES YOU THINK, DON'T IT?

I WONDER WHATEVER HAPPENED TO THAT POSSE? D'YOU THINK THEY GAVE UP, OR WHAT?

I SAID, DO YOU THINK....

OH.

ZZZZZZZZ

14

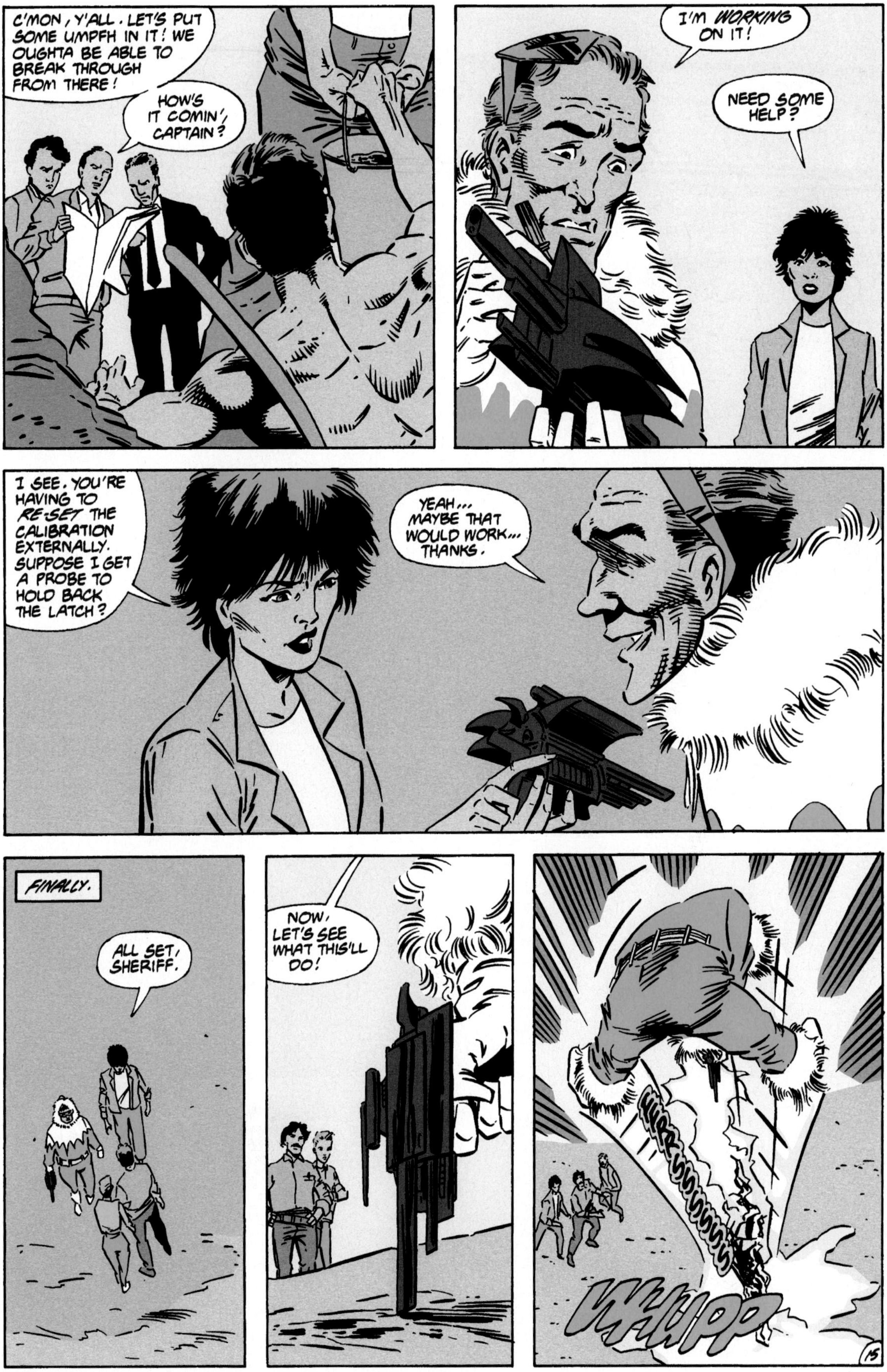
C'MON, Y'ALL. LET'S PUT SOME UMPFH IN IT! WE OUGHTA BE ABLE TO BREAK THROUGH FROM THERE!
HOW'S IT COMIN', CAPTAIN?
I'M WORKING ON IT!
NEED SOME HELP?
I SEE. YOU'RE HAVING TO RE-SET THE CALIBRATION EXTERNALLY. SUPPOSE I GET A PROBE TO HOLD BACK THE LATCH?
YEAH... MAYBE THAT WOULD WORK... THANKS.
FINALLY.
ALL SET, SHERIFF.
NOW, LET'S SEE WHAT THIS'LL DO!
VVHUPP
15

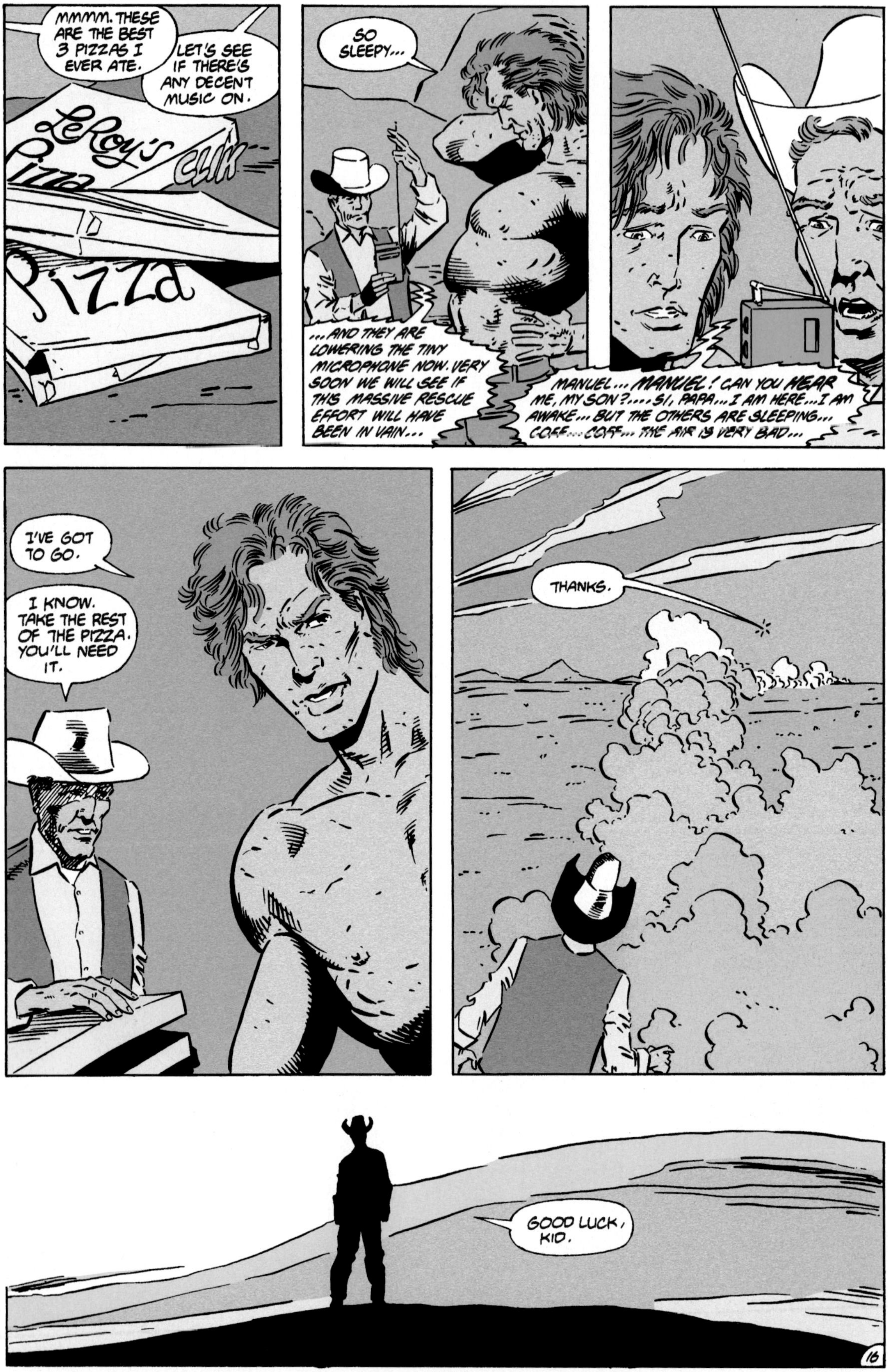
MMMM. THESE ARE THE BEST 3 PIZZAS I EVER ATE.
LET'S SEE IF THERE'S ANY DECENT MUSIC ON.
LeRoy's Pizza
CLIK
Pizza
SO SLEEPY...
...AND THEY ARE LOWERING THE TINY MICROPHONE NOW. VERY SOON WE WILL SEE IF THIS MASSIVE RESCUE EFFORT WILL HAVE BEEN IN VAIN...
MANUEL... MANUEL! CAN YOU HEAR ME, MY SON?.... SI, PAPA... I AM HERE... I AM AWAKE... BUT THE OTHERS ARE SLEEPING... COFF... COFF... THE AIR IS VERY BAD...
I'VE GOT TO GO.
I KNOW. TAKE THE REST OF THE PIZZA. YOU'LL NEED IT.
THANKS.
GOOD LUCK, KID.
16

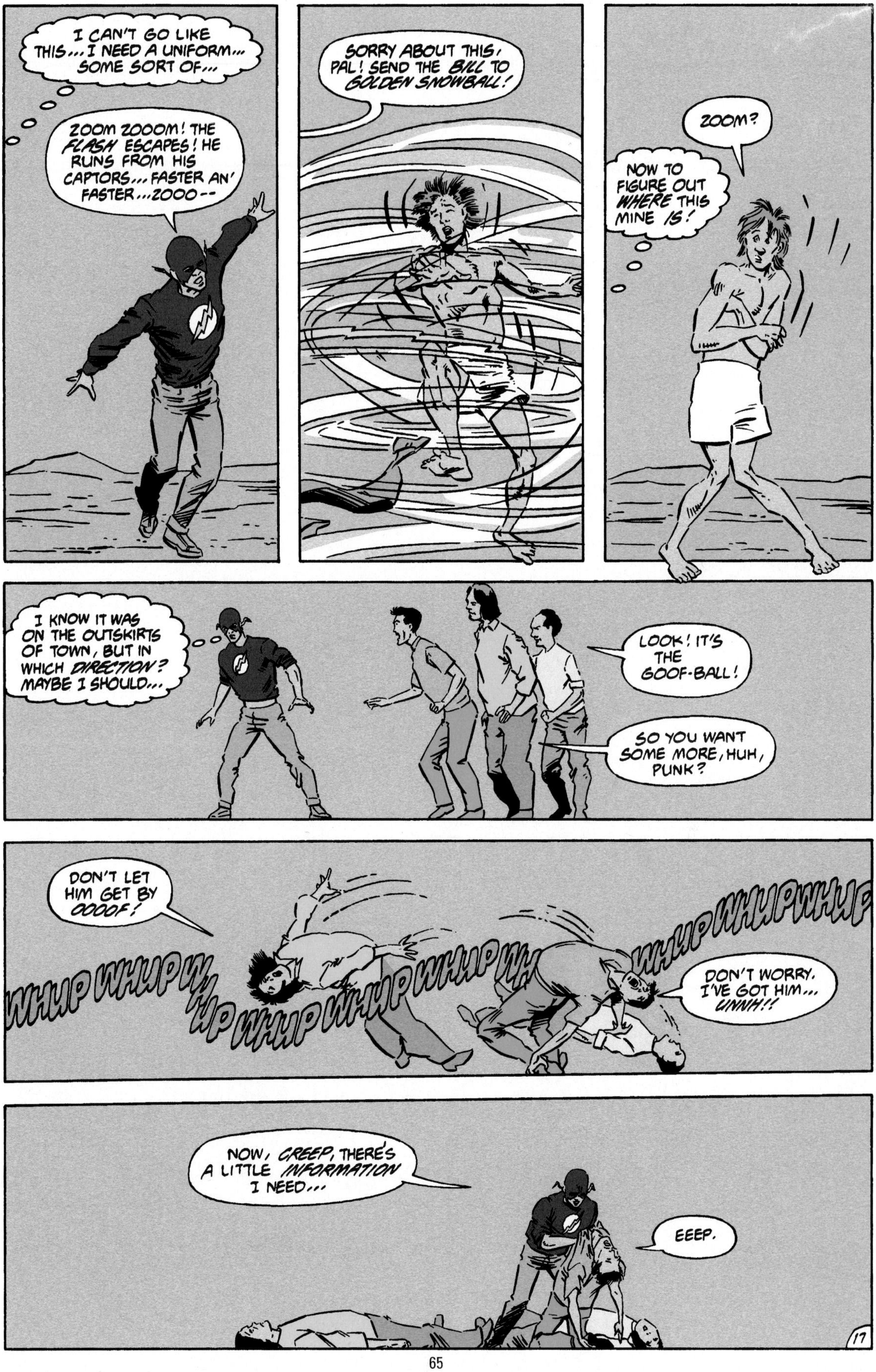
I CAN'T GO LIKE THIS... I NEED A UNIFORM... SOME SORT OF...
ZOOM ZOOOM! THE FLASH ESCAPES! HE RUNS FROM HIS CAPTORS... FASTER AN' FASTER... ZOOO--
SORRY ABOUT THIS, PAL! SEND THE BILL TO GOLDEN SNOWBALL!
ZOOM?
NOW TO FIGURE OUT WHERE THIS MINE IS!
I KNOW IT WAS ON THE OUTSKIRTS OF TOWN, BUT IN WHICH DIRECTION? MAYBE I SHOULD...
LOOK! IT'S THE GOOF-BALL!
SO YOU WANT SOME MORE, HUH, PUNK?
DON'T LET HIM GET BY OOOOF!
WHUP WHUP W
WHUP WHUP WHUP WHUP WH
WHUP WHUP WHUP
DON'T WORRY. I'VE GOT HIM... UNNH!!
NOW, CREEP, THERE'S A LITTLE INFORMATION I NEED...
EEEP.
17

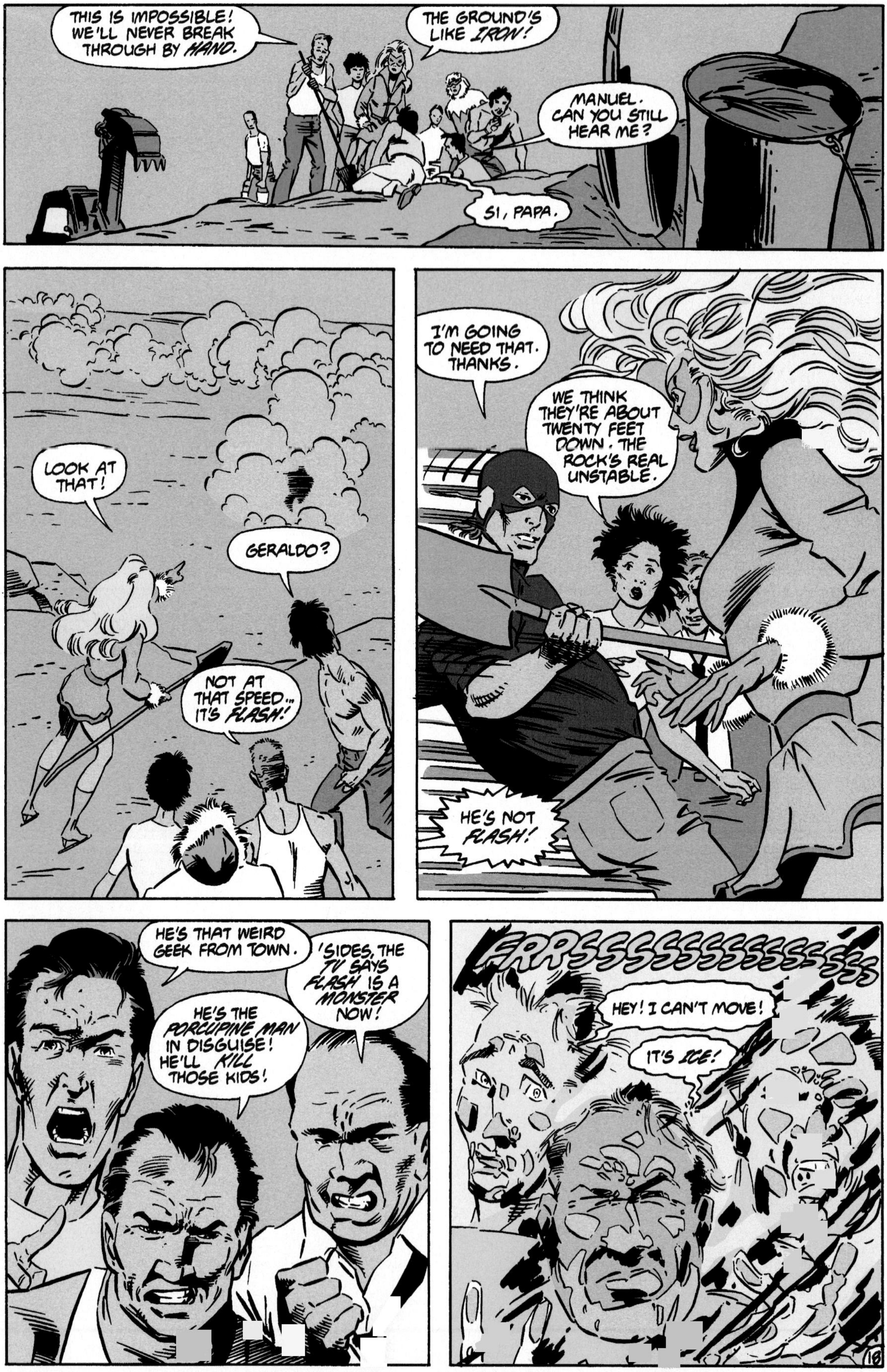
THIS IS IMPOSSIBLE! WE'LL NEVER BREAK THROUGH BY HAND.
THE GROUND'S LIKE IRON!
MANUEL. CAN YOU STILL HEAR ME?
SI, PAPA.
LOOK AT THAT!
GERALDO?
NOT AT THAT SPEED... IT'S FLASH!
I'M GOING TO NEED THAT. THANKS.
WE THINK THEY'RE ABOUT TWENTY FEET DOWN. THE ROCK'S REAL UNSTABLE.
HE'S NOT FLASH!
HE'S THAT WEIRD GEEK FROM TOWN.
'SIDES, THE TV SAYS FLASH IS A MONSTER NOW!
HE'S THE PORCUPINE MAN IN DISGUISE! HE'LL KILL THOSE KIDS!
FRRSSSSSSSSSSSSSSSS
HEY! I CAN'T MOVE!
IT'S ICE!
18

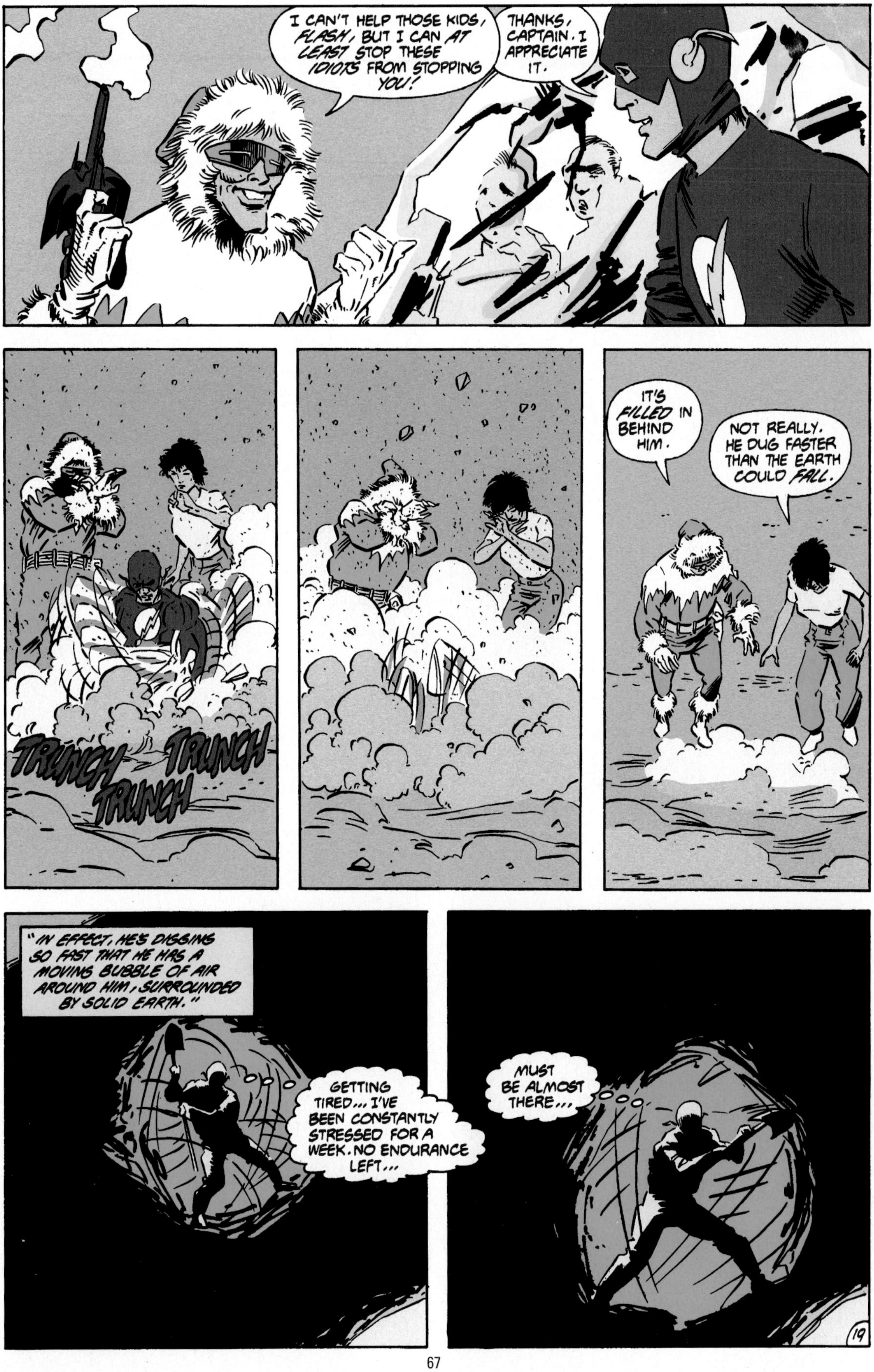
I CAN'T HELP THOSE KIDS, FLASH, BUT I CAN AT LEAST STOP THESE IDIOTS FROM STOPPING YOU!
THANKS, CAPTAIN. I APPRECIATE IT.
TRUNCH TRUNCH TRUNCH
IT'S FILLED IN BEHIND HIM.
NOT REALLY. HE DUG FASTER THAN THE EARTH COULD FALL.
"IN EFFECT, HE'S DIGGING SO FAST THAT HE HAS A MOVING BUBBLE OF AIR AROUND HIM, SURROUNDED BY SOLID EARTH."
GETTING TIRED... I'VE BEEN CONSTANTLY STRESSED FOR A WEEK. NO ENDURANCE LEFT...
MUST BE ALMOST THERE...
19

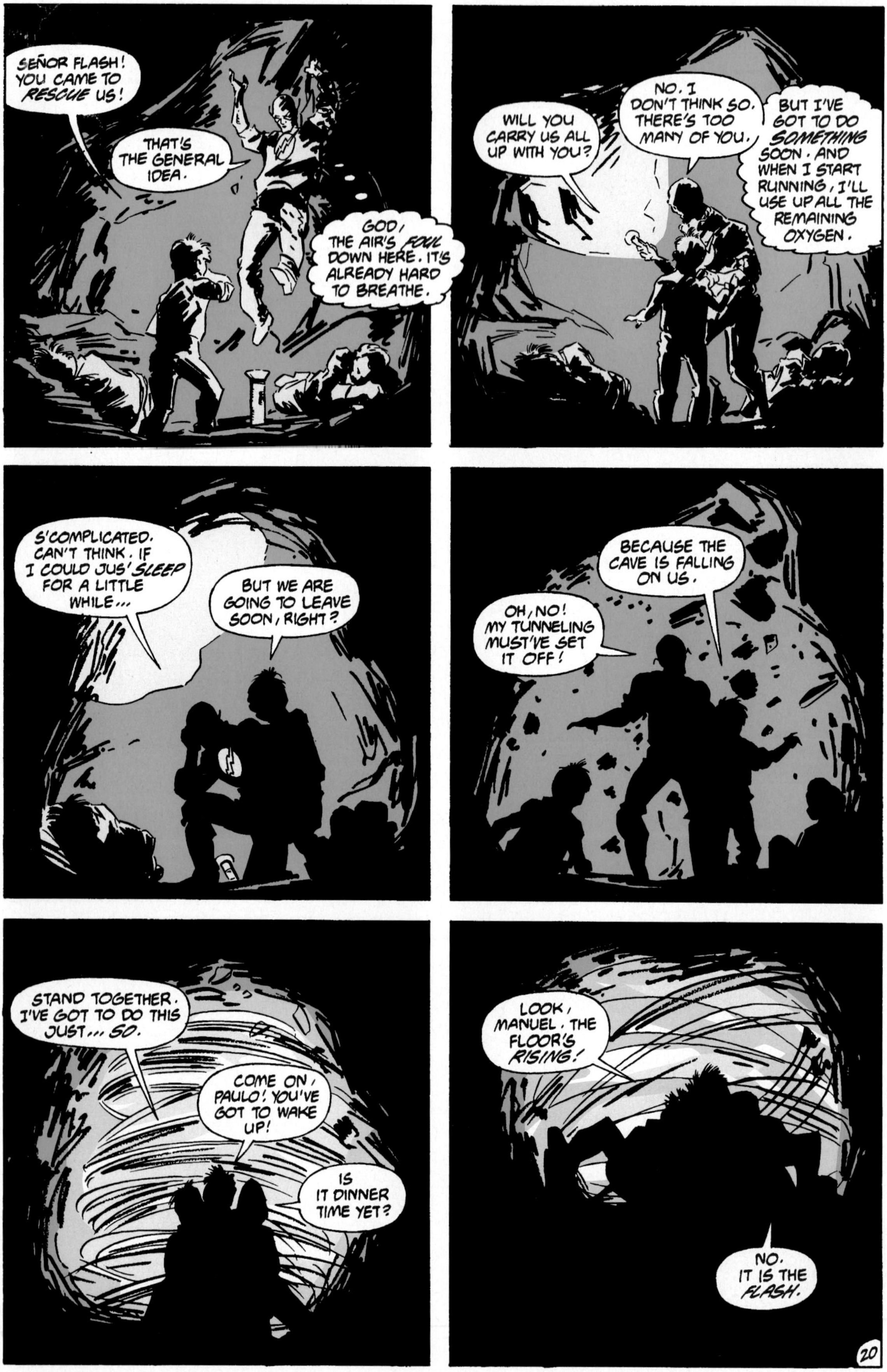
SEÑOR FLASH! YOU CAME TO RESCUE US!
THAT'S THE GENERAL IDEA.
GOD, THE AIR'S FOUL DOWN HERE. IT'S ALREADY HARD TO BREATHE.
WILL YOU CARRY US ALL UP WITH YOU?
NO. I DON'T THINK SO. THERE'S TOO MANY OF YOU.
BUT I'VE GOT TO DO SOMETHING SOON. AND WHEN I START RUNNING, I'LL USE UP ALL THE REMAINING OXYGEN.
S'COMPLICATED. CAN'T THINK. IF I COULD JUS' SLEEP FOR A LITTLE WHILE...
BUT WE ARE GOING TO LEAVE SOON, RIGHT?
BECAUSE THE CAVE IS FALLING ON US.
OH, NO! MY TUNNELING MUST'VE SET IT OFF!
STAND TOGETHER. I'VE GOT TO DO THIS JUST... SO.
COME ON, PAULO! YOU'VE GOT TO WAKE UP!
IS IT DINNER TIME YET?
LOOK, MANUEL. THE FLOOR'S RISING!
NO. IT IS THE FLASH.
20

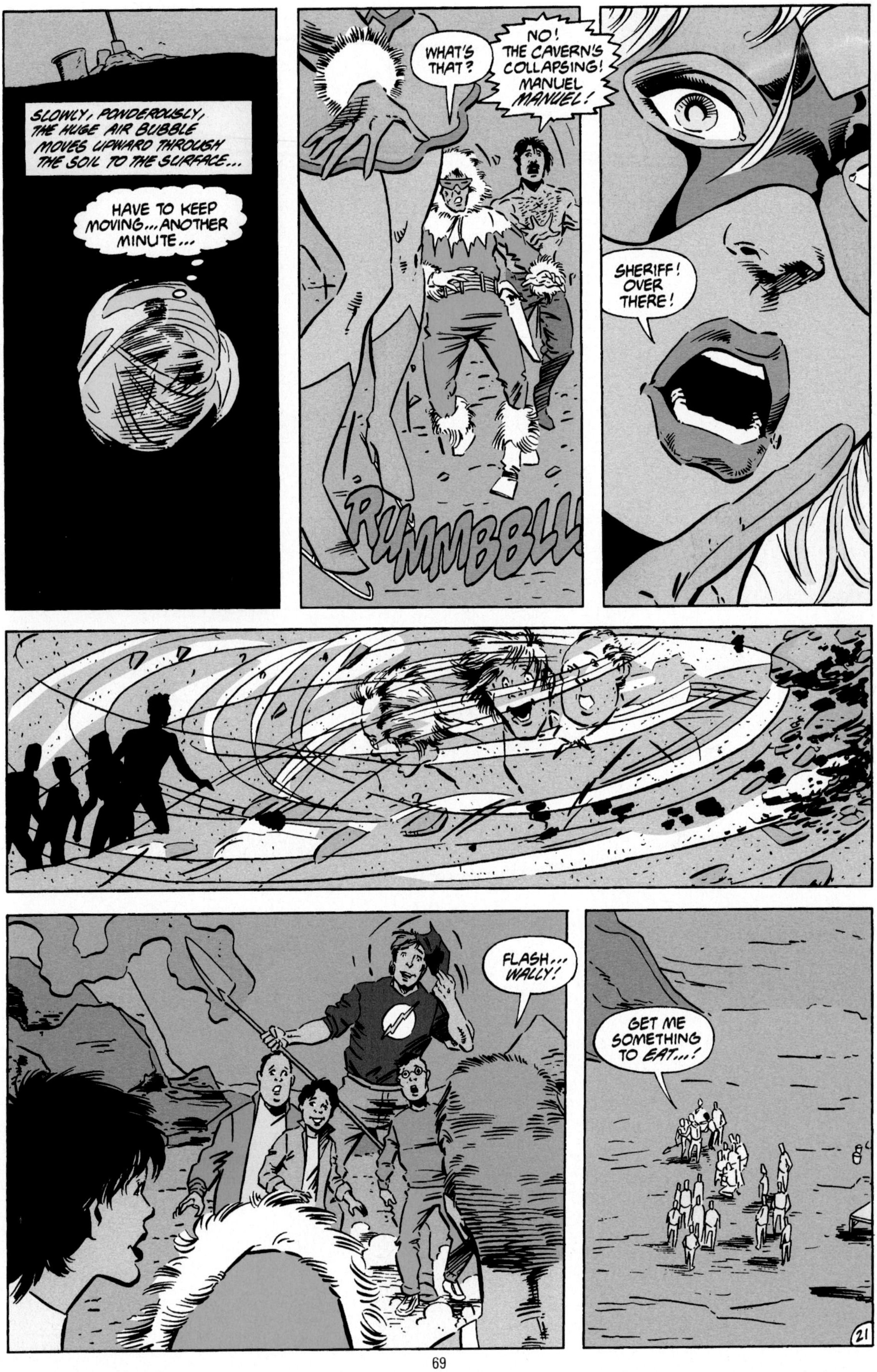
SLOWLY, PONDEROUSLY, THE HUGE AIR BUBBLE MOVES UPWARD THROUGH THE SOIL TO THE SURFACE...
HAVE TO KEEP MOVING...ANOTHER MINUTE...
WHAT'S THAT?
NO! THE CAVERN'S COLLAPSING! MANUEL MANUEL!
RUMMBBLL
SHERIFF! OVER THERE!
FLASH... WALLY!
GET ME SOMETHING TO EAT...!
21

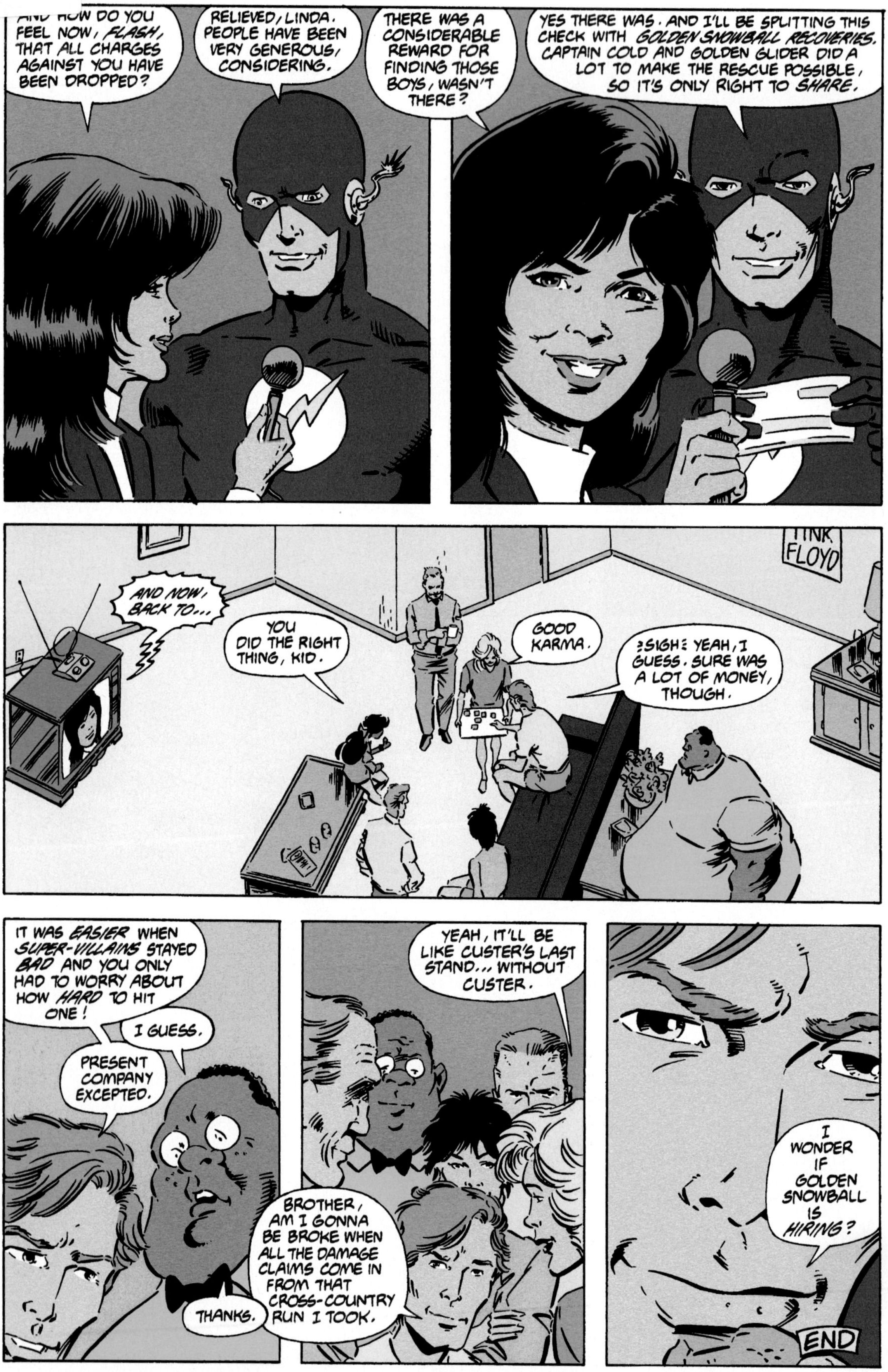
AND HOW DO YOU FEEL NOW, FLASH, THAT ALL CHARGES AGAINST YOU HAVE BEEN DROPPED?
RELIEVED, LINDA. PEOPLE HAVE BEEN VERY GENEROUS, CONSIDERING.
THERE WAS A CONSIDERABLE REWARD FOR FINDING THOSE BOYS, WASN'T THERE?
YES THERE WAS. AND I'LL BE SPLITTING THIS CHECK WITH GOLDEN SNOWBALL RECOVERIES. CAPTAIN COLD AND GOLDEN GLIDER DID A LOT TO MAKE THE RESCUE POSSIBLE, SO IT'S ONLY RIGHT TO SHARE.
AND NOW, BACK TO...
YOU DID THE RIGHT THING, KID.
GOOD KARMA.
:SIGH: YEAH, I GUESS. SURE WAS A LOT OF MONEY, THOUGH.
IT WAS EASIER WHEN SUPER-VILLAINS STAYED BAD AND YOU ONLY HAD TO WORRY ABOUT HOW HARD TO HIT ONE!
I GUESS.
PRESENT COMPANY EXCEPTED.
THANKS.
YEAH, IT'LL BE LIKE CUSTER'S LAST STAND... WITHOUT CUSTER.
BROTHER, AM I GONNA BE BROKE WHEN ALL THE DAMAGE CLAIMS COME IN FROM THAT CROSS-COUNTRY RUN I TOOK.
I WONDER IF GOLDEN SNOWBALL IS HIRING?
END

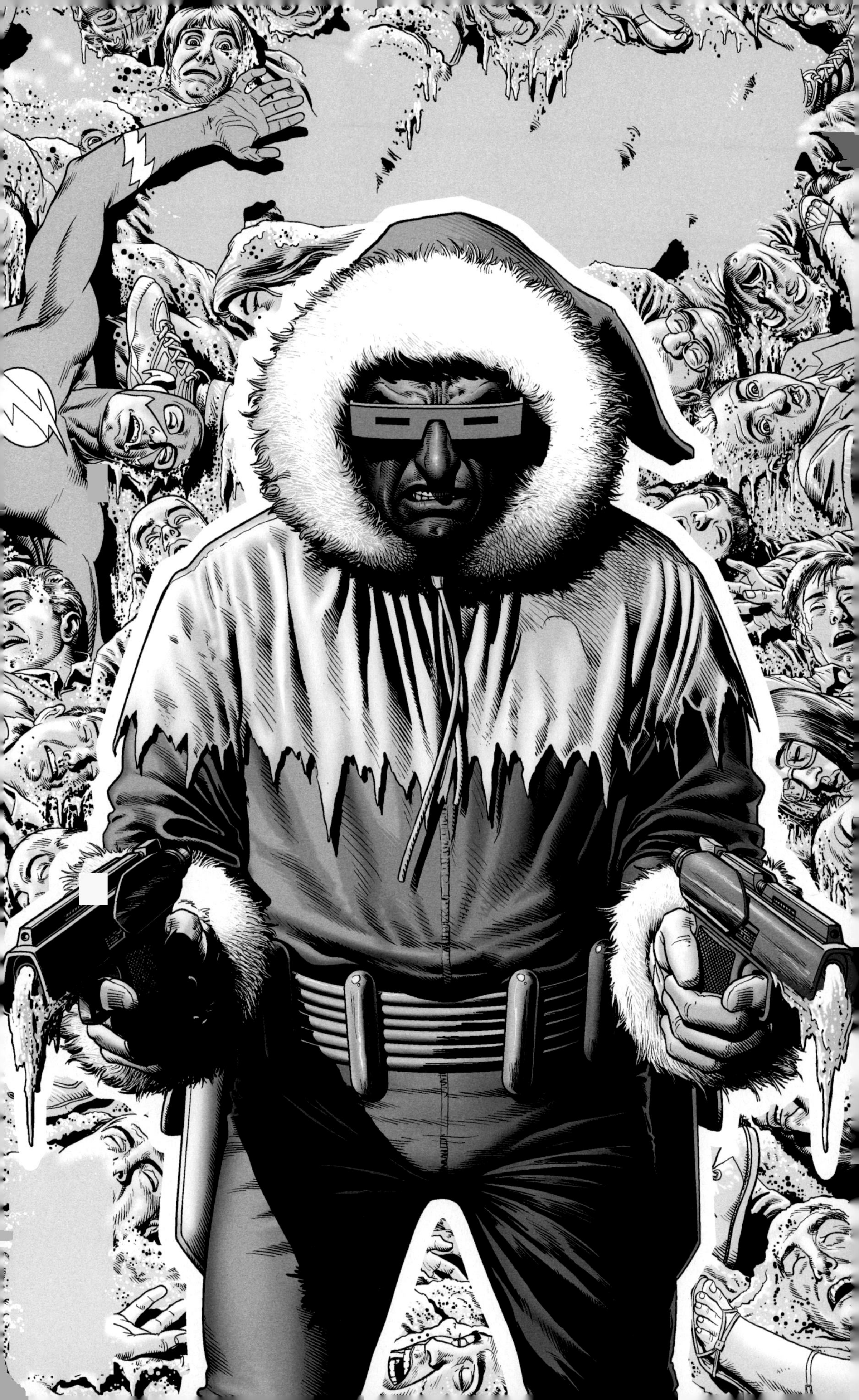

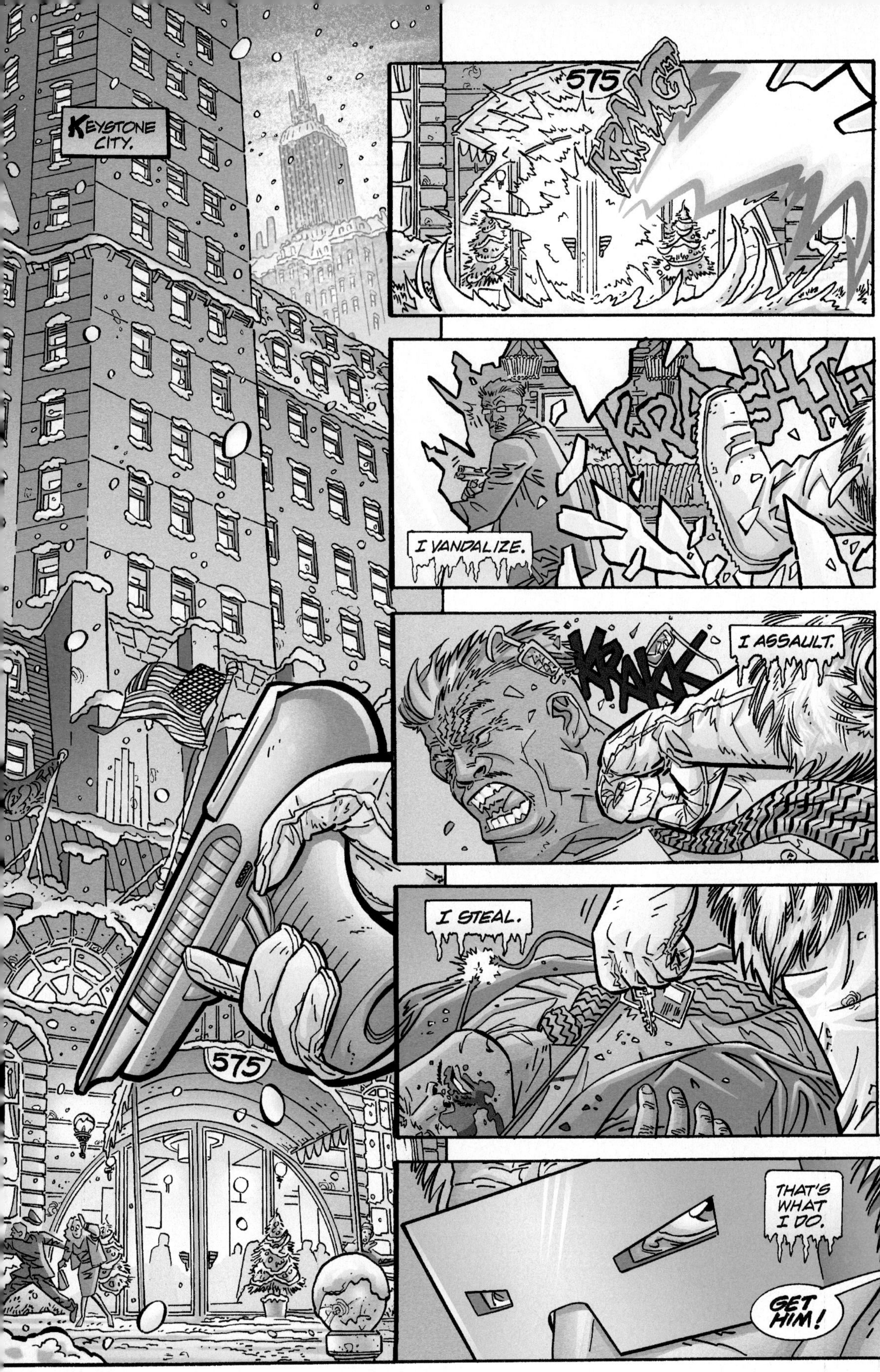
Keystone City.
575
I VANDALIZE.
KRAKK
I ASSAULT.
I STEAL.
THAT'S WHAT I DO.
GET HIM!

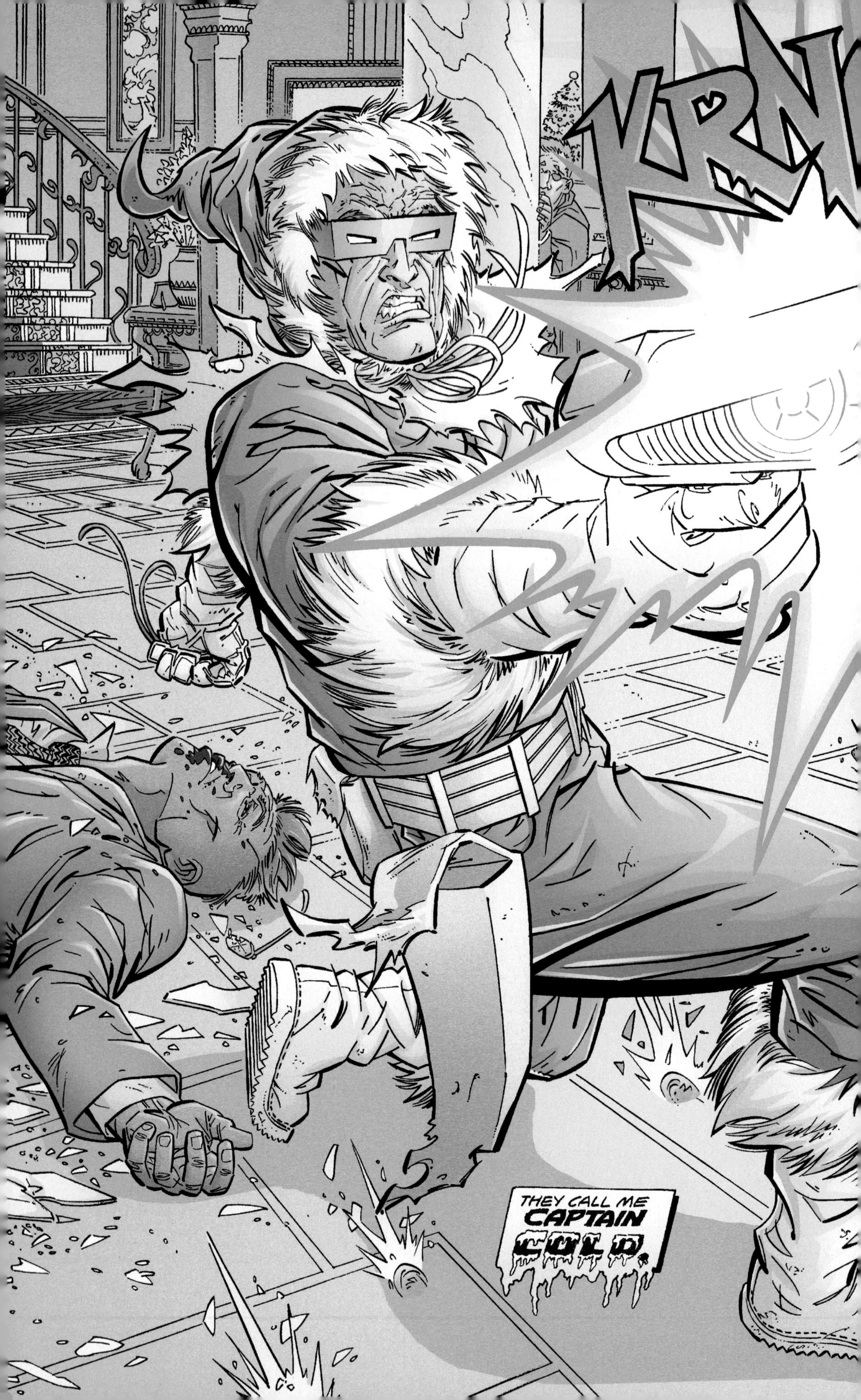
KRN
THEY CALL ME CAPTAIN COLD.

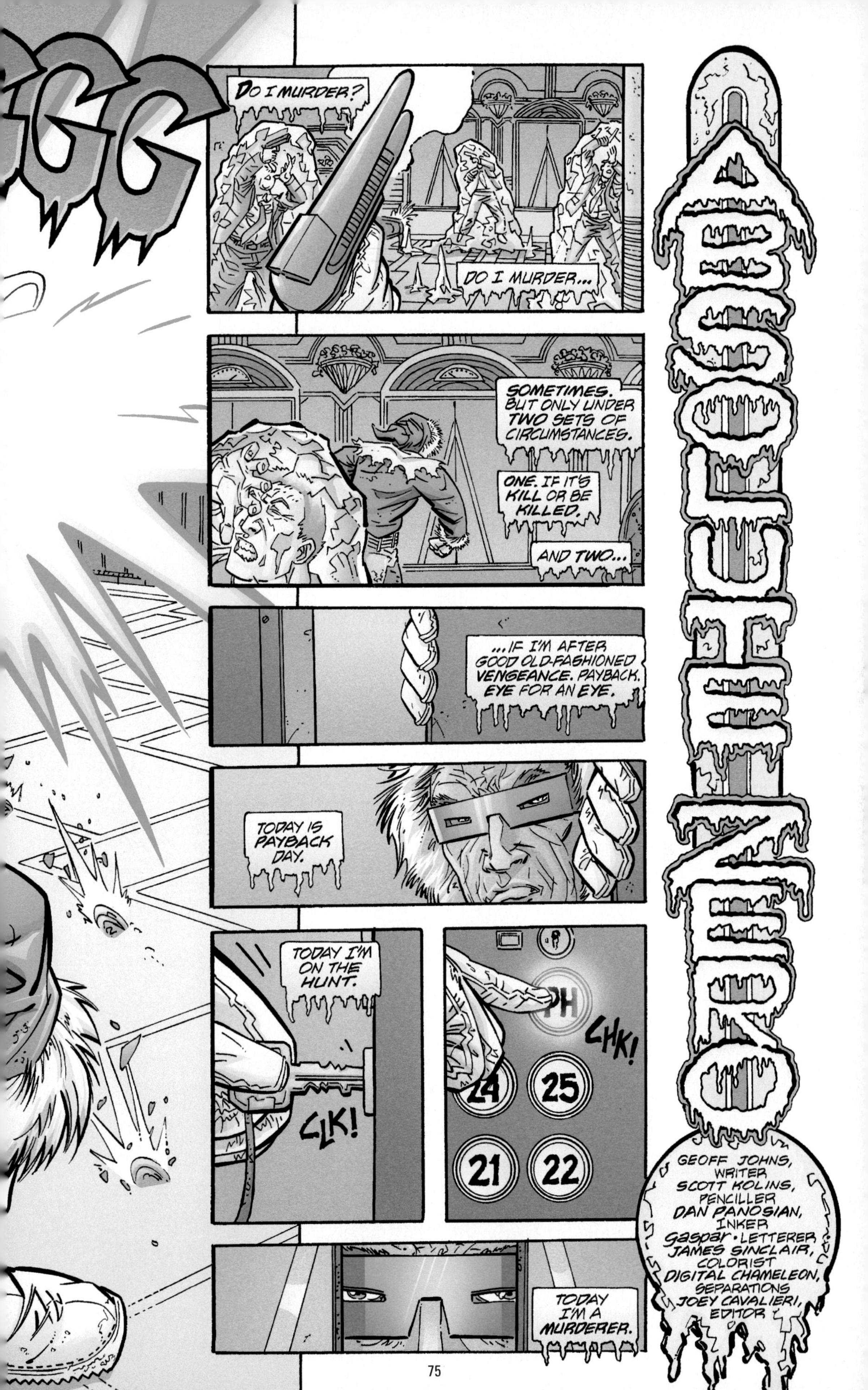
DO I MURDER?
DO I MURDER...
SOMETIMES. BUT ONLY UNDER TWO SETS OF CIRCUMSTANCES.
ONE. IF IT'S KILL OR BE KILLED.
AND TWO...
...IF I'M AFTER GOOD OLD-FASHIONED VENGEANCE. PAYBACK. EYE FOR AN EYE.
TODAY IS PAYBACK DAY.
TODAY I'M ON THE HUNT.
CLK!
PH
CHK!
24
25
21
22
TODAY I'M A MURDERER.
GEOFF JOHNS, WRITER
SCOTT KOLINS, PENCILLER
DAN PANOSIAN, INKER
Gaspar • LETTERER
JAMES SINCLAIR, COLORIST
DIGITAL CHAMELEON, SEPARATIONS
JOEY CAVALIERI, EDITOR

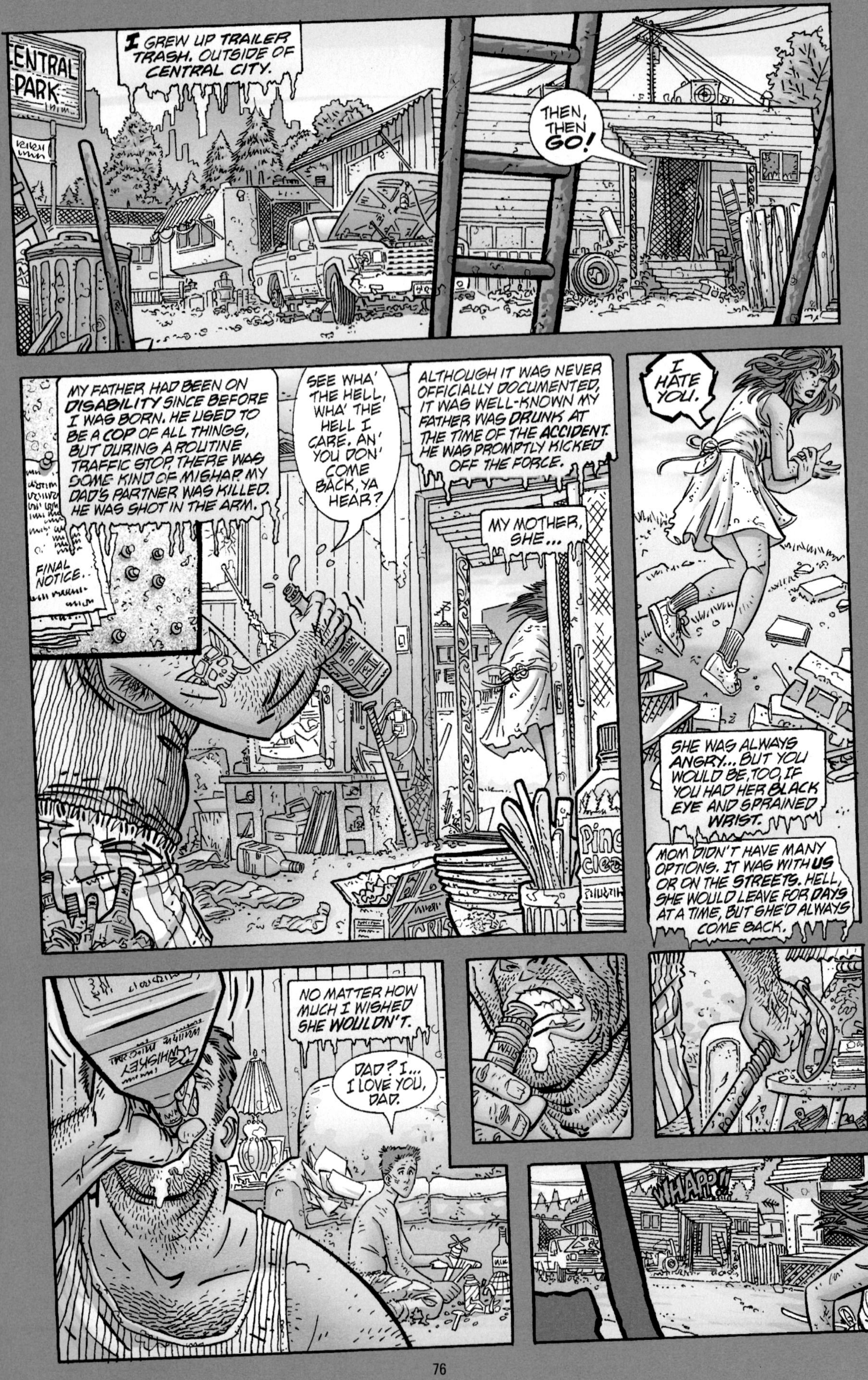
ENTRAL PARK
I GREW UP TRAILER TRASH. OUTSIDE OF CENTRAL CITY.
THEN, THEN GO!
MY FATHER HAD BEEN ON DISABILITY SINCE BEFORE I WAS BORN. HE USED TO BE A COP OF ALL THINGS, BUT DURING A ROUTINE TRAFFIC STOP THERE WAS SOME KIND OF MISHAP. MY DAD'S PARTNER WAS KILLED. HE WAS SHOT IN THE ARM.
SEE WHA' THE HELL, WHA' THE HELL I CARE. AN' YOU DON' COME BACK, YA HEAR?
ALTHOUGH IT WAS NEVER OFFICIALLY DOCUMENTED, IT WAS WELL-KNOWN MY FATHER WAS DRUNK AT THE TIME OF THE ACCIDENT. HE WAS PROMPTLY KICKED OFF THE FORCE.
FINAL NOTICE.
MY MOTHER, SHE...
I HATE YOU.
SHE WAS ALWAYS ANGRY... BUT YOU WOULD BE, TOO, IF YOU HAD HER BLACK EYE AND SPRAINED WRIST.
MOM DIDN'T HAVE MANY OPTIONS. IT WAS WITH US OR ON THE STREETS. HELL, SHE WOULD LEAVE FOR DAYS AT A TIME, BUT SHE'D ALWAYS COME BACK.
NO MATTER HOW MUCH I WISHED SHE WOULDN'T.
DAD? I... I LOVE YOU, DAD.
POLICE
WHAPP!!

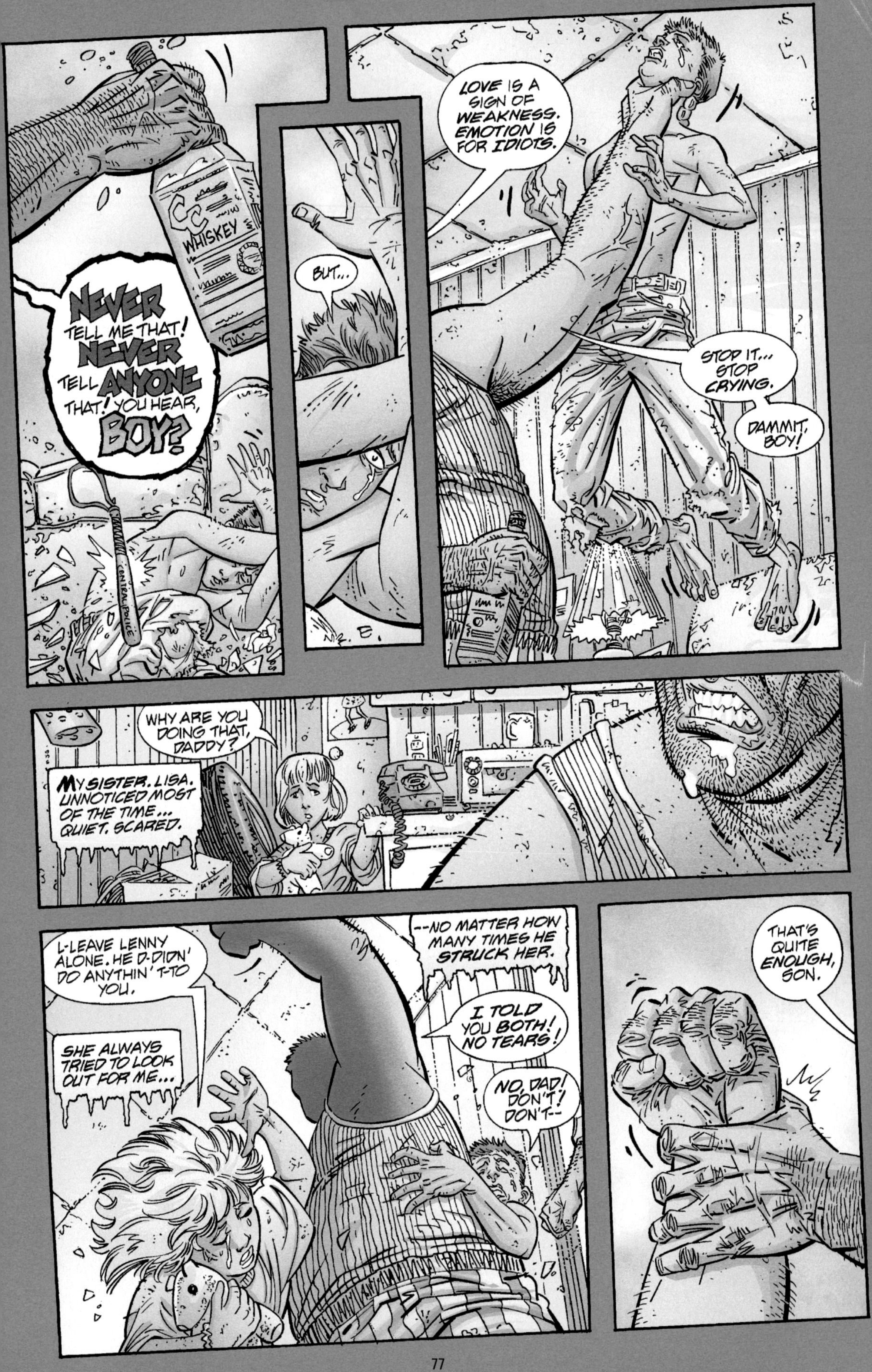
NEVER TELL ME THAT! NEVER TELL ANYONE THAT! YOU HEAR, BOY?
WHISKEY
CENTRAL POLICE
BUT...
LOVE IS A SIGN OF WEAKNESS. EMOTION IS FOR IDIOTS.
STOP IT... STOP CRYING.
DAMMIT, BOY!
WHY ARE YOU DOING THAT, DADDY?
MY SISTER. LISA. UNNOTICED MOST OF THE TIME... QUIET. SCARED.
L-LEAVE LENNY ALONE. HE D-DIDN' DO ANYTHIN' T-TO YOU.
SHE ALWAYS TRIED TO LOOK OUT FOR ME...
--NO MATTER HOW MANY TIMES HE STRUCK HER.
I TOLD YOU BOTH! NO TEARS!
NO, DAD! DON'T! DON'T--
THAT'S QUITE ENOUGH, SON.

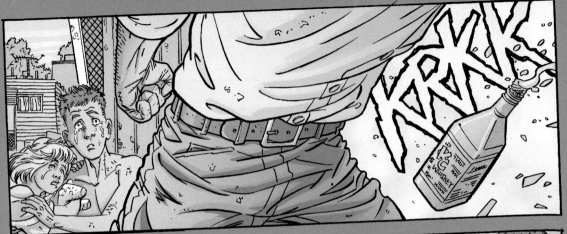

KRKK KK

My grandfather was the only real adult in my young life. He wasn't proud of his son, but with his ailing health I guess he didn't think there was much he could do.

Sleep it off. And stay off this damn poison.

Where's your wife?

Mom left again.

GUG GUG GUG GUG

Well, then, I'm taking you two for the rest of the day.

My grandfather delivered ice. Took it to restaurants, the ball park, fancy places my sister and I never went to.

We thought he had the best job in the world. He got to meet all these nice people.

GOT ICE?

POLAR ICE

It was always a little cold in his truck... but it was always safe, too.

I wish I could remember him better.

He died before I turned twelve.

And all of the good things in our life died with him.

By then, my sister and I had learned not to shed a single tear.

I never cried again. Not for anything.

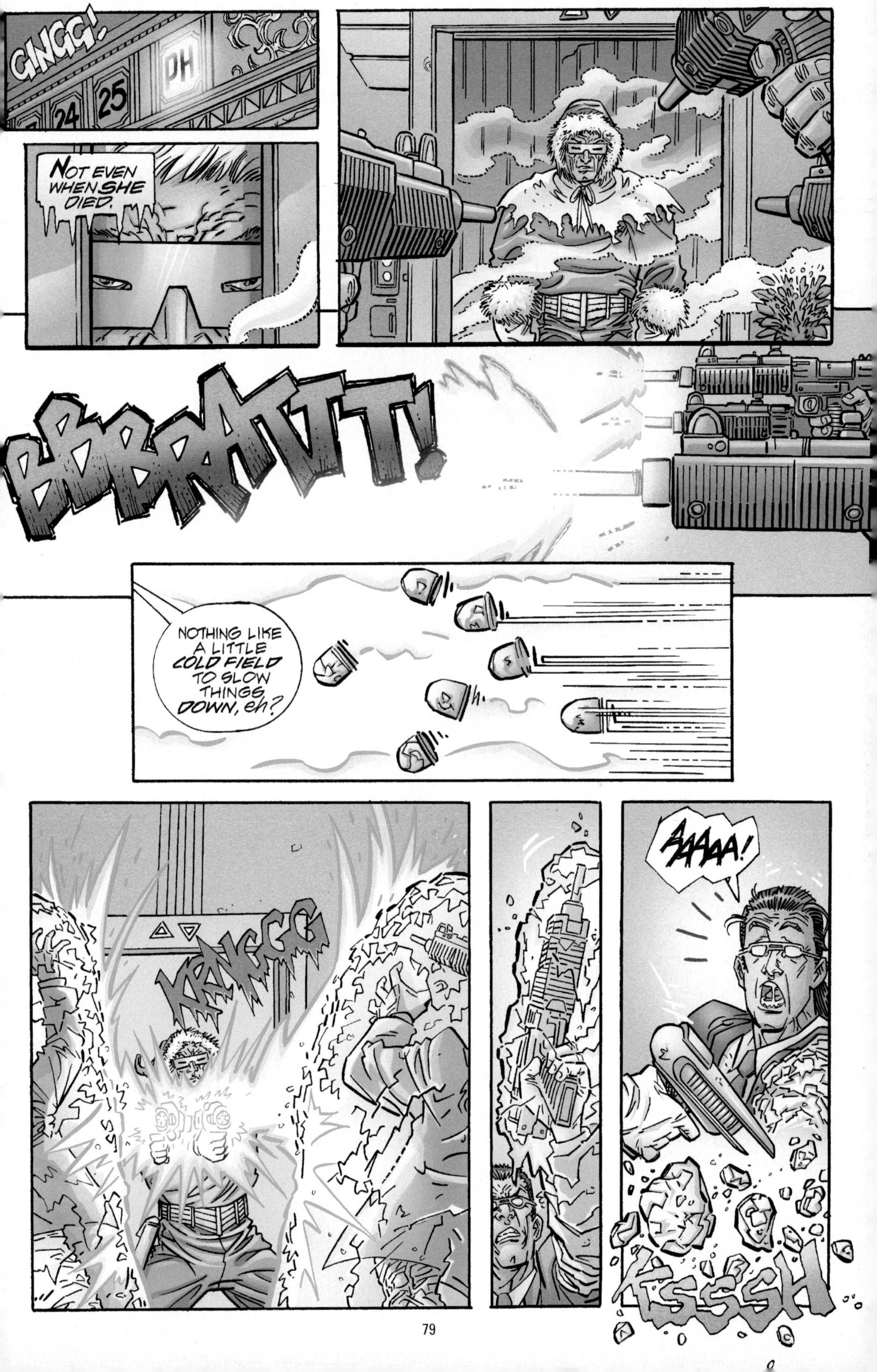
GNGG!
PH
24
25
NOT EVEN WHEN SHE DIED.
BBBRATTT!
NOTHING LIKE A LITTLE COLD FIELD TO SLOW THINGS DOWN, eh?
KRAKGG
AAAAA!
TSSSH

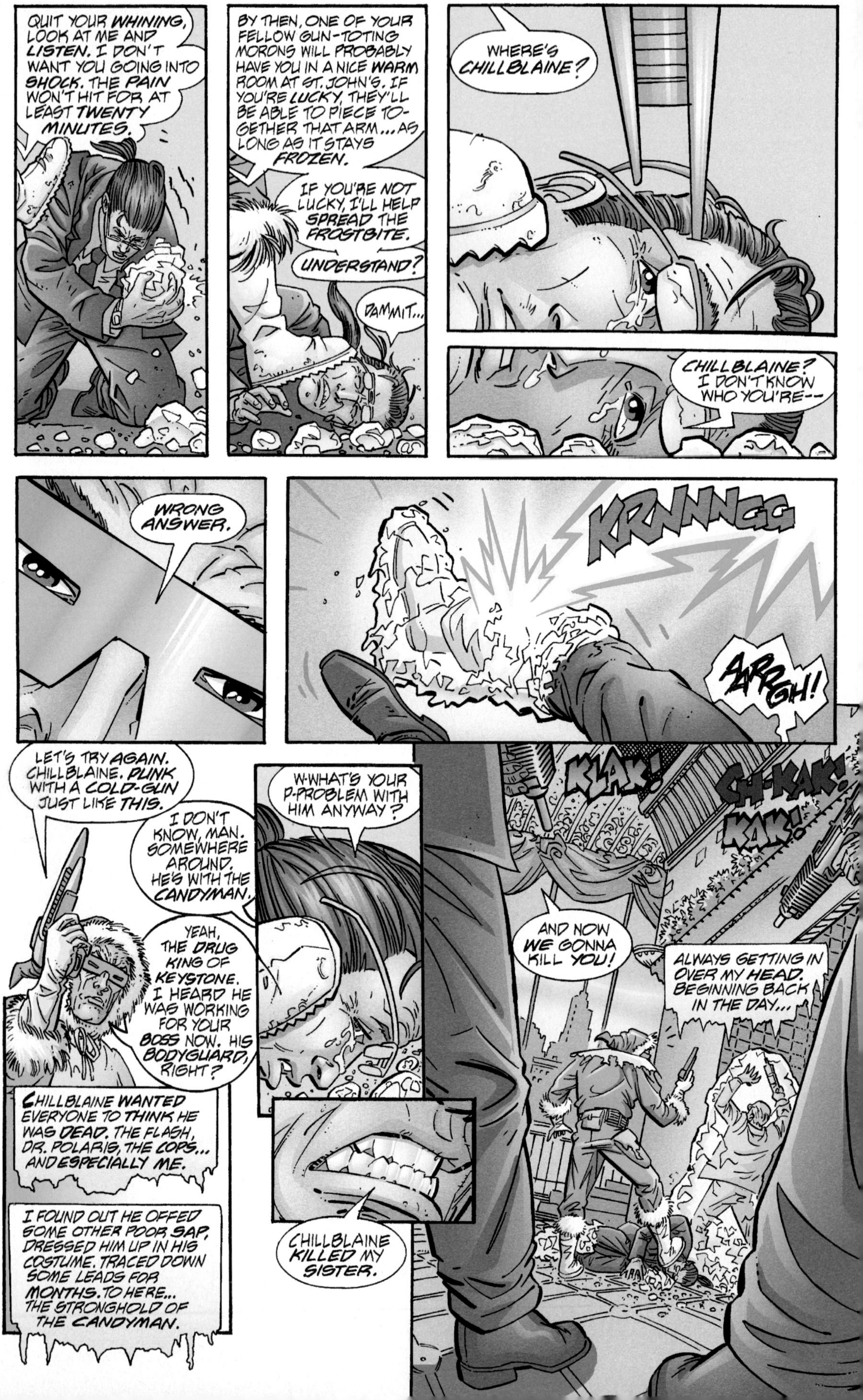
QUIT YOUR WHINING, LOOK AT ME AND LISTEN. I DON'T WANT YOU GOING INTO SHOCK. THE PAIN WON'T HIT FOR AT LEAST TWENTY MINUTES.
BY THEN, ONE OF YOUR FELLOW GUN-TOTING MORONS WILL PROBABLY HAVE YOU IN A NICE WARM ROOM AT ST. JOHN'S. IF YOU'RE LUCKY, THEY'LL BE ABLE TO PIECE TOGETHER THAT ARM... AS LONG AS IT STAYS FROZEN.
IF YOU'RE NOT LUCKY, I'LL HELP SPREAD THE FROSTBITE.
UNDERSTAND?
DAMMIT...
WHERE'S CHILLBLAINE?
CHILLBLAINE? I DON'T KNOW WHO YOU'RE--
WRONG ANSWER.
KRNNNGG
AARRGH!
LET'S TRY AGAIN. CHILLBLAINE. PUNK WITH A COLD-GUN JUST LIKE THIS.
I DON'T KNOW, MAN. SOMEWHERE AROUND. HE'S WITH THE CANDYMAN.
YEAH, THE DRUG KING OF KEYSTONE. I HEARD HE WAS WORKING FOR YOUR BOSS NOW. HIS BODYGUARD, RIGHT?
W-WHAT'S YOUR P-PROBLEM WITH HIM ANYWAY?
CHILLBLAINE WANTED EVERYONE TO THINK HE WAS DEAD. THE FLASH, DR. POLARIS, THE COPS... AND ESPECIALLY ME.
I FOUND OUT HE OFFED SOME OTHER POOR SAP, DRESSED HIM UP IN HIS COSTUME. TRACED DOWN SOME LEADS FOR MONTHS. TO HERE... THE STRONGHOLD OF THE CANDYMAN.
CHILLBLAINE KILLED MY SISTER.
KLAK!
CH-KAK!
KAK!
AND NOW WE GONNA KILL YOU!
ALWAYS GETTING IN OVER MY HEAD. BEGINNING BACK IN THE DAY...

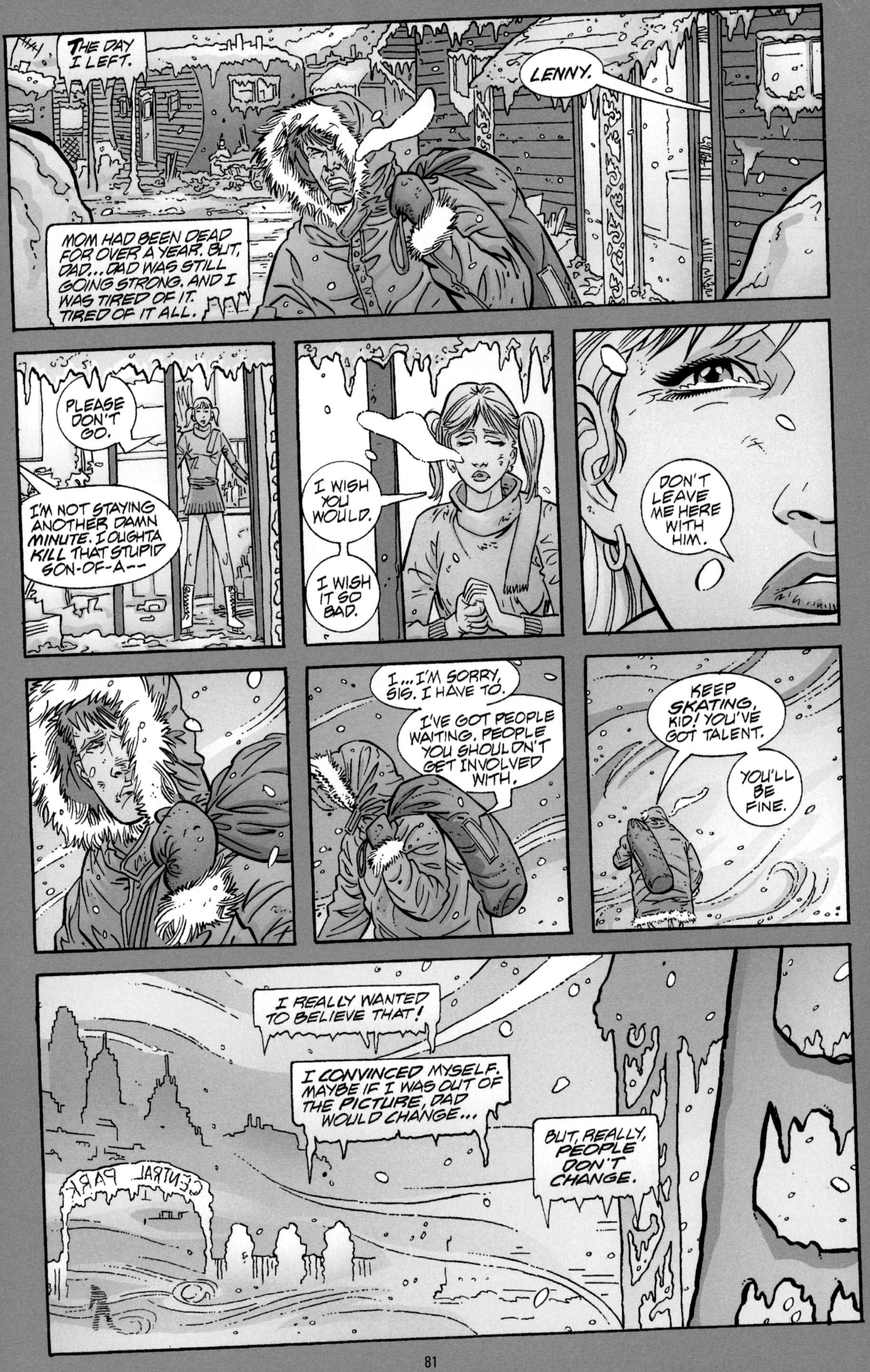

THE DAY I LEFT.
LENNY.
MOM HAD BEEN DEAD FOR OVER A YEAR. BUT, DAD... DAD WAS STILL GOING STRONG. AND I WAS TIRED OF IT. TIRED OF IT ALL.
PLEASE DON'T GO.
I'M NOT STAYING ANOTHER DAMN MINUTE. I OUGHTA KILL THAT STUPID SON-OF-A--
I WISH YOU WOULD.
I WISH IT SO BAD.
DON'T LEAVE ME HERE WITH HIM.
I... I'M SORRY, SIS. I HAVE TO.
I'VE GOT PEOPLE WAITING. PEOPLE YOU SHOULDN'T GET INVOLVED WITH.
KEEP SKATING, KID! YOU'VE GOT TALENT.
YOU'LL BE FINE.
I REALLY WANTED TO BELIEVE THAT!
I CONVINCED MYSELF. MAYBE IF I WAS OUT OF THE PICTURE, DAD WOULD CHANGE...
BUT, REALLY, PEOPLE DON'T CHANGE.
CENTRAL PARK

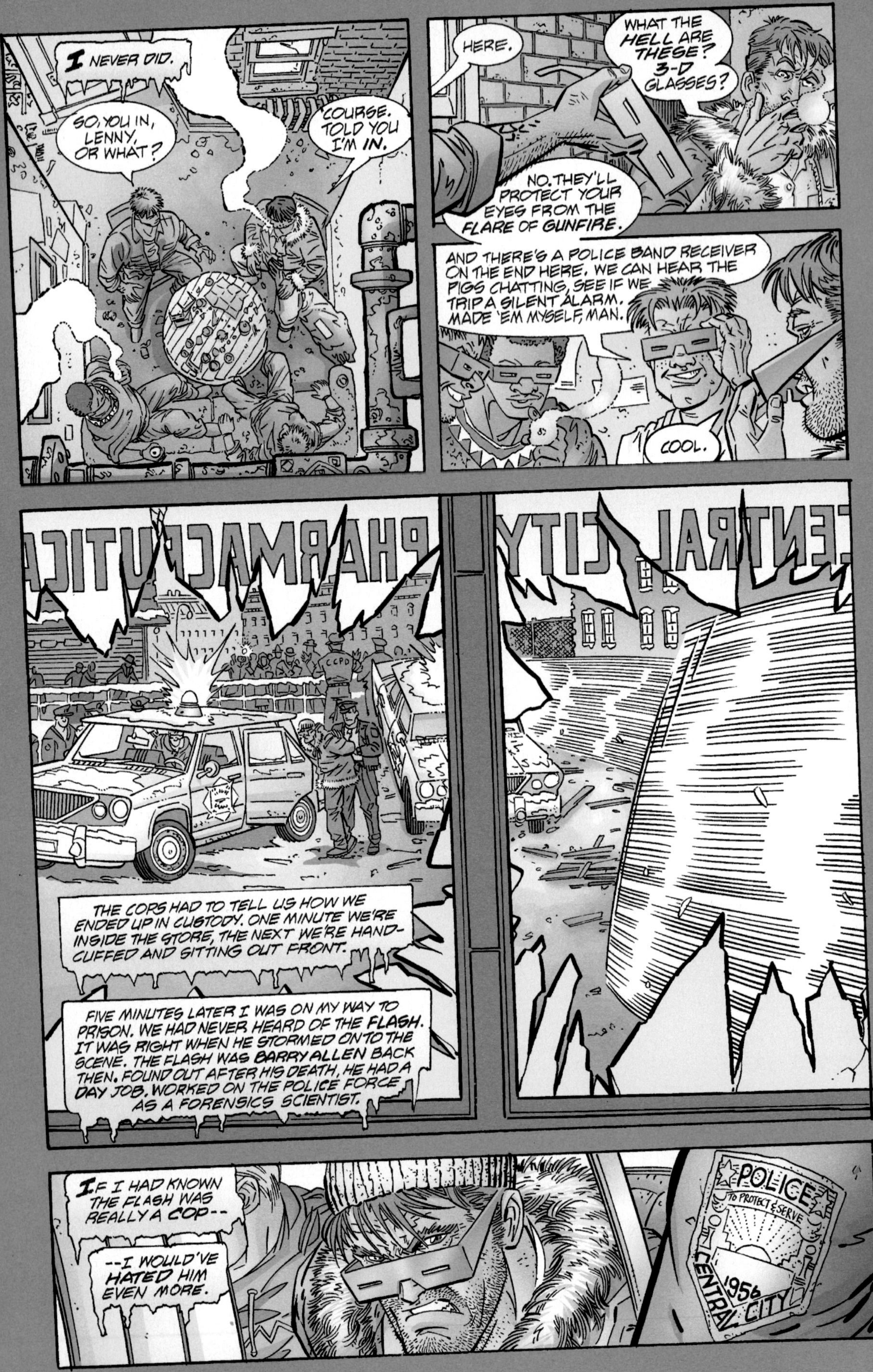

I NEVER DID.
SO, YOU IN, LENNY, OR WHAT?
COURSE. TOLD YOU I'M IN.
HERE.
WHAT THE HELL ARE THESE? 3-D GLASSES?
NO. THEY'LL PROTECT YOUR EYES FROM THE FLARE OF GUNFIRE.
AND THERE'S A POLICE BAND RECEIVER ON THE END HERE. WE CAN HEAR THE PIGS CHATTING, SEE IF WE TRIP A SILENT ALARM. MADE 'EM MYSELF, MAN.
COOL.
PHARMACEUTICA
CENTRAL CITY
CCPD
THE COPS HAD TO TELL US HOW WE ENDED UP IN CUSTODY. ONE MINUTE WE'RE INSIDE THE STORE, THE NEXT WE'RE HAND-CUFFED AND SITTING OUT FRONT.
FIVE MINUTES LATER I WAS ON MY WAY TO PRISON. WE HAD NEVER HEARD OF THE FLASH. IT WAS RIGHT WHEN HE STORMED ONTO THE SCENE. THE FLASH WAS BARRY ALLEN BACK THEN. FOUND OUT AFTER HIS DEATH, HE HAD A DAY JOB. WORKED ON THE POLICE FORCE AS A FORENSICS SCIENTIST.
IF I HAD KNOWN THE FLASH WAS REALLY A COP--
--I WOULD'VE HATED HIM EVEN MORE.
POLICE
TO PROTECT & SERVE
CENTRAL CITY
1956

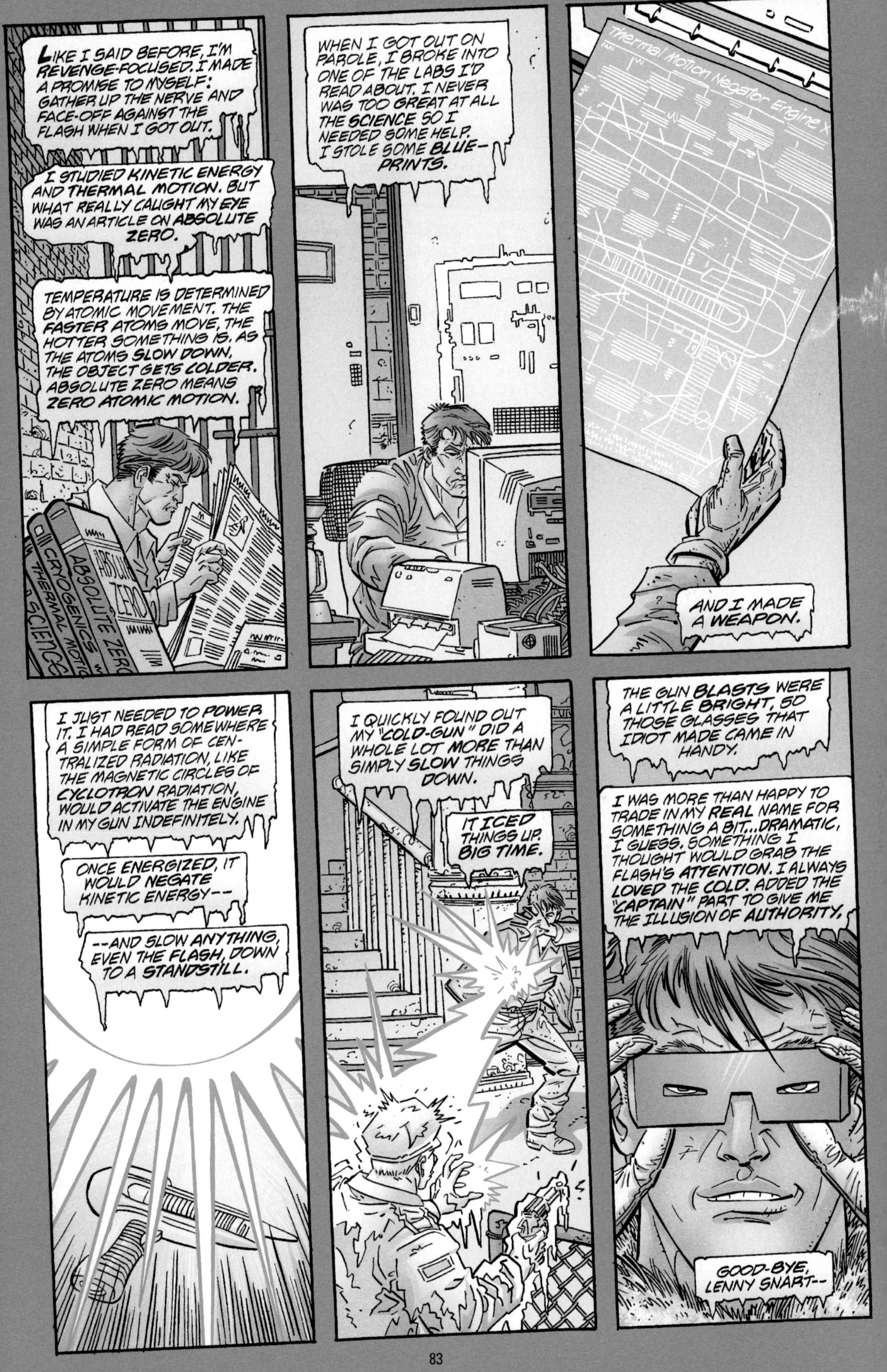

LIKE I SAID BEFORE, I'M REVENGE-FOCUSED. I MADE A PROMISE TO MYSELF: GATHER UP THE NERVE AND FACE-OFF AGAINST THE FLASH WHEN I GOT OUT.
I STUDIED KINETIC ENERGY AND THERMAL MOTION. BUT WHAT REALLY CAUGHT MY EYE WAS AN ARTICLE ON ABSOLUTE ZERO.
TEMPERATURE IS DETERMINED BY ATOMIC MOVEMENT. THE FASTER ATOMS MOVE, THE HOTTER SOMETHING IS. AS THE ATOMS SLOW DOWN, THE OBJECT GETS COLDER. ABSOLUTE ZERO MEANS ZERO ATOMIC MOTION.
ABSOLUTE ZERO
CRYOGENICS
THERMAL MOTI
SCIENCE
WHEN I GOT OUT ON PAROLE, I BROKE INTO ONE OF THE LABS I'D READ ABOUT. I NEVER WAS TOO GREAT AT ALL THE SCIENCE SO I NEEDED SOME HELP. I STOLE SOME BLUE-PRINTS.
Thermal Motion Negator Engine X
AND I MADE A WEAPON.
I JUST NEEDED TO POWER IT. I HAD READ SOMEWHERE A SIMPLE FORM OF CEN-TRALIZED RADIATION, LIKE THE MAGNETIC CIRCLES OF CYCLOTRON RADIATION, WOULD ACTIVATE THE ENGINE IN MY GUN INDEFINITELY.
ONCE ENERGIZED, IT WOULD NEGATE KINETIC ENERGY--
--AND SLOW ANYTHING, EVEN THE FLASH, DOWN TO A STANDSTILL.
I QUICKLY FOUND OUT MY "COLD-GUN" DID A WHOLE LOT MORE THAN SIMPLY SLOW THINGS DOWN.
IT ICED THINGS UP. BIG TIME.
THE GUN BLASTS WERE A LITTLE BRIGHT, SO THOSE GLASSES THAT IDIOT MADE CAME IN HANDY.
I WAS MORE THAN HAPPY TO TRADE IN MY REAL NAME FOR SOMETHING A BIT...DRAMATIC, I GUESS. SOMETHING I THOUGHT WOULD GRAB THE FLASH'S ATTENTION. I ALWAYS LOVED THE COLD. ADDED THE "CAPTAIN" PART TO GIVE ME THE ILLUSION OF AUTHORITY.
GOOD-BYE, LENNY SNART--

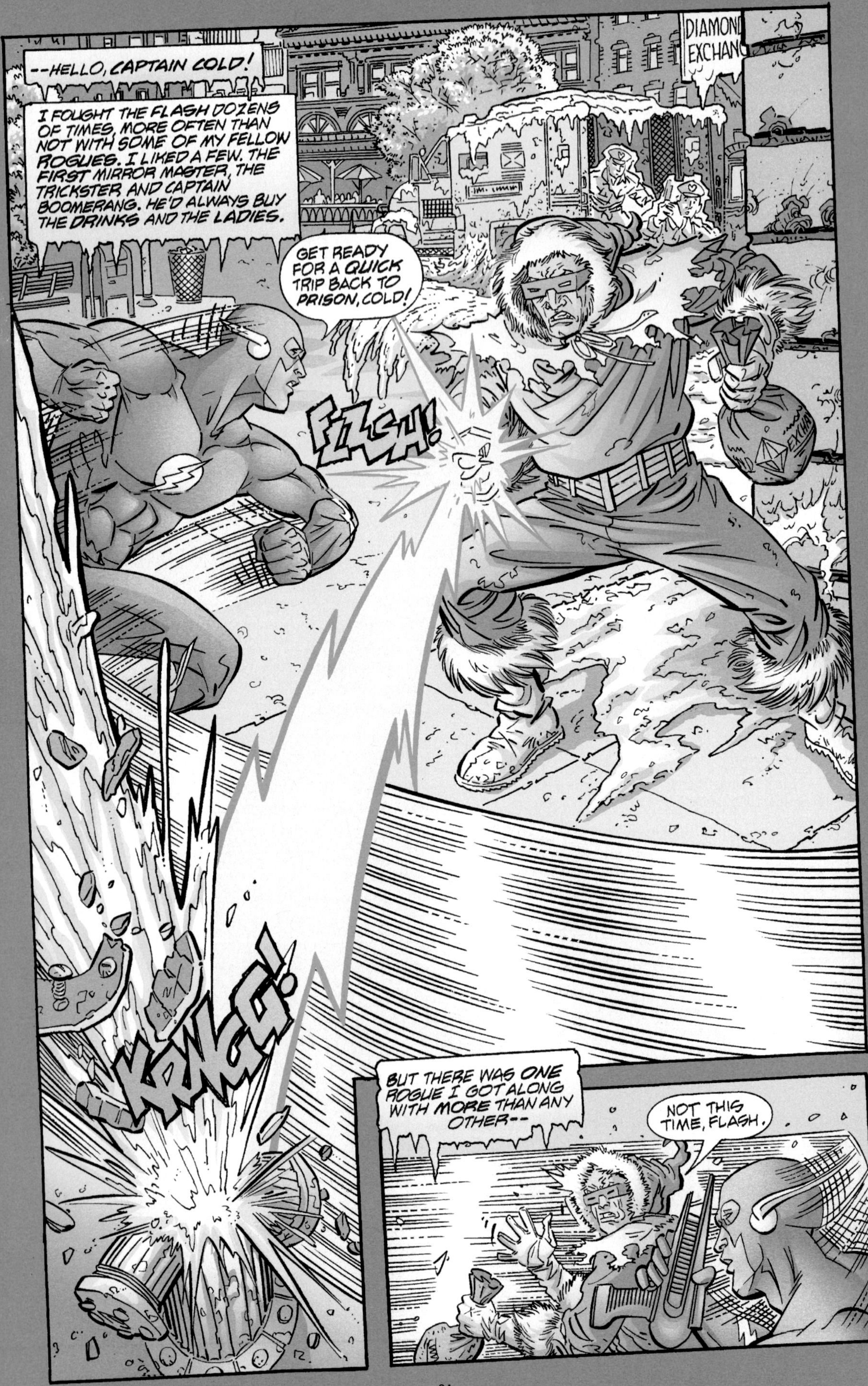

DIAMOND
EXCHANG
--HELLO, CAPTAIN COLD!
I FOUGHT THE FLASH DOZENS OF TIMES, MORE OFTEN THAN NOT WITH SOME OF MY FELLOW ROGUES. I LIKED A FEW. THE FIRST MIRROR MASTER, THE TRICKSTER AND CAPTAIN BOOMERANG. HE'D ALWAYS BUY THE DRINKS AND THE LADIES.
GET READY FOR A QUICK TRIP BACK TO PRISON, COLD!
FZZCH!
KRACG!
BUT THERE WAS ONE ROGUE I GOT ALONG WITH MORE THAN ANY OTHER--
NOT THIS TIME, FLASH.

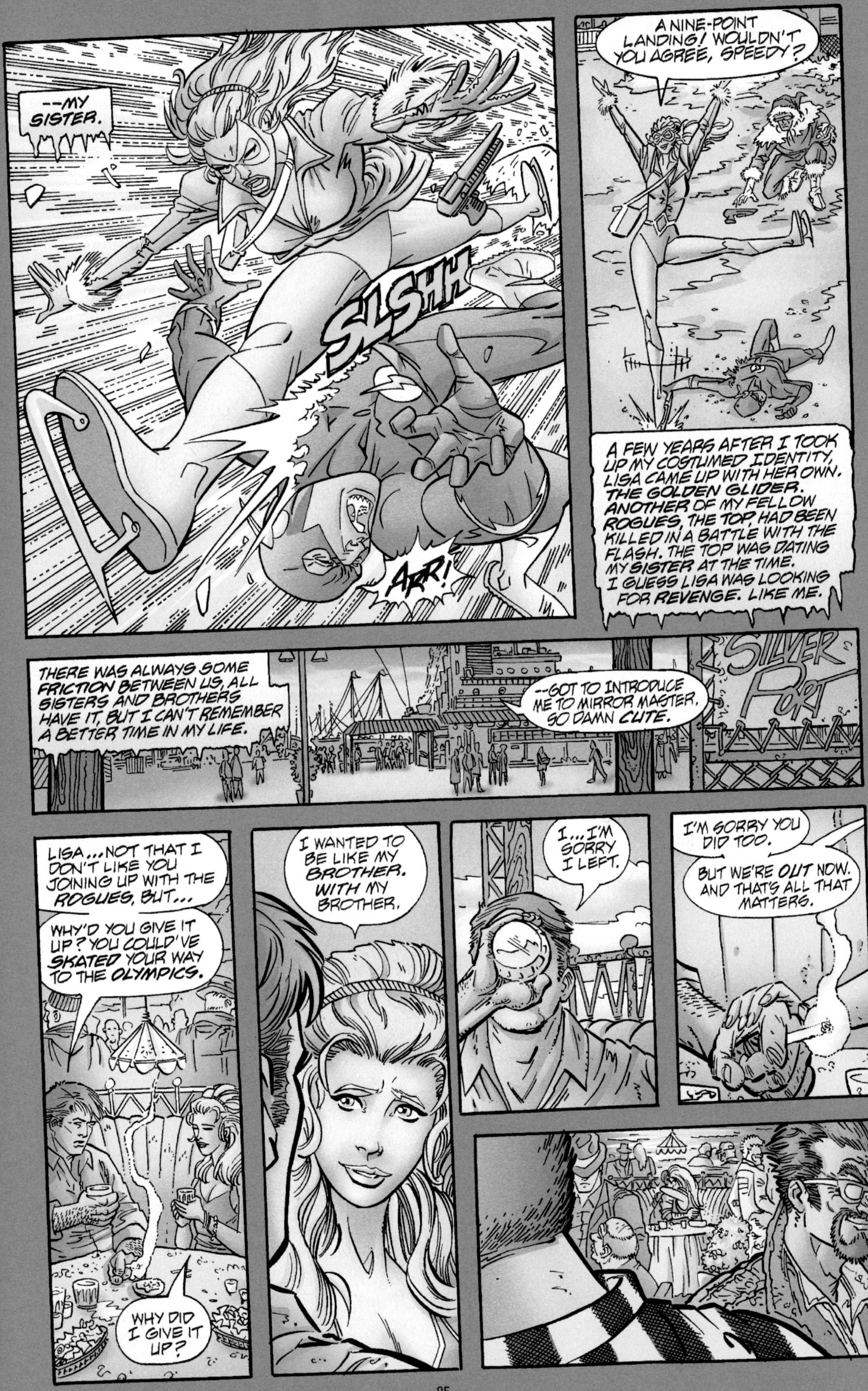

--MY SISTER.
SLSHH
ARR!
A NINE-POINT LANDING! WOULDN'T YOU AGREE, SPEEDY?
A FEW YEARS AFTER I TOOK UP MY COSTUMED IDENTITY, LISA CAME UP WITH HER OWN. THE GOLDEN GLIDER. ANOTHER OF MY FELLOW ROGUES, THE TOP, HAD BEEN KILLED IN A BATTLE WITH THE FLASH. THE TOP WAS DATING MY SISTER AT THE TIME. I GUESS LISA WAS LOOKING FOR REVENGE. LIKE ME.
THERE WAS ALWAYS SOME FRICTION BETWEEN US, ALL SISTERS AND BROTHERS HAVE IT, BUT I CAN'T REMEMBER A BETTER TIME IN MY LIFE.
--GOT TO INTRODUCE ME TO MIRROR MASTER, SO DAMN CUTE.
SILVER PORT
LISA... NOT THAT I DON'T LIKE YOU JOINING UP WITH THE ROGUES, BUT...
WHY'D YOU GIVE IT UP? YOU COULD'VE SKATED YOUR WAY TO THE OLYMPICS.
WHY DID I GIVE IT UP?
I WANTED TO BE LIKE MY BROTHER. WITH MY BROTHER.
I... I'M SORRY I LEFT.
I'M SORRY YOU DID TOO.
BUT WE'RE OUT NOW. AND THAT'S ALL THAT MATTERS.

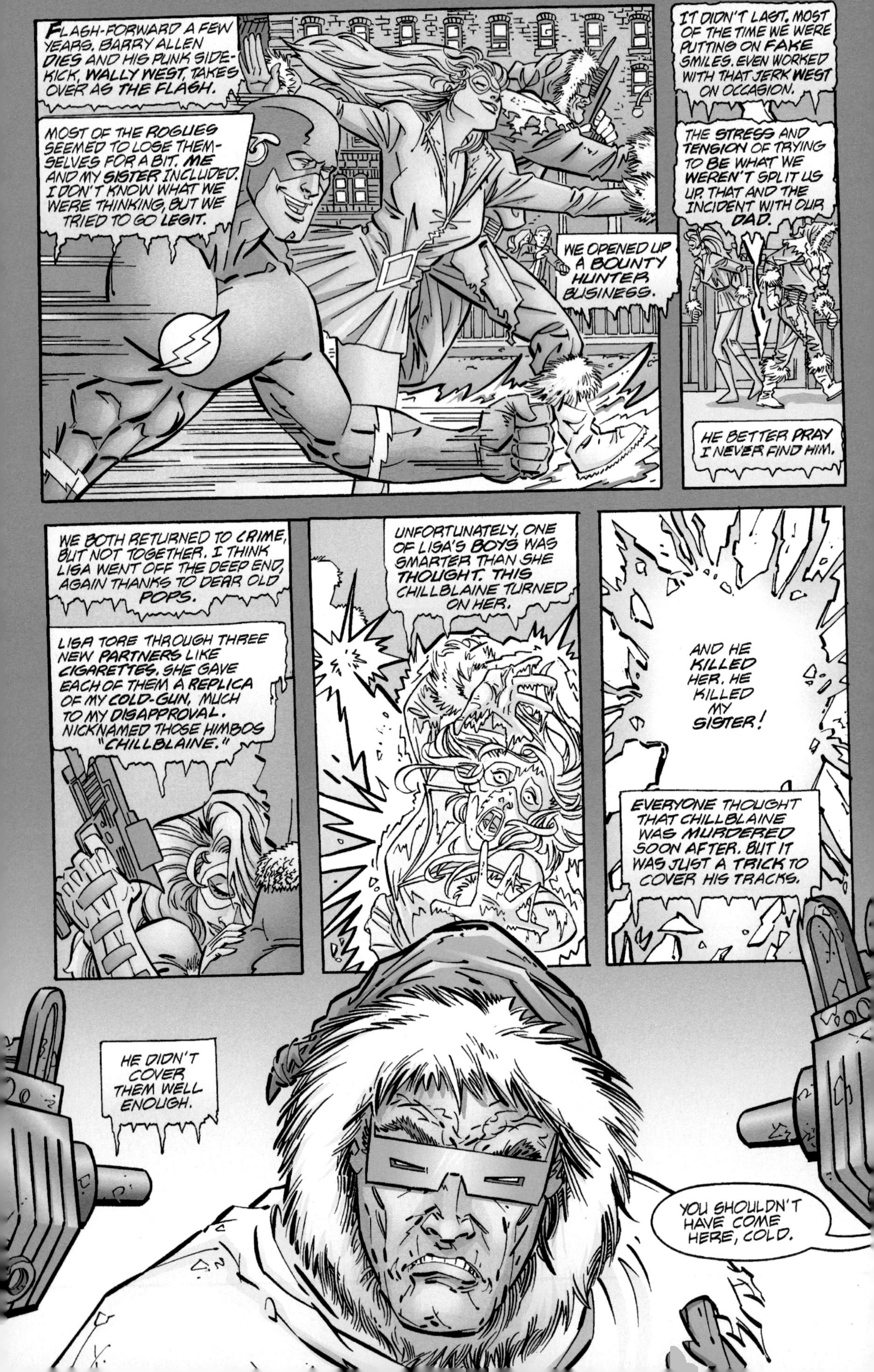
FLASH-FORWARD A FEW YEARS. BARRY ALLEN DIES AND HIS PUNK SIDE-KICK, WALLY WEST, TAKES OVER AS THE FLASH.
MOST OF THE ROGUES SEEMED TO LOSE THEM-SELVES FOR A BIT. ME AND MY SISTER INCLUDED. I DON'T KNOW WHAT WE WERE THINKING, BUT WE TRIED TO GO LEGIT.
WE OPENED UP A BOUNTY HUNTER BUSINESS.
IT DIDN'T LAST. MOST OF THE TIME WE WERE PUTTING ON FAKE SMILES. EVEN WORKED WITH THAT JERK WEST ON OCCASION.
THE STRESS AND TENSION OF TRYING TO BE WHAT WE WEREN'T SPLIT US UP. THAT AND THE INCIDENT WITH OUR DAD.
HE BETTER PRAY I NEVER FIND HIM.
WE BOTH RETURNED TO CRIME, BUT NOT TOGETHER. I THINK LISA WENT OFF THE DEEP END, AGAIN THANKS TO DEAR OLD POPS.
LISA TORE THROUGH THREE NEW PARTNERS LIKE CIGARETTES. SHE GAVE EACH OF THEM A REPLICA OF MY COLD-GUN, MUCH TO MY DISAPPROVAL. NICKNAMED THOSE HIMBOS "CHILLBLAINE."
UNFORTUNATELY, ONE OF LISA'S BOYS WAS SMARTER THAN SHE THOUGHT. THIS CHILLBLAINE TURNED ON HER.
AND HE KILLED HER. HE KILLED MY SISTER!
EVERYONE THOUGHT THAT CHILLBLAINE WAS MURDERED SOON AFTER. BUT IT WAS JUST A TRICK TO COVER HIS TRACKS.
HE DIDN'T COVER THEM WELL ENOUGH.
YOU SHOULDN'T HAVE COME HERE, COLD.

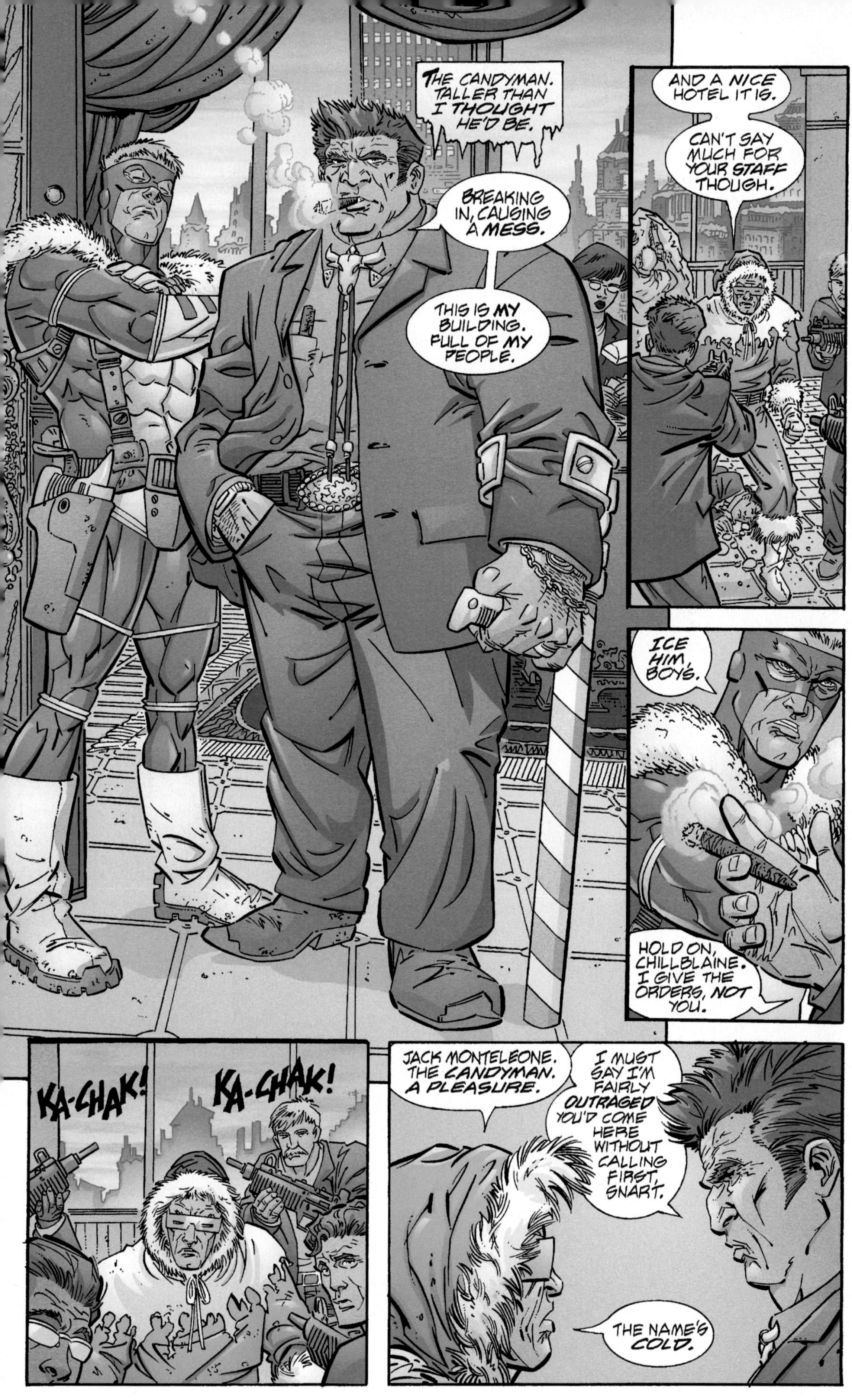
THE CANDYMAN. TALLER THAN I THOUGHT HE'D BE.
BREAKING IN, CAUSING A MESS.
THIS IS MY BUILDING. FULL OF MY PEOPLE.
AND A NICE HOTEL IT IS.
CAN'T SAY MUCH FOR YOUR STAFF THOUGH.
ICE HIM, BOYS.
HOLD ON, CHILLBLAINE. I GIVE THE ORDERS, NOT YOU.
KA-CHAK!
KA-CHAK!
JACK MONTELEONE. THE CANDYMAN. A PLEASURE.
I MUST SAY I'M FAIRLY OUTRAGED YOU'D COME HERE WITHOUT CALLING FIRST, SNART.
THE NAME'S COLD.

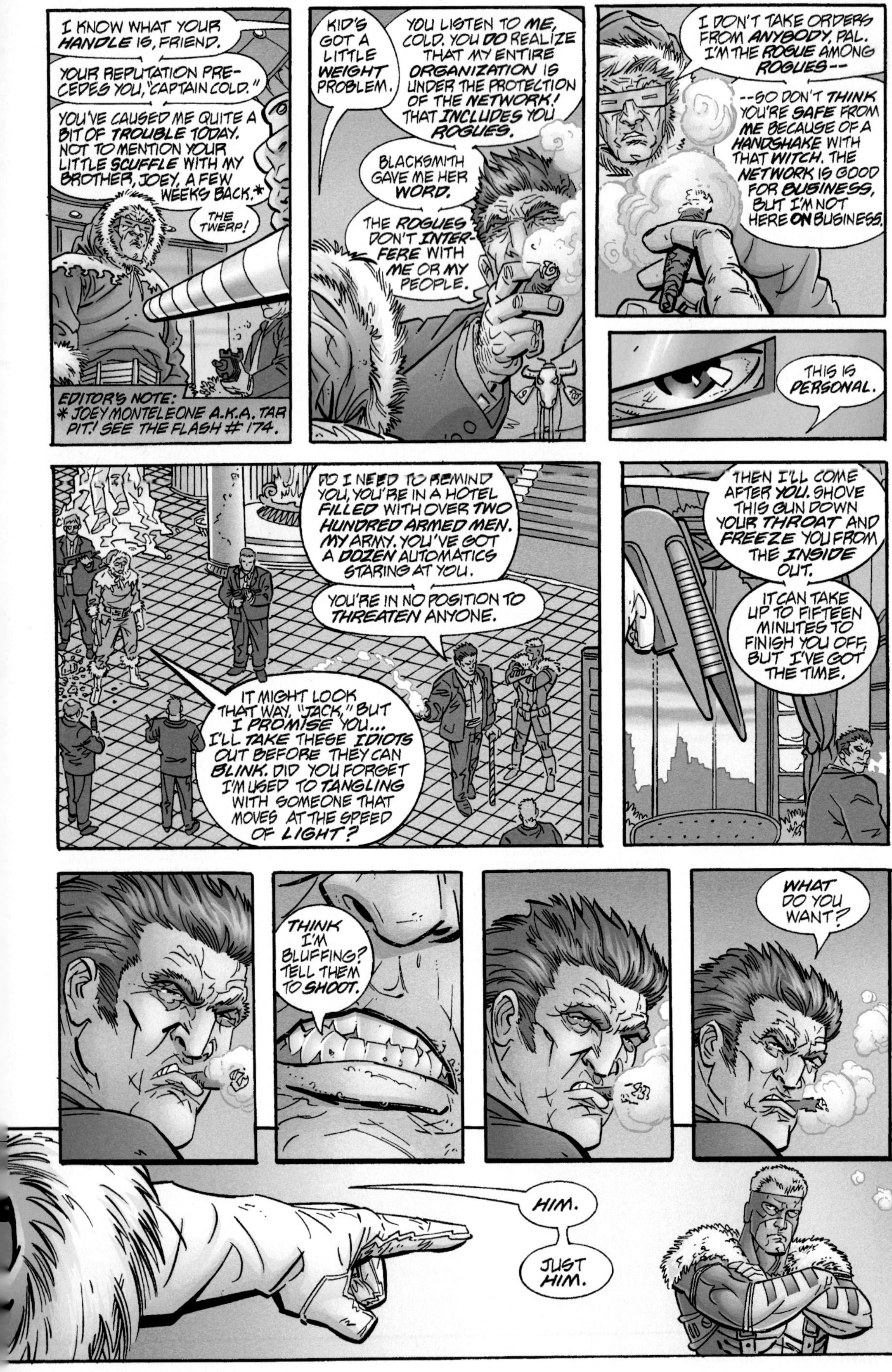
I KNOW WHAT YOUR HANDLE IS, FRIEND.
YOUR REPUTATION PRECEDES YOU, "CAPTAIN COLD."
YOU'VE CAUSED ME QUITE A BIT OF TROUBLE TODAY. NOT TO MENTION YOUR LITTLE SCUFFLE WITH MY BROTHER, JOEY, A FEW WEEKS BACK.*
THE TWERP!
EDITOR'S NOTE: * JOEY MONTELEONE A.K.A. TAR PIT! SEE THE FLASH # 174.
KID'S GOT A LITTLE WEIGHT PROBLEM.
YOU LISTEN TO ME, COLD. YOU DO REALIZE THAT MY ENTIRE ORGANIZATION IS UNDER THE PROTECTION OF THE NETWORK! THAT INCLUDES YOU ROGUES.
BLACKSMITH GAVE ME HER WORD.
THE ROGUES DON'T INTERFERE WITH ME OR MY PEOPLE.
I DON'T TAKE ORDERS FROM ANYBODY, PAL. I'M THE ROGUE AMONG ROGUES--
--SO DON'T THINK YOU'RE SAFE FROM ME BECAUSE OF A HANDSHAKE WITH THAT WITCH. THE NETWORK IS GOOD FOR BUSINESS, BUT I'M NOT HERE ON BUSINESS.
THIS IS PERSONAL.
DO I NEED TO REMIND YOU, YOU'RE IN A HOTEL FILLED WITH OVER TWO HUNDRED ARMED MEN. MY ARMY. YOU'VE GOT A DOZEN AUTOMATICS STARING AT YOU.
YOU'RE IN NO POSITION TO THREATEN ANYONE.
IT MIGHT LOOK THAT WAY, "JACK," BUT I PROMISE YOU... I'LL TAKE THESE IDIOTS OUT BEFORE THEY CAN BLINK. DID YOU FORGET I'M USED TO TANGLING WITH SOMEONE THAT MOVES AT THE SPEED OF LIGHT?
THEN I'LL COME AFTER YOU. SHOVE THIS GUN DOWN YOUR THROAT AND FREEZE YOU FROM THE INSIDE OUT.
IT CAN TAKE UP TO FIFTEEN MINUTES TO FINISH YOU OFF, BUT I'VE GOT THE TIME.
THINK I'M BLUFFING? TELL THEM TO SHOOT.
WHAT DO YOU WANT?
HIM.
JUST HIM.

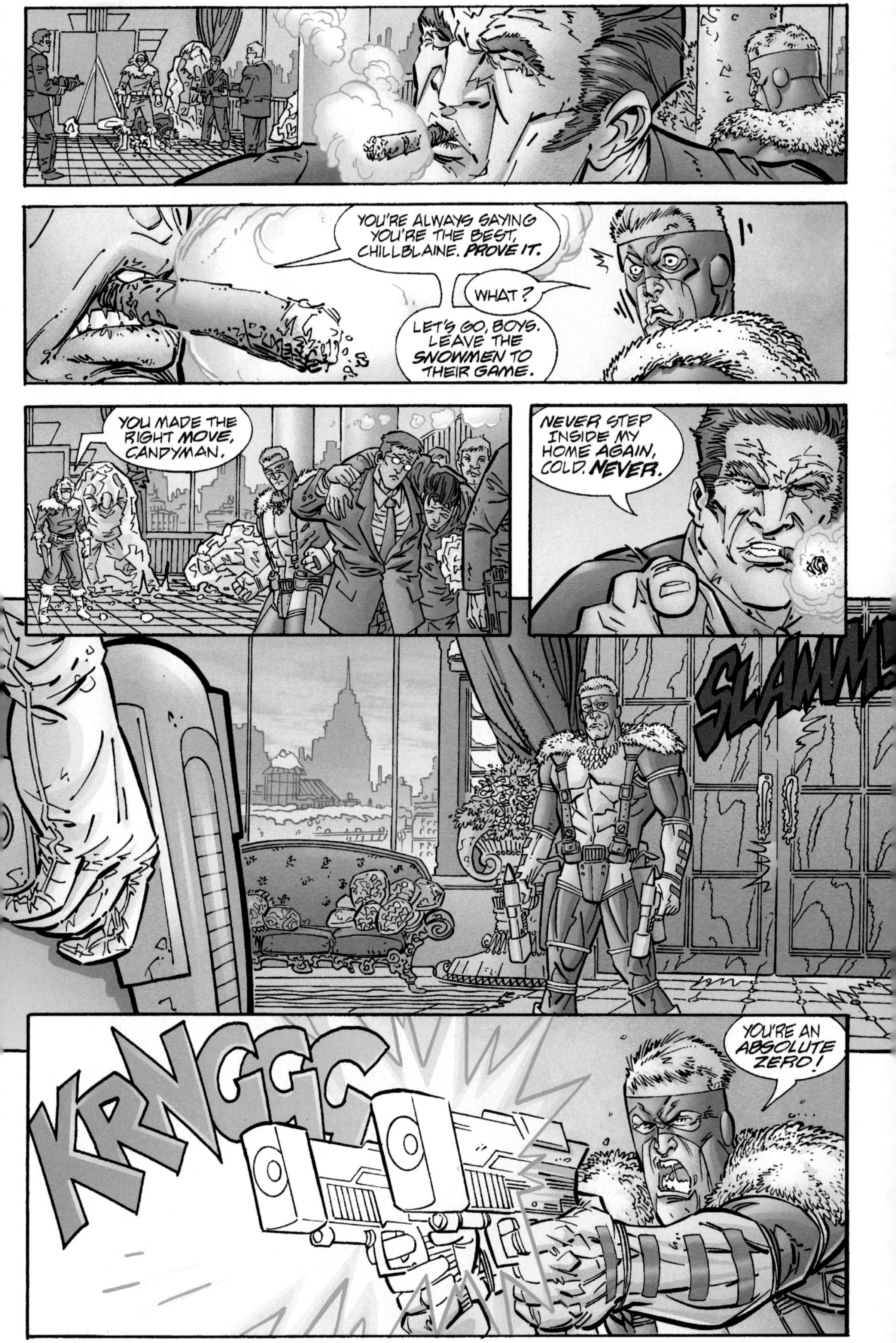

YOU'RE ALWAYS SAYING YOU'RE THE BEST, CHILLBLAINE. PROVE IT.
WHAT?
LET'S GO, BOYS. LEAVE THE SNOWMEN TO THEIR GAME.
YOU MADE THE RIGHT MOVE, CANDYMAN.
NEVER STEP INSIDE MY HOME AGAIN, COLD. NEVER.
SLAMM!
KRNGGC
YOU'RE AN ABSOLUTE ZERO!

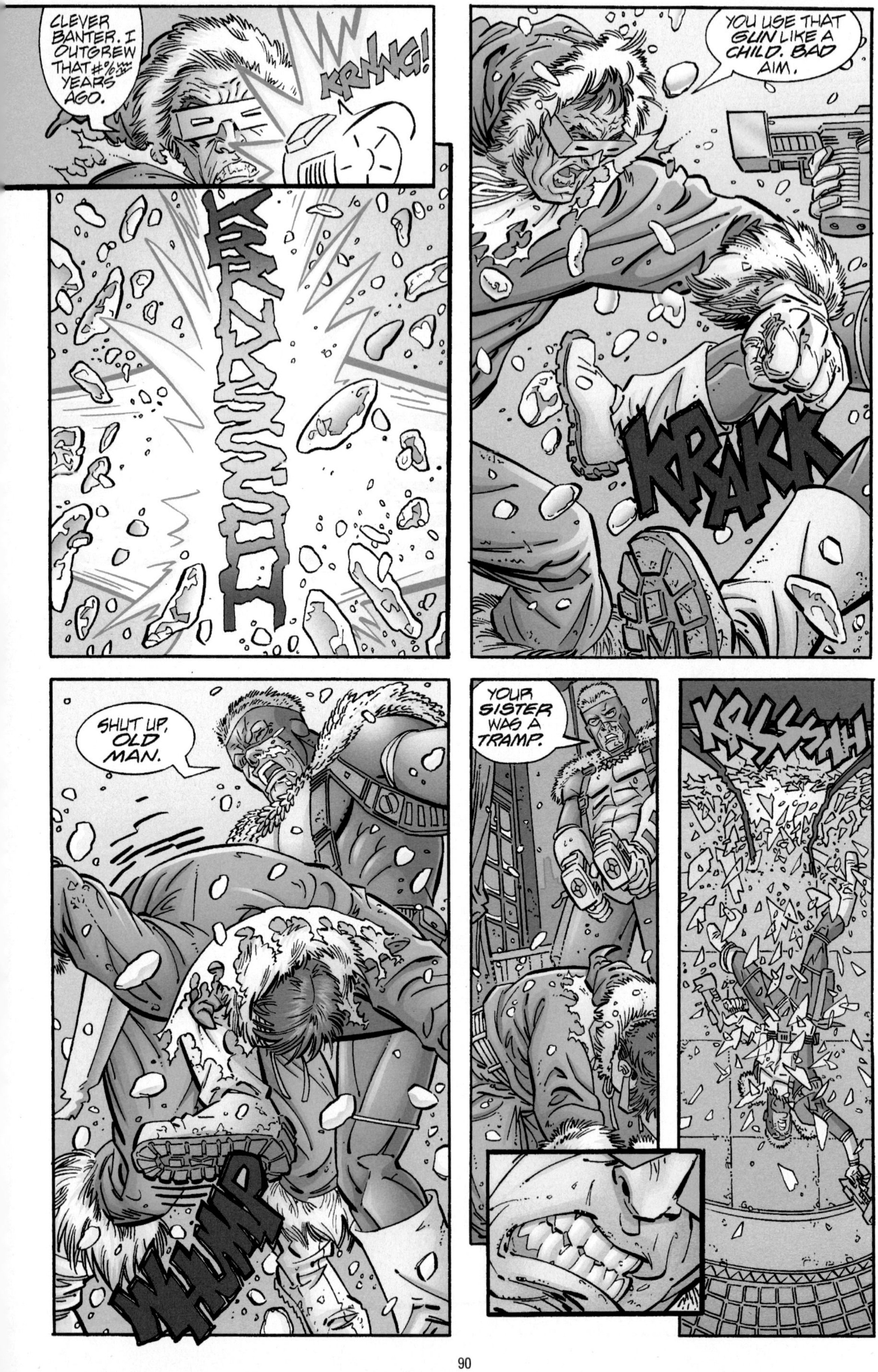
CLEVER BANTER. I OUTGREW THAT #%** YEARS AGO.
KRUNG!
YOU USE THAT GUN LIKE A CHILD. BAD AIM.
KRAKK
SHUT UP, OLD MAN.
WHUMP
YOUR SISTER WAS A TRAMP.
KRSSSH

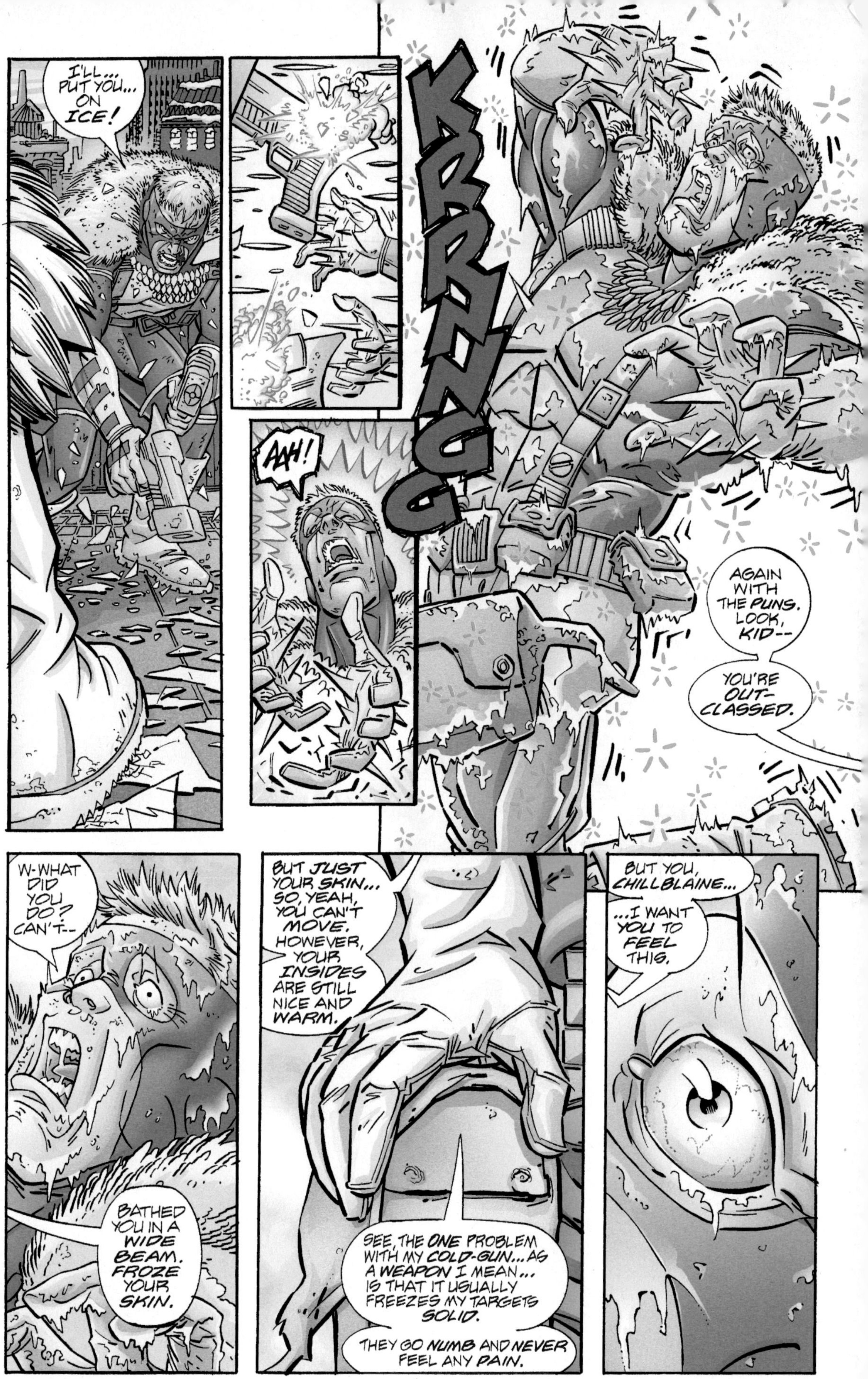

I'LL... PUT YOU... ON ICE!
KRRANG
AAH!
AGAIN WITH THE PUNS. LOOK, KID--
YOU'RE OUT-CLASSED.
W-WHAT DID YOU DO? CAN'T--
BATHED YOU IN A WIDE BEAM. FROZE YOUR SKIN.
BUT JUST YOUR SKIN... SO, YEAH, YOU CAN'T MOVE. HOWEVER, YOUR INSIDES ARE STILL NICE AND WARM.
SEE, THE ONE PROBLEM WITH MY COLD-GUN... AS A WEAPON I MEAN... IS THAT IT USUALLY FREEZES MY TARGETS SOLID.
THEY GO NUMB AND NEVER FEEL ANY PAIN.
BUT YOU, CHILLBLAINE...
...I WANT YOU TO FEEL THIS.

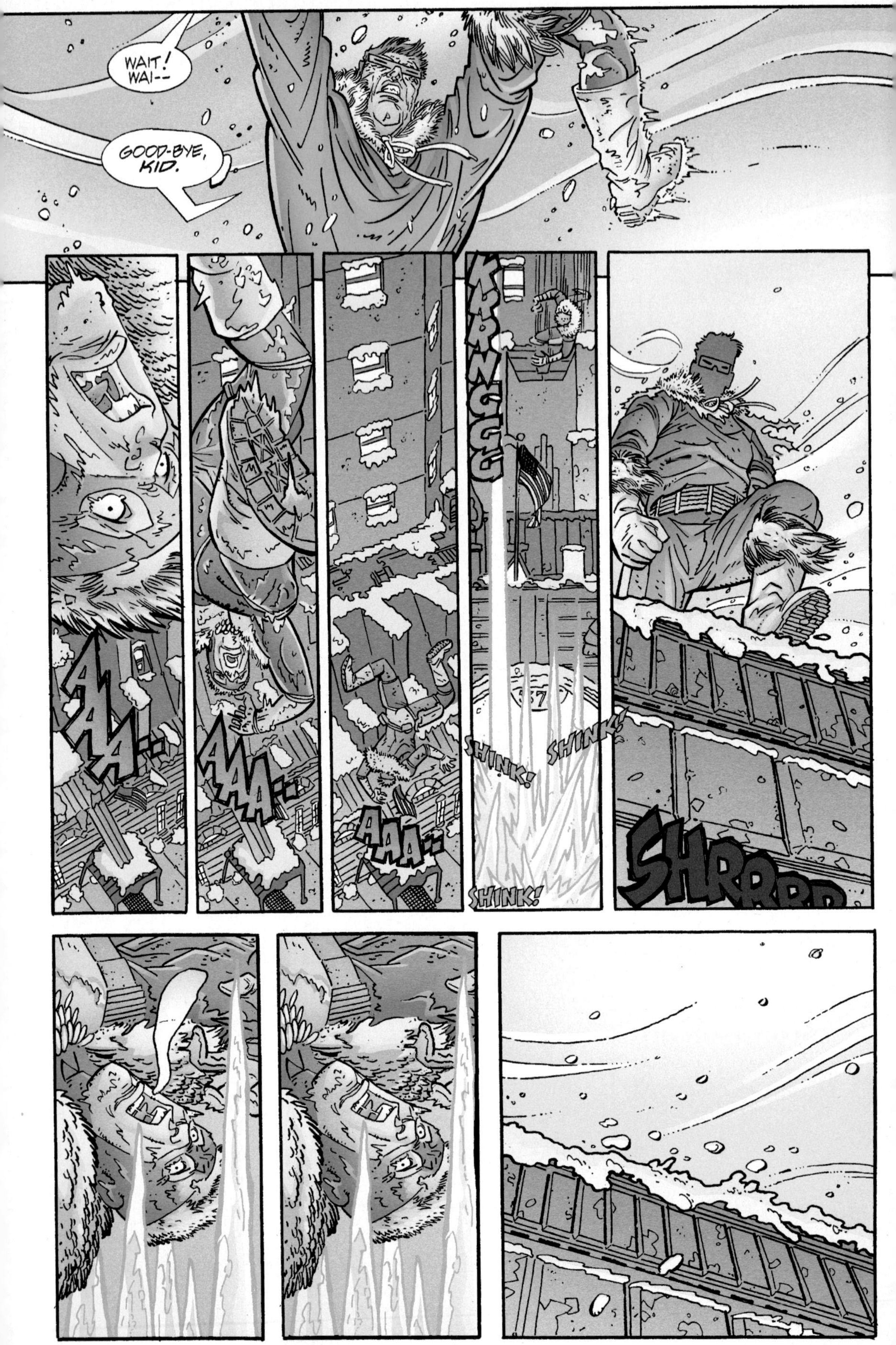
WAIT! WAI--
GOOD-BYE, KID.
AAA--
AAA--
AAA--
KRRNGGG
SHINK!
SHINK!
SHINK!
SHRRRR

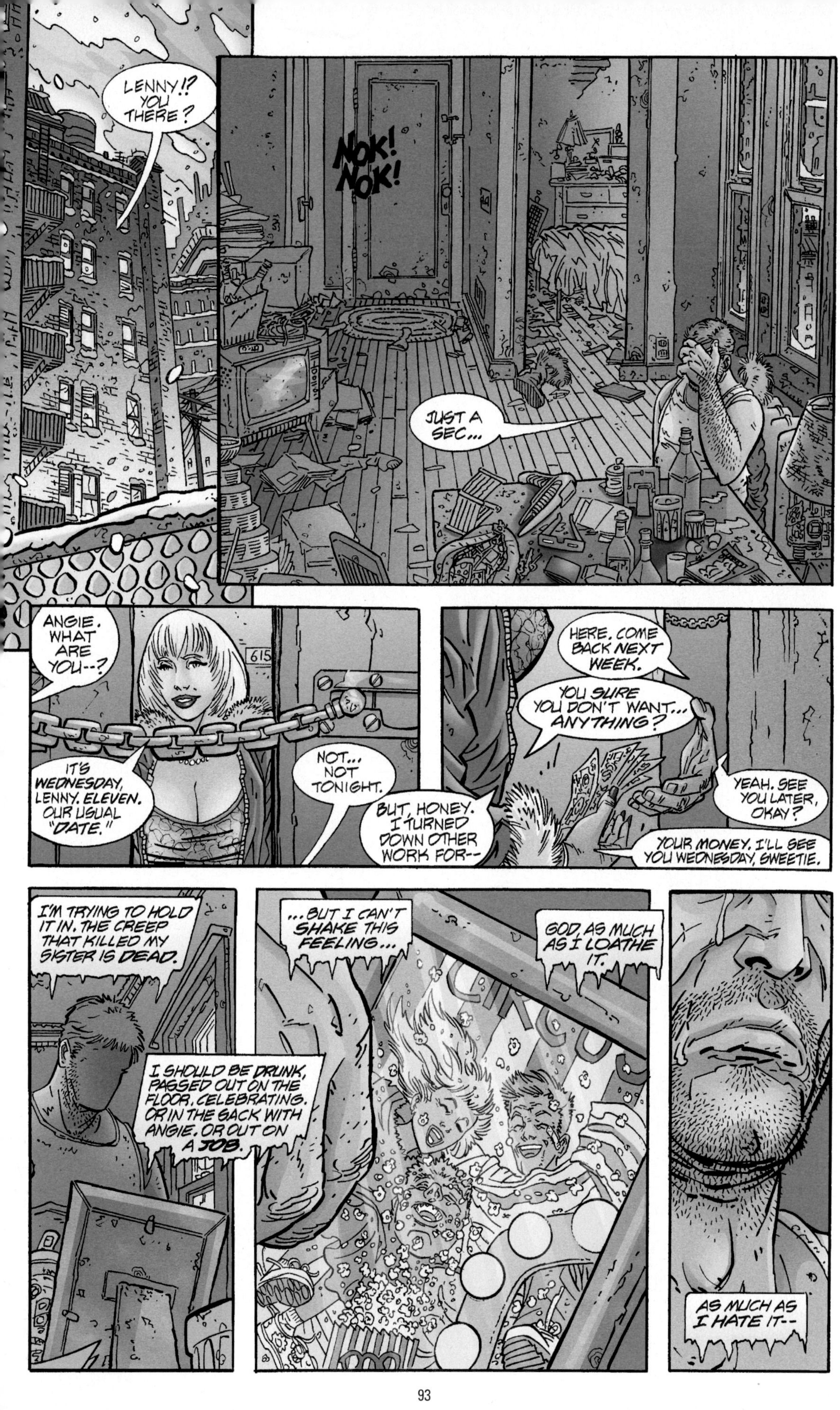
LENNY!? YOU THERE?
NOK! NOK!
JUST A SEC...
ANGIE. WHAT ARE YOU--?
IT'S WEDNESDAY, LENNY. ELEVEN. OUR USUAL "DATE."
NOT... NOT TONIGHT.
BUT, HONEY. I TURNED DOWN OTHER WORK FOR--
HERE. COME BACK NEXT WEEK.
YOU SURE YOU DON'T WANT... ANYTHING?
YEAH. SEE YOU LATER, OKAY?
YOUR MONEY. I'LL SEE YOU WEDNESDAY, SWEETIE.
I'M TRYING TO HOLD IT IN. THE CREEP THAT KILLED MY SISTER IS DEAD.
I SHOULD BE DRUNK, PASSED OUT ON THE FLOOR, CELEBRATING. OR IN THE SACK WITH ANGIE. OR OUT ON A JOB.
...BUT I CAN'T SHAKE THIS FEELING...
GOD, AS MUCH AS I LOATHE IT.
AS MUCH AS I HATE IT--

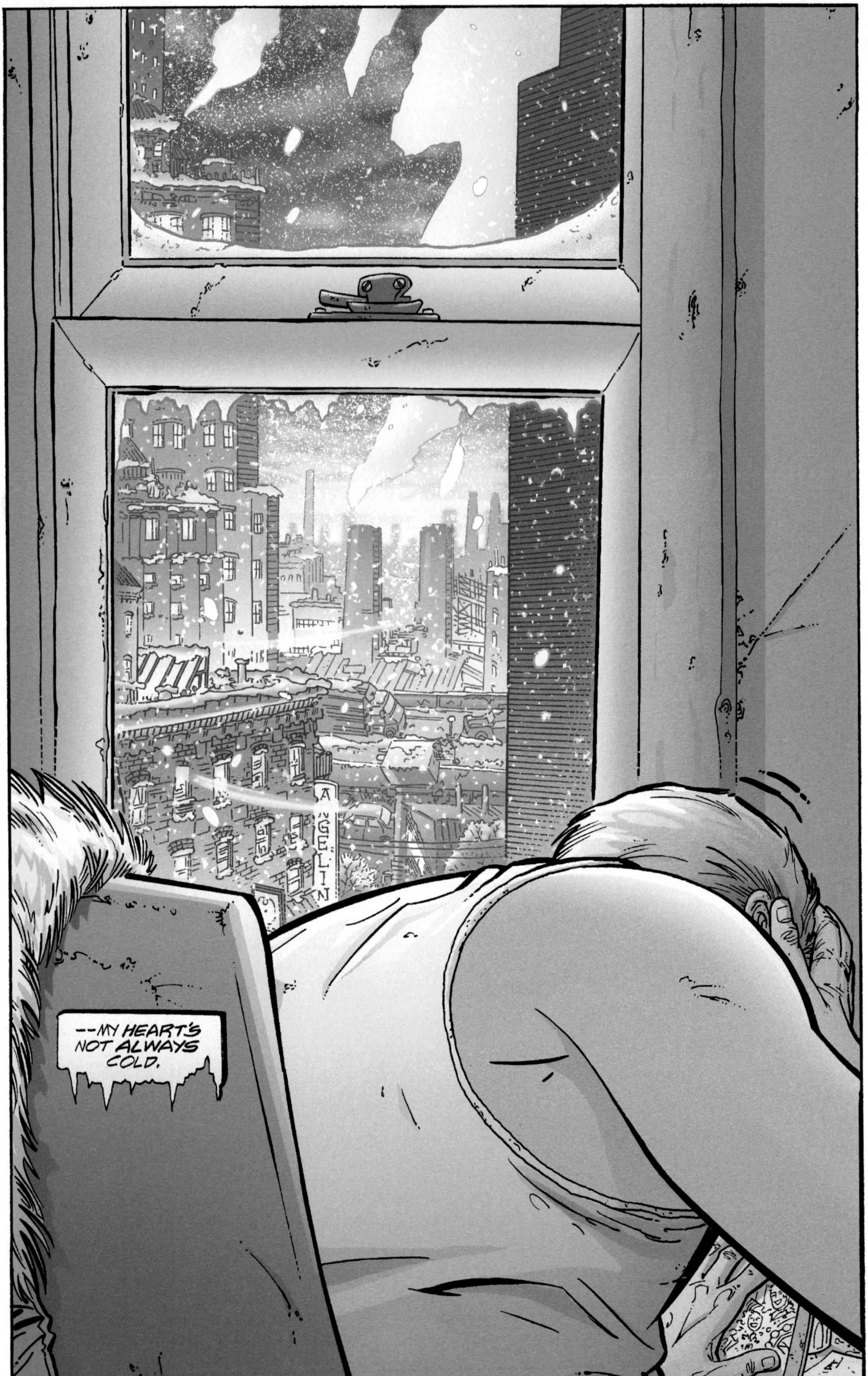
ANGELIN
--MY HEART'S NOT ALWAYS COLD.

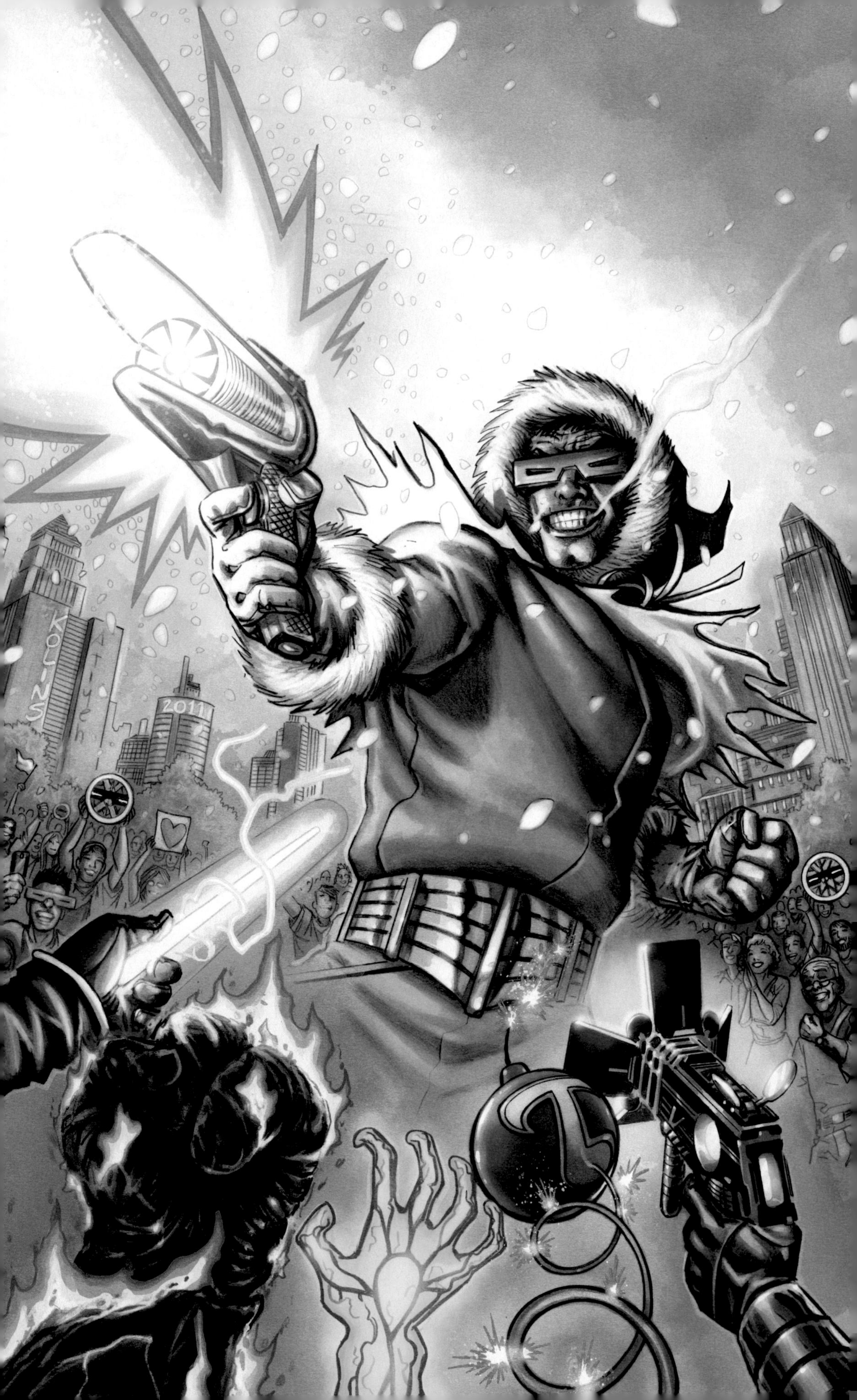
KOLINS
2011

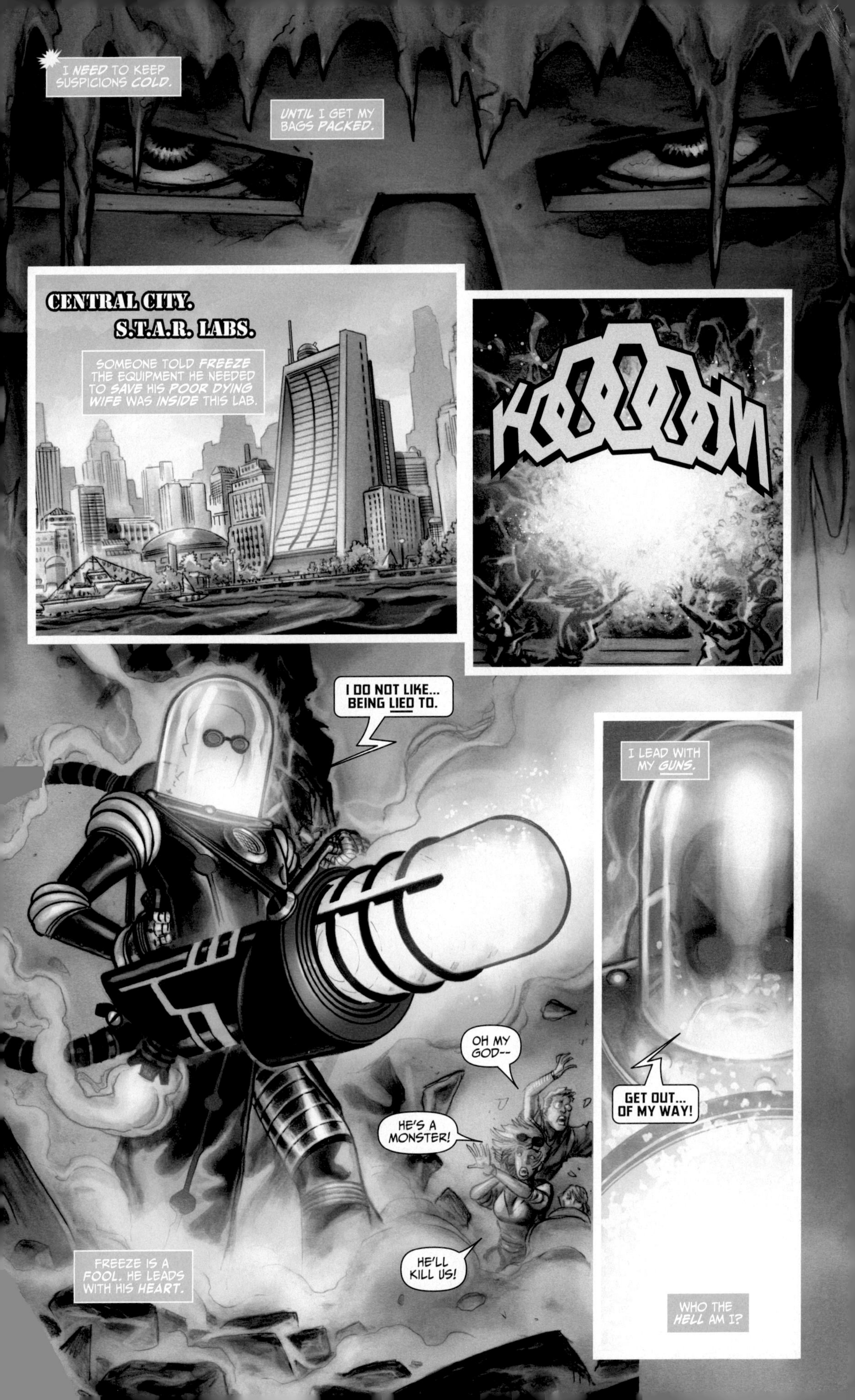

I NEED TO KEEP SUSPICIONS COLD.
UNTIL I GET MY BAGS PACKED.
CENTRAL CITY.
S.T.A.R. LABS.
SOMEONE TOLD FREEZE THE EQUIPMENT HE NEEDED TO SAVE HIS POOR DYING WIFE WAS INSIDE THIS LAB.
KA-BOOM
I DO NOT LIKE... BEING LIED TO.
I LEAD WITH MY GUNS.
OH MY GOD--
GET OUT... OF MY WAY!
HE'S A MONSTER!
FREEZE IS A FOOL. HE LEADS WITH HIS HEART.
HE'LL KILL US!
WHO THE HELL AM I?

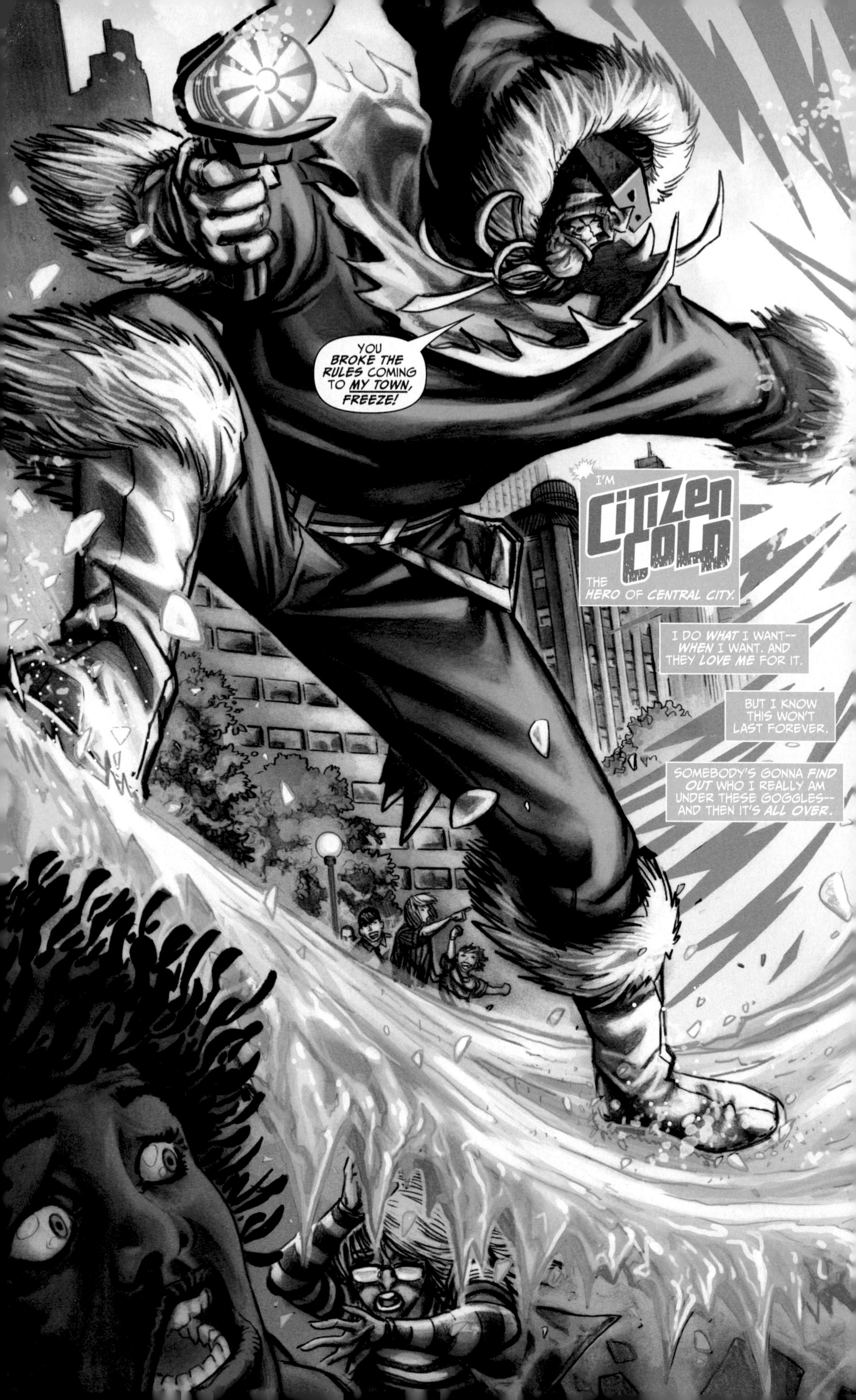
YOU BROKE THE RULES COMING TO MY TOWN, FREEZE!
I'M CITIZEN COLD THE HERO OF CENTRAL CITY.
I DO WHAT I WANT-- WHEN I WANT. AND THEY LOVE ME FOR IT.
BUT I KNOW THIS WON'T LAST FOREVER.
SOMEBODY'S GONNA FIND OUT WHO I REALLY AM UNDER THESE GOGGLES-- AND THEN IT'S ALL OVER.

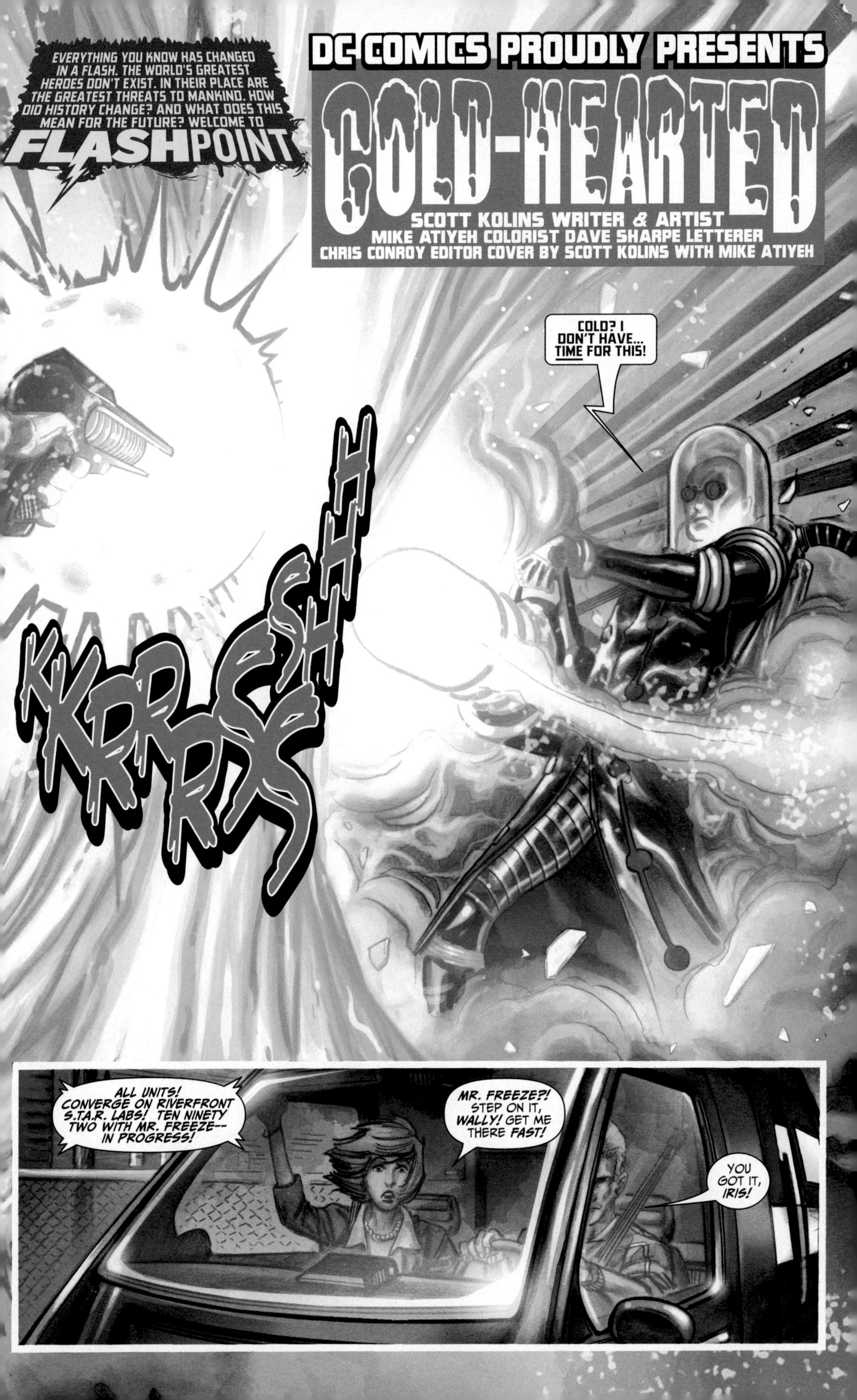

EVERYTHING YOU KNOW HAS CHANGED IN A FLASH. THE WORLD'S GREATEST HEROES DON'T EXIST. IN THEIR PLACE ARE THE GREATEST THREATS TO MANKIND. HOW DID HISTORY CHANGE? AND WHAT DOES THIS MEAN FOR THE FUTURE? WELCOME TO
FLASHPOINT
DC COMICS PROUDLY PRESENTS
COLD-HEARTED
SCOTT KOLINS WRITER & ARTIST
MIKE ATIYEH COLORIST DAVE SHARPE LETTERER
CHRIS CONROY EDITOR COVER BY SCOTT KOLINS WITH MIKE ATIYEH
COLD? I DON'T HAVE... TIME FOR THIS!
KKRRRSSHHH
ALL UNITS! CONVERGE ON RIVERFRONT S.T.A.R. LABS! TEN NINETY TWO WITH MR. FREEZE-- IN PROGRESS!
MR. FREEZE?! STEP ON IT, WALLY! GET ME THERE FAST!
YOU GOT IT, IRIS!

FREEZE'S POWER IS BASED ON CRYOGENIC MEDICINE.

COLD SNAP! COLD SNAP!

DO NOT... MAKE ME-- AHH--

MINE IS A WEAPON.

DON'T LET OUR NAMES FOOL YOU--

MY COLD BEATS *HIS* FREEZE *ANY DAY*.

KKRRNNGGG

COLD SNAP! COLD SNAP!

POK POK

SANCTIMONIOUS... FRAUD...

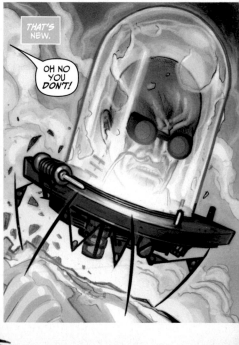

THAT'S NEW.

OH NO YOU DON'T!

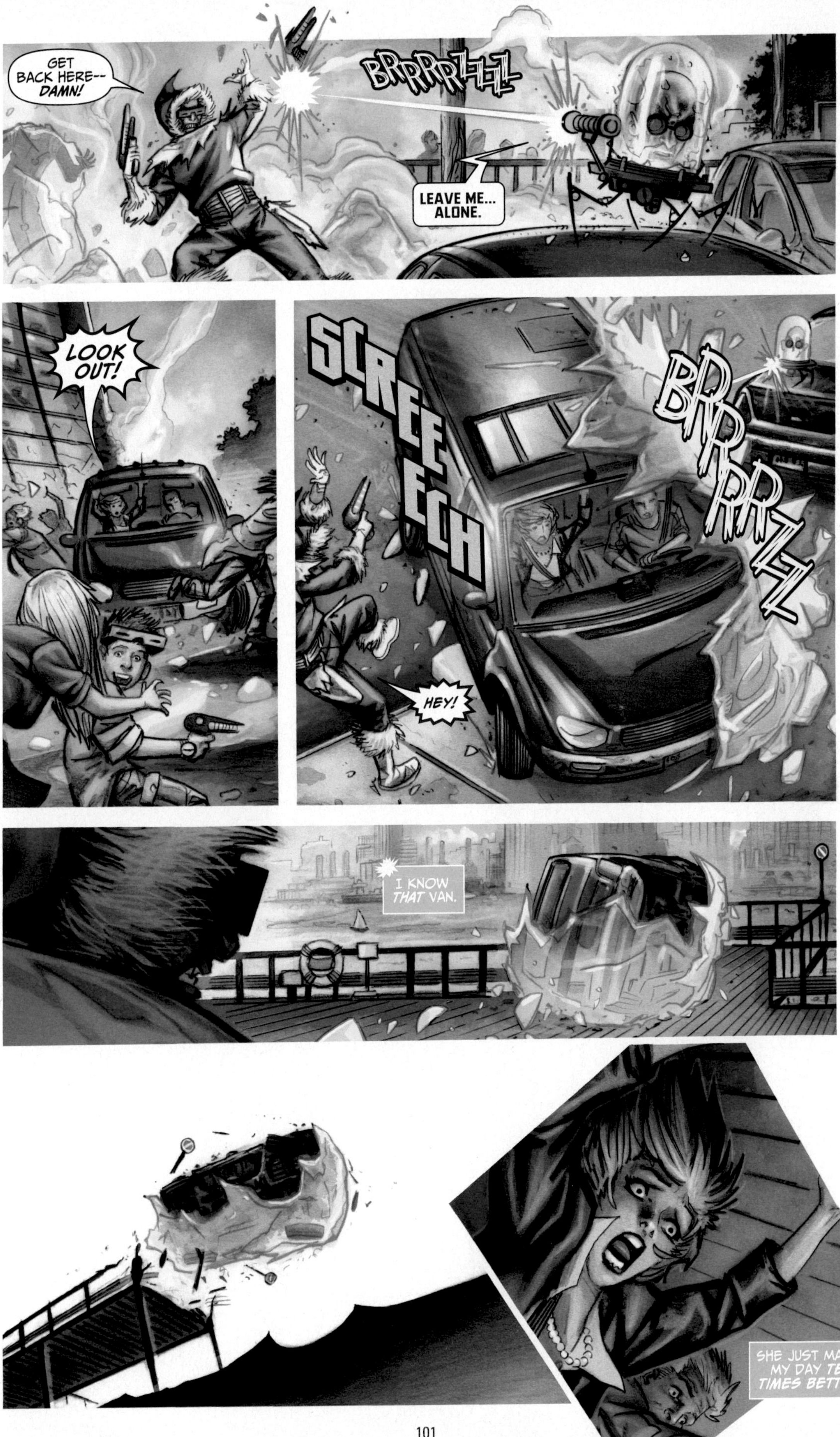

GET BACK HERE-- DAMN!
BRRRRZZZZZ
LEAVE ME... ALONE.
LOOK OUT!
SCREEEECH
BRRRRRZZZ
HEY!
I KNOW THAT VAN.
SHE JUST MADE MY DAY TEN TIMES BETTER.

I'M *TEN TIMES* THE *HERO* WHEN I SAVE THE MOST FAMOUS WOMAN IN THE MIDWEST *AND* BAG THE VILLAIN.

KRRNNGG

SHE JUST PARKED ANOTHER MILLION IN ENDORSEMENTS AT MY DOOR--AND SHE'LL THANK ME FOR IT.

UH-- WE'RE STILL ALIVE?

W-WHAT HAPPENED?

PEOPLE DIE EVERY DAY.

NO! I NEED...TO GET BACK TO--

NORA'S DEAD BY NOW, VICTOR.

(GASP)

YOU DID THIS? YOU SET US UP! YOU COLD-HEARTED BASTAR--

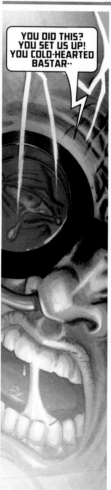

SAY HELLO TO HER FOR ME.

KRRNNGG

DYIN' FOR LOVE IS ABOUT THE *DUMBEST* REASON I CAN THINK OF.

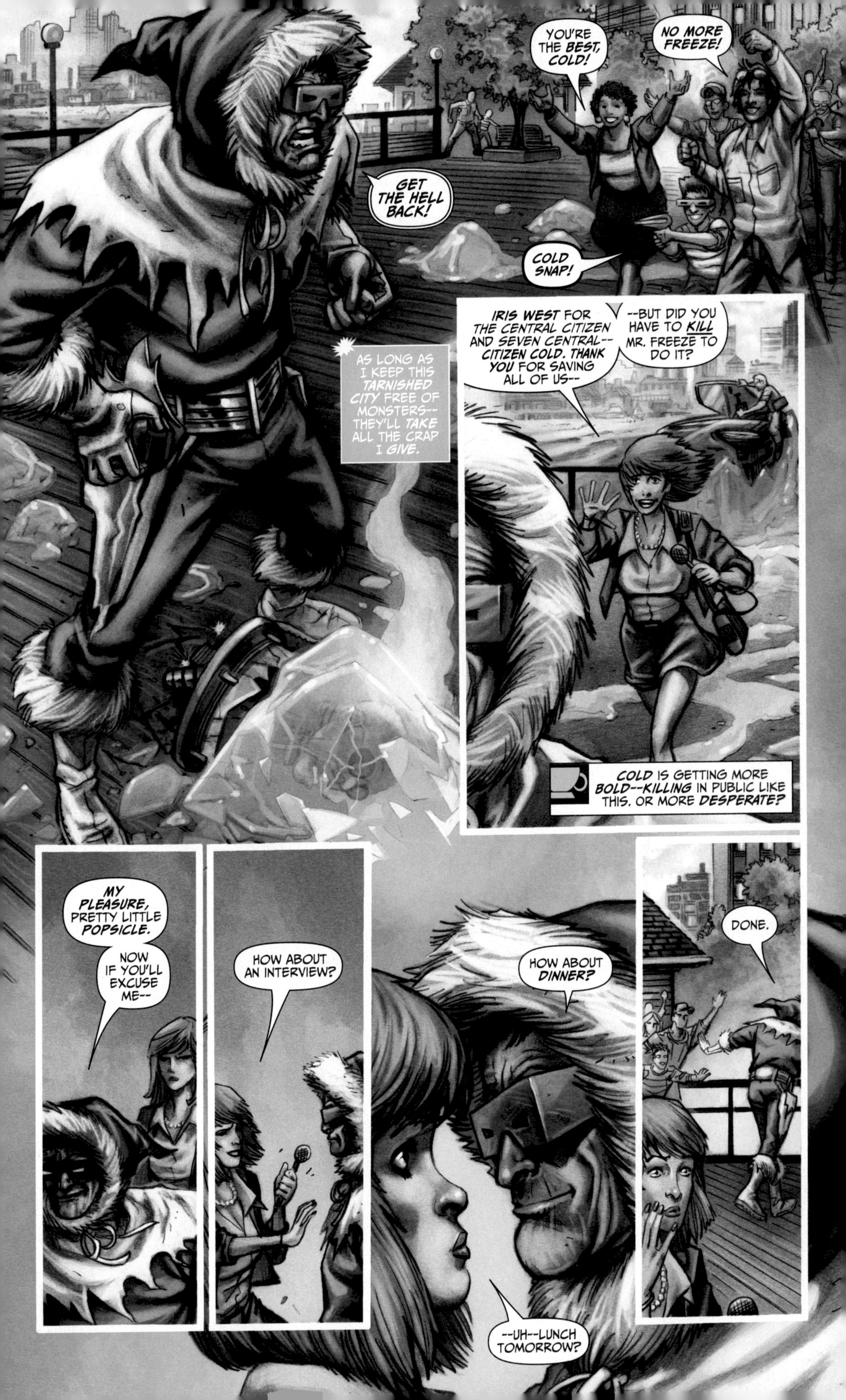
YOU'RE THE BEST, COLD!
NO MORE FREEZE!
GET THE HELL BACK!
COLD SNAP!
AS LONG AS I KEEP THIS TARNISHED CITY FREE OF MONSTERS-- THEY'LL TAKE ALL THE CRAP I GIVE.
IRIS WEST FOR THE CENTRAL CITIZEN AND SEVEN CENTRAL-- CITIZEN COLD. THANK YOU FOR SAVING ALL OF US--
--BUT DID YOU HAVE TO KILL MR. FREEZE TO DO IT?
COLD IS GETTING MORE BOLD--KILLING IN PUBLIC LIKE THIS. OR MORE DESPERATE?
MY PLEASURE, PRETTY LITTLE POPSICLE.
NOW IF YOU'LL EXCUSE ME--
HOW ABOUT AN INTERVIEW?
HOW ABOUT DINNER?
--UH--LUNCH TOMORROW?
DONE.

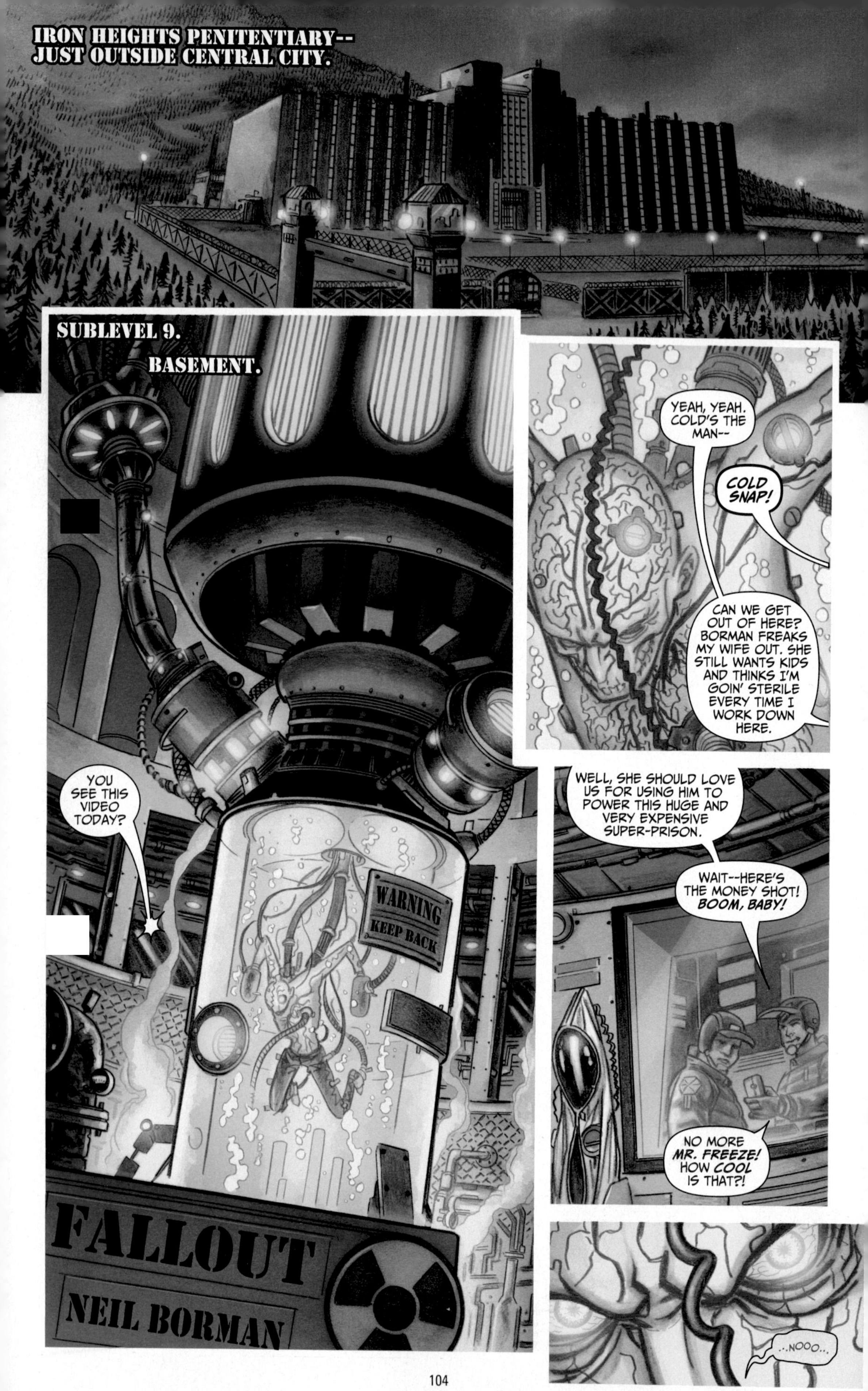
IRON HEIGHTS PENITENTIARY--
JUST OUTSIDE CENTRAL CITY.
SUBLEVEL 9.
BASEMENT.
YOU SEE THIS VIDEO TODAY?
WARNING
KEEP BACK
FALLOUT
NEIL BORMAN
YEAH, YEAH. COLD'S THE MAN--
COLD SNAP!
CAN WE GET OUT OF HERE? BORMAN FREAKS MY WIFE OUT. SHE STILL WANTS KIDS AND THINKS I'M GOIN' STERILE EVERY TIME I WORK DOWN HERE.
WELL, SHE SHOULD LOVE US FOR USING HIM TO POWER THIS HUGE AND VERY EXPENSIVE SUPER-PRISON.
WAIT--HERE'S THE MONEY SHOT! BOOM, BABY!
NO MORE MR. FREEZE! HOW COOL IS THAT?!
..NOOO...

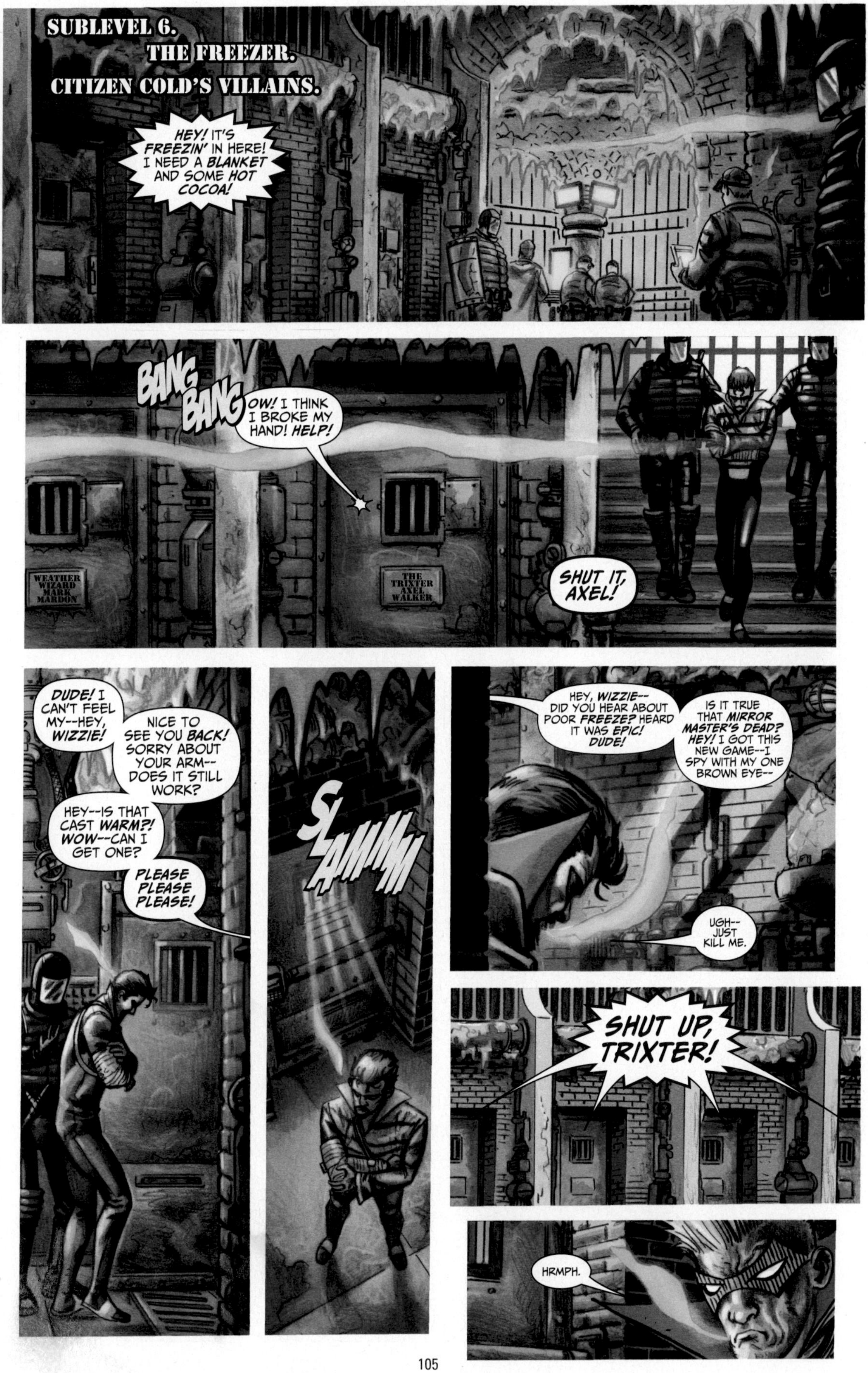
SUBLEVEL 6.
THE FREEZER.
CITIZEN COLD'S VILLAINS.
HEY! IT'S FREEZIN' IN HERE! I NEED A BLANKET AND SOME HOT COCOA!
BANG BANG
OW! I THINK I BROKE MY HAND! HELP!
WEATHER WIZARD MARK MARDON
THE TRIXTER AXEL WALKER
SHUT IT, AXEL!
DUDE! I CAN'T FEEL MY--HEY, WIZZIE!
NICE TO SEE YOU BACK! SORRY ABOUT YOUR ARM--DOES IT STILL WORK?
HEY--IS THAT CAST WARM?! WOW--CAN I GET ONE?
PLEASE PLEASE PLEASE!
SLAMMMM
HEY, WIZZIE--DID YOU HEAR ABOUT POOR FREEZE? HEARD IT WAS EPIC! DUDE!
IS IT TRUE THAT MIRROR MASTER'S DEAD? HEY! I GOT THIS NEW GAME--I SPY WITH MY ONE BROWN EYE--
UGH--JUST KILL ME.
SHUT UP, TRIXTER!
HRMPH.

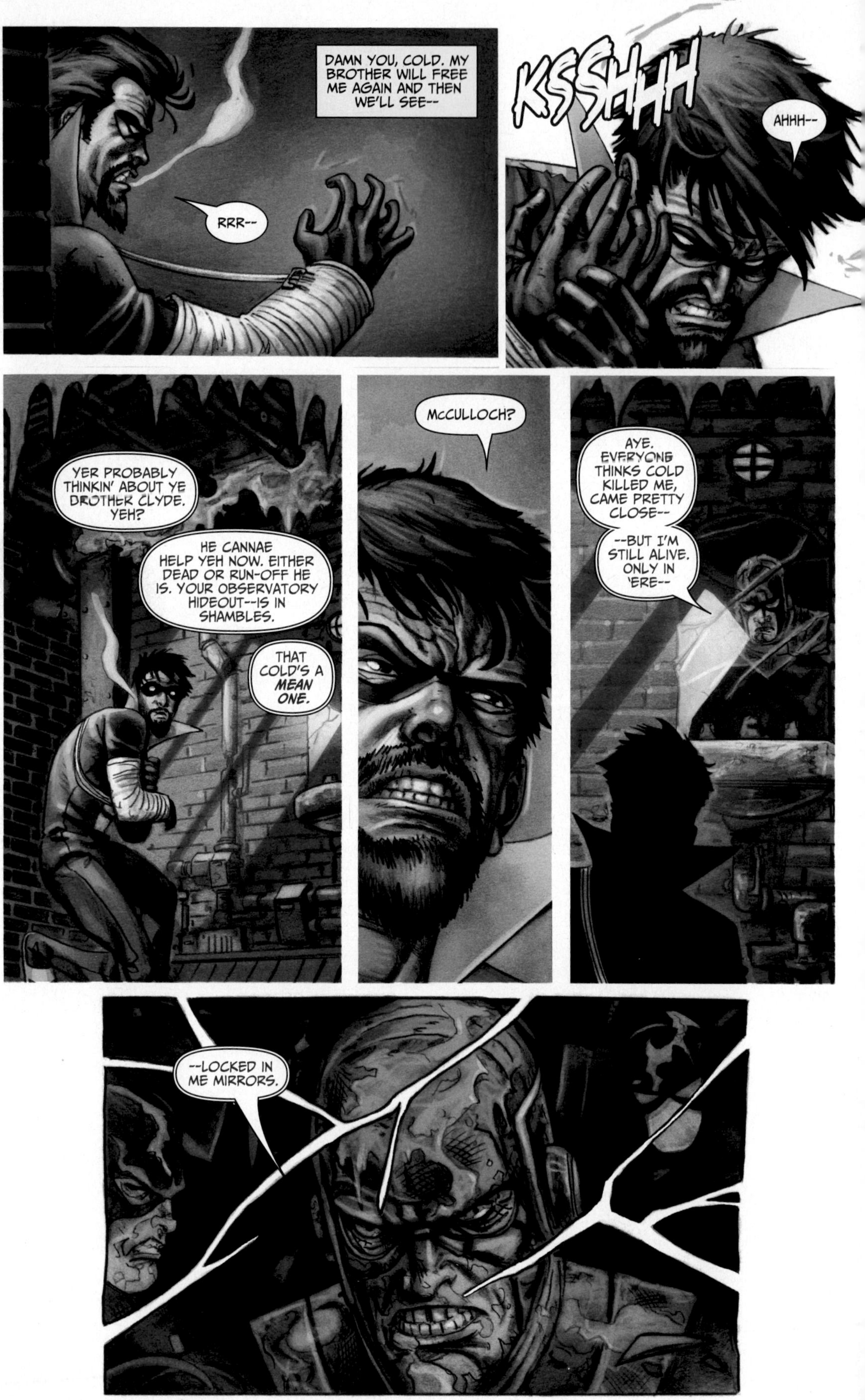
DAMN YOU, COLD. MY BROTHER WILL FREE ME AGAIN AND THEN WE'LL SEE--
RRR--
KSSHHH
AHHH--
YER PROBABLY THINKIN' ABOUT YE BROTHER CLYDE. YEH?
HE CANNAE HELP YEH NOW. EITHER DEAD OR RUN-OFF HE IS. YOUR OBSERVATORY HIDEOUT--IS IN SHAMBLES.
THAT COLD'S A *MEAN ONE.*
McCULLOCH?
AYE. EVERYONE THINKS COLD KILLED ME, CAME PRETTY CLOSE--
--BUT I'M STILL ALIVE. ONLY IN 'ERE--
--LOCKED IN ME MIRRORS.

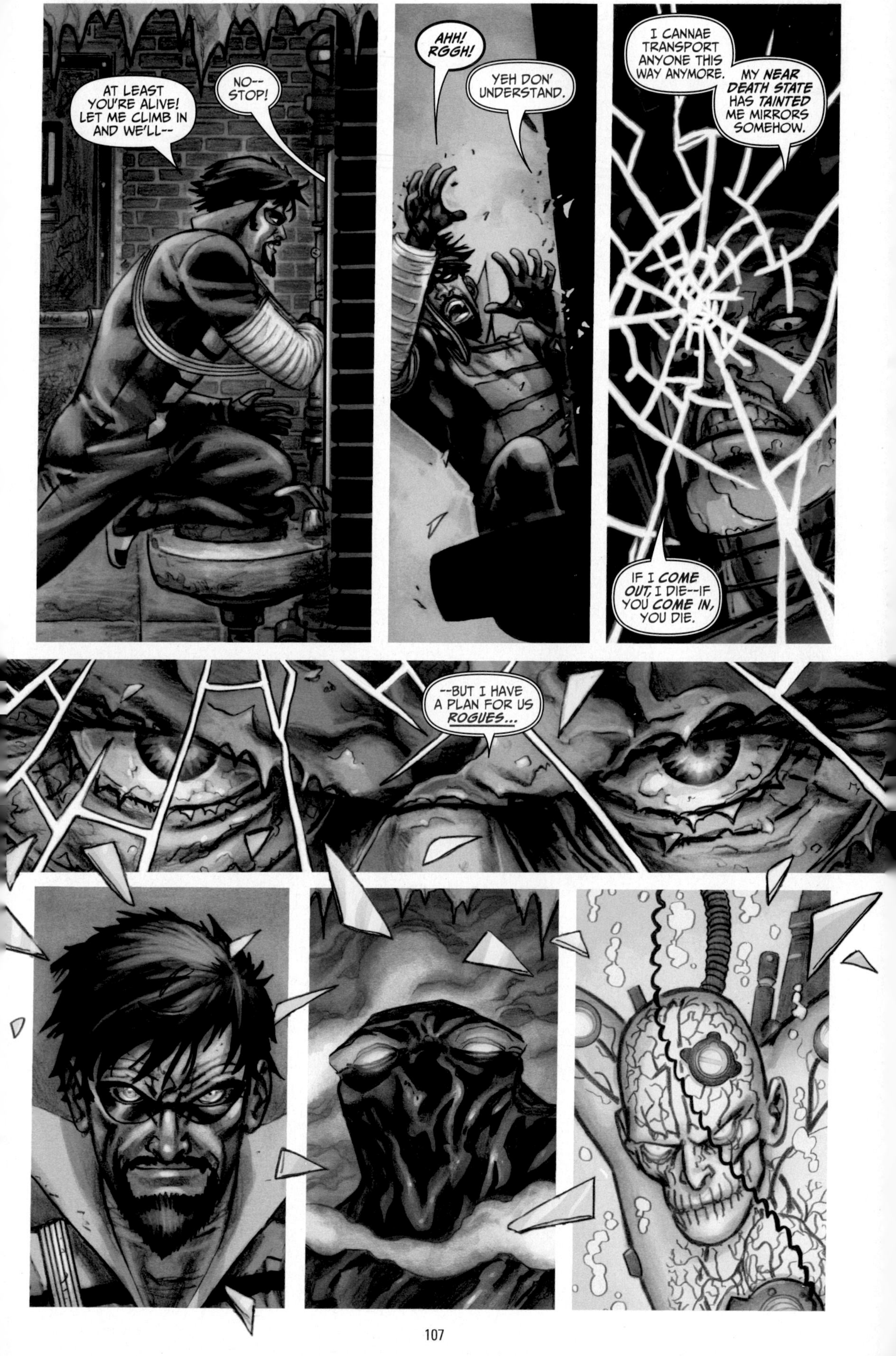
AT LEAST YOU'RE ALIVE! LET ME CLIMB IN AND WE'LL--
NO-- STOP!
AHH! RGGH!
YEH DON' UNDERSTAND.
I CANNAE TRANSPORT ANYONE THIS WAY ANYMORE.
MY NEAR DEATH STATE HAS TAINTED ME MIRRORS SOMEHOW.
IF I COME OUT, I DIE--IF YOU COME IN, YOU DIE.
--BUT I HAVE A PLAN FOR US ROGUES...

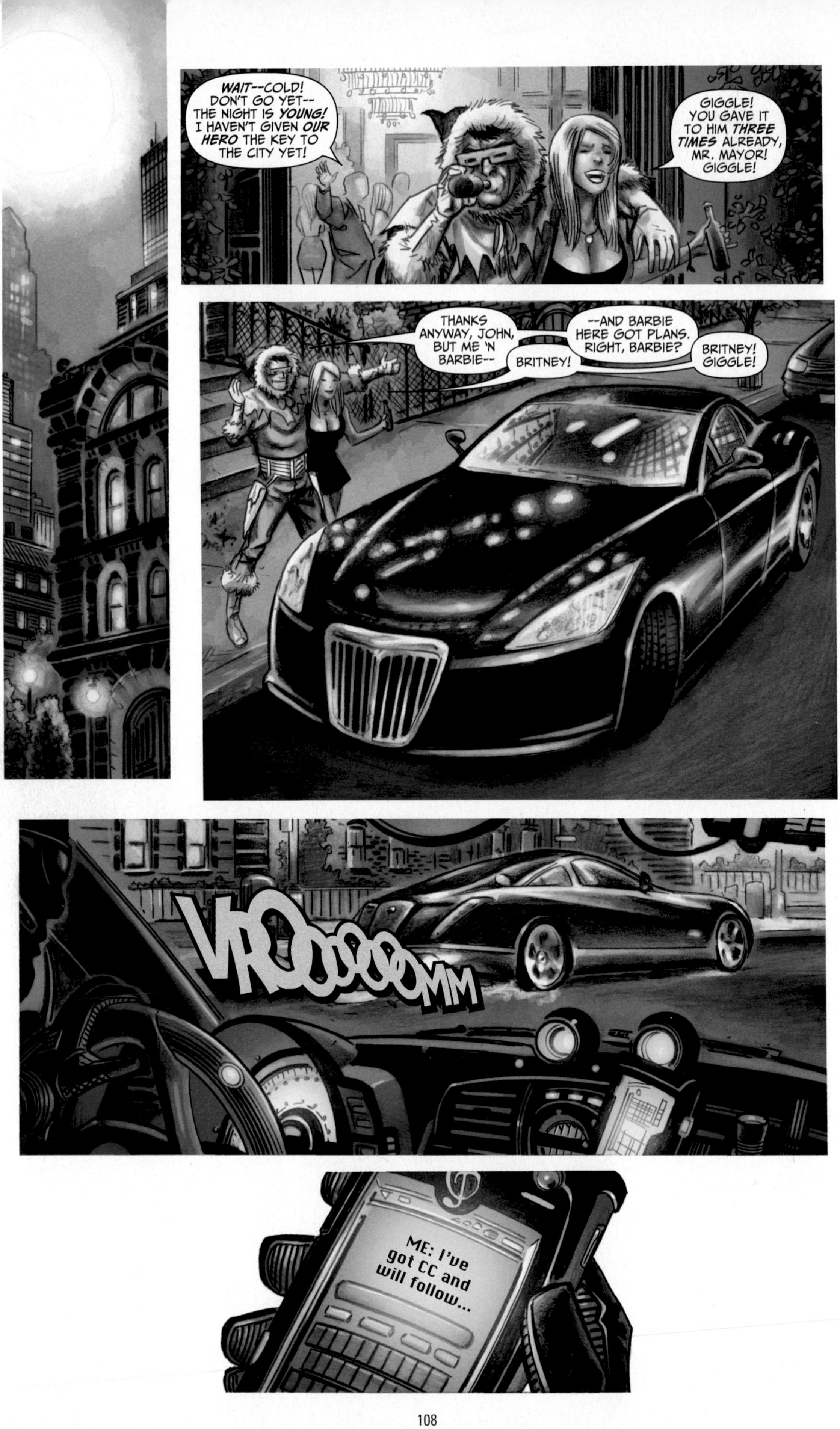
WAIT--COLD! DON'T GO YET-- THE NIGHT IS YOUNG! I HAVEN'T GIVEN OUR HERO THE KEY TO THE CITY YET!
GIGGLE! YOU GAVE IT TO HIM THREE TIMES ALREADY, MR. MAYOR! GIGGLE!
THANKS ANYWAY, JOHN, BUT ME 'N BARBIE--
BRITNEY!
--AND BARBIE HERE GOT PLANS. RIGHT, BARBIE?
BRITNEY! GIGGLE!
VROOOOOOMM
ME: I've got CC and will follow...

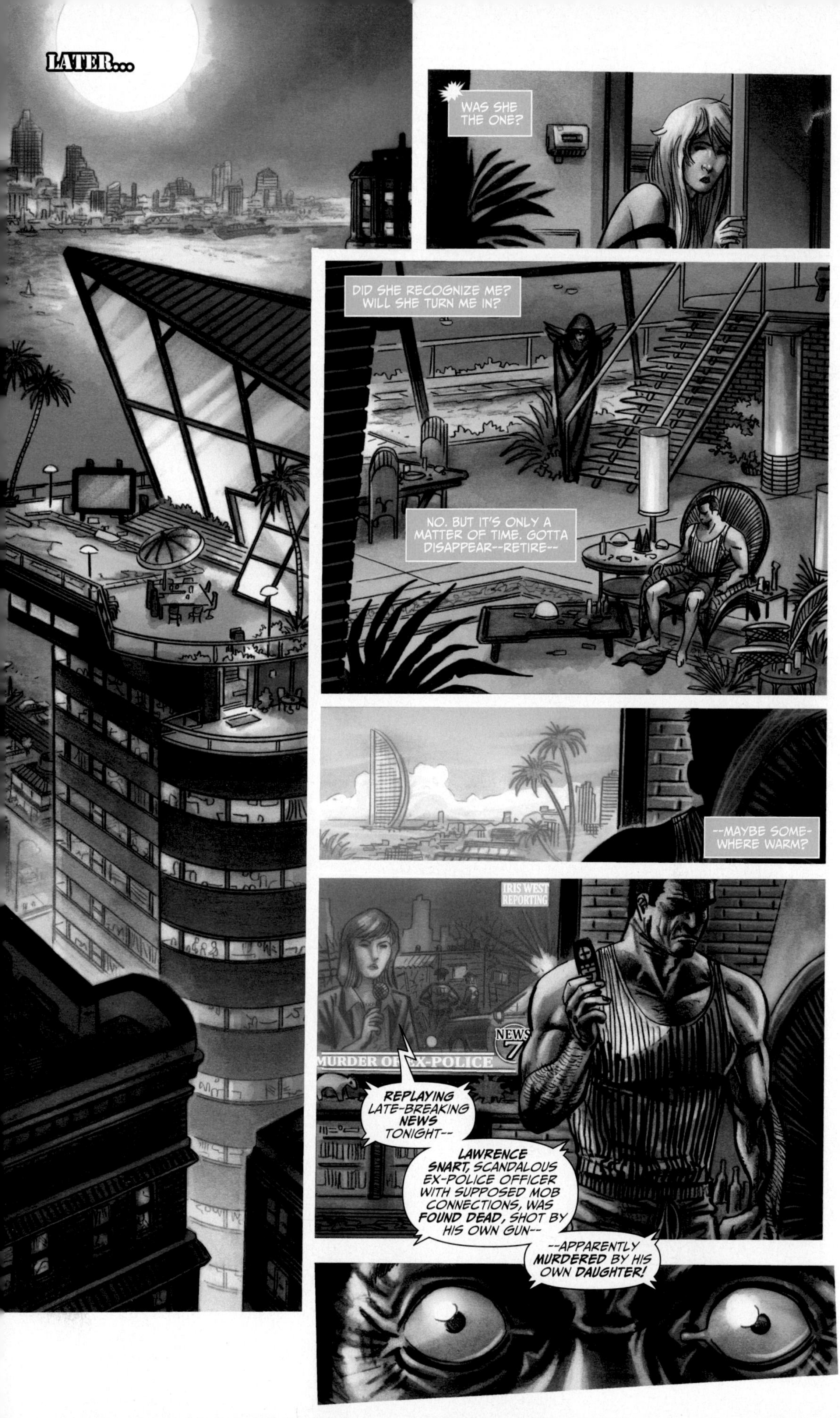
LATER...
WAS SHE THE ONE?
DID SHE RECOGNIZE ME? WILL SHE TURN ME IN?
NO. BUT IT'S ONLY A MATTER OF TIME. GOTTA DISAPPEAR--RETIRE--
--MAYBE SOME-WHERE WARM?
IRIS WEST REPORTING
NEWS 7
MURDER OF EX-POLICE
REPLAYING LATE-BREAKING NEWS TONIGHT--
LAWRENCE SNART, SCANDALOUS EX-POLICE OFFICER WITH SUPPOSED MOB CONNECTIONS, WAS FOUND DEAD, SHOT BY HIS OWN GUN--
--APPARENTLY MURDERED BY HIS OWN DAUGHTER!

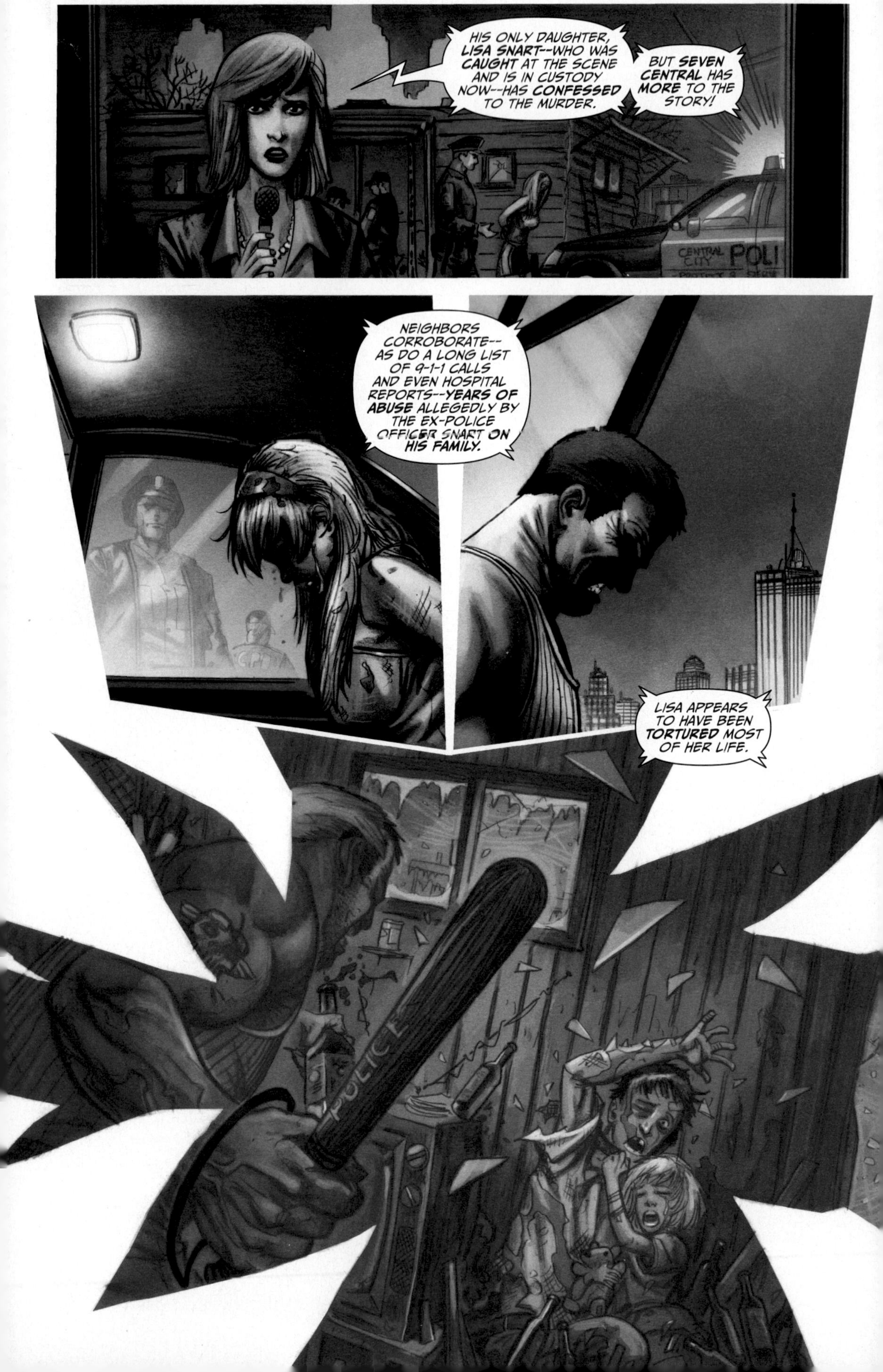
HIS ONLY DAUGHTER, LISA SNART--WHO WAS CAUGHT AT THE SCENE AND IS IN CUSTODY NOW--HAS CONFESSED TO THE MURDER.
BUT SEVEN CENTRAL HAS MORE TO THE STORY!
CENTRAL CITY POLI
NEIGHBORS CORROBORATE-- AS DO A LONG LIST OF 9-1-1 CALLS AND EVEN HOSPITAL REPORTS--YEARS OF ABUSE ALLEGEDLY BY THE EX-POLICE OFFICER SNART ON HIS FAMILY.
LISA APPEARS TO HAVE BEEN TORTURED MOST OF HER LIFE.
POLICE

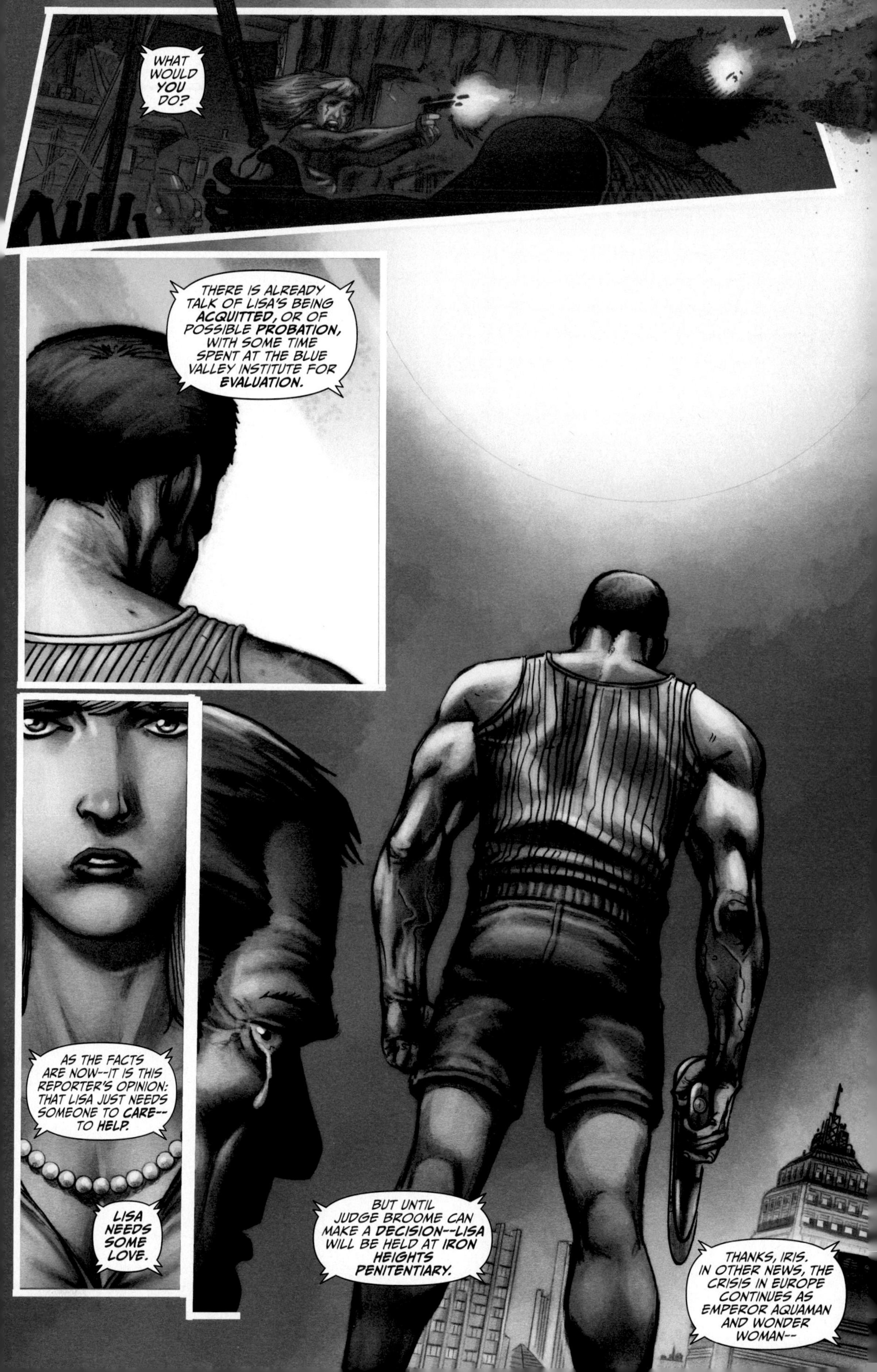
WHAT WOULD YOU DO?
THERE IS ALREADY TALK OF LISA'S BEING ACQUITTED, OR OF POSSIBLE PROBATION, WITH SOME TIME SPENT AT THE BLUE VALLEY INSTITUTE FOR EVALUATION.
AS THE FACTS ARE NOW--IT IS THIS REPORTER'S OPINION: THAT LISA JUST NEEDS SOMEONE TO CARE--TO HELP.
LISA NEEDS SOME LOVE.
BUT UNTIL JUDGE BROOME CAN MAKE A DECISION--LISA WILL BE HELD AT IRON HEIGHTS PENITENTIARY.
THANKS, IRIS. IN OTHER NEWS, THE CRISIS IN EUROPE CONTINUES AS EMPEROR AQUAMAN AND WONDER WOMAN--

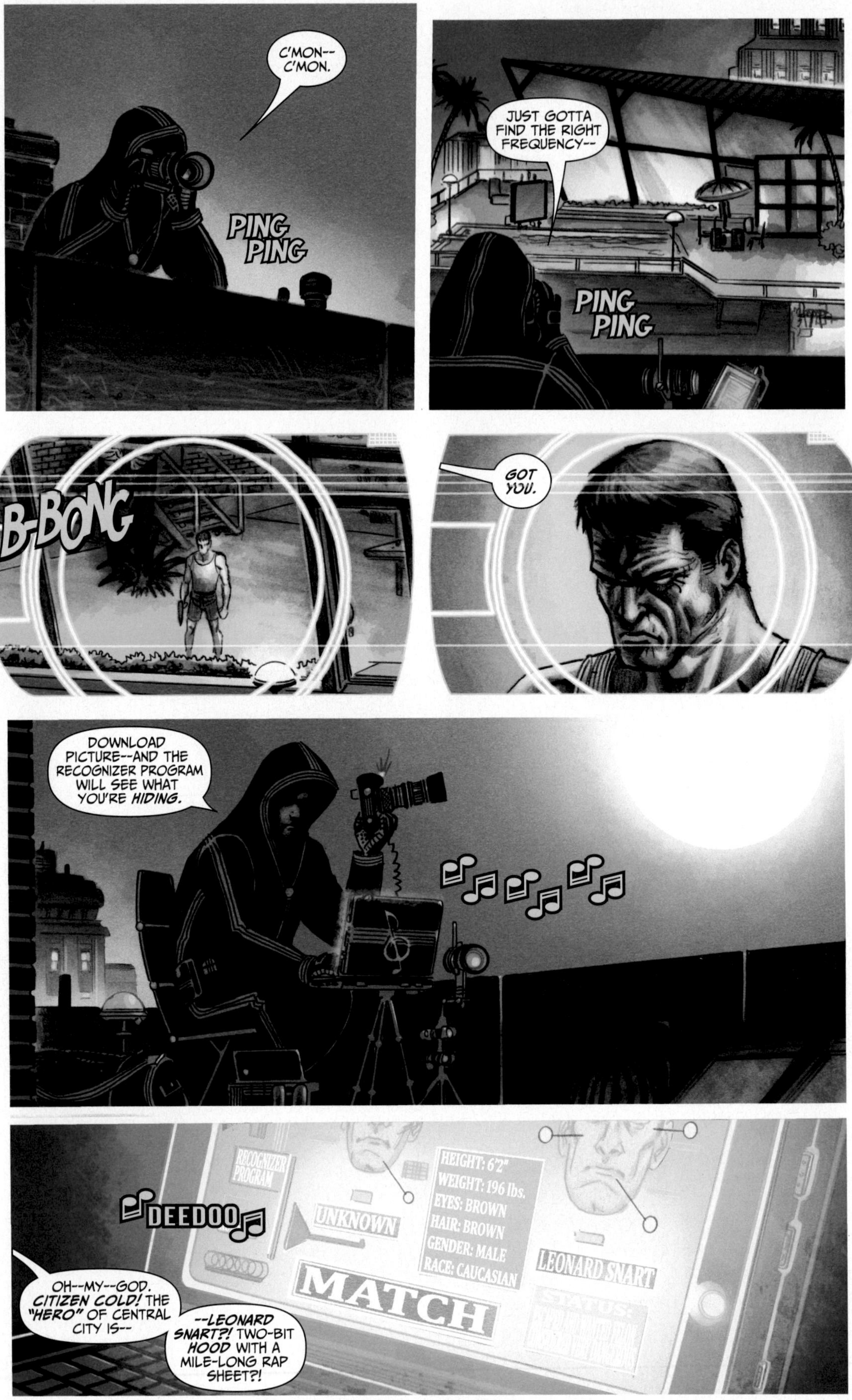
C'MON--
C'MON.
PING
PING
JUST GOTTA FIND THE RIGHT FREQUENCY--
PING
PING
B-BONG
GOT YOU.
DOWNLOAD PICTURE--AND THE RECOGNIZER PROGRAM WILL SEE WHAT YOU'RE *HIDING*.
DEEDOO
RECOGNIZER PROGRAM
UNKNOWN
HEIGHT: 6'2"
WEIGHT: 196 lbs.
EYES: BROWN
HAIR: BROWN
GENDER: MALE
RACE: CAUCASIAN
LEONARD SNART
MATCH
STATUS:
OH--MY--GOD. *CITIZEN COLD!* THE *"HERO"* OF CENTRAL CITY IS--
--LEONARD SNART?! TWO-BIT *HOOD* WITH A MILE-LONG RAP SHEET?!

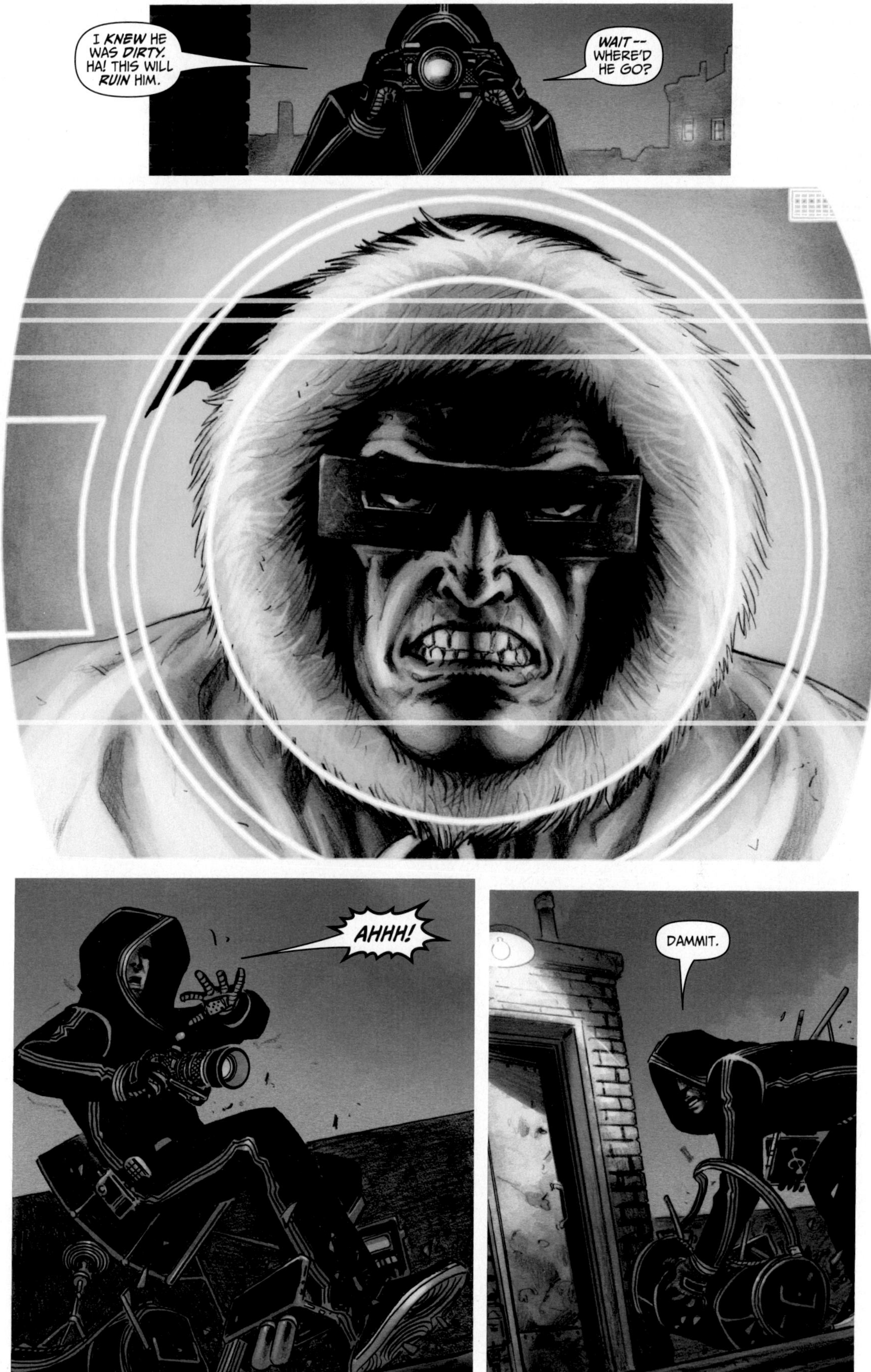
I KNEW HE WAS DIRTY. HA! THIS WILL RUIN HIM.
WAIT-- WHERE'D HE GO?
AHHH!
DAMMIT.

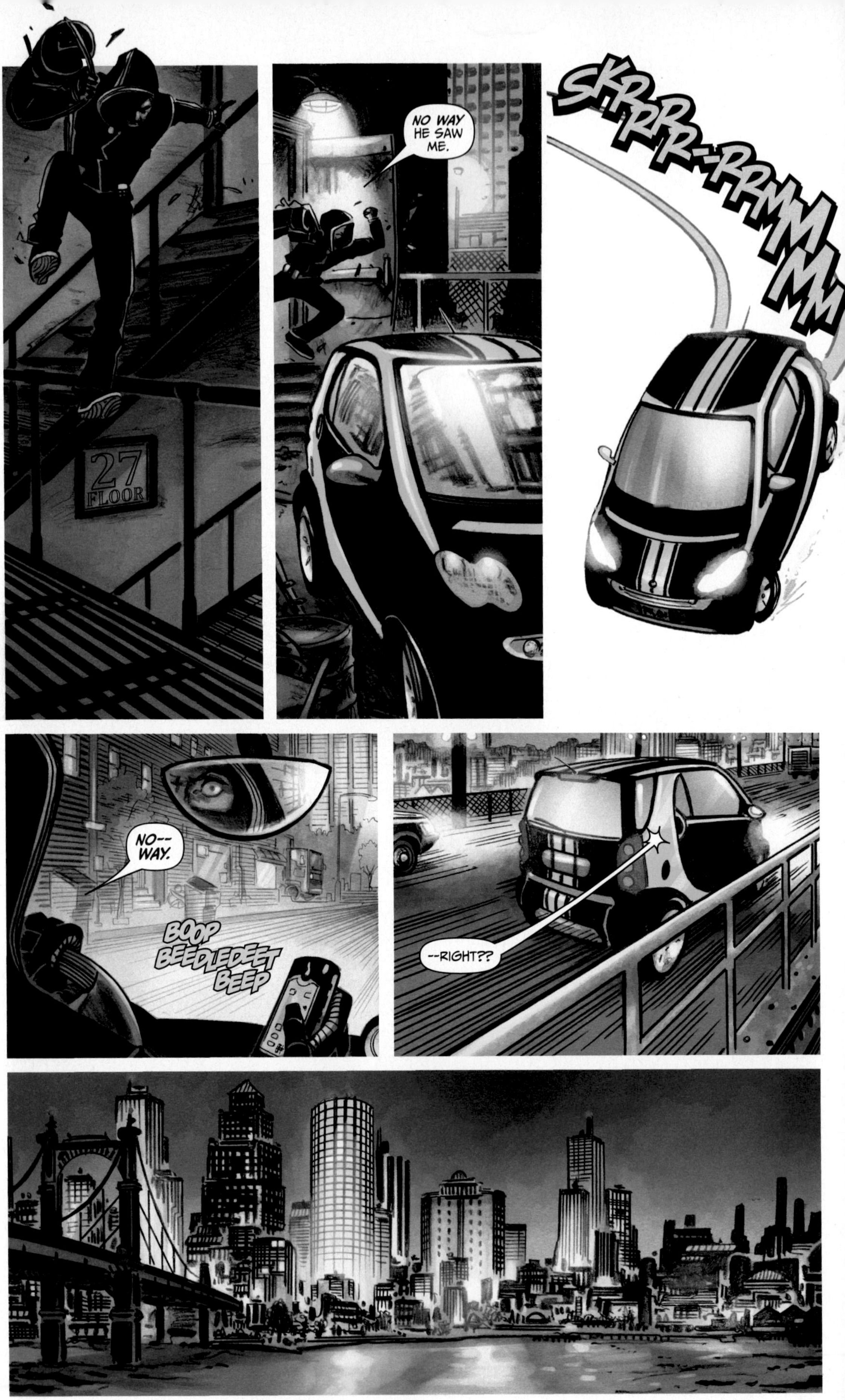
27
FLOOR
NO WAY HE SAW ME.
SKRRRR--RRMMMM
NO--WAY.
BOOP BEEDLEDEET BEEP
--RIGHT??

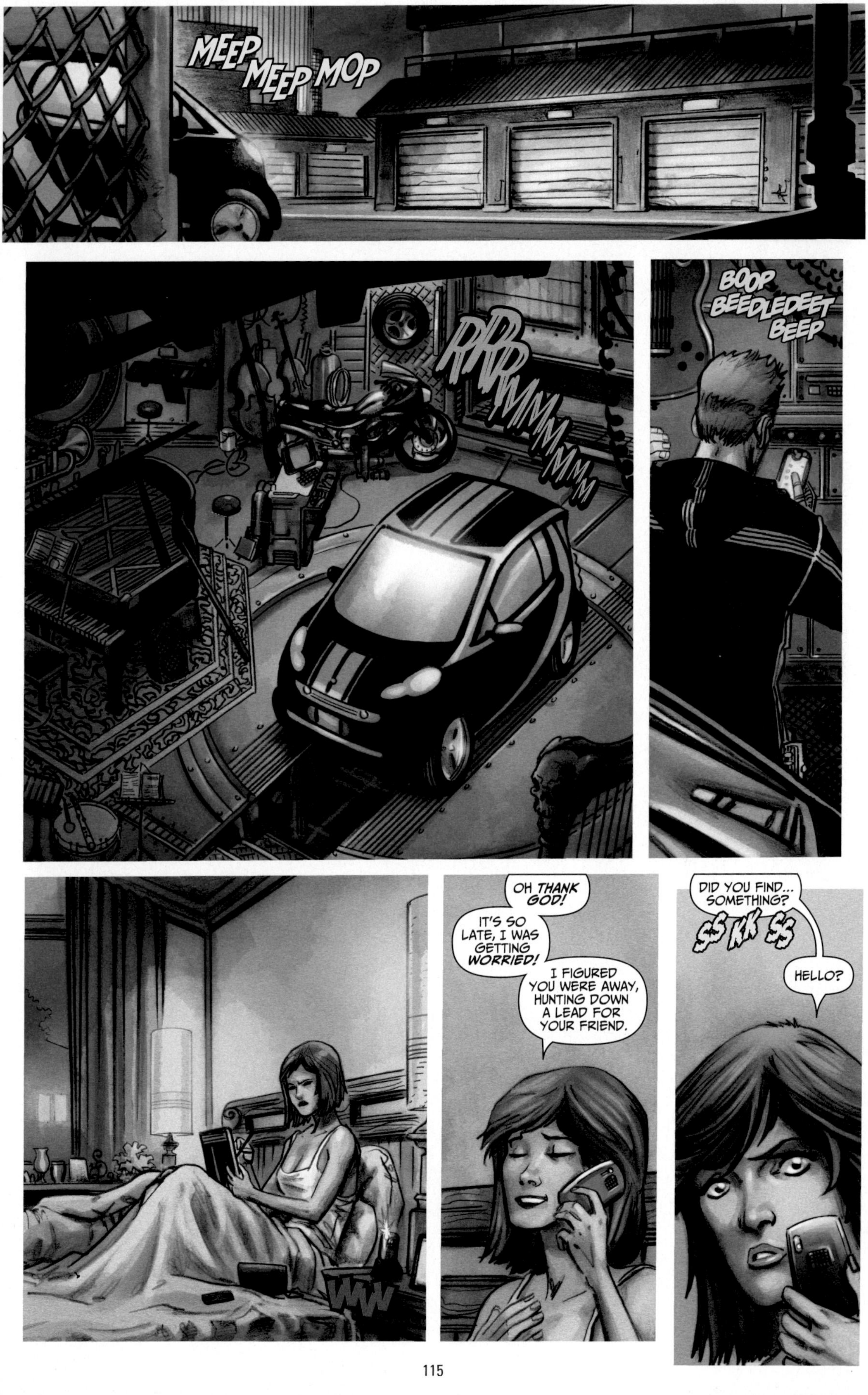
MEEP MEEP MOP
RRRMMMMMM
BOOP BEEDLEDEET BEEP
OH THANK GOD!
IT'S SO LATE, I WAS GETTING WORRIED!
I FIGURED YOU WERE AWAY, HUNTING DOWN A LEAD FOR YOUR FRIEND.
DID YOU FIND... SOMETHING?
SS KK SS
HELLO?

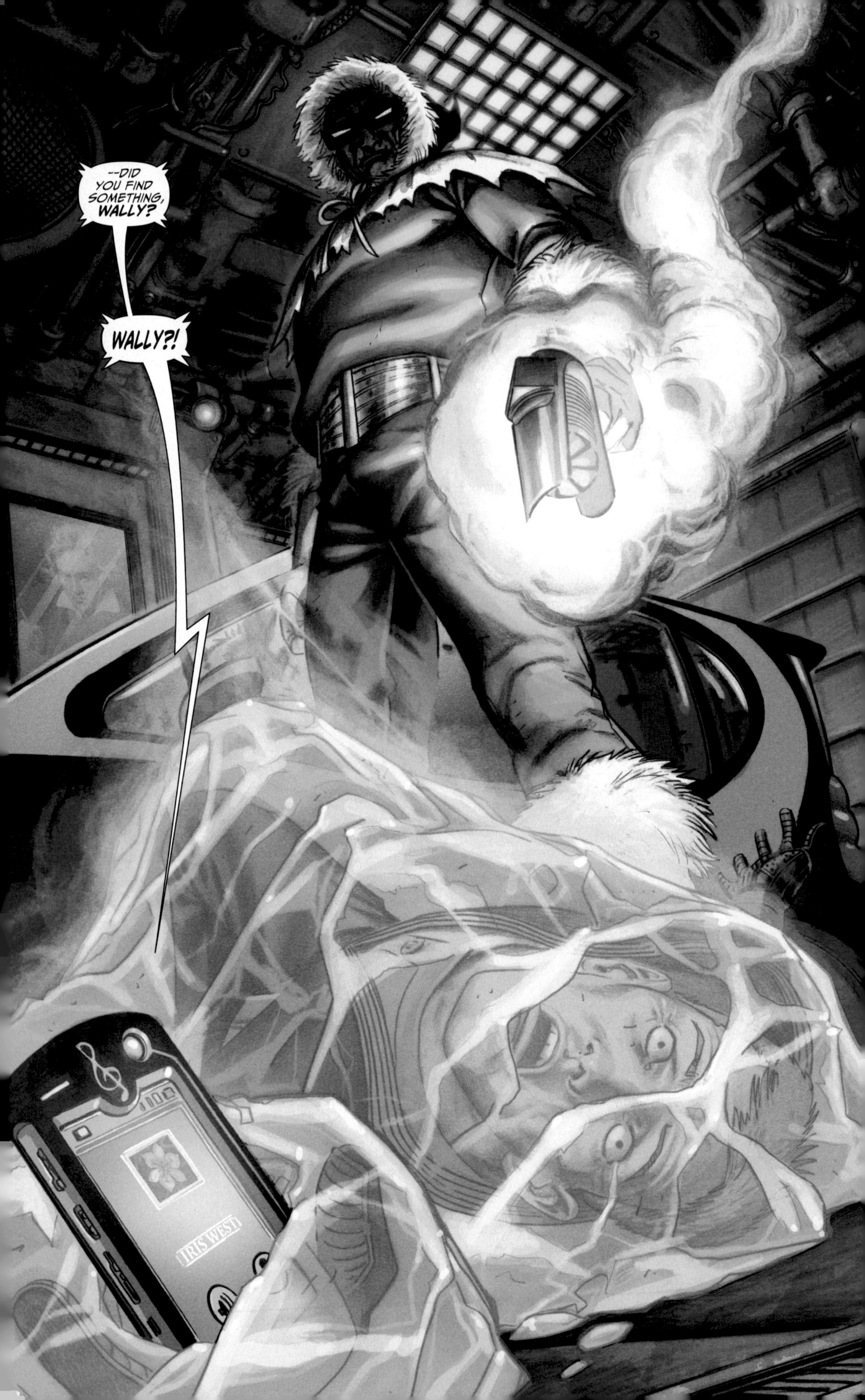
--DID YOU FIND SOMETHING, WALLY?
WALLY?!
IRIS WEST

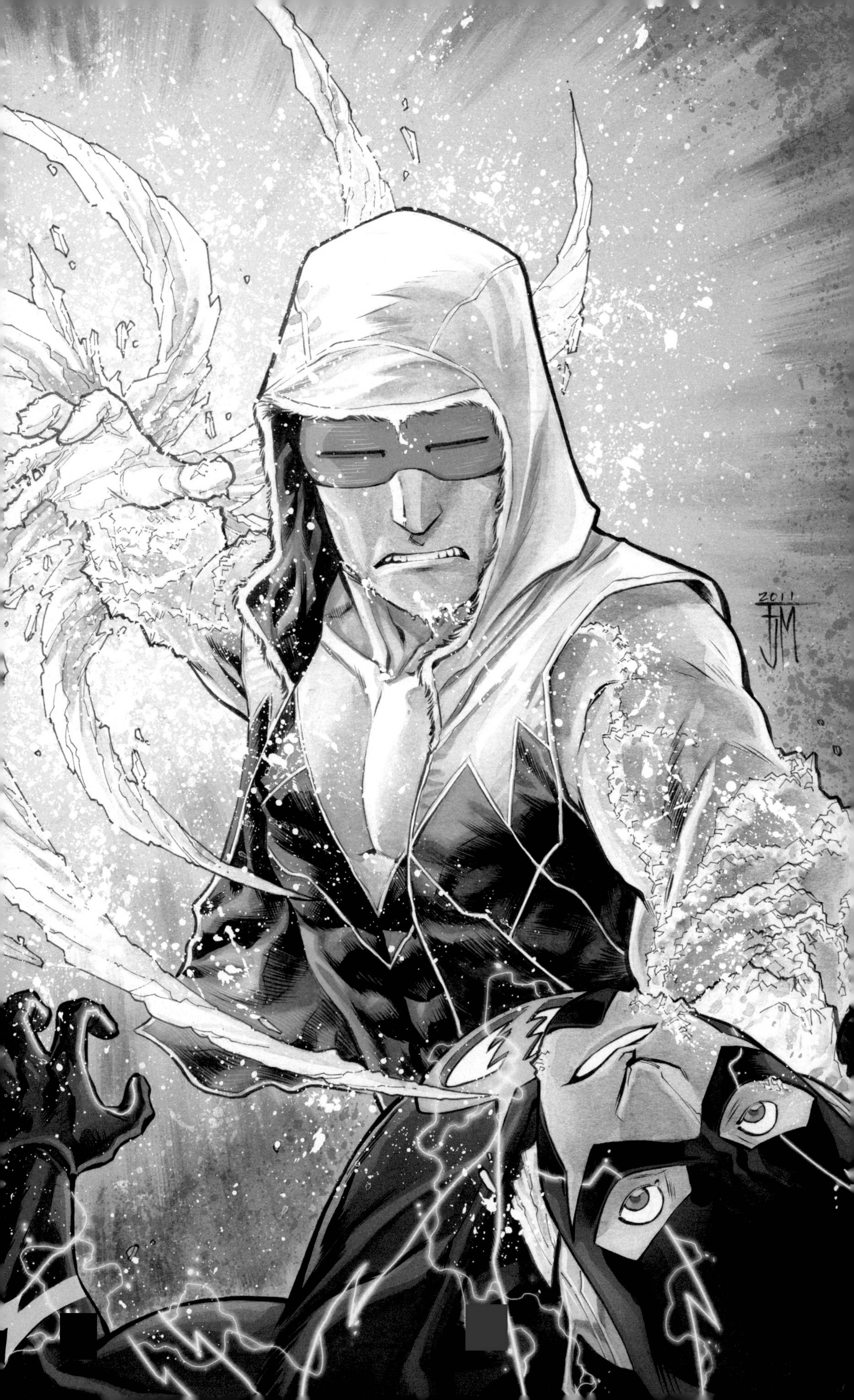

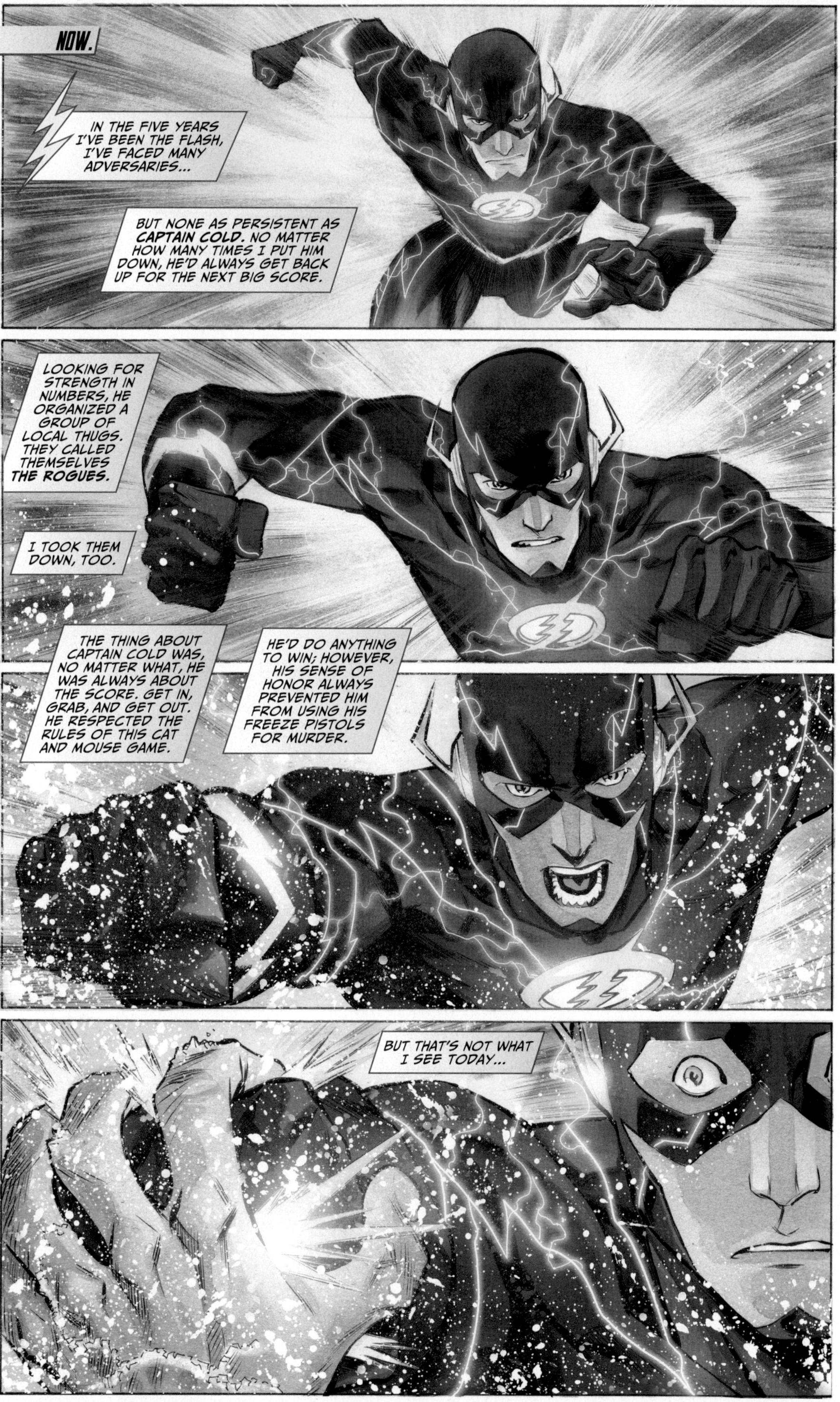
NOW.
IN THE FIVE YEARS I'VE BEEN THE FLASH, I'VE FACED MANY ADVERSARIES...
BUT NONE AS PERSISTENT AS **CAPTAIN COLD.** NO MATTER HOW MANY TIMES I PUT HIM DOWN, HE'D ALWAYS GET BACK UP FOR THE NEXT BIG SCORE.
LOOKING FOR STRENGTH IN NUMBERS, HE ORGANIZED A GROUP OF LOCAL THUGS. THEY CALLED THEMSELVES **THE ROGUES.**
I TOOK THEM DOWN, TOO.
THE THING ABOUT CAPTAIN COLD WAS, NO MATTER WHAT, HE WAS ALWAYS ABOUT THE SCORE. GET IN, GRAB, AND GET OUT. HE RESPECTED THE RULES OF THIS CAT AND MOUSE GAME.
HE'D DO ANYTHING TO WIN; HOWEVER, HIS SENSE OF HONOR ALWAYS PREVENTED HIM FROM USING HIS FREEZE PISTOLS FOR MURDER.
BUT THAT'S NOT WHAT I SEE TODAY...

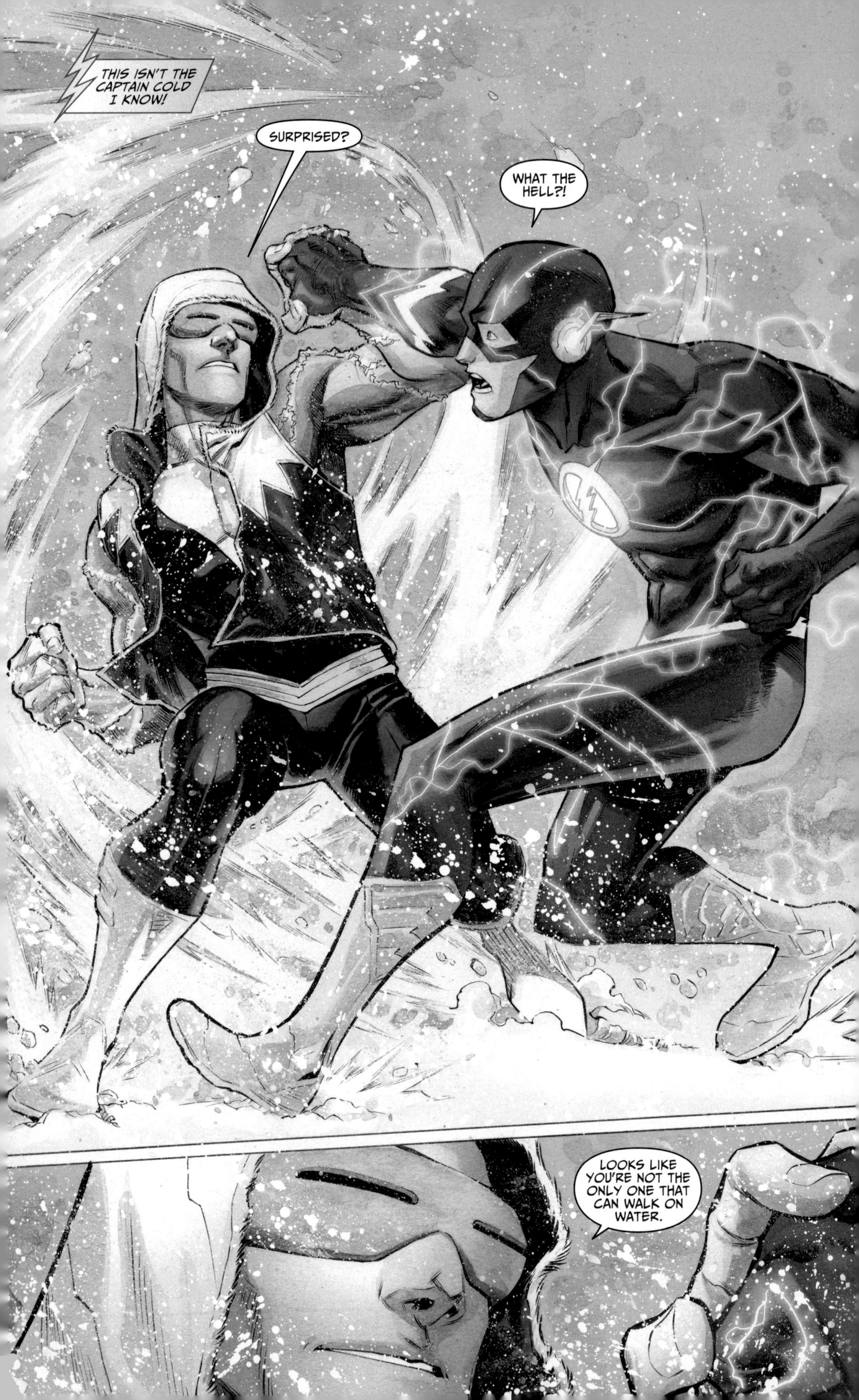
THIS ISN'T THE CAPTAIN COLD I KNOW!
SURPRISED?
WHAT THE HELL?!
LOOKS LIKE YOU'RE NOT THE ONLY ONE THAT CAN WALK ON WATER.

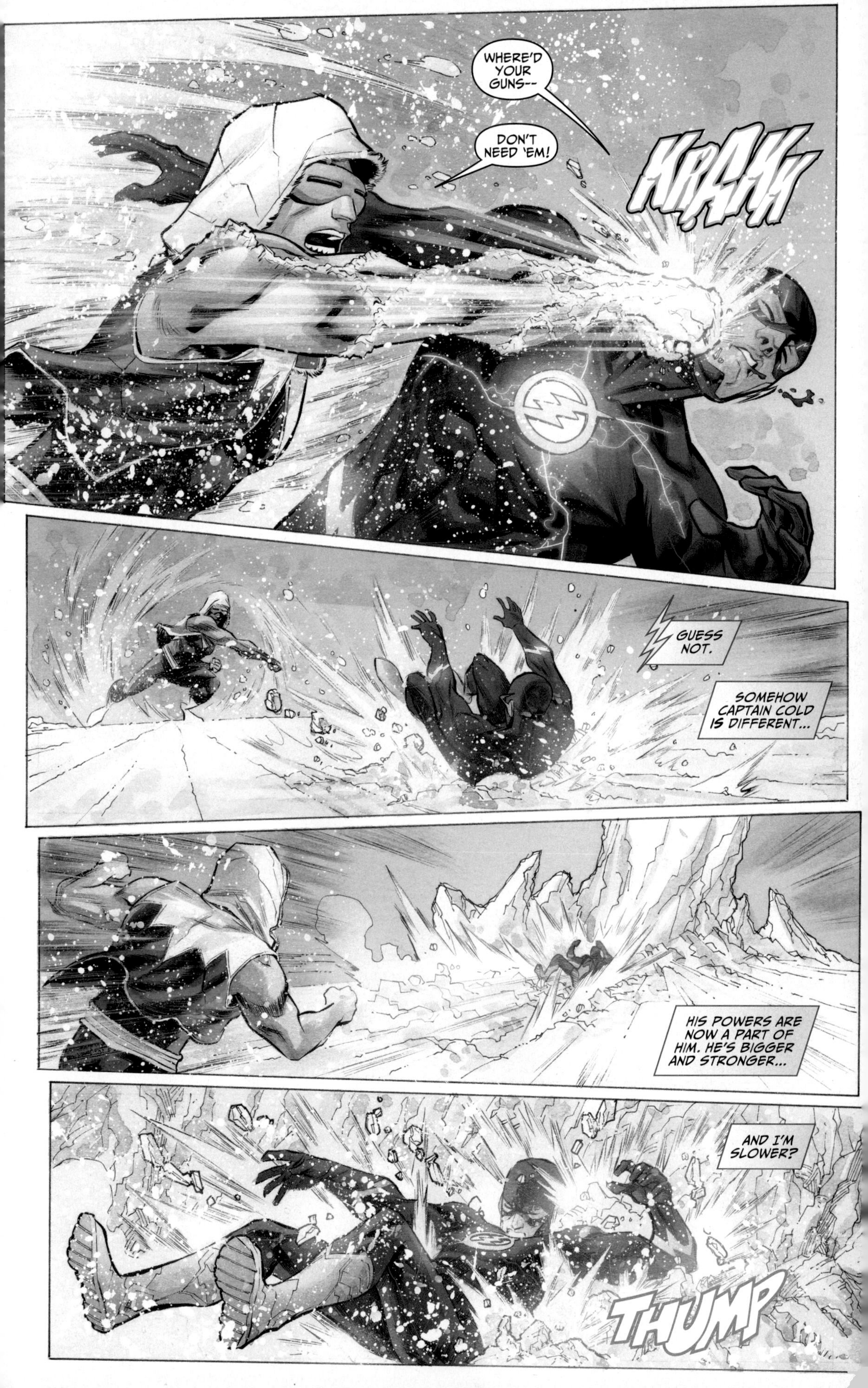
WHERE'D YOUR GUNS--
DON'T NEED 'EM!
KRAKK
GUESS NOT.
SOMEHOW CAPTAIN COLD IS DIFFERENT...
HIS POWERS ARE NOW A PART OF HIM. HE'S BIGGER AND STRONGER...
AND I'M SLOWER?
THUMP

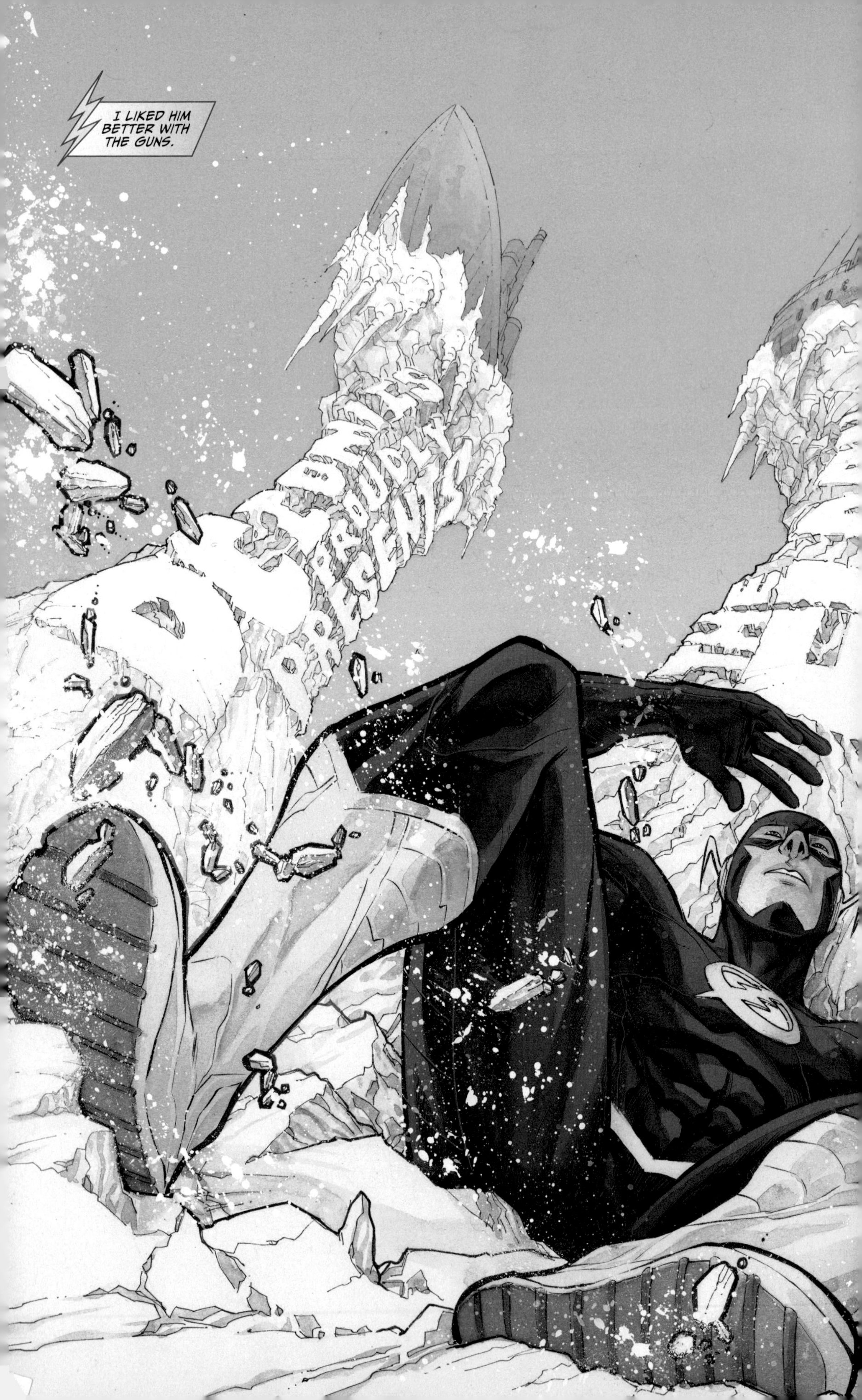
I LIKED HIM BETTER WITH THE GUNS.

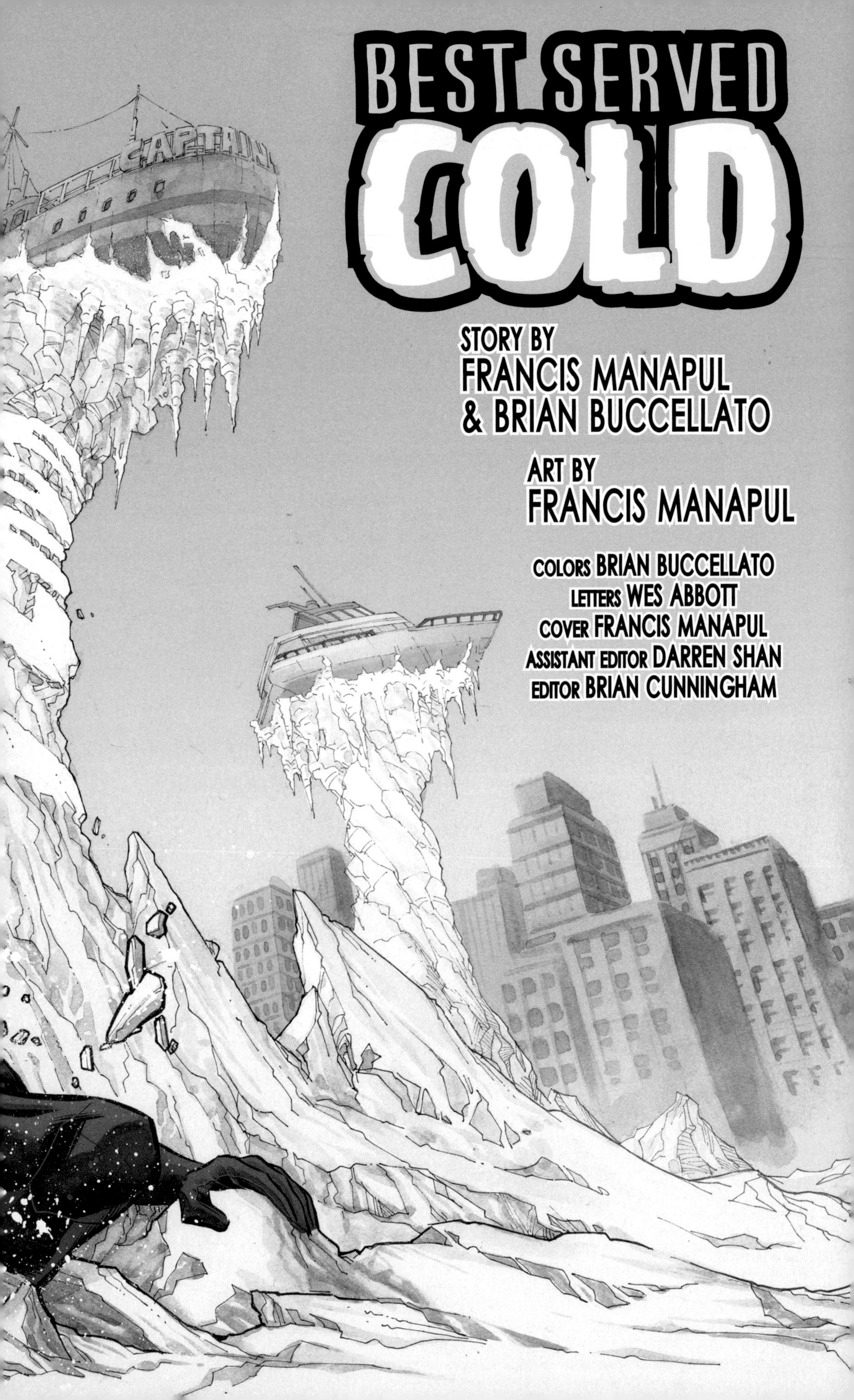
BEST SERVED
COLD
STORY BY
FRANCIS MANAPUL
& BRIAN BUCCELLATO
ART BY
FRANCIS MANAPUL
COLORS BRIAN BUCCELLATO
LETTERS WES ABBOTT
COVER FRANCIS MANAPUL
ASSISTANT EDITOR DARREN SHAN
EDITOR BRIAN CUNNINGHAM

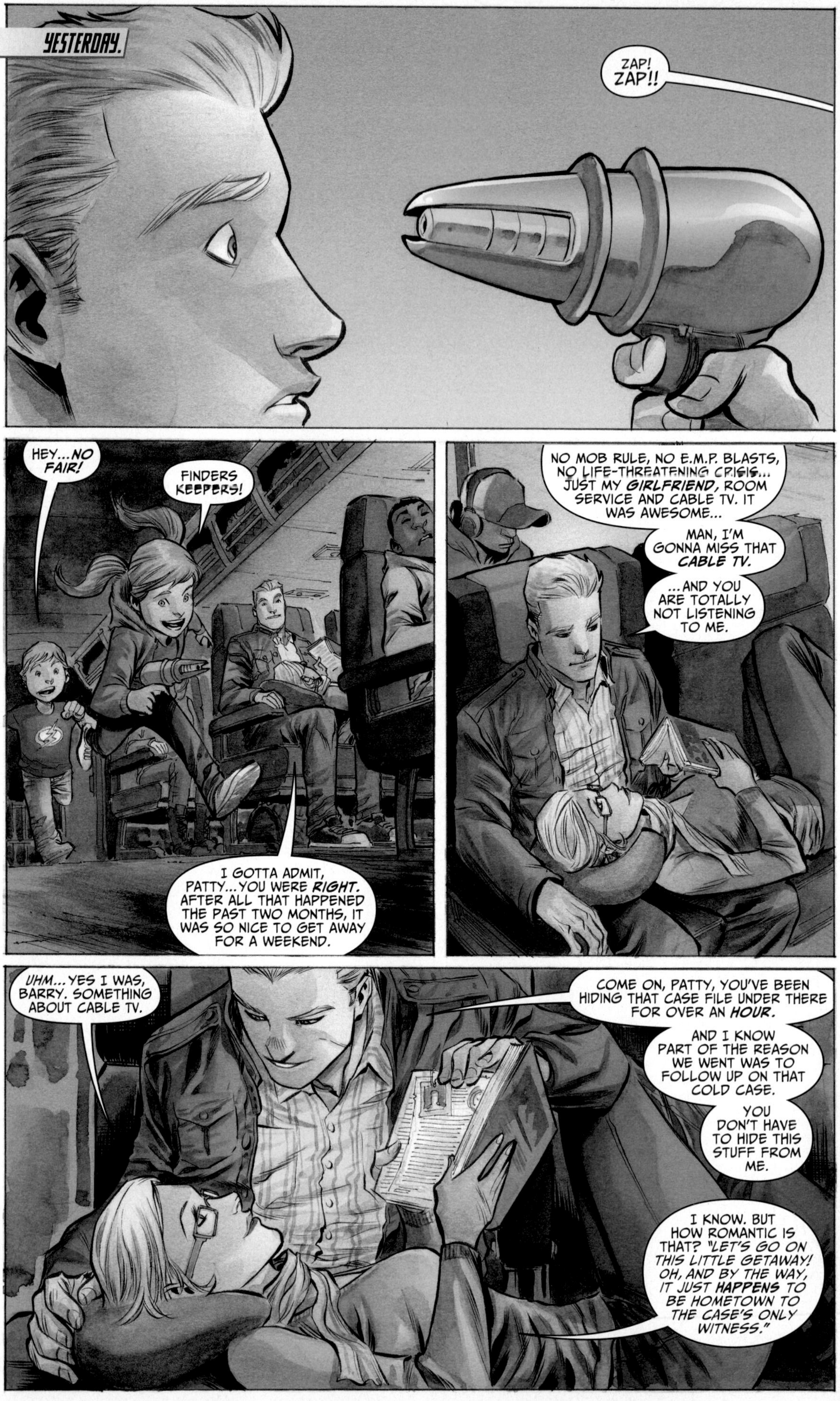
YESTERDAY.
ZAP! ZAP!!
HEY...NO FAIR!
FINDERS KEEPERS!
I GOTTA ADMIT, PATTY...YOU WERE RIGHT. AFTER ALL THAT HAPPENED THE PAST TWO MONTHS, IT WAS SO NICE TO GET AWAY FOR A WEEKEND.
NO MOB RULE, NO E.M.P. BLASTS, NO LIFE-THREATENING CRISIS... JUST MY GIRLFRIEND, ROOM SERVICE AND CABLE TV. IT WAS AWESOME...
MAN, I'M GONNA MISS THAT CABLE TV.
...AND YOU ARE TOTALLY NOT LISTENING TO ME.
UHM...YES I WAS, BARRY. SOMETHING ABOUT CABLE TV.
COME ON, PATTY, YOU'VE BEEN HIDING THAT CASE FILE UNDER THERE FOR OVER AN HOUR.
AND I KNOW PART OF THE REASON WE WENT WAS TO FOLLOW UP ON THAT COLD CASE.
YOU DON'T HAVE TO HIDE THIS STUFF FROM ME.
I KNOW. BUT HOW ROMANTIC IS THAT? "LET'S GO ON THIS LITTLE GETAWAY! OH, AND BY THE WAY, IT JUST HAPPENS TO BE HOMETOWN TO THE CASE'S ONLY WITNESS."

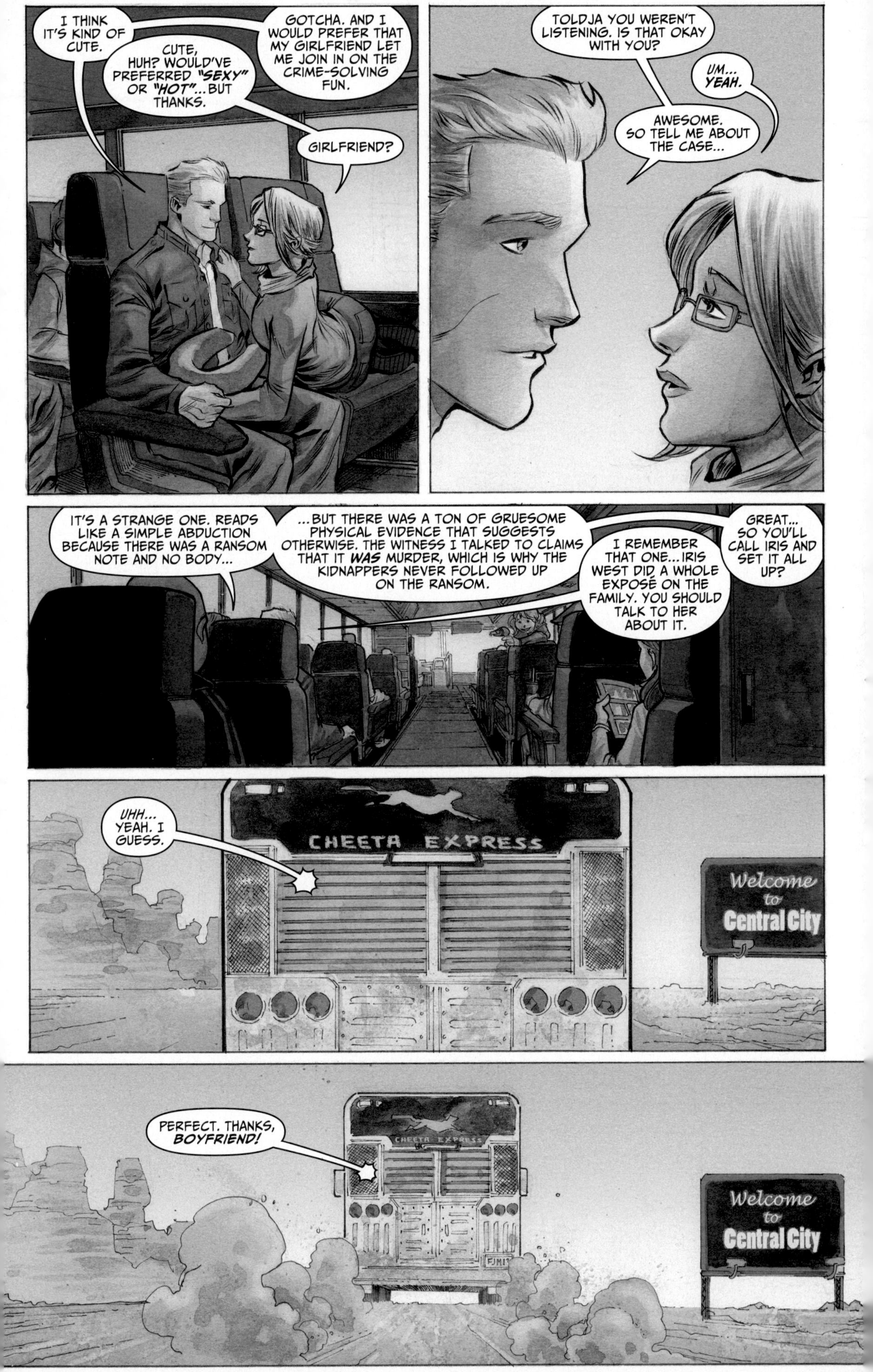
I THINK IT'S KIND OF CUTE.
GOTCHA. AND I WOULD PREFER THAT MY GIRLFRIEND LET ME JOIN IN ON THE CRIME-SOLVING FUN.
CUTE, HUH? WOULD'VE PREFERRED "SEXY" OR "HOT"... BUT THANKS.
GIRLFRIEND?
TOLDJA YOU WEREN'T LISTENING. IS THAT OKAY WITH YOU?
UM... YEAH.
AWESOME. SO TELL ME ABOUT THE CASE...
IT'S A STRANGE ONE. READS LIKE A SIMPLE ABDUCTION BECAUSE THERE WAS A RANSOM NOTE AND NO BODY...
...BUT THERE WAS A TON OF GRUESOME PHYSICAL EVIDENCE THAT SUGGESTS OTHERWISE. THE WITNESS I TALKED TO CLAIMS THAT IT WAS MURDER, WHICH IS WHY THE KIDNAPPERS NEVER FOLLOWED UP ON THE RANSOM.
I REMEMBER THAT ONE... IRIS WEST DID A WHOLE EXPOSÉ ON THE FAMILY. YOU SHOULD TALK TO HER ABOUT IT.
GREAT... SO YOU'LL CALL IRIS AND SET IT ALL UP?
CHEETA EXPRESS
UHH... YEAH. I GUESS.
Welcome to Central City
PERFECT. THANKS, BOYFRIEND!
CHEETA EXPRESS
Welcome to Central City

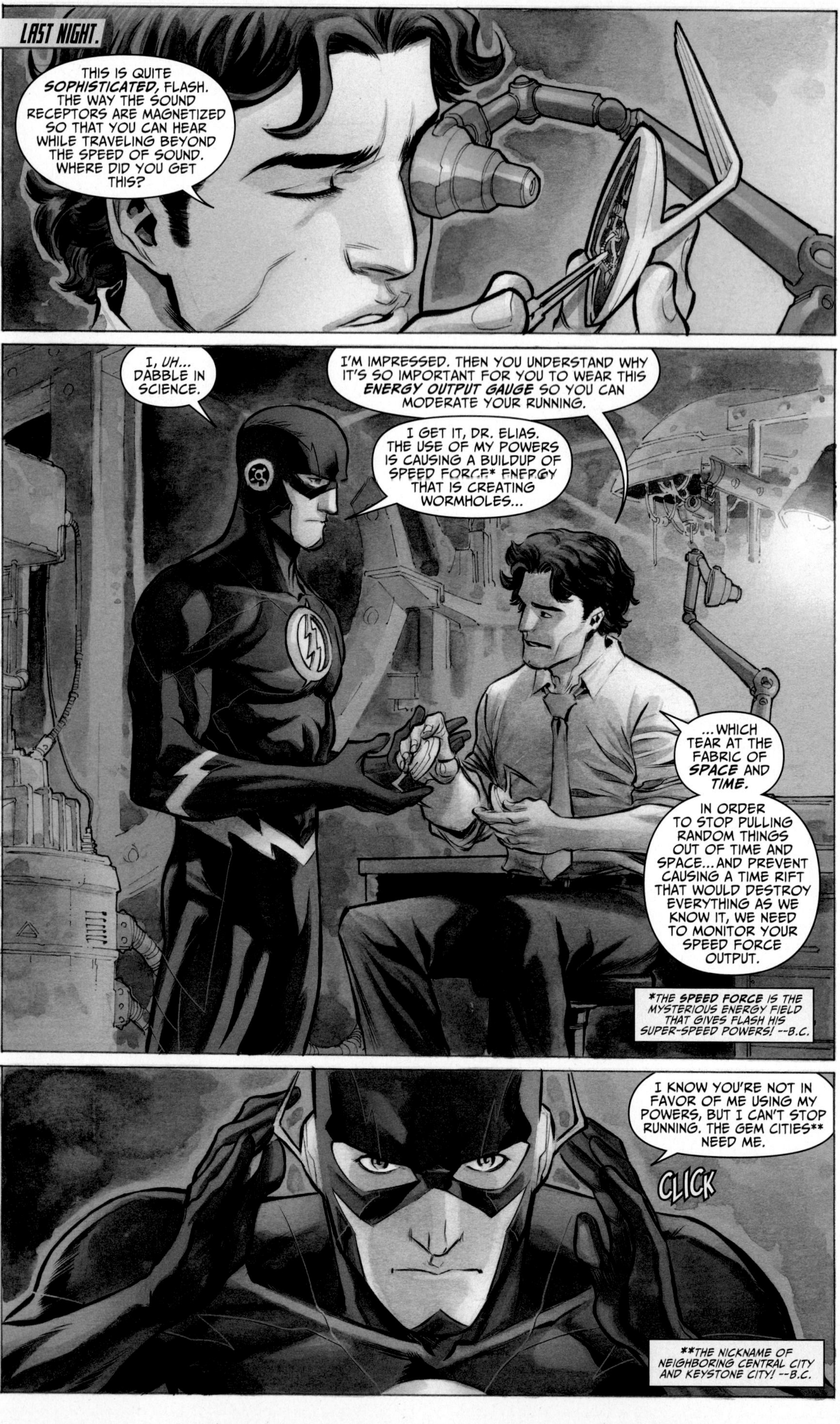
LAST NIGHT.
THIS IS QUITE SOPHISTICATED, FLASH. THE WAY THE SOUND RECEPTORS ARE MAGNETIZED SO THAT YOU CAN HEAR WHILE TRAVELING BEYOND THE SPEED OF SOUND. WHERE DID YOU GET THIS?
I, UH... DABBLE IN SCIENCE.
I'M IMPRESSED. THEN YOU UNDERSTAND WHY IT'S SO IMPORTANT FOR YOU TO WEAR THIS ENERGY OUTPUT GAUGE SO YOU CAN MODERATE YOUR RUNNING.
I GET IT, DR. ELIAS. THE USE OF MY POWERS IS CAUSING A BUILDUP OF SPEED FORCE* ENERGY THAT IS CREATING WORMHOLES...
...WHICH TEAR AT THE FABRIC OF SPACE AND TIME.
IN ORDER TO STOP PULLING RANDOM THINGS OUT OF TIME AND SPACE...AND PREVENT CAUSING A TIME RIFT THAT WOULD DESTROY EVERYTHING AS WE KNOW IT, WE NEED TO MONITOR YOUR SPEED FORCE OUTPUT.
*THE SPEED FORCE IS THE MYSTERIOUS ENERGY FIELD THAT GIVES FLASH HIS SUPER-SPEED POWERS! --B.C.
I KNOW YOU'RE NOT IN FAVOR OF ME USING MY POWERS, BUT I CAN'T STOP RUNNING. THE GEM CITIES** NEED ME.
CLICK
**THE NICKNAME OF NEIGHBORING CENTRAL CITY AND KEYSTONE CITY! --B.C.

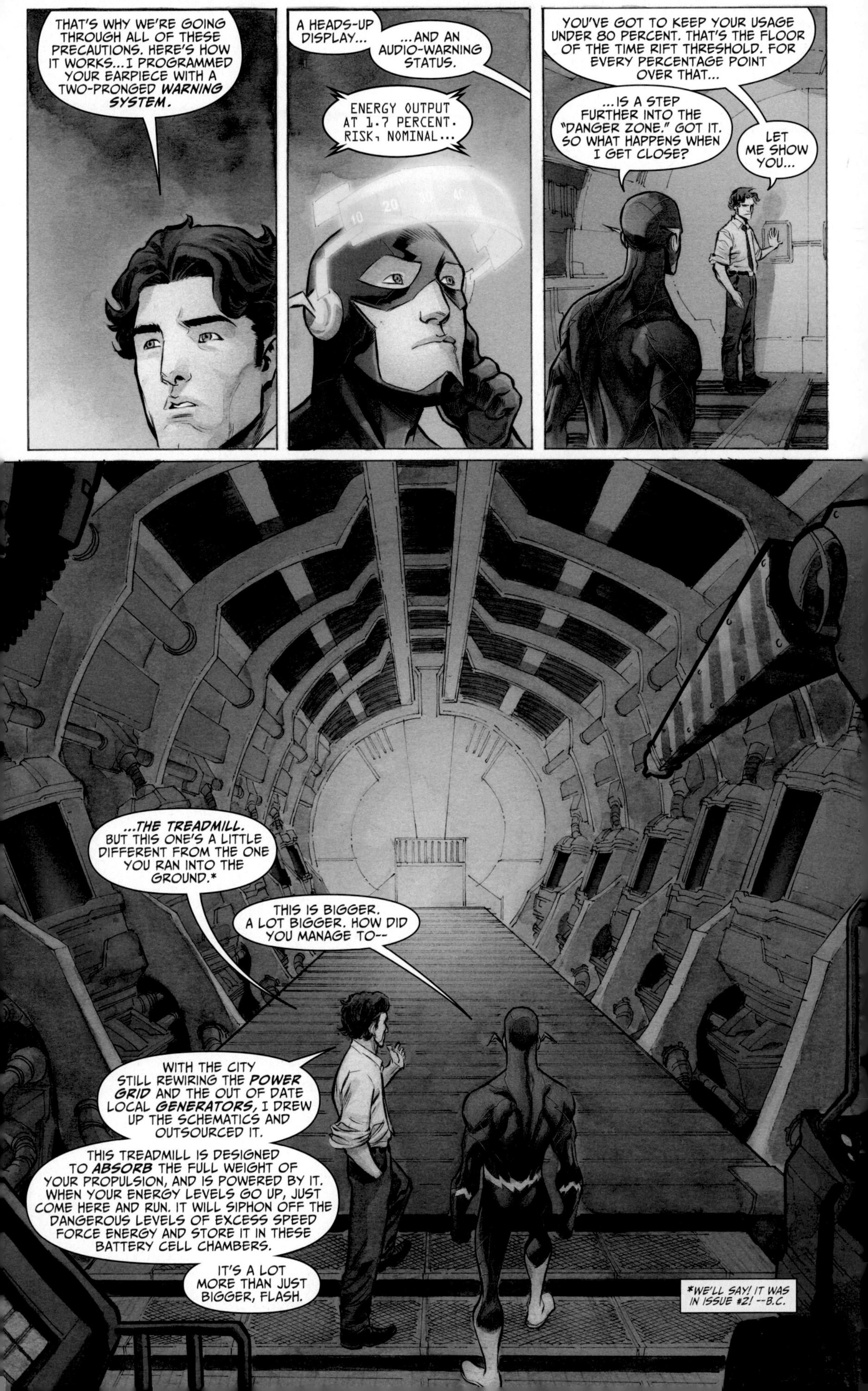
THAT'S WHY WE'RE GOING THROUGH ALL OF THESE PRECAUTIONS. HERE'S HOW IT WORKS... I PROGRAMMED YOUR EARPIECE WITH A TWO-PRONGED WARNING SYSTEM.
A HEADS-UP DISPLAY...
...AND AN AUDIO-WARNING STATUS.
ENERGY OUTPUT AT 1.7 PERCENT. RISK, NOMINAL...
10 20 30 40
YOU'VE GOT TO KEEP YOUR USAGE UNDER 80 PERCENT. THAT'S THE FLOOR OF THE TIME RIFT THRESHOLD. FOR EVERY PERCENTAGE POINT OVER THAT...
...IS A STEP FURTHER INTO THE "DANGER ZONE." GOT IT. SO WHAT HAPPENS WHEN I GET CLOSE?
LET ME SHOW YOU...
...THE TREADMILL. BUT THIS ONE'S A LITTLE DIFFERENT FROM THE ONE YOU RAN INTO THE GROUND.*
THIS IS BIGGER. A LOT BIGGER. HOW DID YOU MANAGE TO--
WITH THE CITY STILL REWIRING THE POWER GRID AND THE OUT OF DATE LOCAL GENERATORS, I DREW UP THE SCHEMATICS AND OUTSOURCED IT.
THIS TREADMILL IS DESIGNED TO ABSORB THE FULL WEIGHT OF YOUR PROPULSION, AND IS POWERED BY IT. WHEN YOUR ENERGY LEVELS GO UP, JUST COME HERE AND RUN. IT WILL SIPHON OFF THE DANGEROUS LEVELS OF EXCESS SPEED FORCE ENERGY AND STORE IT IN THESE BATTERY CELL CHAMBERS.
IT'S A LOT MORE THAN JUST BIGGER, FLASH.
*WE'LL SAY! IT WAS IN ISSUE #2! --B.C.

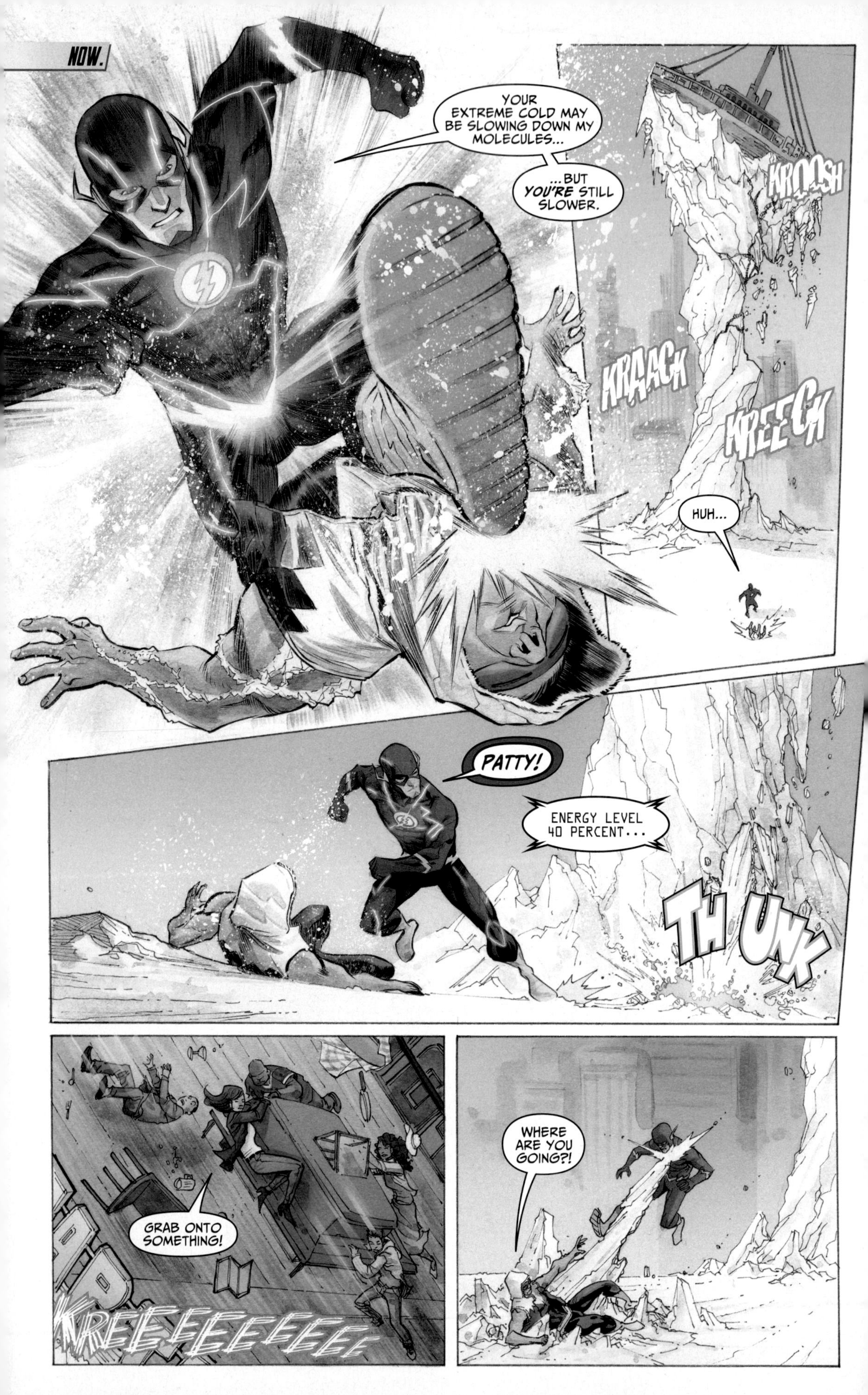
NOW.
YOUR EXTREME COLD MAY BE SLOWING DOWN MY MOLECULES...
...BUT YOU'RE STILL SLOWER.
KROOSH
KRAACK
KREECH
HUH...
PATTY!
ENERGY LEVEL 40 PERCENT...
THUNK
GRAB ONTO SOMETHING!
KREEEEEEEEEEEE
WHERE ARE YOU GOING?!

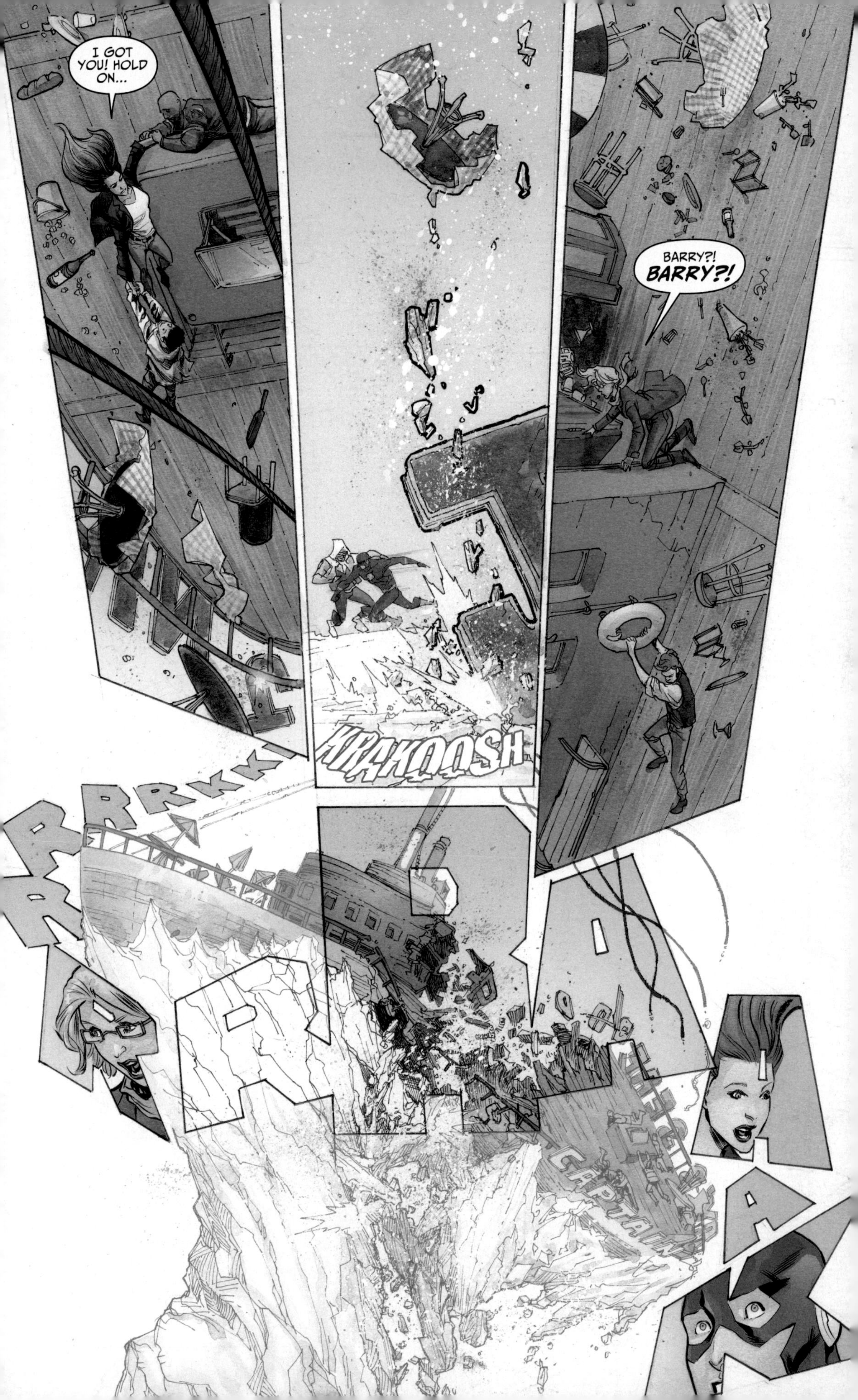
I GOT YOU! HOLD ON...
KRAKOOSH
BARRY?! BARRY?!
RRRKK
CAPTAIN

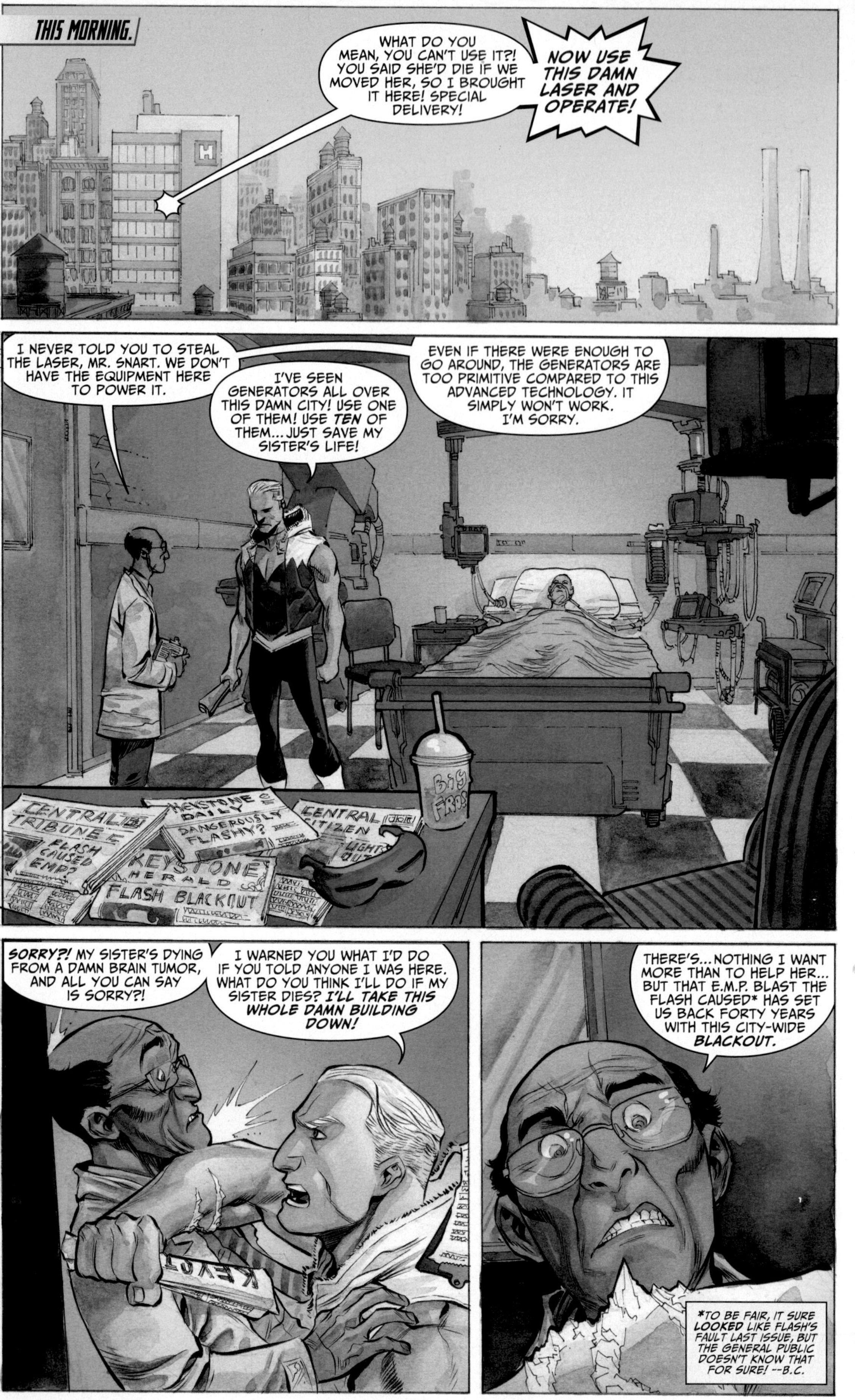

THIS MORNING.
WHAT DO YOU MEAN, YOU CAN'T USE IT?! YOU SAID SHE'D DIE IF WE MOVED HER, SO I BROUGHT IT HERE! SPECIAL DELIVERY!
NOW USE THIS DAMN LASER AND OPERATE!
I NEVER TOLD YOU TO STEAL THE LASER, MR. SNART. WE DON'T HAVE THE EQUIPMENT HERE TO POWER IT.
I'VE SEEN GENERATORS ALL OVER THIS DAMN CITY! USE ONE OF THEM! USE *TEN* OF THEM... JUST SAVE MY SISTER'S LIFE!
EVEN IF THERE WERE ENOUGH TO GO AROUND, THE GENERATORS ARE TOO PRIMITIVE COMPARED TO THIS ADVANCED TECHNOLOGY. IT SIMPLY WON'T WORK. I'M SORRY.
CENTRAL TRIBUNE
FLASH CAUSED EMP?
KEYSTONE DAILY
DANGEROUSLY FLASHY?
CENTRAL CITIZEN
KEYSTONE HERALD
FLASH BLACKOUT
SORRY?! MY SISTER'S DYING FROM A DAMN BRAIN TUMOR, AND ALL YOU CAN SAY IS SORRY?!
I WARNED YOU WHAT I'D DO IF YOU TOLD ANYONE I WAS HERE. WHAT DO YOU THINK I'LL DO IF MY SISTER DIES? ***I'LL TAKE THIS WHOLE DAMN BUILDING DOWN!***
THERE'S... NOTHING I WANT MORE THAN TO HELP HER... BUT THAT E.M.P. BLAST THE FLASH CAUSED* HAS SET US BACK FORTY YEARS WITH THIS CITY-WIDE ***BLACKOUT.***
*TO BE FAIR, IT SURE ***LOOKED*** LIKE FLASH'S FAULT LAST ISSUE, BUT THE GENERAL PUBLIC DOESN'T KNOW THAT FOR SURE! --B.C.

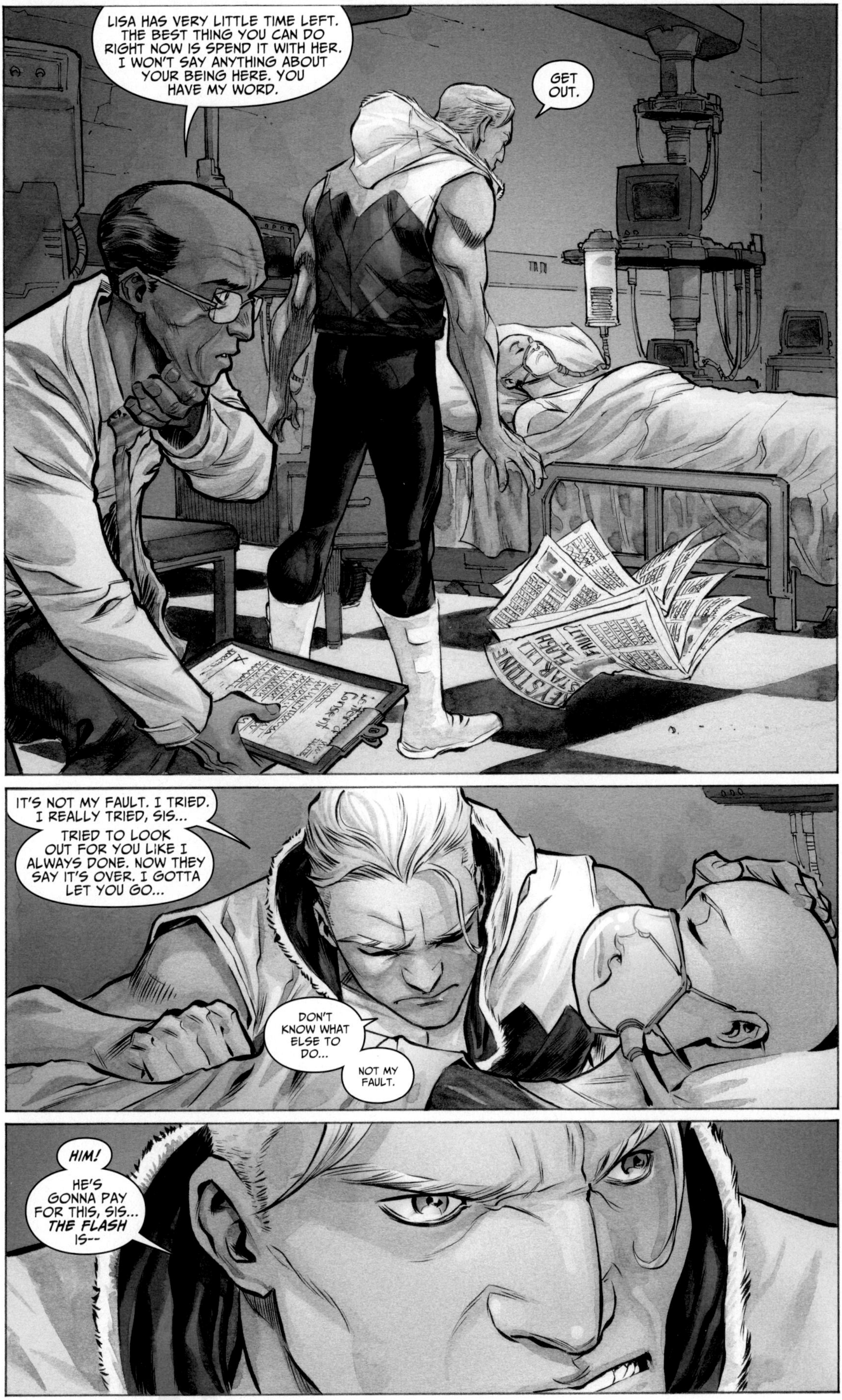
LISA HAS VERY LITTLE TIME LEFT. THE BEST THING YOU CAN DO RIGHT NOW IS SPEND IT WITH HER. I WON'T SAY ANYTHING ABOUT YOUR BEING HERE. YOU HAVE MY WORD.
GET OUT.
IT'S NOT MY FAULT. I TRIED. I REALLY TRIED, SIS...
TRIED TO LOOK OUT FOR YOU LIKE I ALWAYS DONE. NOW THEY SAY IT'S OVER. I GOTTA LET YOU GO...
DON'T KNOW WHAT ELSE TO DO...
NOT MY FAULT.
HIM!
HE'S GONNA PAY FOR THIS, SIS... THE FLASH IS--

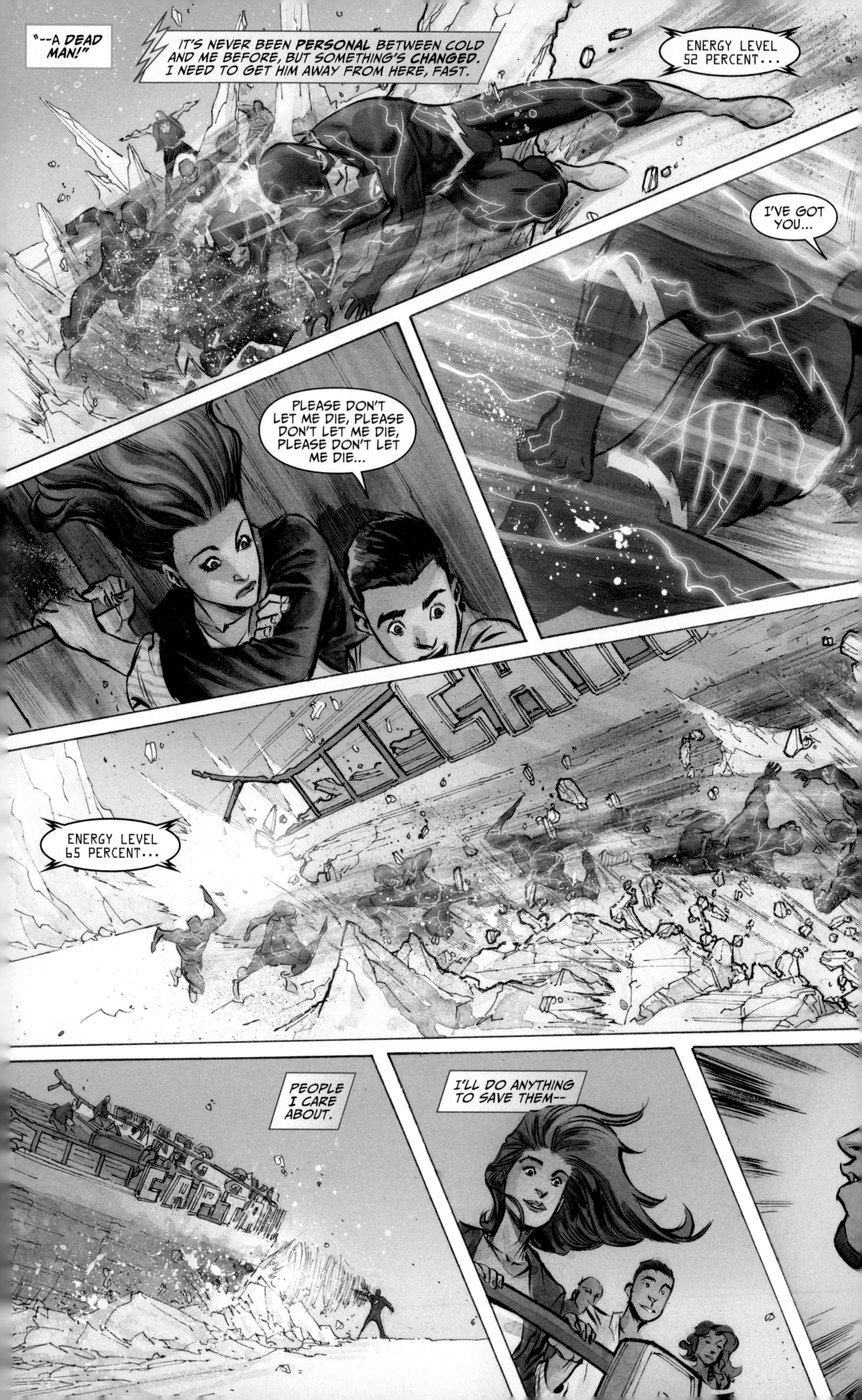
"--A DEAD MAN!"
IT'S NEVER BEEN PERSONAL BETWEEN COLD AND ME BEFORE, BUT SOMETHING'S CHANGED. I NEED TO GET HIM AWAY FROM HERE, FAST.
ENERGY LEVEL 52 PERCENT...
I'VE GOT YOU...
PLEASE DON'T LET ME DIE, PLEASE DON'T LET ME DIE, PLEASE DON'T LET ME DIE...
ENERGY LEVEL 65 PERCENT...
PEOPLE I CARE ABOUT.
I'LL DO ANYTHING TO SAVE THEM--

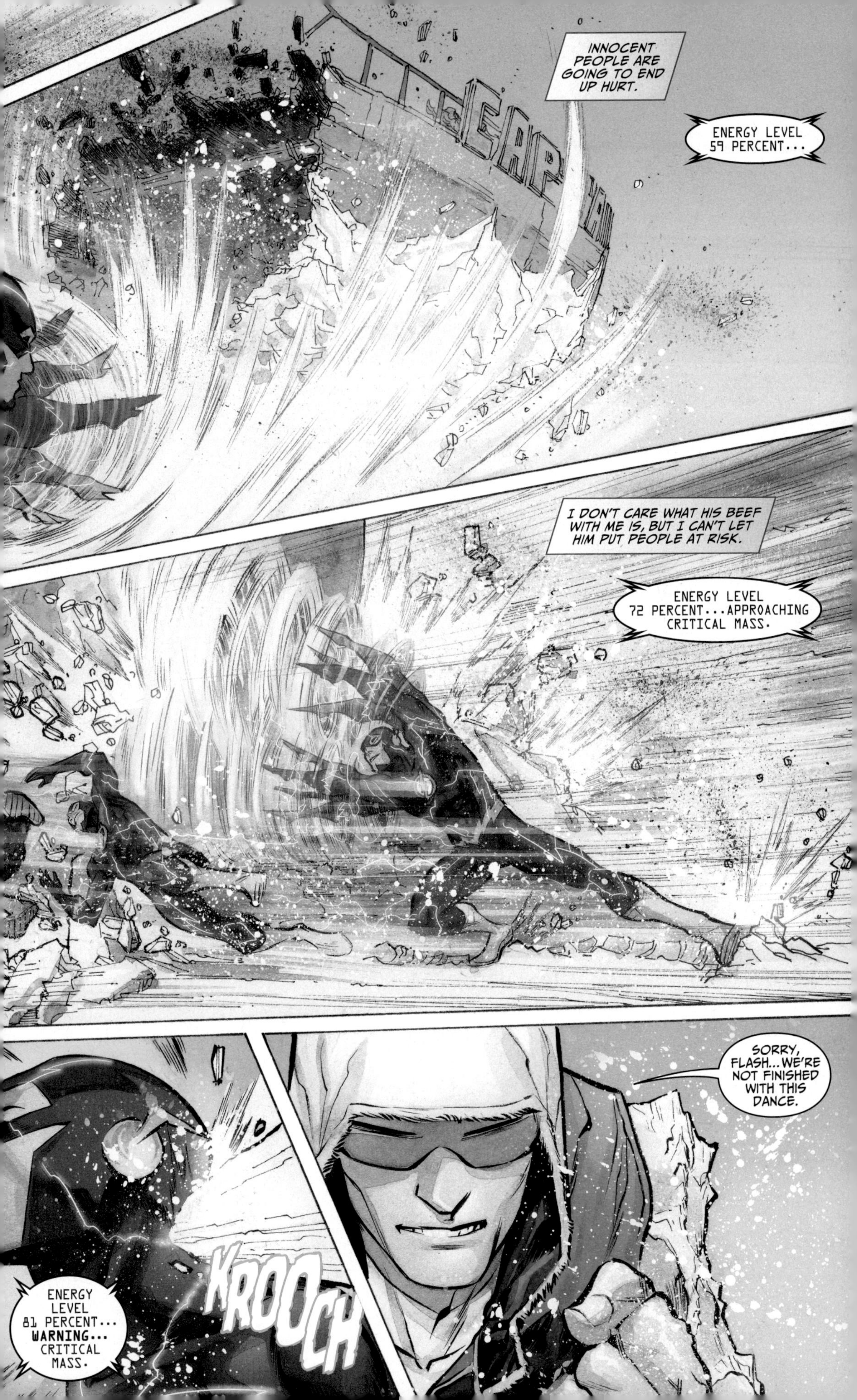
INNOCENT PEOPLE ARE GOING TO END UP HURT.
ENERGY LEVEL 59 PERCENT...
I DON'T CARE WHAT HIS BEEF WITH ME IS, BUT I CAN'T LET HIM PUT PEOPLE AT RISK.
ENERGY LEVEL 72 PERCENT...APPROACHING CRITICAL MASS.
SORRY, FLASH...WE'RE NOT FINISHED WITH THIS DANCE.
KROOCH
ENERGY LEVEL 81 PERCENT... WARNING... CRITICAL MASS.

SO WHAT DO YOU THINK, IRIS... IT WAS A MURDER, RIGHT?

PROBABLY, PATTY. BUT I HAVE TO BE HONEST, THERE'S NOT MUCH ABOUT THAT CASE THAT MAKES SENSE. I BROUGHT COPIES OF MY RESEARCH, BUT I DOUBT YOU'RE GOING TO FIND ANYTHING THE DETECTIVES DIDN'T. IT DOESN'T ADD UP.

AND YOU CAN FORGET ABOUT THE LANDLORD WHO FOUND THE NOTE. HE WENT BACK TO GUATEMALA. SUPPOSEDLY LIVES IN THE JUNGLES.

OH. THAT STINKS.

SORRY, I WISH THERE WAS MORE THAT I COULD TELL YOU.

AND I'M SORRY TO DRAG YOU OUT OF THE OFFICE ON A BUSY WORKDAY. I'M SURE YOU'VE GOT NEWS TO BREAK...

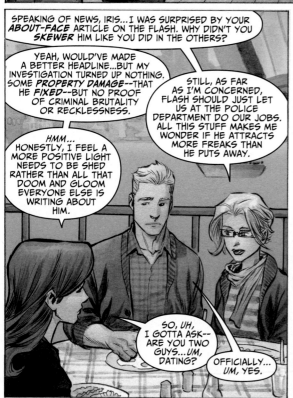

SPEAKING OF NEWS, IRIS... I WAS SURPRISED BY YOUR *ABOUT-FACE* ARTICLE ON THE FLASH. WHY DIDN'T YOU *SKEWER* HIM LIKE YOU DID IN THE OTHERS?

YEAH, WOULD'VE MADE A BETTER HEADLINE...BUT MY INVESTIGATION TURNED UP NOTHING. SOME *PROPERTY DAMAGE*--THAT HE *FIXED*--BUT NO PROOF OF CRIMINAL BRUTALITY OR RECKLESSNESS.

STILL, AS FAR AS I'M CONCERNED, FLASH SHOULD JUST LET US AT THE POLICE DEPARTMENT DO OUR JOBS. ALL THIS STUFF MAKES ME WONDER IF HE ATTRACTS MORE FREAKS THAN HE PUTS AWAY.

HMM... HONESTLY, I FEEL A MORE POSITIVE LIGHT NEEDS TO BE SHED RATHER THAN ALL THAT DOOM AND GLOOM EVERYONE ELSE IS WRITING ABOUT HIM.

SO, UH, I GOTTA ASK-- ARE YOU TWO GUYS...UM, DATING?

OFFICIALLY... UM, YES.

THAT'S... THAT'S GREAT. YOU MAKE A CUTE COUPLE. HOW LONG HAS IT BEEN?

A COUPLE MONTHS. *UHM...*EXCUSE ME, I'M GONNA USE THE BATHROOM...

SORRY, THAT WAS AWKWARD.

KIND OF HILARIOUS. YOU SEE HOW *RED* HE GOT?

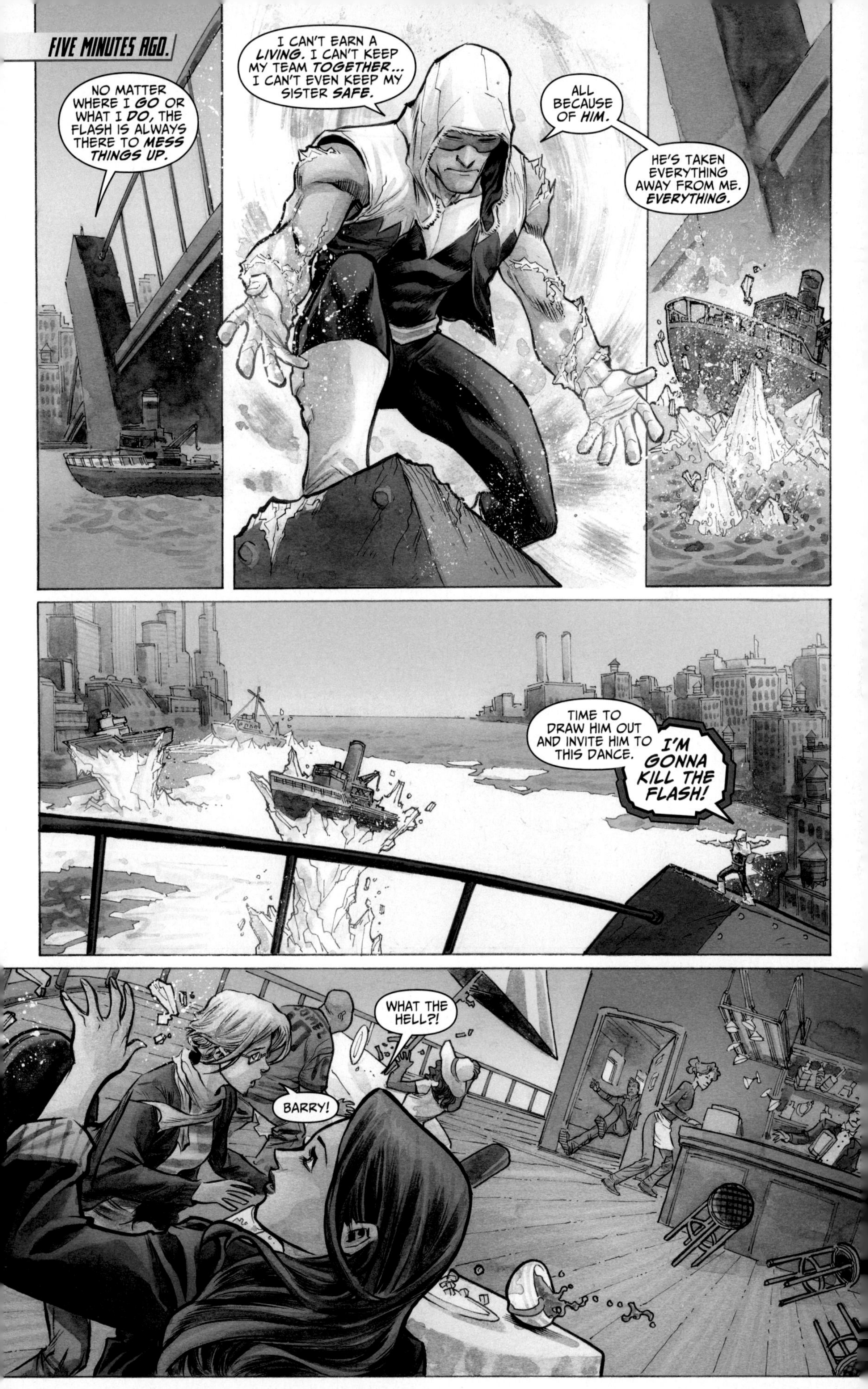
FIVE MINUTES AGO.
NO MATTER WHERE I GO OR WHAT I DO, THE FLASH IS ALWAYS THERE TO MESS THINGS UP.
I CAN'T EARN A LIVING. I CAN'T KEEP MY TEAM TOGETHER... I CAN'T EVEN KEEP MY SISTER SAFE.
ALL BECAUSE OF HIM.
HE'S TAKEN EVERYTHING AWAY FROM ME. EVERYTHING.
TIME TO DRAW HIM OUT AND INVITE HIM TO THIS DANCE.
I'M GONNA KILL THE FLASH!
WHAT THE HELL?!
BARRY!

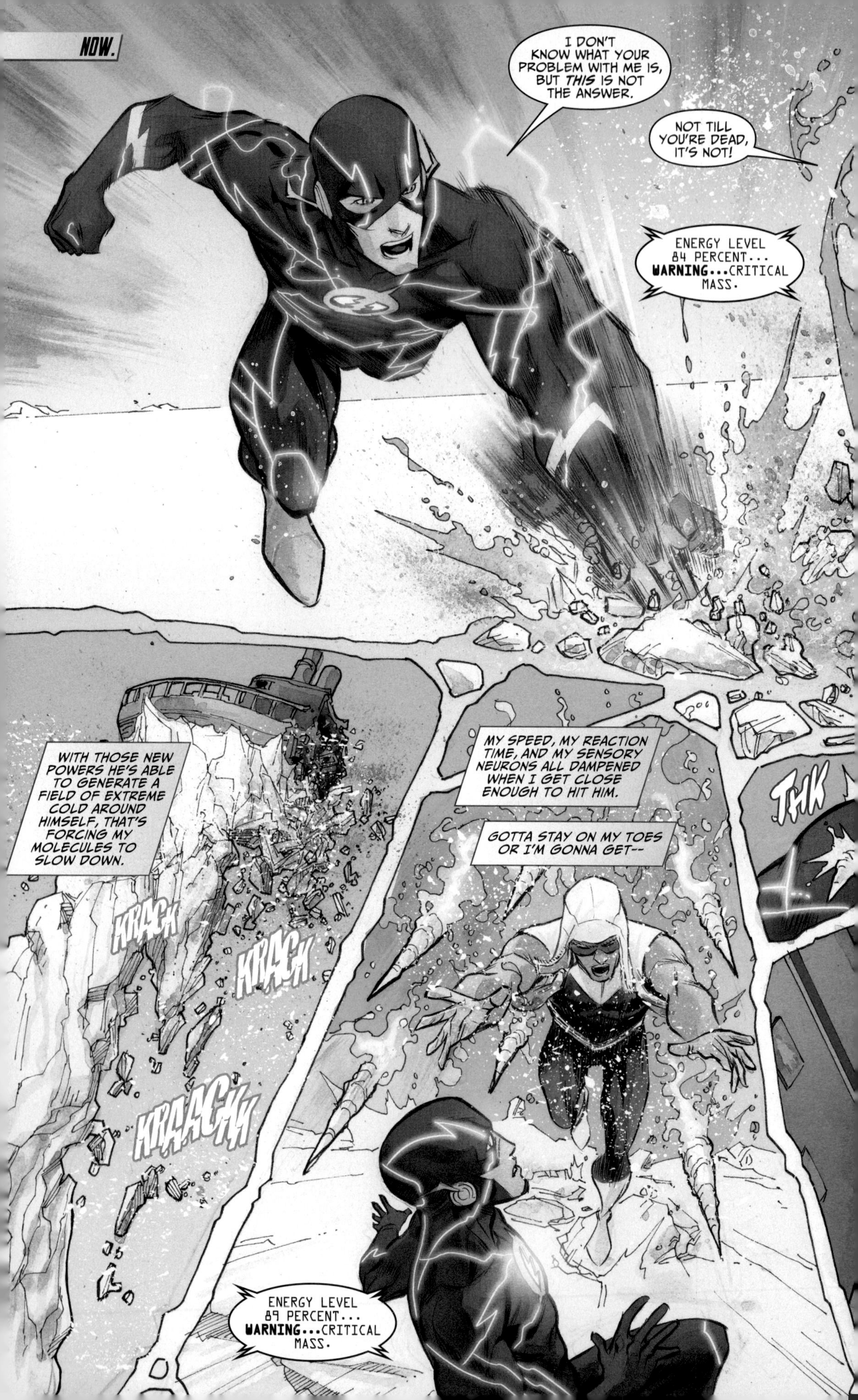
NOW.
I DON'T KNOW WHAT YOUR PROBLEM WITH ME IS, BUT THIS IS NOT THE ANSWER.
NOT TILL YOU'RE DEAD, IT'S NOT!
ENERGY LEVEL 84 PERCENT... WARNING...CRITICAL MASS.
WITH THOSE NEW POWERS HE'S ABLE TO GENERATE A FIELD OF EXTREME COLD AROUND HIMSELF, THAT'S FORCING MY MOLECULES TO SLOW DOWN.
KRACK
KRACK
KRAACKK
MY SPEED, MY REACTION TIME, AND MY SENSORY NEURONS ALL DAMPENED WHEN I GET CLOSE ENOUGH TO HIT HIM.
GOTTA STAY ON MY TOES OR I'M GONNA GET--
THK
ENERGY LEVEL 89 PERCENT... WARNING...CRITICAL MASS.

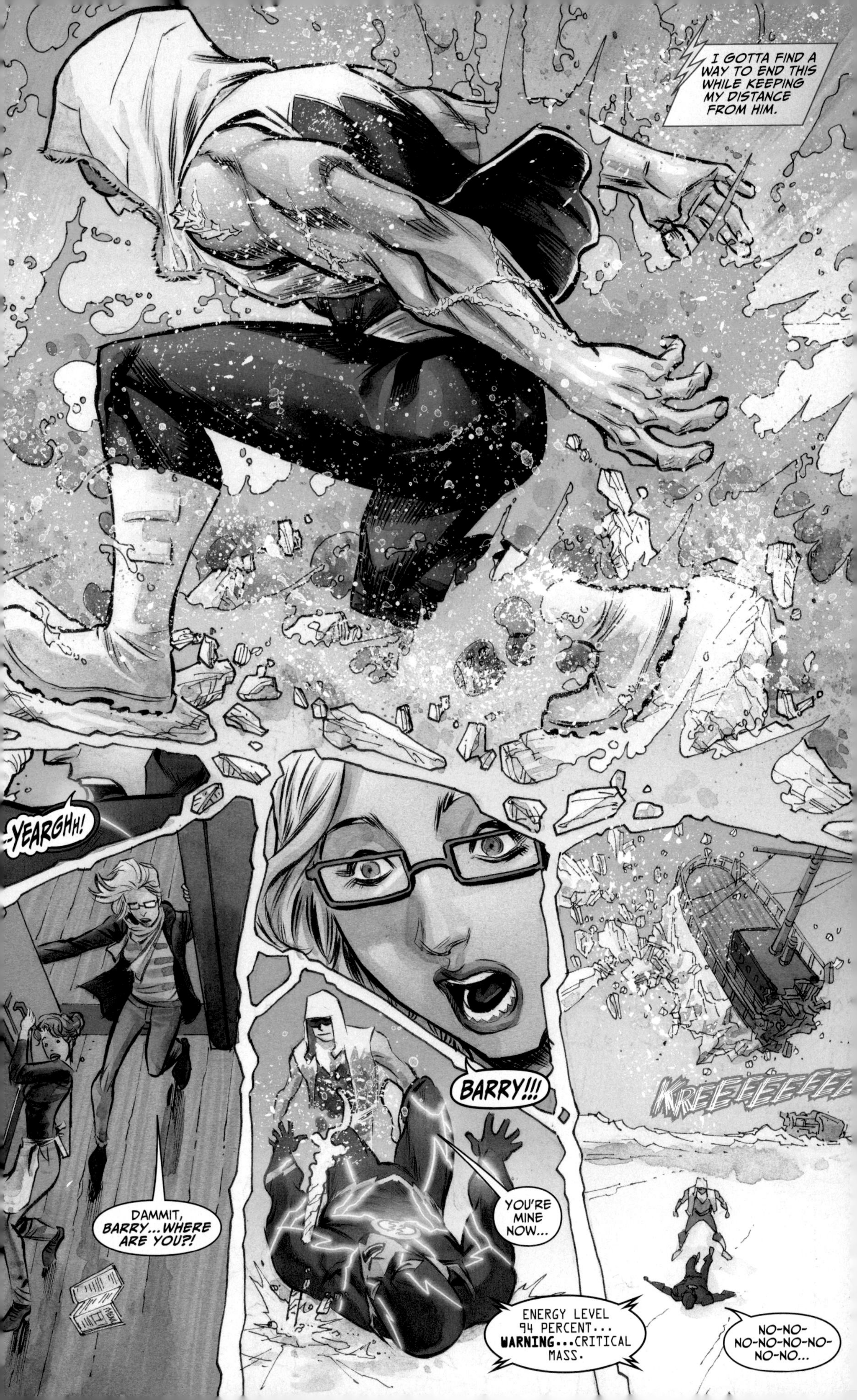
I GOTTA FIND A WAY TO END THIS WHILE KEEPING MY DISTANCE FROM HIM.
-YEARGHH!
DAMMIT, BARRY... WHERE ARE YOU?!
BARRY!!!
YOU'RE MINE NOW...
ENERGY LEVEL 94 PERCENT... WARNING...CRITICAL MASS.
KREEEEEEEE
NO-NO-NO-NO-NO-NO-NO-NO...

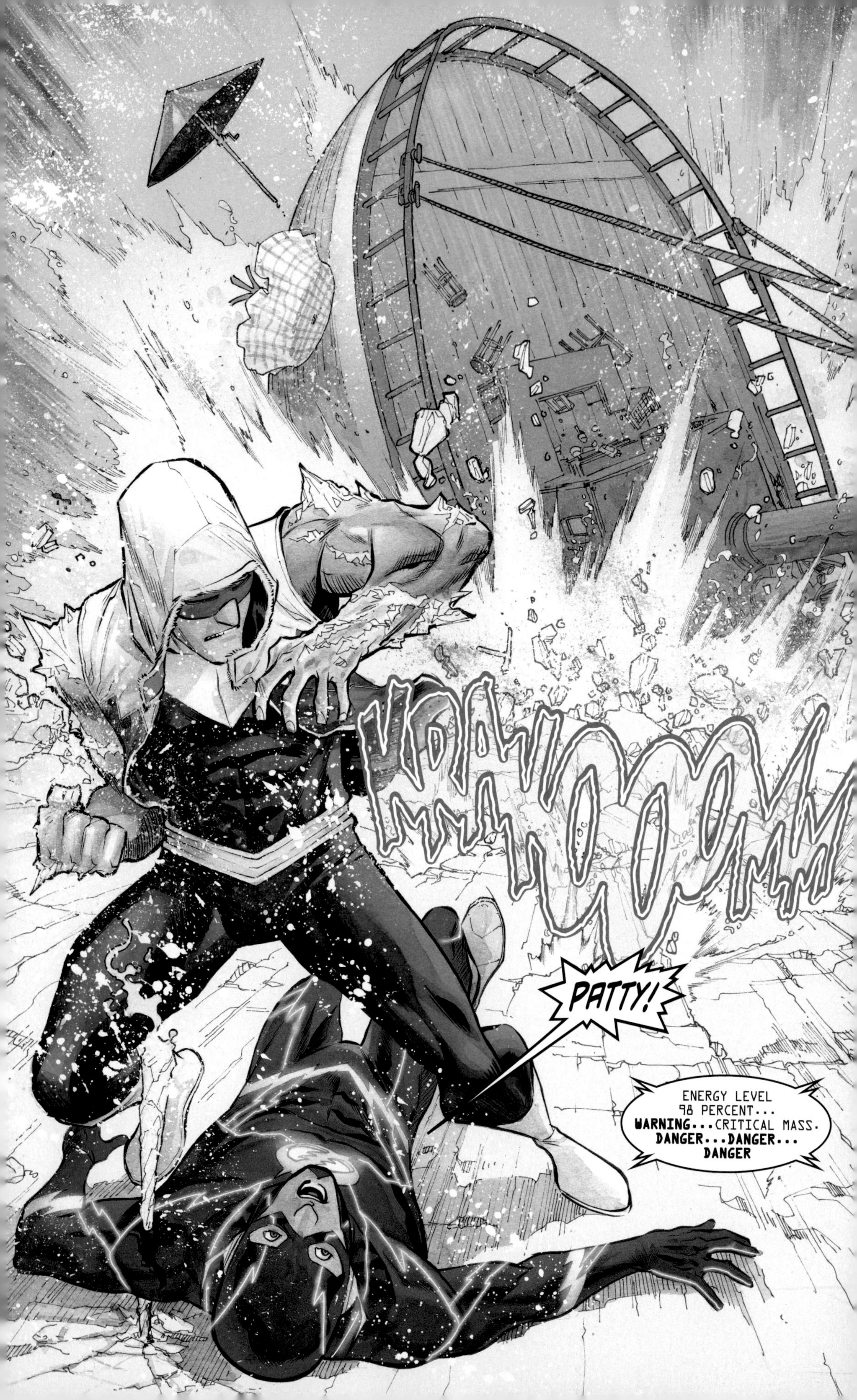
VRAWOOOMM
PATTY!
ENERGY LEVEL
98 PERCENT...
WARNING...CRITICAL MASS.
DANGER...DANGER...
DANGER

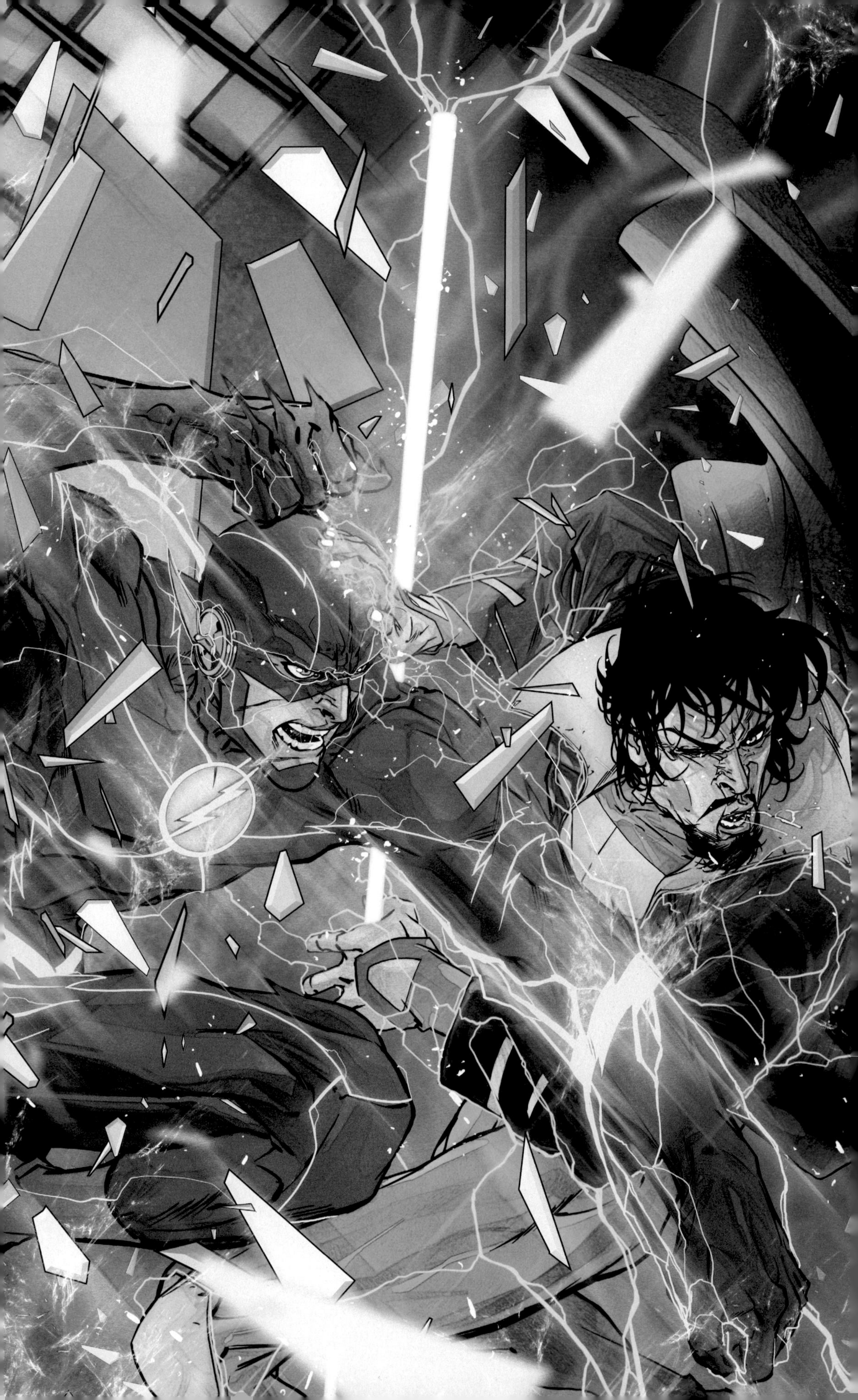

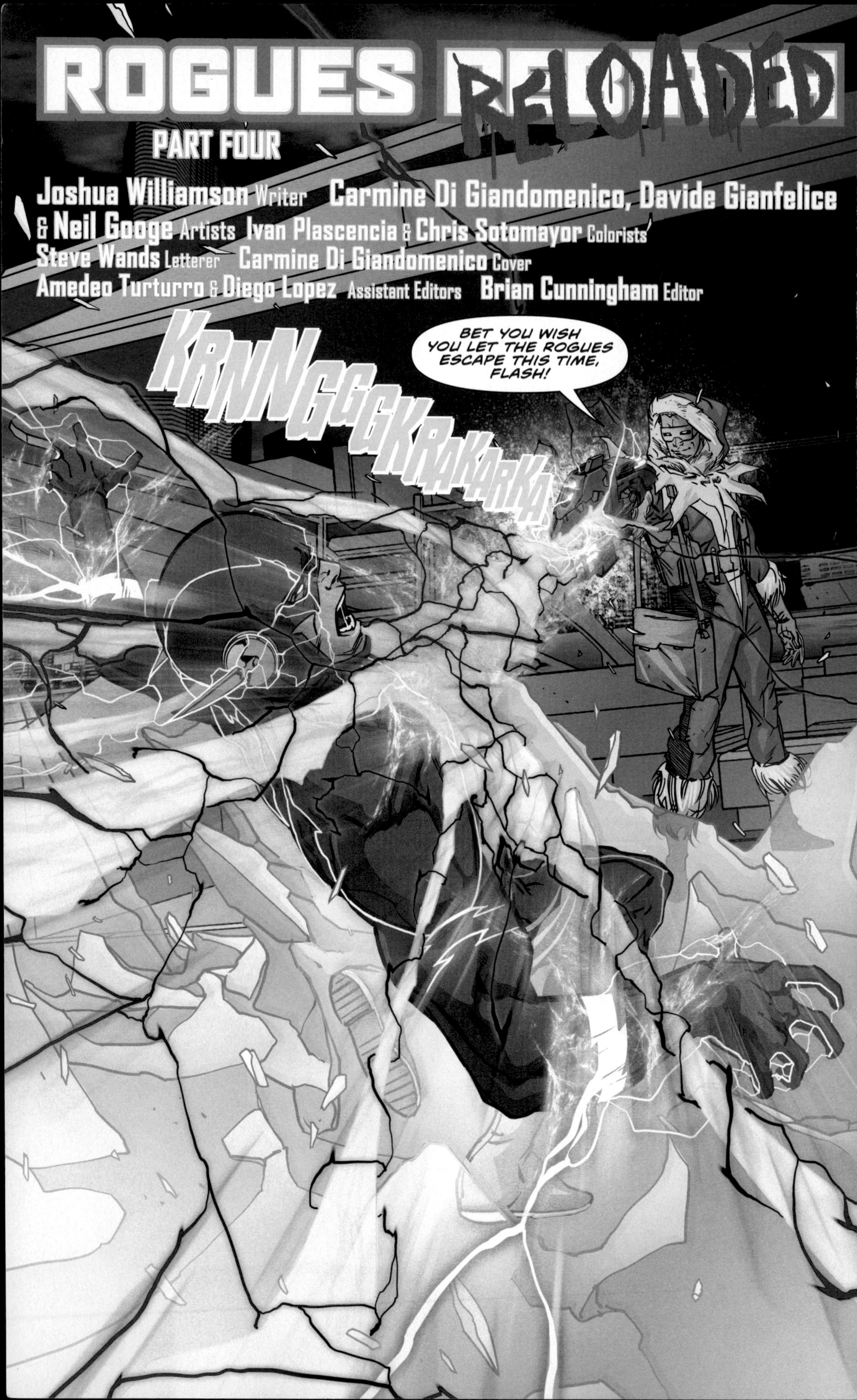
ROGUES RELOADED
PART FOUR
Joshua Williamson Writer Carmine Di Giandomenico, Davide Gianfelice & Neil Googe Artists Ivan Plascencia & Chris Sotomayor Colorists
Steve Wands Letterer Carmine Di Giandomenico Cover
Amedeo Turturro & Diego Lopez Assistant Editors Brian Cunningham Editor
KRNNGGGKRAKARKA
BET YOU WISH YOU LET THE ROGUES ESCAPE THIS TIME, FLASH!

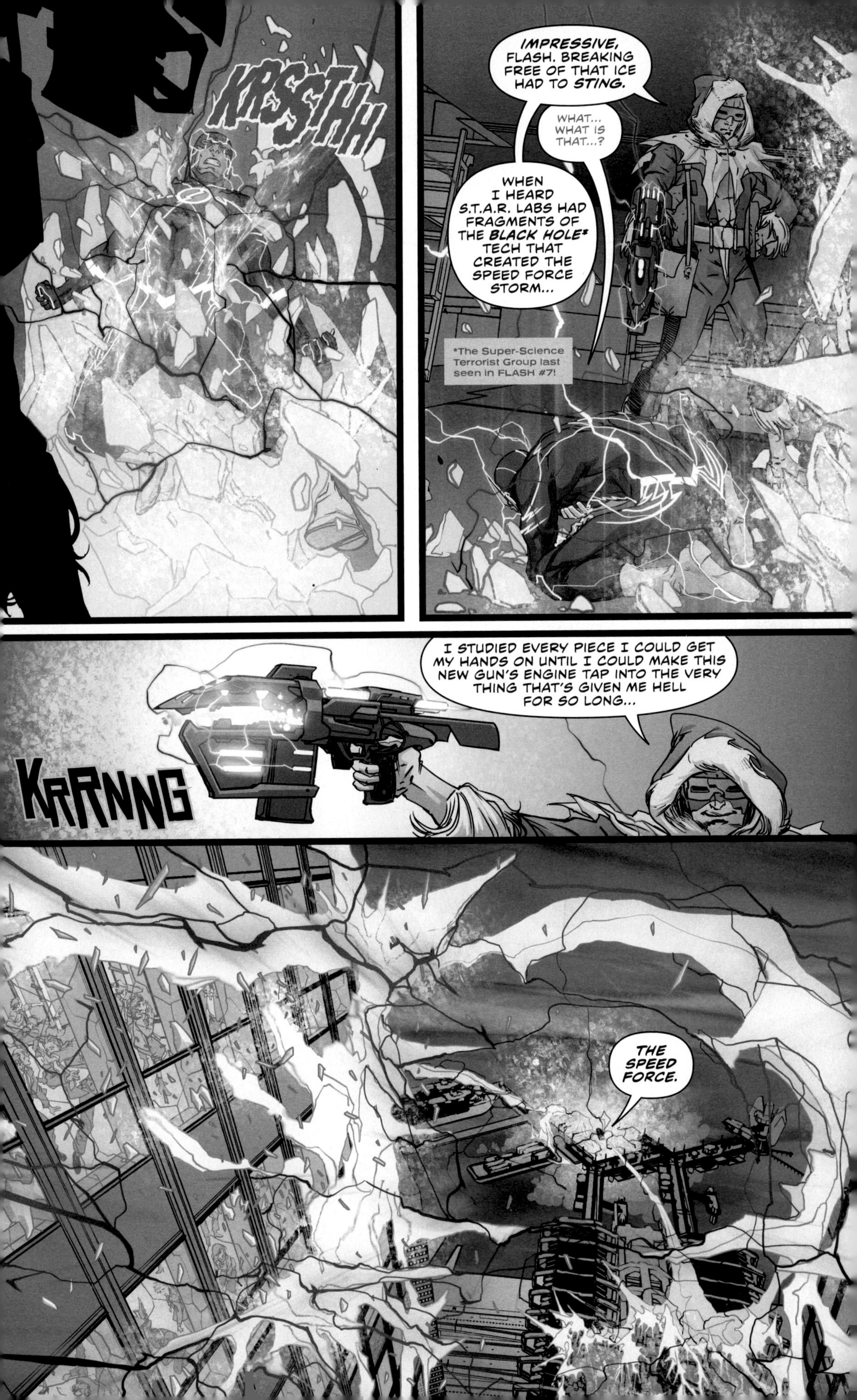
KRSSTHH!
IMPRESSIVE, FLASH. BREAKING FREE OF THAT ICE HAD TO STING.
WHAT... WHAT IS THAT...?
WHEN I HEARD S.T.A.R. LABS HAD FRAGMENTS OF THE BLACK HOLE* TECH THAT CREATED THE SPEED FORCE STORM...
*The Super-Science Terrorist Group last seen in FLASH #7!
I STUDIED EVERY PIECE I COULD GET MY HANDS ON UNTIL I COULD MAKE THIS NEW GUN'S ENGINE TAP INTO THE VERY THING THAT'S GIVEN ME HELL FOR SO LONG...
KRRNNG
THE SPEED FORCE.

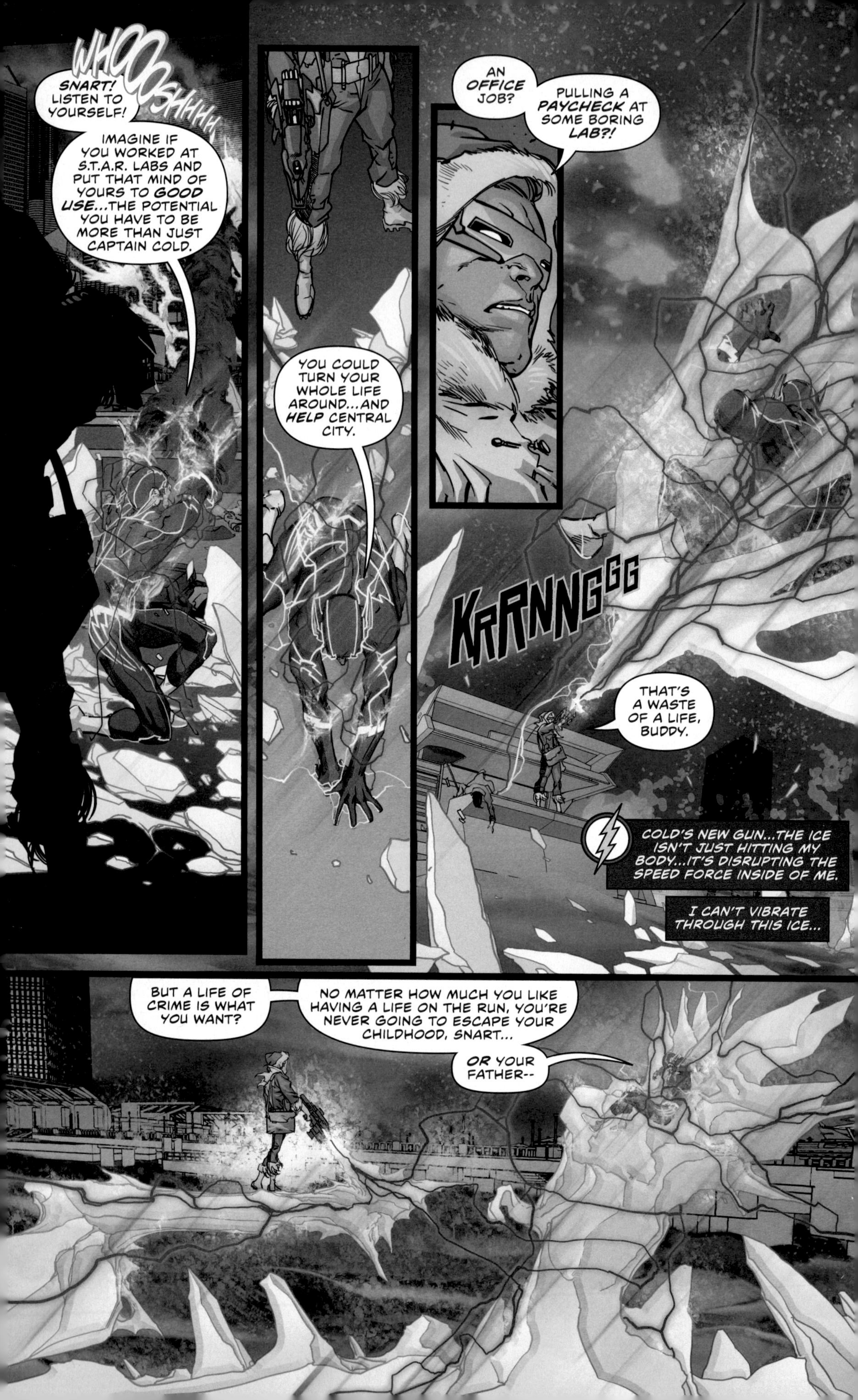
WHOOOOSHHHH
SNART! LISTEN TO YOURSELF!
IMAGINE IF YOU WORKED AT S.T.A.R. LABS AND PUT THAT MIND OF YOURS TO GOOD USE...THE POTENTIAL YOU HAVE TO BE MORE THAN JUST CAPTAIN COLD.
YOU COULD TURN YOUR WHOLE LIFE AROUND...AND HELP CENTRAL CITY.
AN OFFICE JOB?
PULLING A PAYCHECK AT SOME BORING LAB?!
KRRNNGGG
THAT'S A WASTE OF A LIFE, BUDDY.
COLD'S NEW GUN...THE ICE ISN'T JUST HITTING MY BODY...IT'S DISRUPTING THE SPEED FORCE INSIDE OF ME.
I CAN'T VIBRATE THROUGH THIS ICE...
BUT A LIFE OF CRIME IS WHAT YOU WANT?
NO MATTER HOW MUCH YOU LIKE HAVING A LIFE ON THE RUN, YOU'RE NEVER GOING TO ESCAPE YOUR CHILDHOOD, SNART...
OR YOUR FATHER--

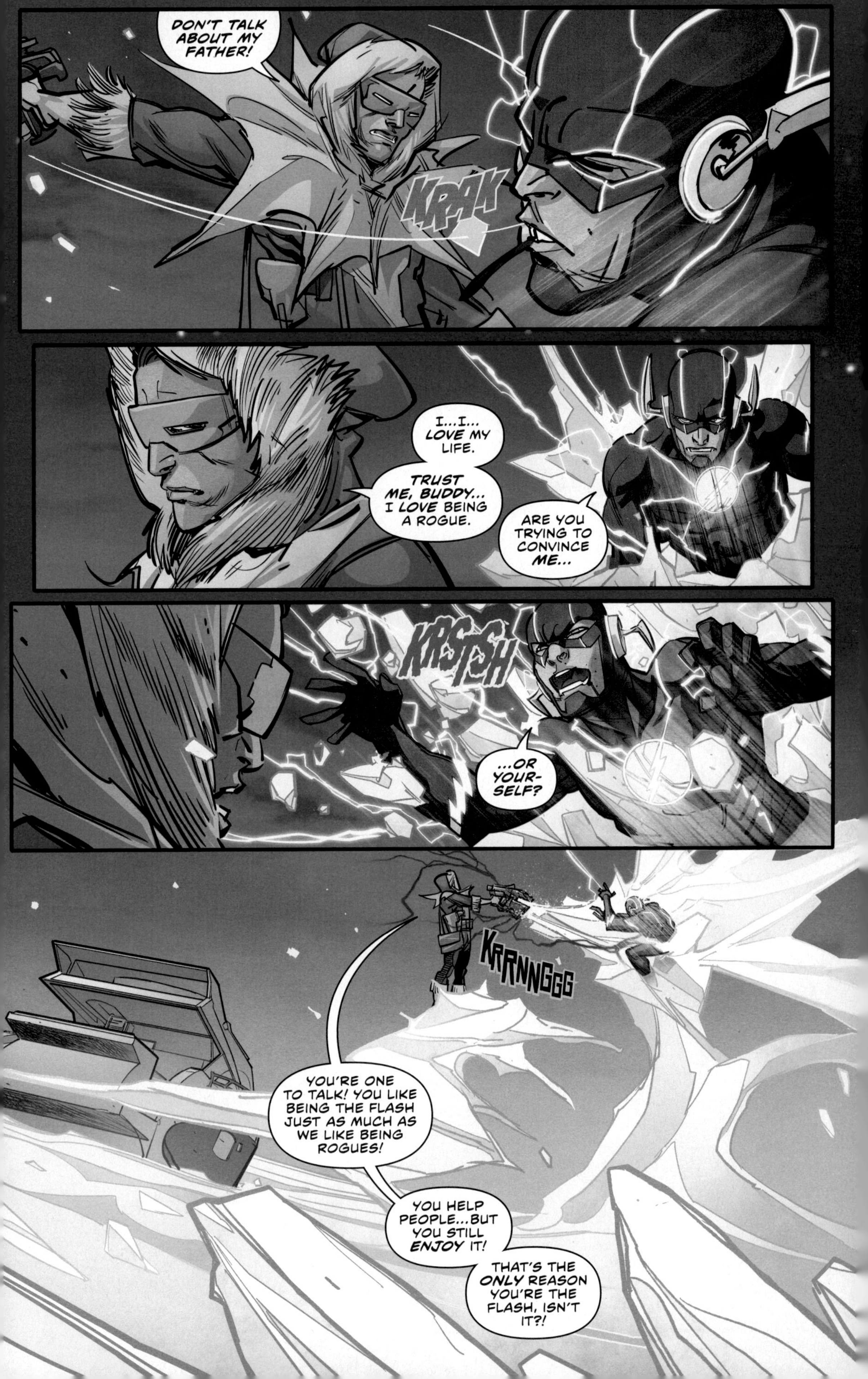
DON'T TALK ABOUT MY FATHER!
KRAK
I...I... LOVE MY LIFE.
TRUST ME, BUDDY... I LOVE BEING A ROGUE.
ARE YOU TRYING TO CONVINCE ME...
KRSTSH
...OR YOURSELF?
KRRNNGGG
YOU'RE ONE TO TALK! YOU LIKE BEING THE FLASH JUST AS MUCH AS WE LIKE BEING ROGUES!
YOU HELP PEOPLE...BUT YOU STILL ENJOY IT!
THAT'S THE ONLY REASON YOU'RE THE FLASH, ISN'T IT?!

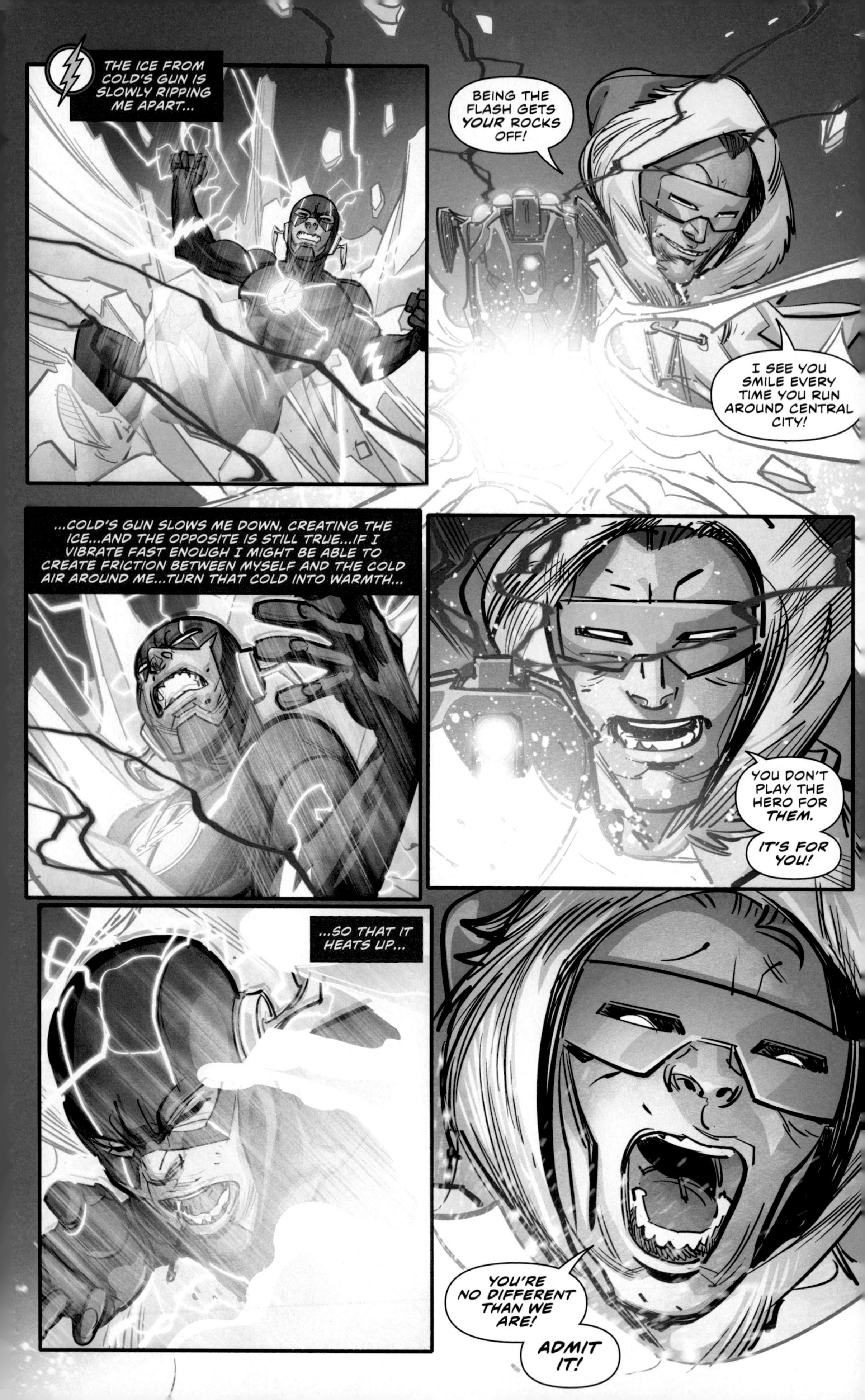
THE ICE FROM COLD'S GUN IS SLOWLY RIPPING ME APART...
BEING THE FLASH GETS *YOUR* ROCKS OFF!
I SEE YOU SMILE EVERY TIME YOU RUN AROUND CENTRAL CITY!
...COLD'S GUN SLOWS ME DOWN, CREATING THE ICE...AND THE OPPOSITE IS STILL TRUE...IF I VIBRATE FAST ENOUGH I MIGHT BE ABLE TO CREATE FRICTION BETWEEN MYSELF AND THE COLD AIR AROUND ME...TURN THAT COLD INTO WARMTH...
YOU DON'T PLAY THE HERO FOR *THEM.*
IT'S FOR YOU!
...SO THAT IT HEATS UP...
YOU'RE NO DIFFERENT THAN WE ARE!
ADMIT IT!

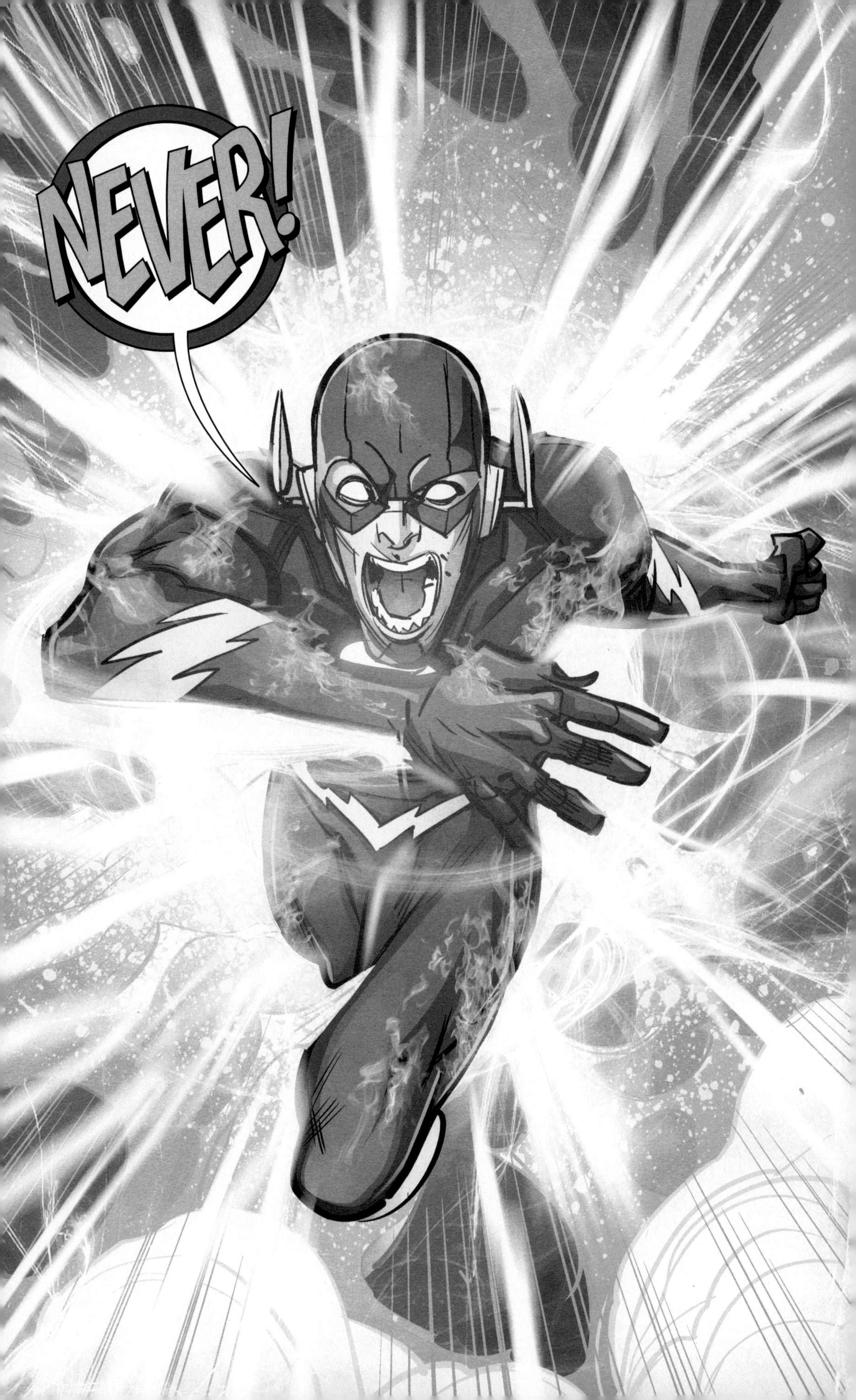
NEVER!

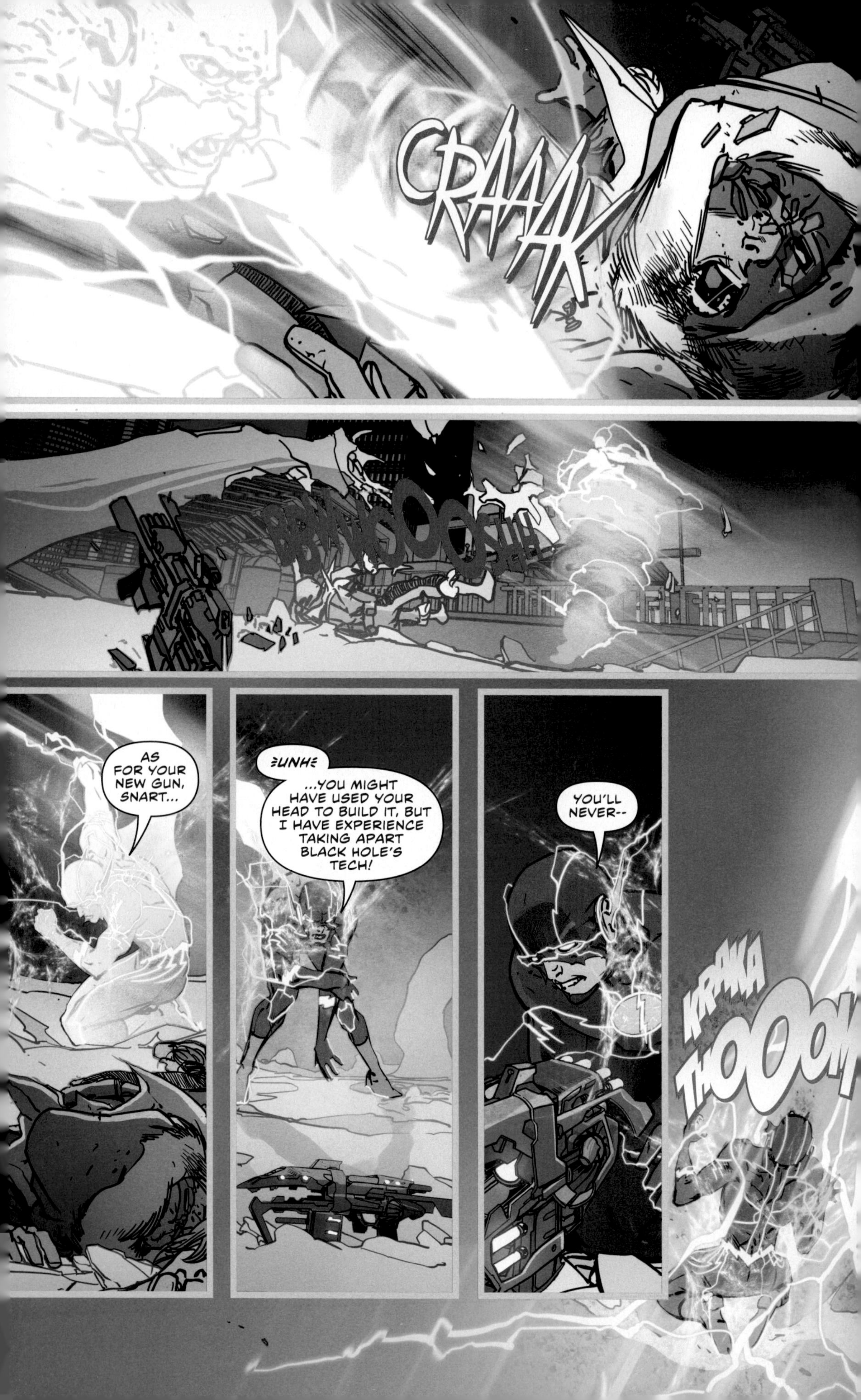
CRAAAK
BDWOOOSHH
AS FOR YOUR NEW GUN, SNART...
UNH
...YOU MIGHT HAVE USED YOUR HEAD TO BUILD IT, BUT I HAVE EXPERIENCE TAKING APART BLACK HOLE'S TECH!
YOU'LL NEVER--
KRAKA THOOOM

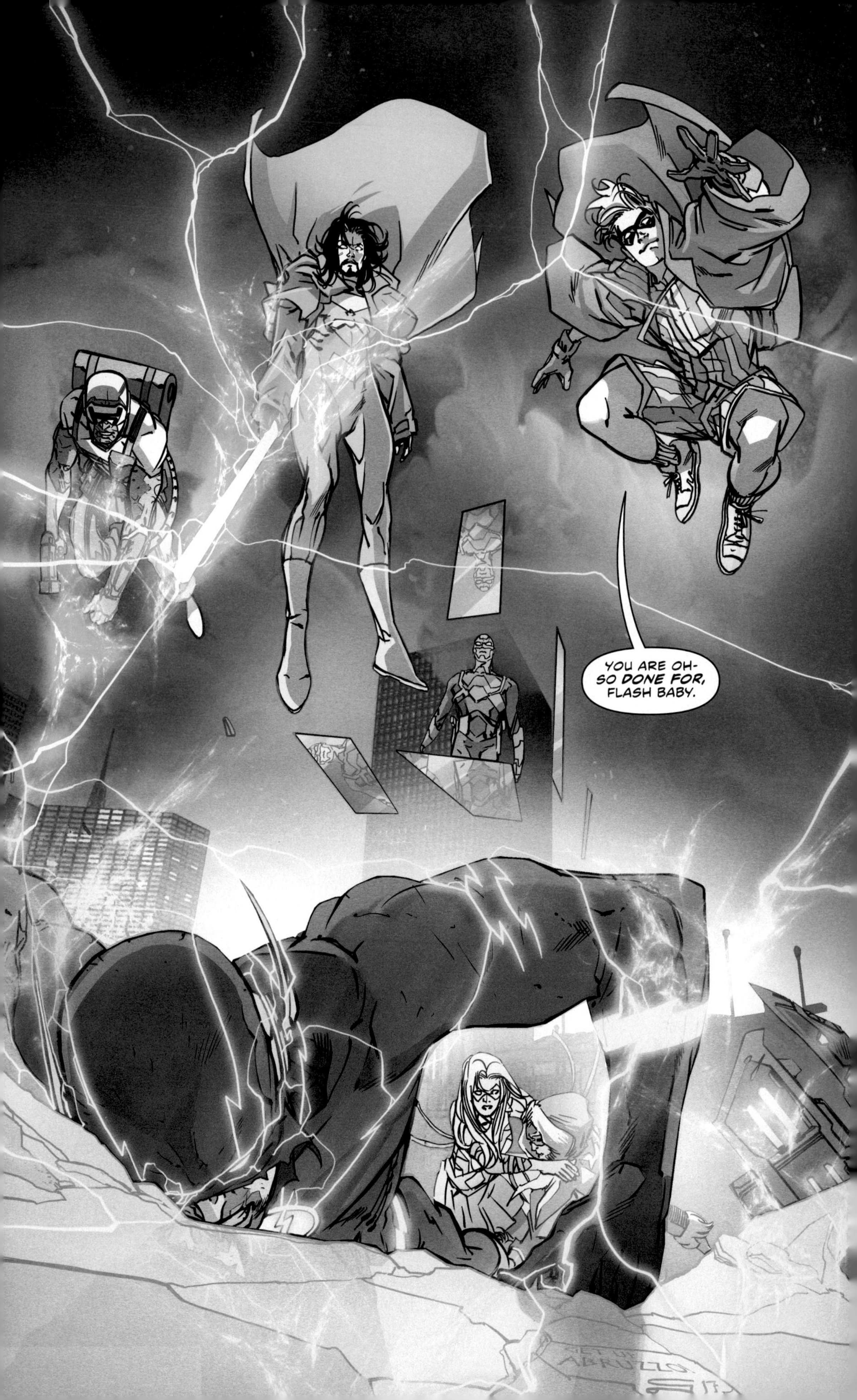
YOU ARE OH-SO DONE FOR, FLASH BABY.

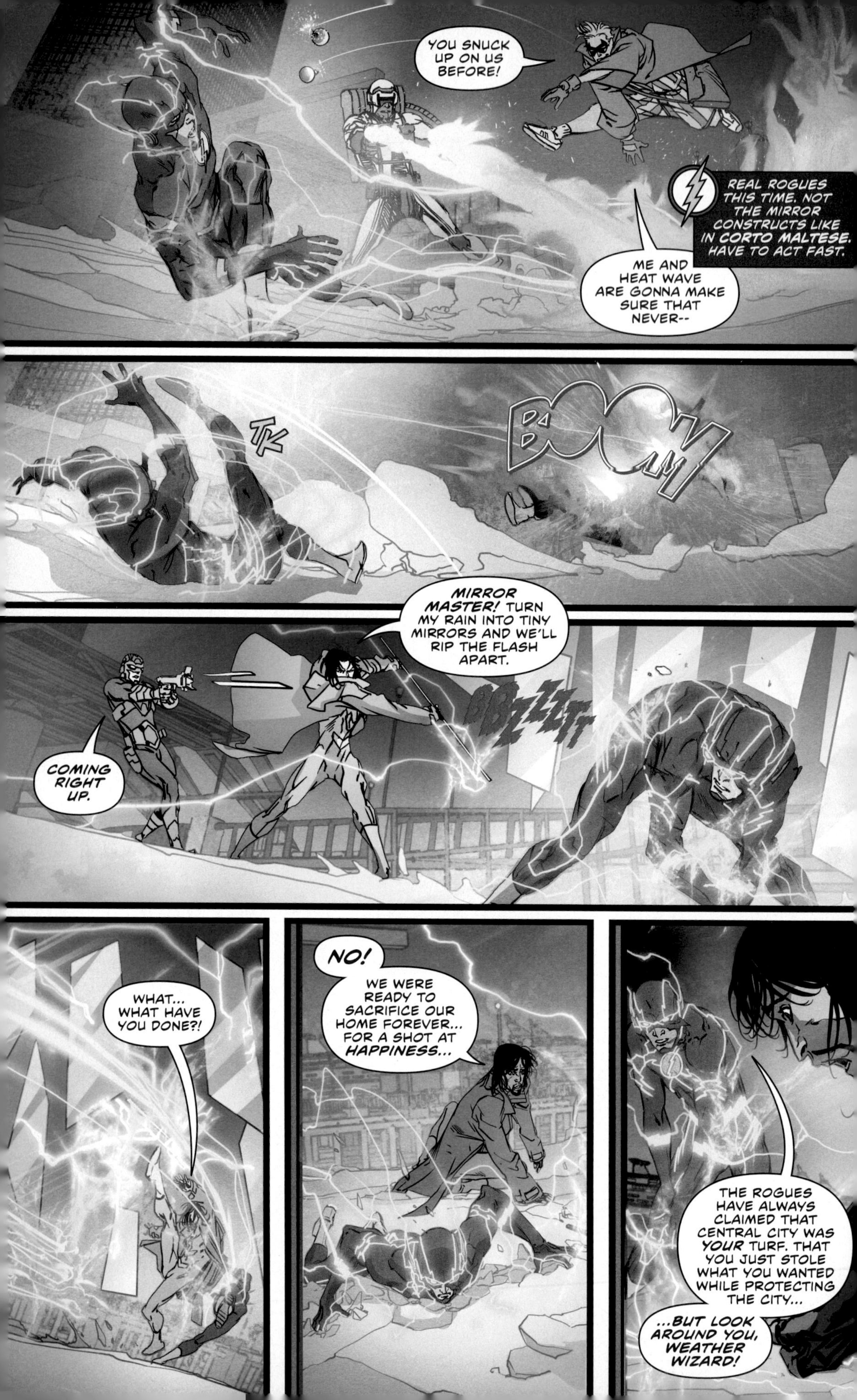
YOU SNUCK UP ON US BEFORE!
REAL ROGUES THIS TIME. NOT THE MIRROR CONSTRUCTS LIKE IN *CORTO MALTESE.* HAVE TO ACT FAST.
ME AND HEAT WAVE ARE GONNA MAKE SURE THAT NEVER--
TK
BOOM
MIRROR MASTER! TURN MY RAIN INTO TINY MIRRORS AND WE'LL RIP THE FLASH APART.
COMING RIGHT UP.
WHAT... WHAT HAVE YOU DONE?!
NO!
WE WERE READY TO SACRIFICE OUR HOME FOREVER... FOR A SHOT AT *HAPPINESS...*
THE ROGUES HAVE ALWAYS CLAIMED THAT CENTRAL CITY WAS *YOUR* TURF. THAT YOU JUST STOLE WHAT YOU WANTED WHILE PROTECTING THE CITY...
...BUT LOOK AROUND YOU, WEATHER WIZARD!

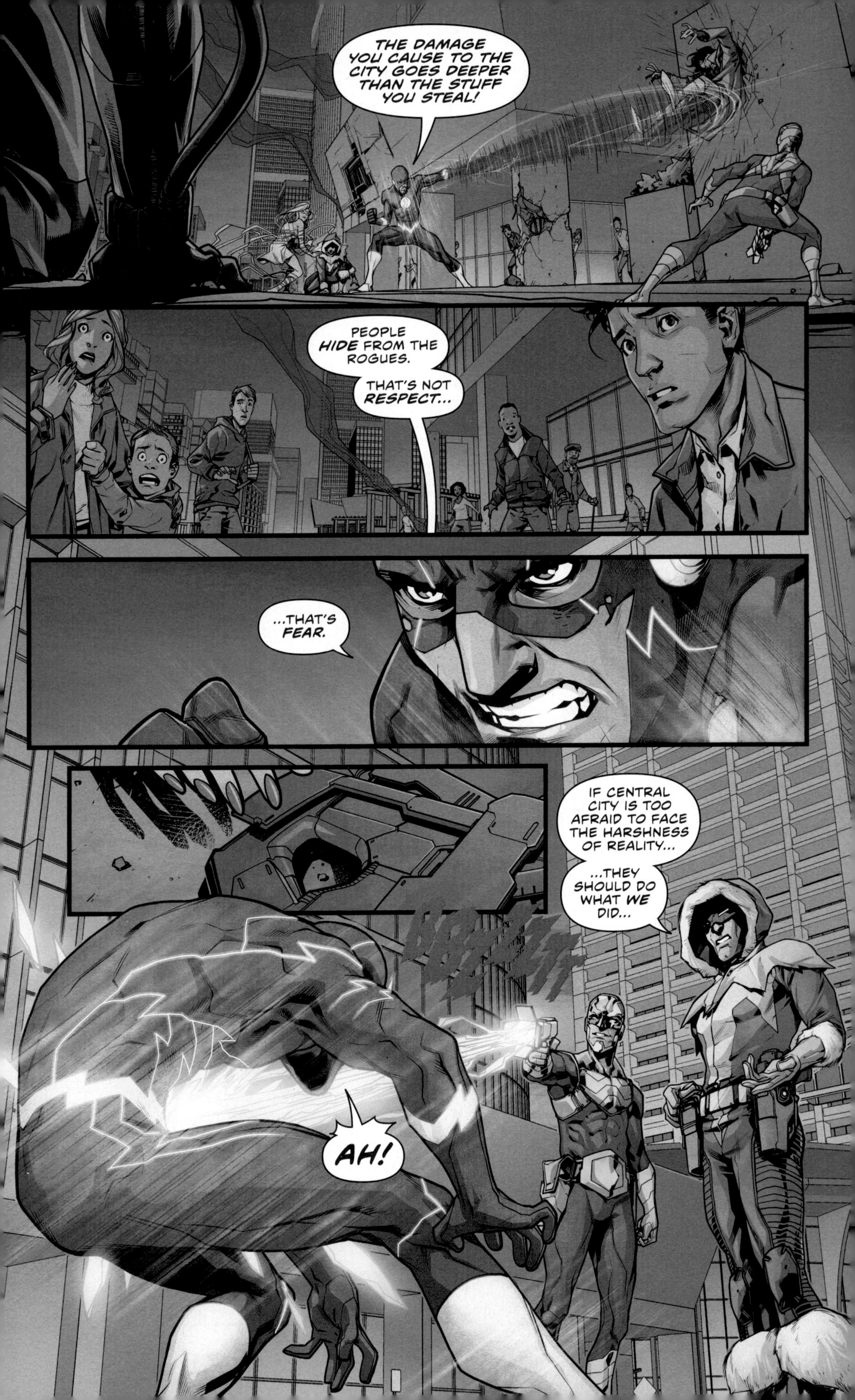
THE DAMAGE YOU CAUSE TO THE CITY GOES DEEPER THAN THE STUFF YOU STEAL!
PEOPLE HIDE FROM THE ROGUES.
THAT'S NOT RESPECT...
...THAT'S FEAR.
IF CENTRAL CITY IS TOO AFRAID TO FACE THE HARSHNESS OF REALITY...
...THEY SHOULD DO WHAT WE DID...
AH!

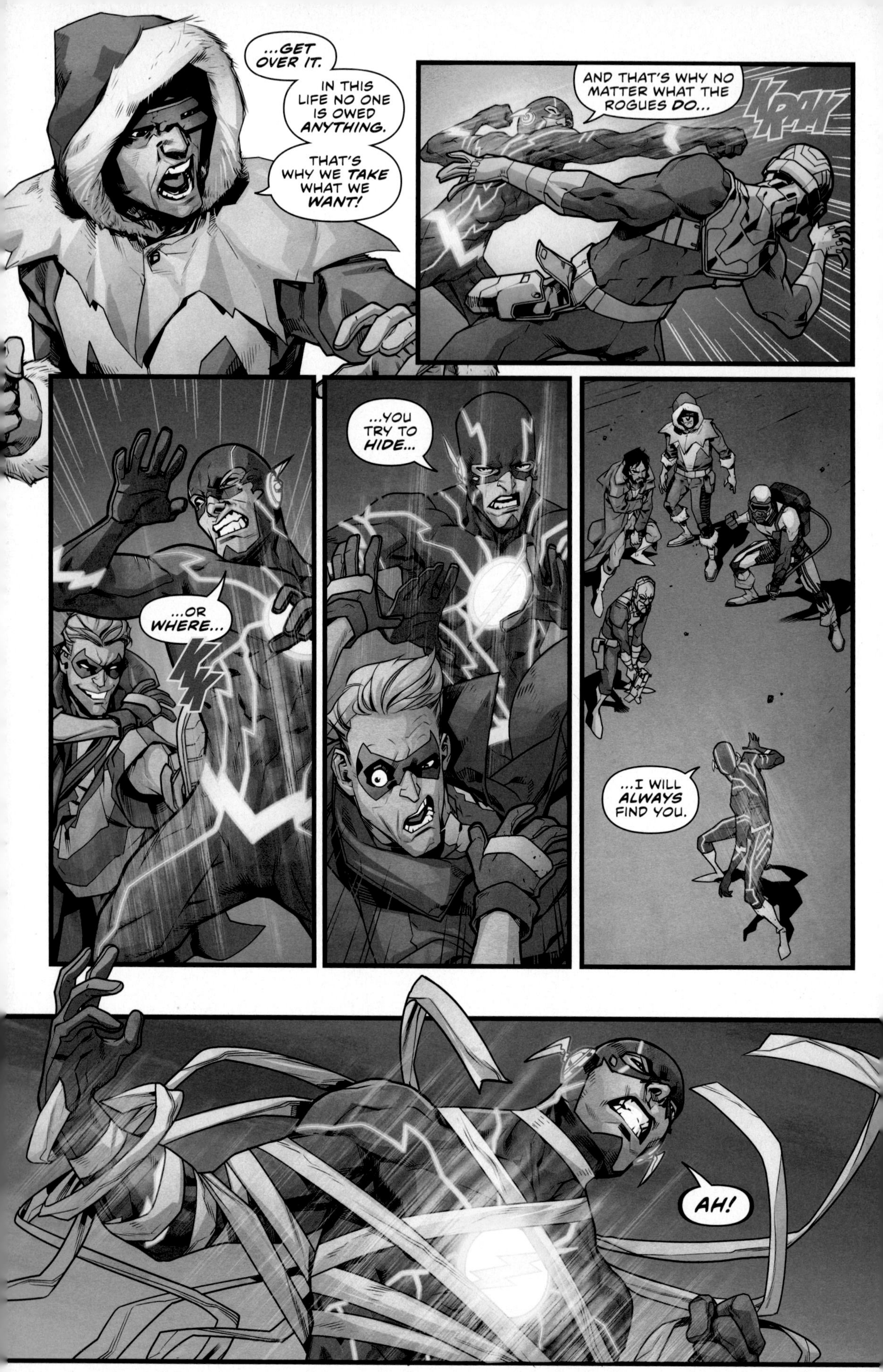
...GET OVER IT.
IN THIS LIFE NO ONE IS OWED ANYTHING.
THAT'S WHY WE TAKE WHAT WE WANT!
AND THAT'S WHY NO MATTER WHAT THE ROGUES DO...
KRAK
...OR WHERE...
...YOU TRY TO HIDE...
...I WILL ALWAYS FIND YOU.
AH!

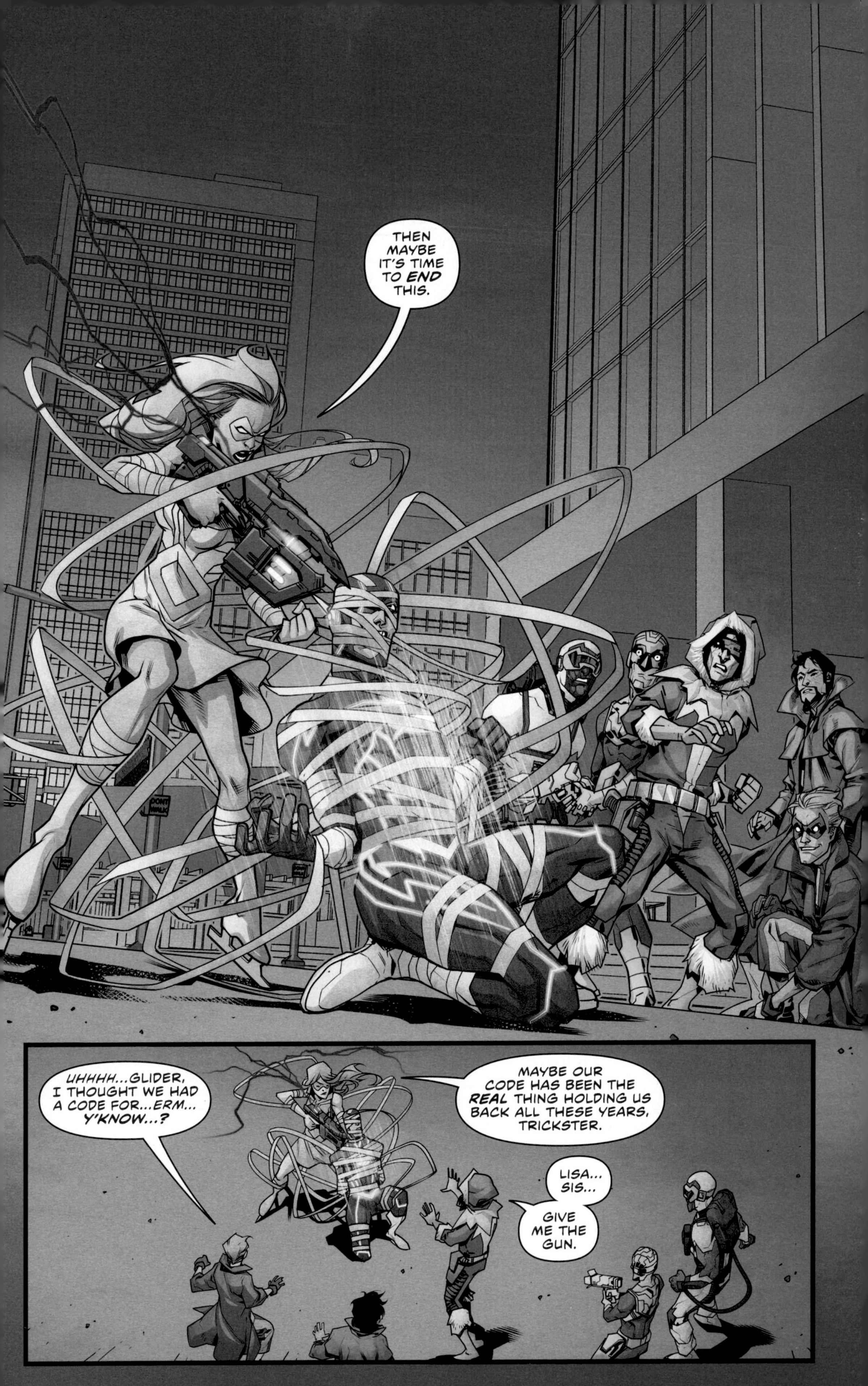
THEN MAYBE IT'S TIME TO END THIS.
UHHHH...GLIDER, I THOUGHT WE HAD A CODE FOR...ERM... Y'KNOW...?
MAYBE OUR CODE HAS BEEN THE REAL THING HOLDING US BACK ALL THESE YEARS, TRICKSTER.
LISA... SIS...
GIVE ME THE GUN.

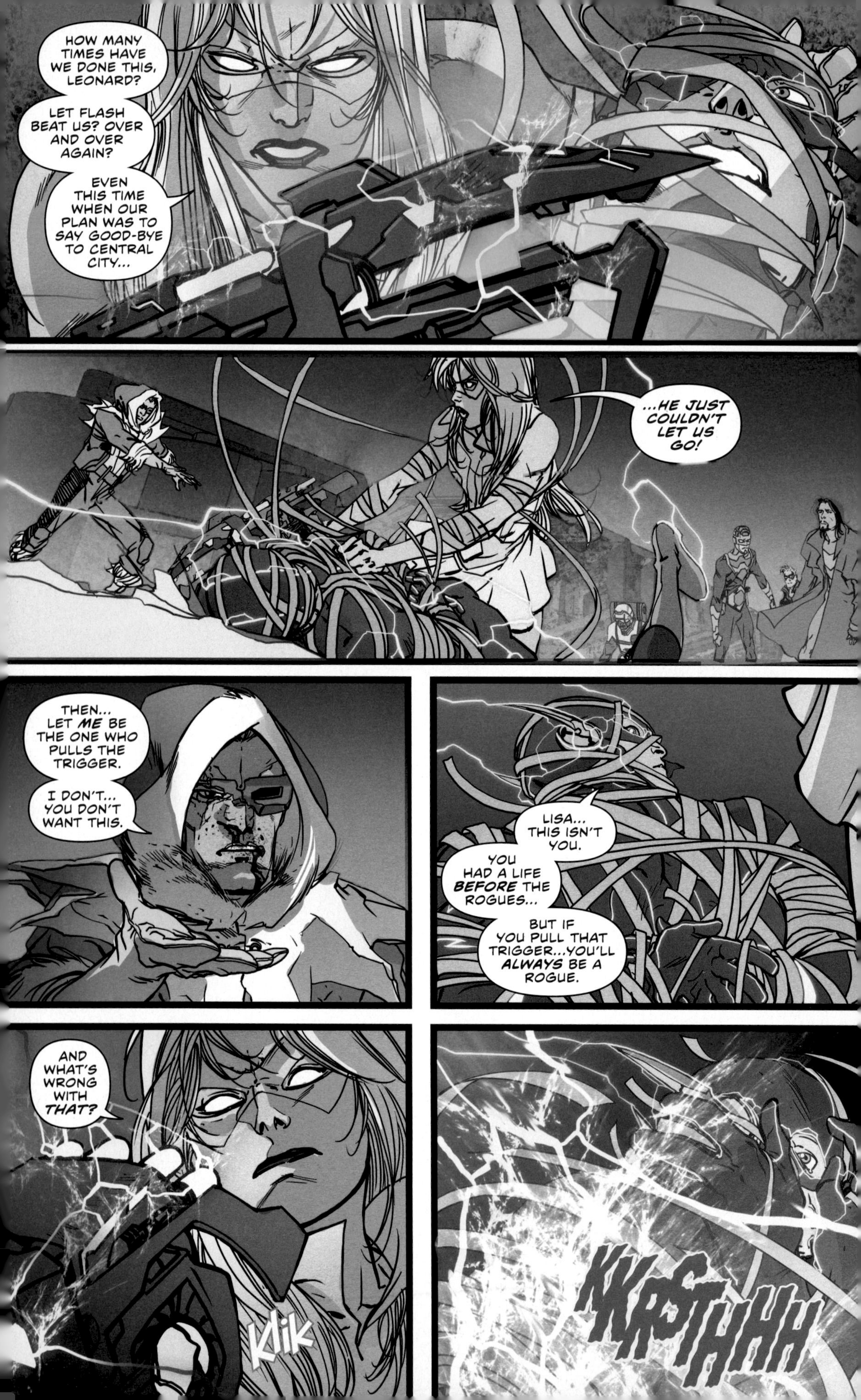
HOW MANY TIMES HAVE WE DONE THIS, LEONARD?
LET FLASH BEAT US? OVER AND OVER AGAIN?
EVEN THIS TIME WHEN OUR PLAN WAS TO SAY GOOD-BYE TO CENTRAL CITY...
...HE JUST COULDN'T LET US GO!
THEN... LET *ME* BE THE ONE WHO PULLS THE TRIGGER.
I DON'T... YOU DON'T WANT THIS.
LISA... THIS ISN'T YOU.
YOU HAD A LIFE *BEFORE* THE ROGUES...
BUT IF YOU PULL THAT TRIGGER...YOU'LL *ALWAYS* BE A ROGUE.
AND WHAT'S WRONG WITH *THAT*?
Klik
KKRSSTHHH

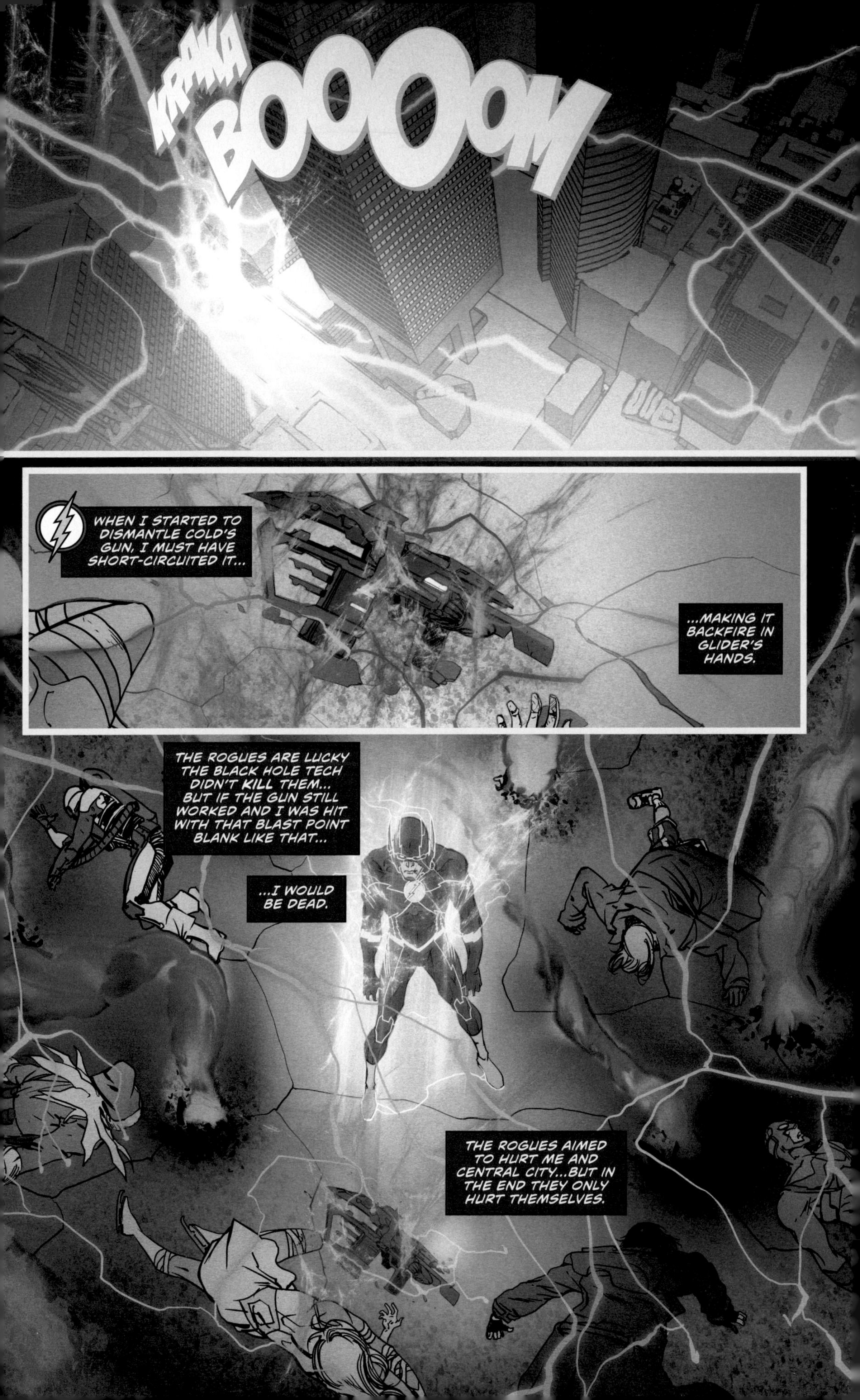
KRAKA
BOOOOOM
WHEN I STARTED TO DISMANTLE COLD'S GUN, I MUST HAVE SHORT-CIRCUITED IT...
...MAKING IT BACKFIRE IN GLIDER'S HANDS.
THE ROGUES ARE LUCKY THE BLACK HOLE TECH DIDN'T KILL THEM... BUT IF THE GUN STILL WORKED AND I WAS HIT WITH THAT BLAST POINT BLANK LIKE THAT...
...I WOULD BE DEAD.
THE ROGUES AIMED TO HURT ME AND CENTRAL CITY...BUT IN THE END THEY ONLY HURT THEMSELVES.

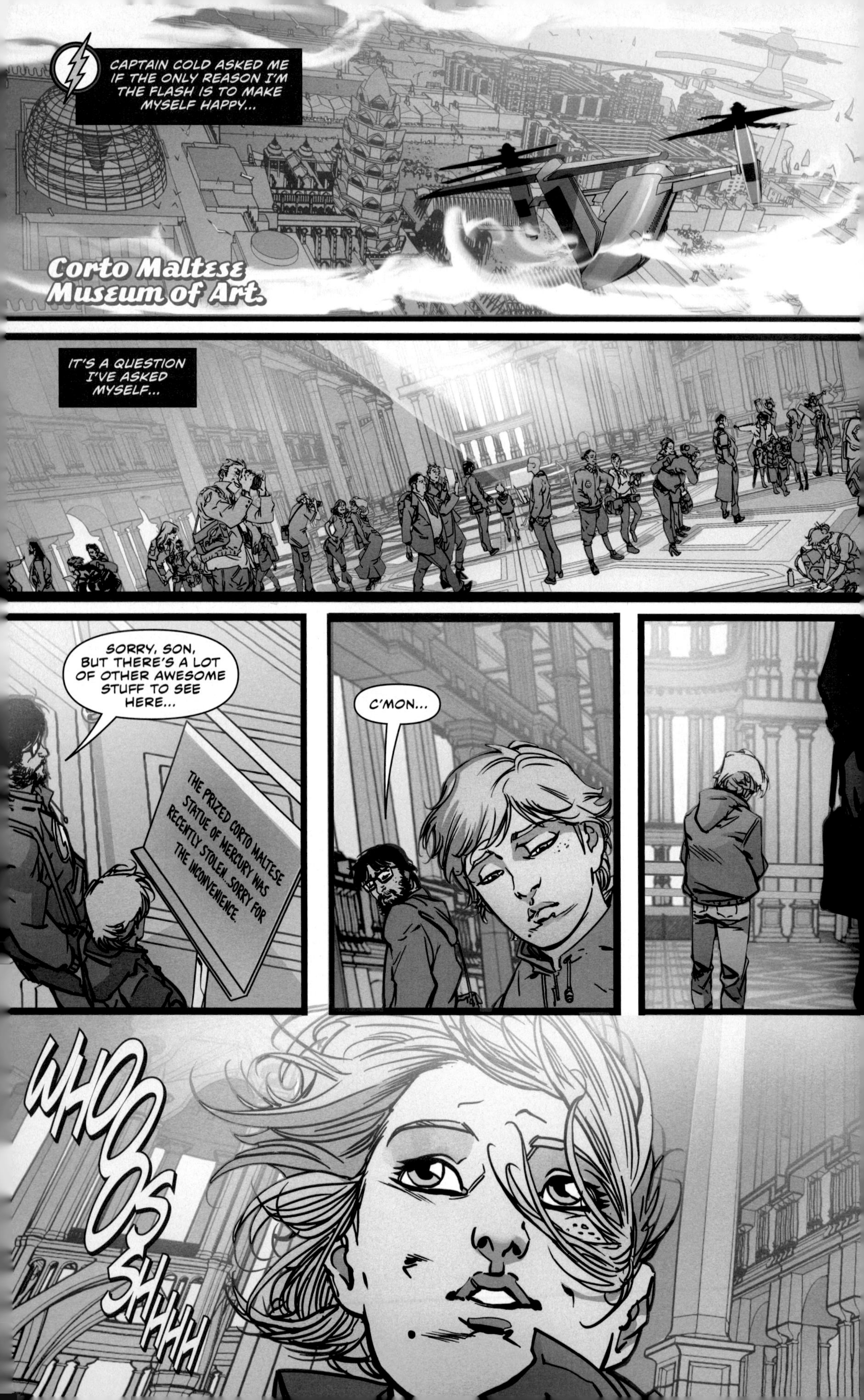
CAPTAIN COLD ASKED ME IF THE ONLY REASON I'M THE FLASH IS TO MAKE MYSELF HAPPY...
Corto Maltese Museum of Art.
IT'S A QUESTION I'VE ASKED MYSELF...
SORRY, SON, BUT THERE'S A LOT OF OTHER AWESOME STUFF TO SEE HERE...
THE PRIZED CORTO MALTESE STATUE OF MERCURY WAS RECENTLY STOLEN...SORRY FOR THE INCONVENIENCE.
C'MON...
WHOOOSHHHH

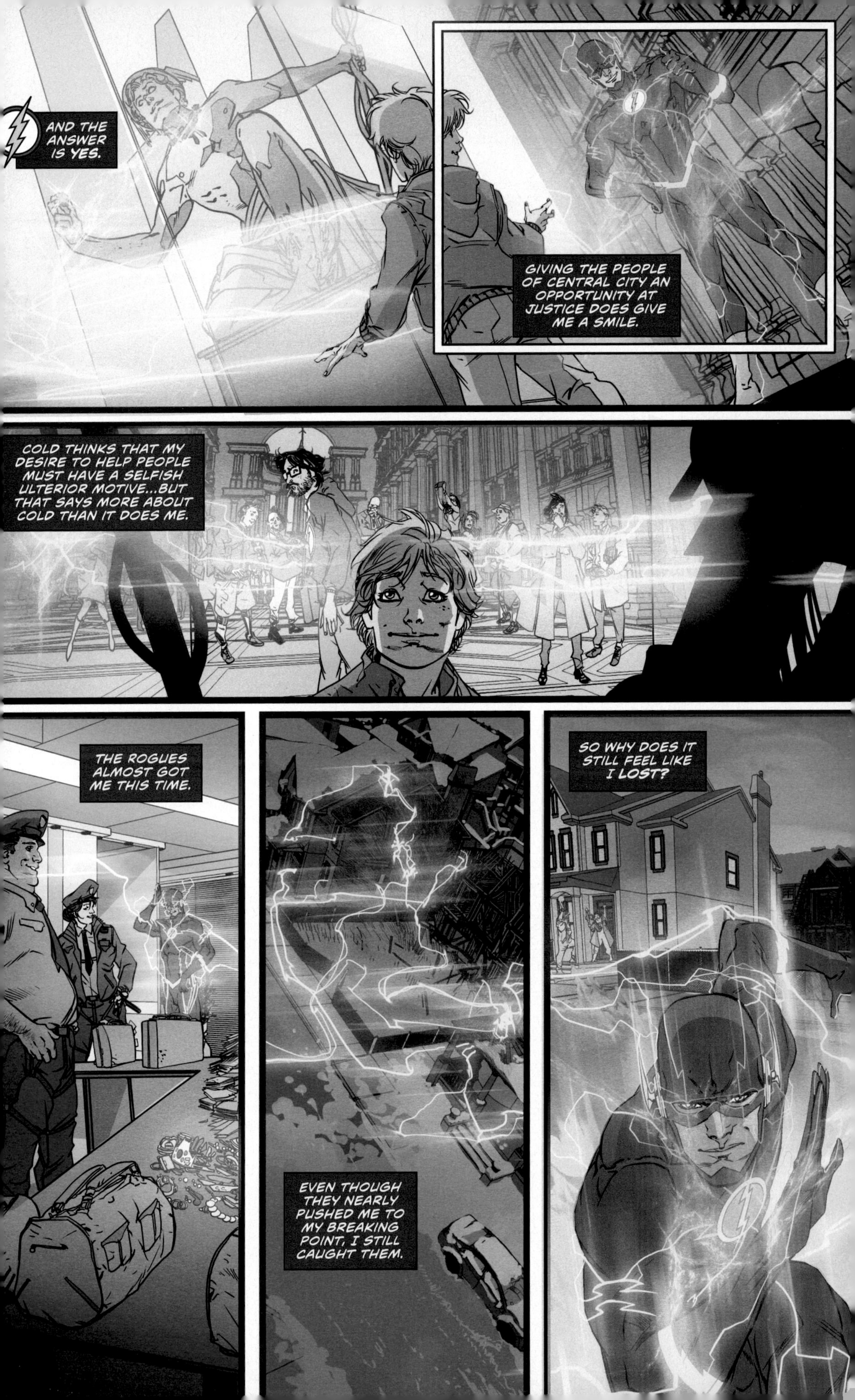
AND THE ANSWER IS YES.
GIVING THE PEOPLE OF CENTRAL CITY AN OPPORTUNITY AT JUSTICE DOES GIVE ME A SMILE.
COLD THINKS THAT MY DESIRE TO HELP PEOPLE MUST HAVE A SELFISH ULTERIOR MOTIVE...BUT THAT SAYS MORE ABOUT COLD THAN IT DOES ME.
THE ROGUES ALMOST GOT ME THIS TIME.
EVEN THOUGH THEY NEARLY PUSHED ME TO MY BREAKING POINT, I STILL CAUGHT THEM.
SO WHY DOES IT STILL FEEL LIKE I LOST?

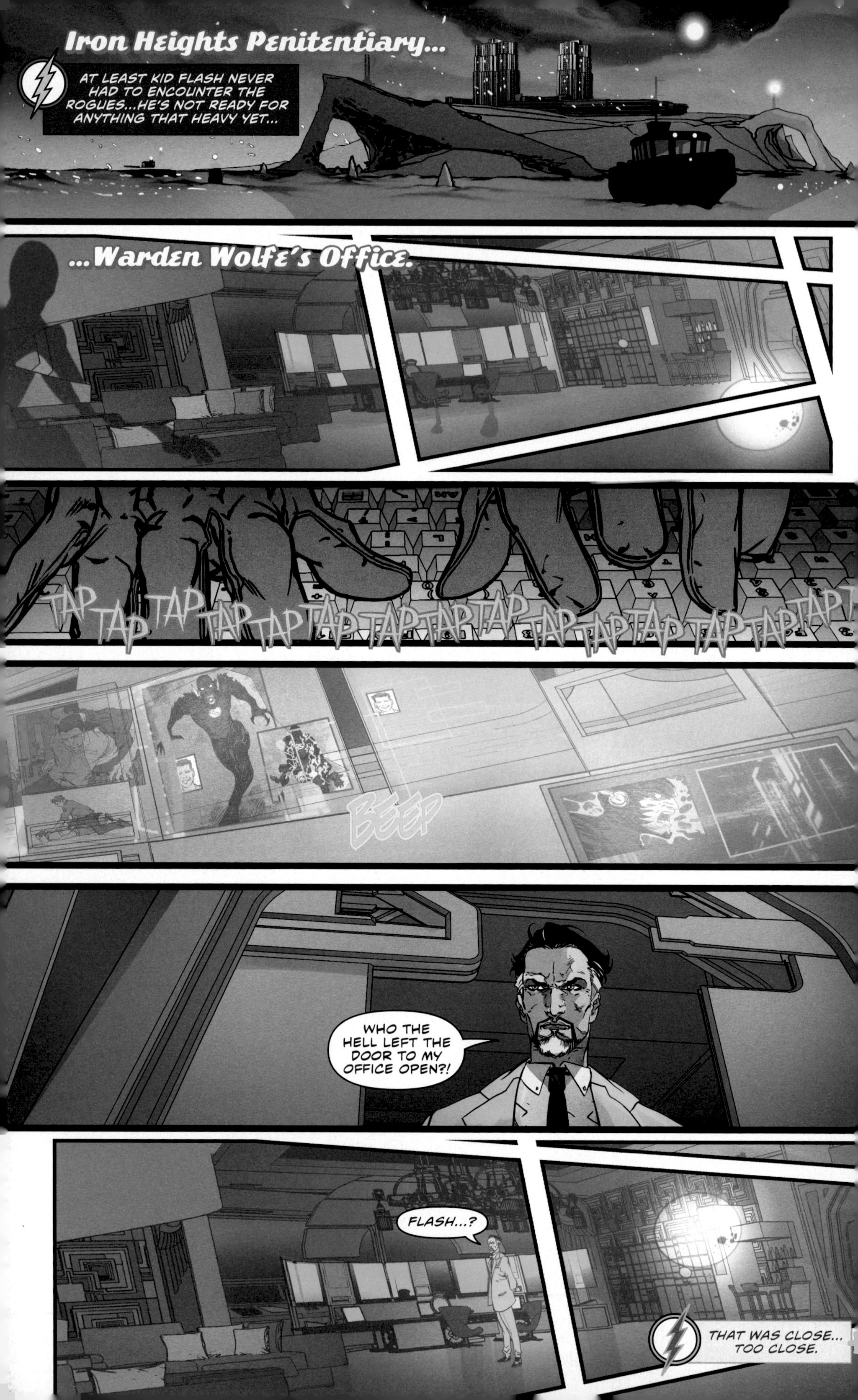
Iron Heights Penitentiary...
AT LEAST KID FLASH NEVER HAD TO ENCOUNTER THE ROGUES...HE'S NOT READY FOR ANYTHING THAT HEAVY YET...
...Warden Wolfe's Office.
TAP TAP TAP TAP TAP TAP TAP TAP TAP TAP TAP TAP TAP TAP TAP TAP
BEEP
WHO THE HELL LEFT THE DOOR TO MY OFFICE OPEN?!
FLASH...?
THAT WAS CLOSE... TOO CLOSE.

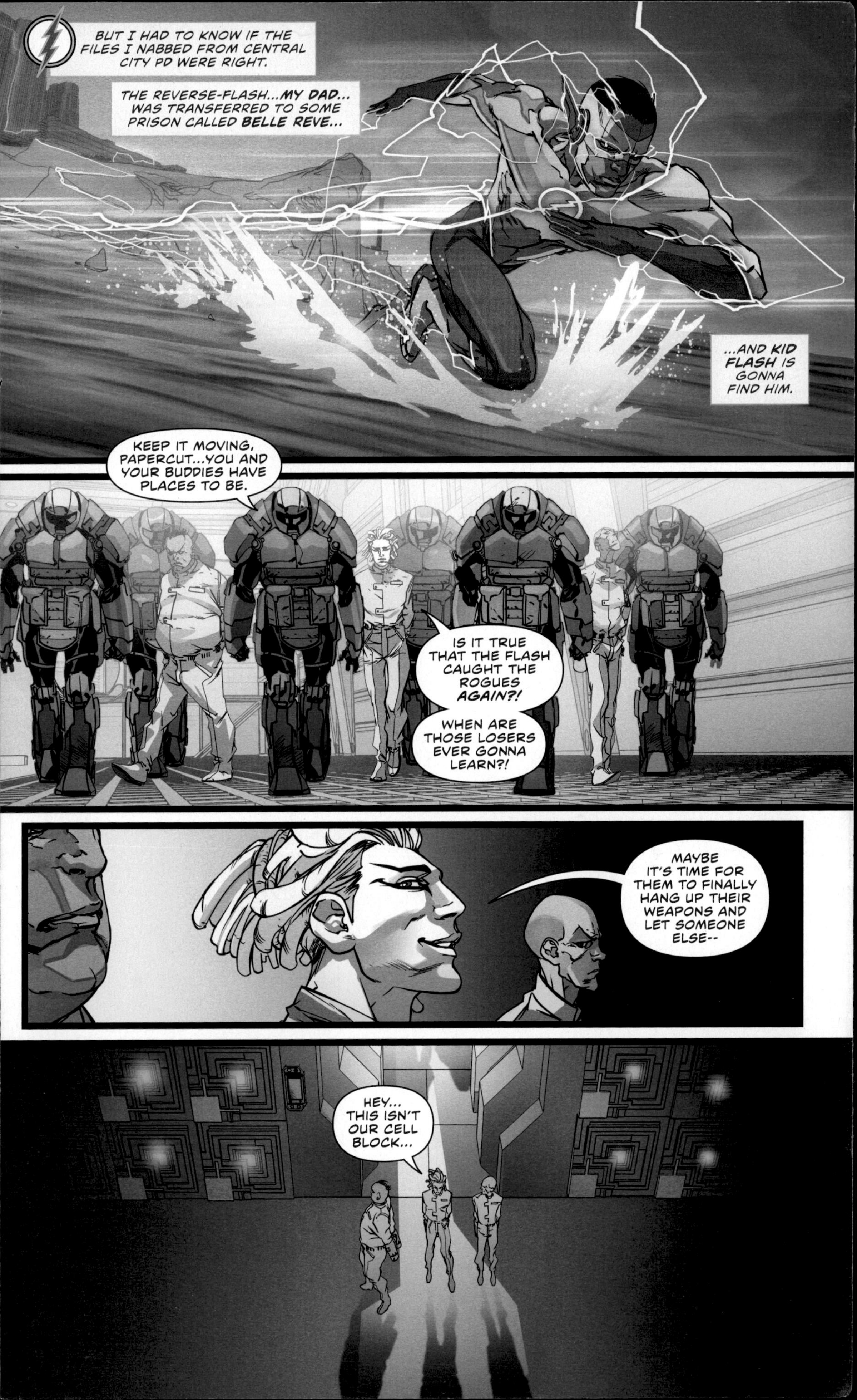
BUT I HAD TO KNOW IF THE FILES I NABBED FROM CENTRAL CITY PD WERE RIGHT.
THE REVERSE-FLASH...MY DAD... WAS TRANSFERRED TO SOME PRISON CALLED BELLE REVE...
...AND KID FLASH IS GONNA FIND HIM.
KEEP IT MOVING, PAPERCUT...YOU AND YOUR BUDDIES HAVE PLACES TO BE.
IS IT TRUE THAT THE FLASH CAUGHT THE ROGUES AGAIN?!
WHEN ARE THOSE LOSERS EVER GONNA LEARN?!
MAYBE IT'S TIME FOR THEM TO FINALLY HANG UP THEIR WEAPONS AND LET SOMEONE ELSE--
HEY... THIS ISN'T OUR CELL BLOCK...

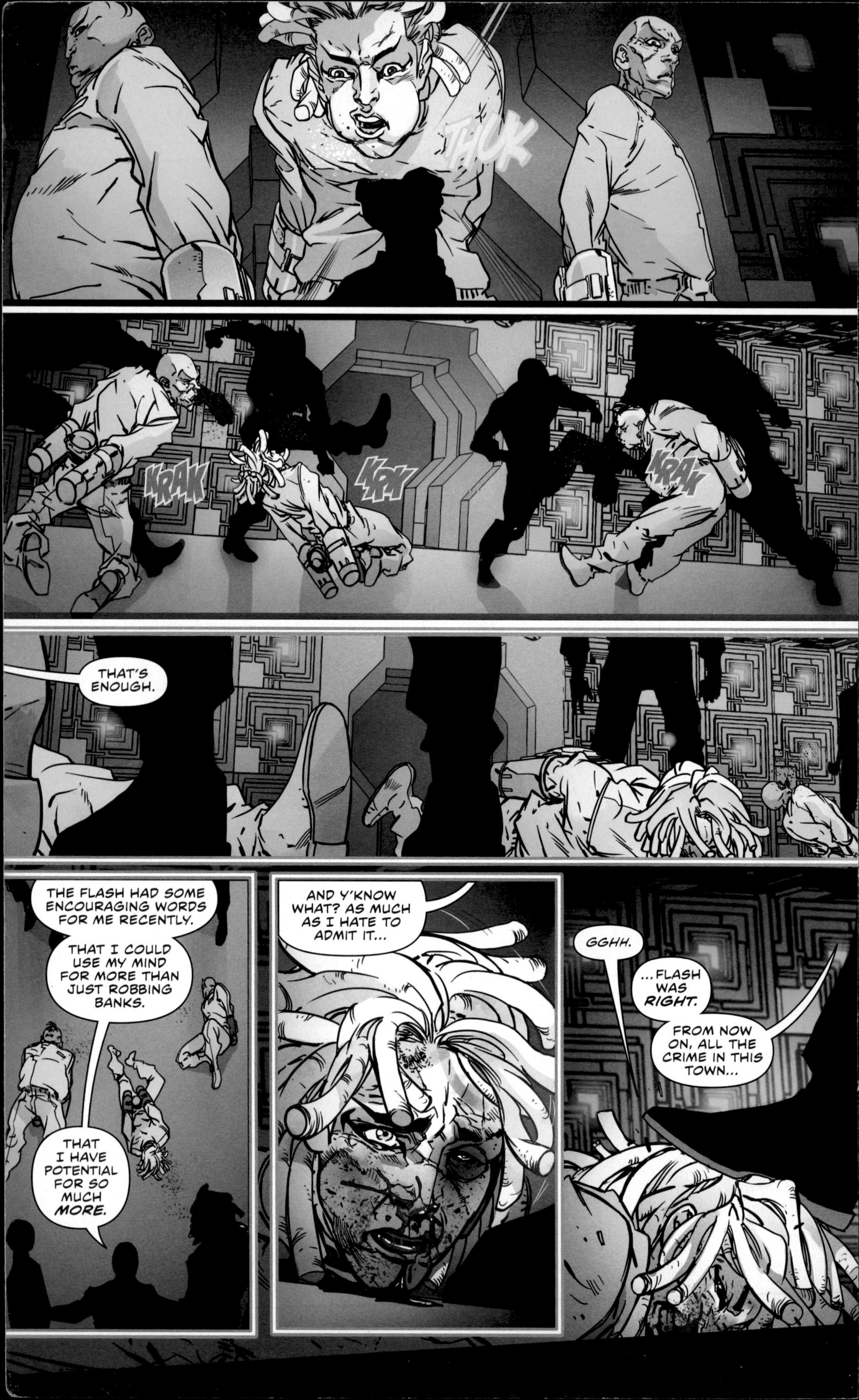
THUK
KRAK
KRAK
KRAK
THAT'S ENOUGH.
THE FLASH HAD SOME ENCOURAGING WORDS FOR ME RECENTLY.
THAT I COULD USE MY MIND FOR MORE THAN JUST ROBBING BANKS.
THAT I HAVE POTENTIAL FOR SO MUCH MORE.
AND Y'KNOW WHAT? AS MUCH AS I HATE TO ADMIT IT...
GGHH.
...FLASH WAS RIGHT.
FROM NOW ON, ALL THE CRIME IN THIS TOWN...

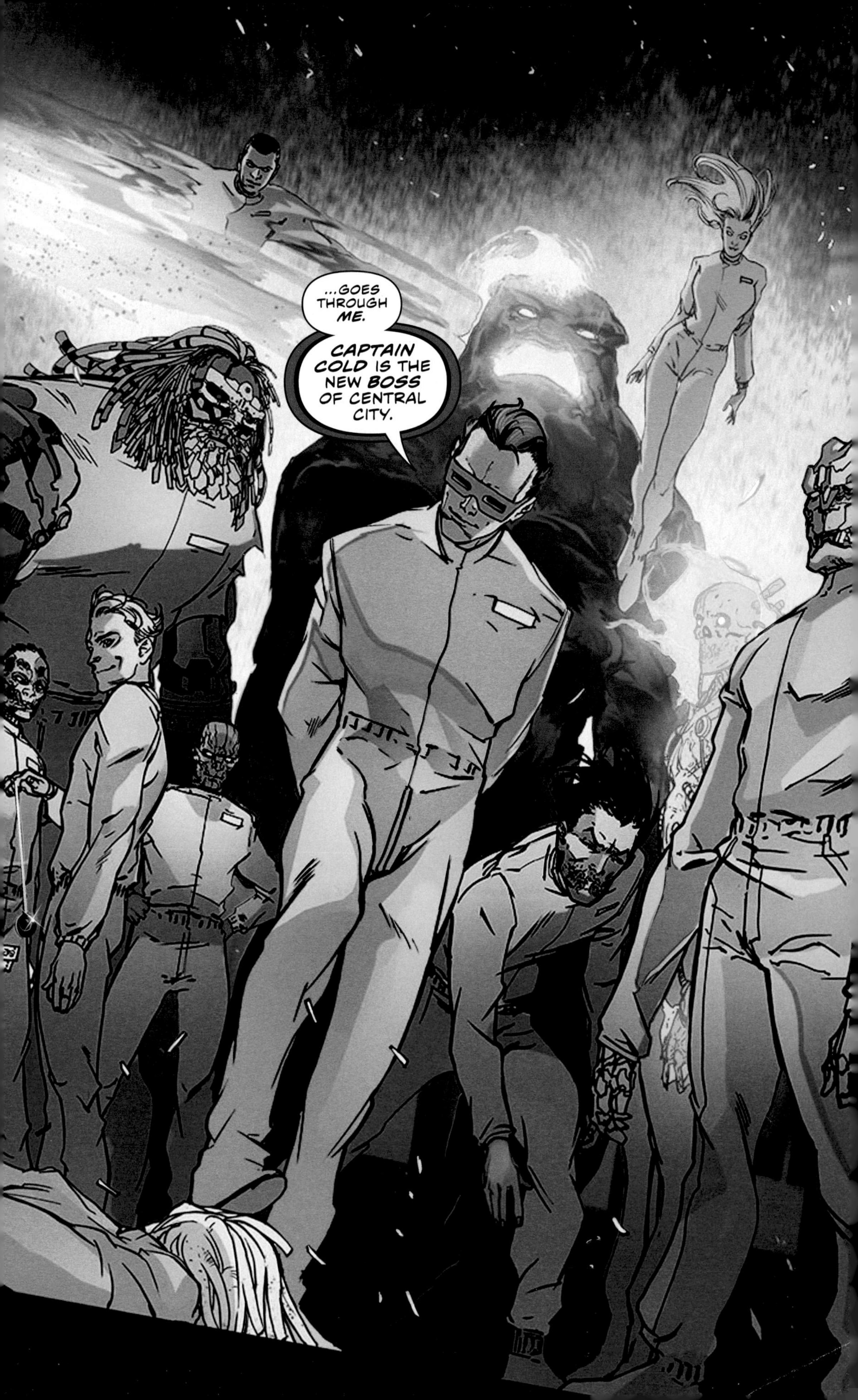
...GOES THROUGH ME.
CAPTAIN COLD IS THE NEW BOSS OF CENTRAL CITY.

CAPTAIN COLD

Real Name: Leonard Snart
Occupation: Professional Criminal
Marital Status: Single
Ht: 6' 2" Wt: 196 lbs.
Eyes: Brown Hair: Brown
First Appearance: SHOWCASE #8 (May-June, 1957)

Leonard Snart grew up in a trailer park outside of Central City with an alcoholic father and a verbally abusive mother. His only fond memories are of his younger sister, Lisa. The two would shoplift together, beat up the neighbor kids and steal from their own parents. When Snart turned eighteen, he moved out, becoming a small-time thief, and began drinking excessively and experimenting with drugs.

After graduating to armed robbery, Snart was caught by Barry Allen (the second Flash) in Central City and imprisoned. During his jail time, he studied thermal motion, hoping to find a way to slow Flash down. When he was released, Snart broke into a lab and used an unknown radiation to charge a special gun of his own design.

Snart's cold-gun has the unique ability to halt movement at the atomic level, thereby achieving Absolute Zero. It can also create a "cold field" which Snart – renamed Captain Cold – used to slow Flash down so that he could be seen.

After Barry Allen died, Cold briefly teamed with his sister, now a super-villain called the Golden Glider, and the two eventually formed a quasi-legitimate business as bounty hunters. But "good" was not in their blood and it quickly fell apart. Soon after, the Golden Glider was murdered, thrusting Cold back into a life of crime.

Cold often goes on binges with his illicit earnings, spending his money on booze and professional escorts. He has recently returned to Keystone City for reasons yet to be revealed.

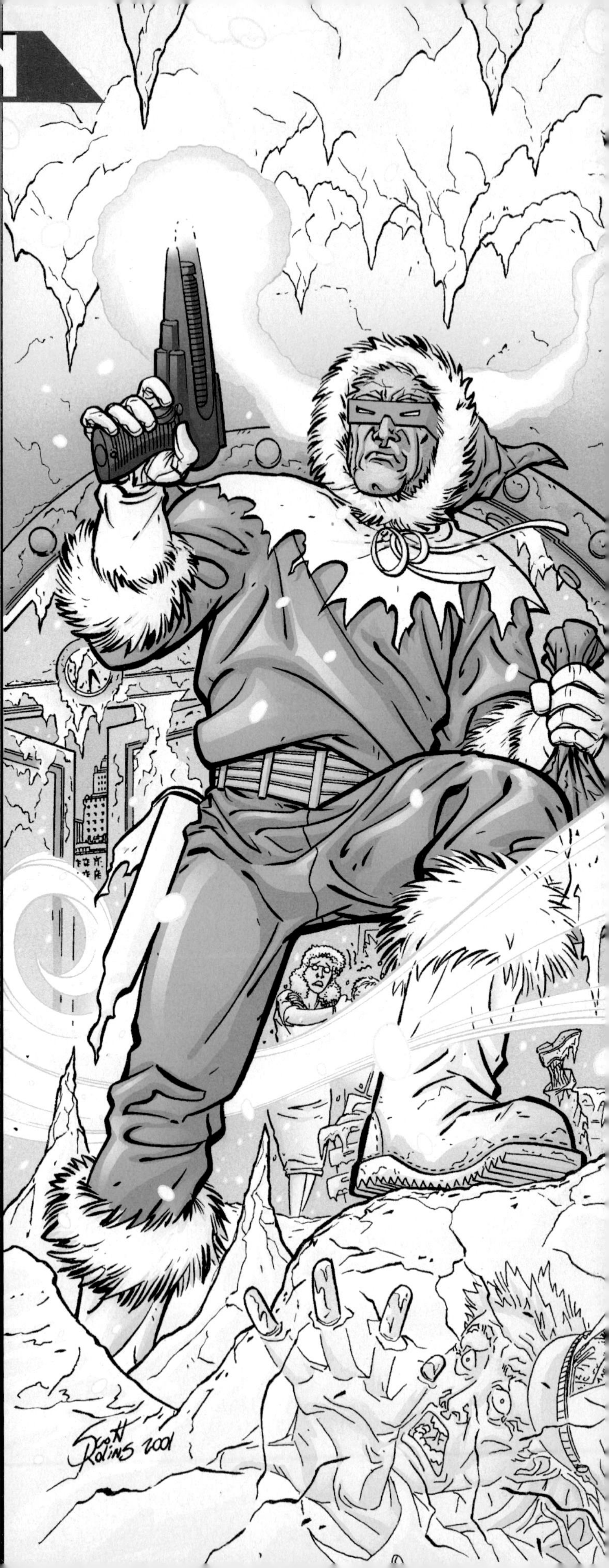